DESIGNING USABLE TEXTS

THE EDUCATIONAL TECHNOLOGY SERIES

Edited by

Harold F. O'Neil, Jr.

U.S. Army Research Institute for
the Behavioral and Social Sciences
Alexandria, Virginia

DESIGNING USABLE TEXTS

Edited by

Thomas M. Duffy

Communications Design Center
Carnegie–Mellon University
Pittsburgh, Pennsylvania

Robert Waller

Institute of Educational Technology
The Open University
Milton Keynes, England

1985

ACADEMIC PRESS, INC.

(Harcourt Brace Jovanovich, Publishers)

Orlando   San Diego   New York   London
Toronto   Montreal   Sydney   Tokyo

ACADEMIC PRESS, INC.
Orlando, Florida 32887

United Kingdom Edition published by
ACADEMIC PRESS INC. (LONDON) LTD.
24-28 Oval Road, London NW1 7DX

LIBRARY OF CONGRESS CATALOGING IN PUBLICATION DATA

Main entry under title:

Designing usable texts.

Includes index.
1. Examinations—Design and construction—Addresses,
essays, lectures. I. Duffy, Thomas M. II. Waller,
Robert (Robert W.)
LB3060.65D47   1985   371.2'61   84-6314
ISBN 0-12-223260-7 (alk. paper)

PRINTED IN THE UNITED STATES OF AMERICA

85 86 87 88   9 8 7 6 5 4 3 2 1

Contents

PART IV   IDENTIFYING INFORMATION REQUIREMENTS

12.   Understanding Readers and Their Uses of Text
T. Sticht

13.   Modeling Users and Their Use of Technical Manuals
Richard P. Kern

14. Testing Design Alternatives: A Comparison of Procedures
Gary M. Schumacher and Robert Waller

Contributors

Numbers in parentheses indicate the pages on which the authors' contributions begin.

THOMAS H. ANDERSON (159), Center for the Study of Reading, University of Illinois, Champaign, Illinois 61820

BONNIE B. ARMBRUSTER (159), Center for the Study of Reading, University of Illinois, Champaign, Illinois 61820

JOHN F. CARTER (145), International Correspondence Institute, Brussels, Belgium, and Southern California College, Costa Mesa, California 92626

THOMAS M. DUFFY (113), Communication Design Center, Carnegie–Mellon University, Pittsburgh, Pennsylvania 15213

DANIEL B. FELKER (43), Document Design Center, American Institutes for Research, Washington, D.C. 20007

LAWRENCE T. FRASE (97), AT&T Bell Laboratories, Summit, New Jersey 07901

ROBERT E. HORN (179), Information Mapping Inc., Waltham, Massachusetts 02154

STACEY A. KEENAN (97), AT&T Bell Laboratories, Summit, New Jersey 07901

RICHARD P. KERN (341), U.S. Army Research Institute for the Behavioral and Social Sciences, Alexandria, Virginia 22333

NINA H. MACDONALD (97), AT&T Bell Laboratories, Summit, New Jersey 07901

DAVID R. OLSON (3), Applied Psychology Department, Ontario Institute for Studies in Education, Toronto, Ontario M5S 1V6, Canada

ELIZABETH ORNA (19), Information, Editorial and Typographical Design Consultancy, Norwich, Norfolk, England

JANE PETERSON[1] (43), Document Design Center, American Institutes for Research, Washington, D.C. 20007

---

[1]Present address: Richland College of the Dallas County Community College District, Dallas, Texas 75243.

JANICE C. REDISH (43), Document Design Center, American Institutes for Research, Washington, D.C. 20007

GARY M. SCHUMACHER (377), Department of Psychology, Ohio University, Athens, Ohio 45701

ROBERT J. SMILLIE (213), Navy Personnel Research and Developmental Center, San Diego, California 92152

T. STICHT (315), U.S. Naval Postgraduate School, Monterey, California 93940

MICHAEL TWYMAN (245), Department of Typography & Graphic Communication, University of Reading, Whiteknights, Reading RG6 2AU, England

ROBERT WALLER (377), Institute of Educational Technology, Open University, Milton Keynes, England

PATRICIA WRIGHT (63), Medical Research Council, Applied Psychology Unit, Cambridge, CB2 2EF England

Preface

At one time it was fashionable for prophets of the electronic age to predict the demise of text in favor of electronic audiovisual media. Instead, it is now apparent that these media themselves generate large quantities of text, on which their own operation and maintenance depend. For example, a colleague recently bought a portable computer that arrived with a manual twice its size in volume and weight.

Even the most ordinary domestic appliances, such as washing machines, now require quite complex programming to operate their microprocessor controls, where once there was just a single switch. And the literacy component of industrial jobs continues to grow, too. Technical manuals are long and difficult, and for large and complex systems they can weigh literally thousands of pounds: In the military context this poses something of a problem for field repairs—I once read of a battle tank that came equipped with an armor-plated microfiche reader and a complete set of microfilm manuals.

It is not in dispute that texts exist for, among other things, the purpose of communication—messages are recorded in them to be interpreted at a later date—but in practice there is rather more to it than that. Although recall of text content is still the dominant criterion encountered in the empirical research literature, there is a growing realization among researchers that it is often inappropriate. Even when we leave aside the large proportion of texts that are simply for the purpose of entertainment, only a small number of the functional texts that remain are intended to be learned, and few are designed to be read in the conventional sense of a linear processing from beginning to end. Hence the title of this volume; it addresses the issue not only of comprehensible texts, but of their usability in the fullest sense.

The alternative is to see texts as just one component of a complete system: the text, the user, the environment, and the purposive context. This suggests, though, that if research outcomes are themselves to be usable by text producers, they need to be context-sensitive in the way they are determined and the way they are expressed. Data from reductionist scientific experiments may support theories that may in turn inform practice, but the link is often tenuous. In the practical world, knowledge has traditionally been passed on aphoristically, as rules, guidelines, and examples. However, text technologies are changing so fast that there is no time for these to evolve in the old way. Research—of the right kind— has never been needed more in the world of practice.

Text can be considered as arguments, as linguistic entities, as programs of instruction, as components of a system, mechanism, task, or procedure, and even as art objects. Each text is simultaneously part of a number of different systems: A typical college textbook, for example, can be seen as part of its author's corpus of work, as part of the discipline of psychology or education, as part of the English-speaking culture, and as part of the students' task environment. Functional texts thus have too many facets for any one approach or level of analysis to tackle comprehensively.

It is because of the broadness of the usability criterion that the authors of this volume represent a number of special fields from both academic and practical traditions. They are traditions that have sometimes been antagonistic—the one caricatured as insensitive to practical matters of text production, the other as unreasoning and arbitrary. However, those on either side who exhibit these tendencies err in similar ways: Sidetracked into methodological or aesthetic debate, they lose sight of the real-world goals and applications of their professions. One of the problems is that we lack a common language for discussing functional text. Psychologists traditionally deal in theories, writers and designers in feelings. Whether these are manifested in contrived stimulus materials for experiments or in prize-winning creative works, they each refer to a tidy world of ideal texts. This book has been compiled, though, in the belief that recommendations about text design from whatever source must be soundly argued, properly tested, consistent with the research evidence, but also realistic, affordable, and intuitively acceptable. It is for this reason that the authors in this volume address themselves directly to the analysis of textual communication processes in the real world of publishing systems and work sites.

In the introductory chapter, Olson places text in the general theoretical framework of communications in which text is an utterance. The dilemma faced by the writer–designer and the competence he or she must possess become evident in the contrast of design requirements for text and for oral utterances. Part II, "Authoring, Editing, and the Production Process," examines what writers do and how they can be trained (Felker et al.; Orna), what editors do (Wright) and perhaps what they should do (Carter), and appropriate and inappropriate use of linguistic guidelines (Frase et al.; Duffy). In Part III, several alternative design systems and strategies for instructional text (Anderson and Armbruster), reference text (Horn), and procedural text (Smillie), and for the use of pictorial representation in all of these text types (Twyman) are presented. In Part IV, "Identifying Information Requirements," the focus is on how an understanding of the use of text can be a basis for the design of text. Sticht provides a theoretical perspective on literacy and the use of text. Schumacher and Waller discuss alternative text-evaluation strategies that have or may have practical usefulness, and Kern provides a strong case for what might be called the experimental-ethnography approach to text evaluation.

The typography of the volume conforms to the standards of The Educational Technology Series. We would like to thank the authors for their patience and cooperation with us as we muddled through the trans-Atlantic editorial process. The opportunities for providing us with ''editorial guidelines'' were many, and we appreciate their resistance to temptation. We are grateful to Elizabeth Orna for compiling the index for us and we would also like to express our appreciation to Cindy Thomas Duffy and Jenny Waller for their patience and encouragement throughout this endeavor.

PART I

Introduction

CHAPTER 1

On the Designing and Understanding of Written Texts

DAVID R. OLSON

INTRODUCTION

Three issues appropriately dominate the chapters in this book. The first has to do with the relations between the structures of texts and the mental resources, processes, goals, and interests of their readers–users. The second issue has to do with the production of comprehensible, utilizable texts, through the creation, design, and management of text structure, from the typographic and linguistic to textual and discourse levels. The third issue has to do with more immediate practical design problems and their relation to the preceding theoretical problems.

CONSTRUCTING AND USING TEXTS

Discussions of texts and their uses tend to hide one fundamental consideration: texts are *one* side of a very basic system—that of communication by means of ordinary language. In an analysis of everyday discourse, it is relatively easy to keep track of the primary *social* relation that is maintained between conversational partners and to note that language is simply their means for mediating their interactions and sharing their intentions. Many of our misperceptions of texts could be avoided if we realized that fundamentally texts mediate a reader and a writer, even if the writer frequently loses track of his or her audience and even if the reader frequently forgets that the text being read is, basically, merely the expression of some person.

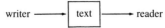

DESIGNING USABLE TEXTS

If we recognize that texts are extended utterances, we see our way past the first hurdle. The differentiation of an author from his or her text allows unprecedented scope for revision and design, but on the other hand, it creates the illusion of autonomy, authority, and objectivity, as we see presently. Nevertheless, a text is ultimately not different from the utterance of a speech act that is directed from one person to another in the attempt to construct a social relationship, to issue a command, to make a request, to get the listener to change a belief, and so on.

Once texts are seen as derivative of ordinary uses of language, we can lay to rest the naively optimistic assumption that authors and designers can create, by means of successive approximations and empirical trial and error, universally effective texts. It is, of course, simply nonsense that one could create a symbol, let alone a text, that had the effect of being not only immediately comprehensible but completely persuasive to any reader. One may recall the attempts in the 1940s by the armed forces to prevent the spread of venereal diseases through the construction of a persuasive film showing the horrors of disease and some means for avoiding it. Yet, for rather obvious reasons, the film had no effect whatever. It was not basically a problem of communication, but rather of the competing goals and interests of the viewers. Ultimately, I believe, the only way to make a person do something is through force, not communication. What, then, can design be expected to do to improve the usability of texts?

The problem in designing texts is to attempt to achieve some goals without seriously losing access to others. The problem is analogous to designing a car with both good acceleration and low fuel consumption; the two goals are somewhat incompatible. There is no one stone that can kill these two birds.

What then are some options and how do we choose among them? Fortunately, they are relatively clear. We can make better texts that make fewer assumptions about the readers, *or* we can train better readers so that they can cope with almost any texts. Hence, discussions of text design are complementary to those of increasing literacy skills. Let us see if we can specify more fully how these considerations are interdependent.

Any symbolic form makes some assumption about its users. The once-popular view that pictorial media are self-explanatory is no longer plausible. Twyman points out in Chapter 11 of the present volume, symbols of any greater complexity than those portraying simple objects require knowledge of the symbolic form to be intelligible. Sir Ernst Gombrich (1974) made this point in his analysis of the picture left on the moon by an Apollo mission, to be ''read'' or ''deciphered'' by itinerant space men: The upraised hand on the pictured man and woman, for example, is simply a pictorial convention; unless the reader knows the convention for greeting, the symbol is meaningless. Every symbol makes assumptions about the comprehender (or reader of a text). Psychologists may be expected to help discover how readers understand and use texts? One of the contributions of psychologists is to discover how various readers understand and interpret written texts and thereby make clear just what writers can safely assume about readers.

A MODEL OF COMPREHENSION

To handle the question of how readers understand and use text, we need a richer theory of the comprehension of utterances and texts. We may begin with the following:

Speaker ⟶ Text ⟶ Reader

and elaborate it thus:

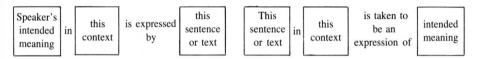

We shall consider only the logical form of the relation, a relation that is symmetrical for the speaker and hearer if we assume that what the reader recovers is the speaker's intention. The critical dimensions are shown in Figure 1 in terms of the relationship between the semantic structure (S), which is sometimes called the text structure, sometimes the sentence meaning, and sometimes "the meaning in the text"; the context or knowledge of the world or simply a possible word (PW); and the intended meaning (M), which is sometimes called either the speaker's meaning, the speaker's intention, or sometimes simply the interpreted or comprehended meaning.

Informally, we may describe these constituents as (1) what we "say," (2) a context or a possible word, and (3) what we "mean." Formally, the claim is that S is a function from PW to M. That is, for any value of PW, S will determine the possible meanings M. Conversely S without PW does not "mean" anything.

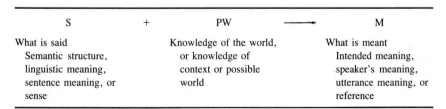

S	+	PW	⟶	M
What is said Semantic structure, linguistic meaning, sentence meaning, or sense		Knowledge of the world, or knowledge of context or possible world		What is meant Intended meaning, speaker's meaning, utterance meaning, or reference

Fig. 1.   The relation between a sentence and its context in the specification of meaning.

Before I use this theory to comment on the theories and arguments raised in this book, let me make clear that the theory has both a decent pedigree and some empirical support. The pedigree arises from combining Bierwisch's formal semantic theory with Searle's analysis of speech acts (see Olson & Hildyard, 1983). The data come from some experiments (which I do not discuss in detail here) that my colleagues—Angela Hildyard, Nancy Torrance, Hillel Goelman—and I have carried out at the Ontario Institute for Studies in Education (See Olson, Torrance & Hildyard, 1984) as well as from other researchers.

First, let me show that S and M are interdependent in just the way I have indicated. Consider the following linguistic structures:

S Structure	+	PW (context)	⟶	M (meaning)
"You're standing on my toes."		(really are)		"Move your foot."
"You're standing on my toes."		(not really)		"You're invading my space."
"I hear talking."		(a classroom)		"Be quiet."
"I hear talking."		(long-distance phone call)		"Speak louder."

These sentences illustrate the fact that if you alter PW, the meaning of the S changes correspondingly. Such observations in the early days of transformational grammar were raised (by people like me) to show that sentences did not have fixed meaning. It is the meaning M in Figure 1 that depends on context PW, not the S (what transformational linguists call linguistic meaning). By differentiating S from M we can eat our cake and have it too. We can say that meaning depends on context and yet admit that a sentence has a linguistic form that is generated by the formal rules described by linguists. Moreover, we can discuss differences in the PW entertained or presupposed by the writer and the PW in which the reader understands the text; these are the central issues in designing usable texts.

TEXT STRUCTURES AND THE CONTEXTS OF COMPREHENSION

The chapters in this book can be arranged in terms of the preceding model. On the one hand we have those that deal primarily with the structure of text—from the graphemic, to the lexical, to the syntactic and textual levels–structures examined especially in the present volume by Anderson and Armbruster (Chapter 8), by Duffy (Chapter 6), by Frase, Macdonald, and Keenan (Chapter 5), by Horn (Chapter 9), and by Smillie (Chapter 10). All the procedures they discuss for clarifying the structure of the text for what, in Figure 1, I have called "What is said" are both enlightening and useful, and we consider them in more detail presently. But as I have already suggested, many alterations in text, especially attempts to make texts autonomous expressions of meaning, makes particularly strong assumptions about the reader's linguistic knowledge and about the reader's knowledge of the PW.

On the other side of the model, in the present volume, we have Wright's chapter (4), with its emphasis on understanding; Kern's (Chapter 13), Smillie's (Chapter 10), and Schumacher's and Waller's (Chapter 14) discussion of user-centered as opposed to text-centered texts; and Orna's (Chapter 2) and Wright's (Chapter 4), concern for audience.[1] In fact, most authors have sympathy both for the structure of texts and for their usefulness and comprehensibility by user, an issue of particular concern to the chapters by Carter (7) and Sticht (12). Hence, it is clear that the dominant issue of all of these chapters is that of relationship between the structure of texts and their processing and use by readers. Let us see if we can formalize or at least tidy up the relations between these considerations.

First, notice that texts play one part (the part subject to design, admittedly) but only one part in the determination of meaning. Sentences and texts may be seen as linguistic structures that in a broad sense include phonological–graphemic, typographic, syntactic, lexical, and textual structures. These structures, together with the context or PW, mean something to a comprehender (or for that matter a producer). If a listener–reader fails to arrive at an M, either he or she does not know the rules of S (i.e., he or she has limited literacy–linguistic skills); S is faulty as Anderson and Armbruster (Chapter 8) show in their examples; or the listener–reader does not share the appropriate PW. Any use of S, however, assumes that the user knows the structure of S—that is he or she knows how S expresses M in PW. If one does not, one cannot determine M. However, even if one knows S, unless one shares PW, one cannot construct M. Furthermore, as more is known about the readers' PW, the writer can eliminate some of the structures of S because the reader is able to make the required assumptions. Winograd (1980) has discussed this in some detail. Suppose one were reading a text: "Tommy had just been given a new set of blocks. He was opening the box when he saw Jimmy coming in." Winograd continues, "There is no mention of what is in the box—no clue as to what box it is at all. But a person reading the text makes the immediate assumption that the box contains the set of blocks. We can do this because we know that new items often come in boxes, and that opening the box is a usual thing to do" (p. 215). Similar arguments have been made by Bransford and Franks (1971) and Paris (1975).

Such inferences are reliably made by readers and listeners; writers can often count on readers to make just the appropriate inferences. Suppose, to take another example, a reader read this text: "The policeman drew his revolver and fired. The burglar slumped to the floor." The reader is invited to make the

---

[1] Orna is largely concerned with the interactions between authors and text designers and editors. She discusses the effects of these interactions on the eventual readers of the text.

inference that the policeman shot the burglar, even though the text does not explicitly say so, and even though it is logically possible that the burglar merely fainted from fright, and so on. All elaborated explanations have to end somewhere and that end point is where the reader can contribute the critical knowledge from his or her PW. To tell the reader the obvious is as inconsiderate as to overlook telling the essentials.

Now let us apply this to our texts. What we need, of course, to mediate an S, and its M is the provision of an adequate context or PW. S means M only in the PW. The text writer–producer constructs a text, an S, that in some PW expresses M. The readers have their *own* PWs that they use to determine an M from S. Does the writer correctly anticipate the readers' PW? Not if the reader does not completely share the set of beliefs, prior knowledge, and so on that make up the PW in which S specifies M for the writer. There are two options open. Either the writer can try to guess the PW of the reader, a possibility we examine presently, *or* the writer can make fewer assumptions about the reader's prior knowledge and attempt to build up a common PW through the use of text. Anderson and Armbruster (Chapter 8) suggest, as do Horn (Chapter 9) and Smillie (Chapter 10), that the writer may completely determine the reader's PW via the text so that the reader will, given S, recover M. Certainly, that is one important function of text but that assumes an extremely high degree of literacy on the part of the reader. This point requires some elaboration.

EXPLICIT TEXTS AND CONTEXT-DEPENDENT TEXTS

In ordinary discourse, the listener–reader already brings a PW, composed of some prior knowledge and some contextual knowledge, and the sentence assumes or presupposes that exact PW, and so the listener–reader can recover the intended meaning. But writers can rarely, if ever, correctly guess the prior knowledge, let alone the purpose and goals, held by a reader. Thus, as Smillie, Anderson and Armbruster, and Horn propose, texts may be constructed that do not presuppose an appropriate PW but that actually construct the appropriate context or PW through the text. Let us call such texts *explicit texts*. In such texts, the burden of comprehension falls on the interpretation of S rather than on the PW previously held by the listener. Put more simply, if you want the listener to understand S appropriately, then teach him or her the appropriate PW through the text, rather than find a PW already in the listener's mind, into which S can be tied. In this case, S is primary; whereas in ordinary discourse, PW—the expectancies, beliefs, interests of the listener—is primary. Nonetheless, PW can to some extent be constructed through S—that is through the text—and to the extent that that is required, the structure of the text—at a logical, syntactic, lexical, and textual level—will be crucial. To oversimplify, the more the text is to teach a reader, the greater the weight that falls onto the S of the text and the less it falls on the listener's existing PW.

But note that as the burden of constructing the PW falls increasingly on S, the greater the demands placed on the literacy skills of the reader. Hence, explicit text is needed at precisely the point that it is least useful—for the poor or uninformed reader. Texts that assume the least prior knowledge of PW by the reader necessarily assume the greatest degree of knowledge of S—the highest levels of literary skills. This is the primary limitation of explicit logical prose text.

Thus, if a writer attempts to construct the PW through text, an enormous burden falls on the linguistic skills of the reader. For some ideas, however, there is no alternative; new theories, for example, require readers to reassemble PW on the basis of the literal meaning of the text. Understandably, such texts are difficult to read.

Let us, then, back away from the attempt to make S an adequate and explicit representation of meaning and see what we can do from the reader's side. The reader already perceives a PW through which he or she can interpret a text. A live speaker *knowing* the listener's PW can usually generate an S to specify an intended meaning. But, in principle, a text writer cannot know a reader's PW— the reader is separated in time and space and in many cases is not even known to the writer except in the most general terms. Nonetheless, to some extent the writer can anticipate the PW of many readers, as did the Gideon Bible in my hotel room, which says:

> Need a tonic? Read Psalm 27.
> Lonely? Read Psalm 23.

(I had the feeling the writer of the questions did not anticipate my needs exactly.)

It is doubtful if a text writer can ever anticipate the PWs of all readers, especially those of lively readers who are likely to try out their own ideas, who read for their own purposes, and so on. But by knowing probable knowledge and expectancies, and problems of a certain class of readers, one can create texts that exploit as far as possible the PW of that class of readers. Surely such texts are easier to read and to use than those that make no assumptions about prior PW of readers or, worse still, wrongly assume it.

This point is central to Wright's comments (Chapter 4 in the present volume) on contextualizing text. Formal text does not easily provide (construct) its own context, and thus the reader is left with the job of providing a PW in which the formal text (S) can mean something. The reader can read what is said and yet not know what is meant. Comprehension of S is immensely facilitated if the reader already knows the context or PW; and a good text writer will play into the PW existing in the reader. The formal structure will then be understood by seeing how it maps into and extends an already known PW. Easy texts, in a word, are appropriate to the reader's existing PW.

In summary, then, text is a function from a *PW* to a meaning. If readers know the relevant PW, comprehension is easy; if too difficult, readers may find it easier to simply memorize S rather than to build the appropriate PW. To make text comprehension easy you must appeal to the reader's PW.

But written texts, unlike oral language, cannot be tailored easily, if ever, to the reader's PW. Readers bring PW to text. That is our dilemma. To return to our automobile analogy, How do you balance the goal of good acceleration with that of low gasoline consumption? One does not solve such a problem, one accepts a workable compromise. I suggest that good text preserves logical form such that, given the logical form and given high levels of linguistic and literacy skill, a diligent reader could imagine a PW of which that text is an appropriate description. On the other hand, good texts are also geared to many diverse PWs and hence to many uses by readers.

That, then, is our dilemma. On the one hand, we can design highly structured explicit texts that explicitly create a PW, largely ignoring the PWs that readers bring to the text. In this case readers will need extremely high degrees of linguistic competence to deal with them, and that is a level of competence we can expect only in experts. Hence such texts are of restricted usefulness.

On the other hand, we can guess, sometimes correctly, the PW of the readers and write texts that map directly into their existing PWs. Such texts are readily comprehended, but because a writer can only guess a particular PW of any particular readers, such texts are again of restricted usefulness. We minimize our losses by anticipating reader's PW and by attempting to make texts as autonomous and self-explanatory as possible. Because it is so difficult to know just what knowledge and interest a reader has, text writers may be tempted to ignore the reader and simply construct explicit logical texts. Contrary to my earlier views on the "meaning in the text" (Olson, 1977) this seems not to be a realistic goal.

Such explicit logical texts are *primarily* of use to the expert reader who already possesses the basic stock of concepts, not to the average reader. To be useful to the average user, the text simultaneously should be geared to may PWs and hence to many uses. If texts are intended for children, for example, they should raise many considerations in addition to the logical form of the argument. In discussing the role of the Krebcycle in metabolism, texts for children should not only spell out the equations but also raise such questions as Who was Kreb? Why did he attack such a question? What was he up to? Is his a good theory? How do we know? How was the theory tested? Do scientists secrete theories? Is this a problem area in science, or is it a closed case? And in schools, at least, I would have these ideas discussed by teachers as well as read by students.

As an aside, we may note that universal literacy encouraged the idea of the individual silent reader—everyone tied to his or her own book. Why not go back, for some situations at least, to the manuscript era when the one copy of the book was chained to the pulpit, and it was assumed that the average reader would often need a clergyman to help in understanding it correctly. The teacher's role in this scenario is to show the student how to correctly interpret the text. But if texts are to stand up to careful, critical reading, they must be informationally adequate and logically coherent as Anderson and Armbruster (Chapter 8 in the present volume) and Horn (Chapter 9) show. Stripping text of its complex concepts merely to meet the requirements of readibility formulas degrades rather than simplifies text.

OPTIMAL DESIGN OF TEXTS

Now, let us see how our general schema may apply to the design of S, that is, the design of text. Recall that all design in S assumes the reader's knowledge of the rules of S but it does not necessarily presuppose PW. However, good design is a matter of interrelating the two. Good design consists of finding an appropriate form S to express a M in a PW. Finding an appropriate form to represent a problem, as Twyman (Chapter 11 in the present volume), Sticht, (Chapter 12), and Smillie (Chapter 10) suggest, is to make the problem solvable. This is no less true for pictures than for words or for flow charts. Recall the story of Ramon y Cajal, the Spanish neurologist who in the early part of the century won the Nobel prize for his descriptions of the neuron. Others looked at neurons with a microscope but they saw only what for them resembled a mass of felt. Cajal, looked at the same mass but saw interrelated neurons, of which he made remarkable drawings.[2] Cajal claimed that he succeeded at this task because of his early training as an artist, a career that had been forceably ended by his father's decision that being a physician was a good career while being an artist was not. This training in the visual arts led him to see the structure of nerve cells where others could not. To this day Cajal's drawings serve as models in many neurology texts (Cajal, 1973).

The same point is true, I believe, for the creation of texts. Authors, editors, and publishers are looking for optimal forms of expression that will most comprehensibly express M in PW. That is the heart of designing usable text. This is what Twyman (Chapter 11 in the present volume) looks for in his study of depictions. A similar point was both stated and illustrated by Alexander Pope (1711/1966) in his *Essay on Criticism* when he urged that "The sound must seem an echo to the sense." Notice how the word *sense* literally echoes the word

---

[2]Foster said that, thanks to Cajal's work, "The impenetrable forest of the neurons system had been converted into a well laid out and delightful park" (p. 421).

sound so that both literally and metaphorically the point is made. It is not enough that meaning is expressed; it is a matter of finding the characteristics of the form of expression that highlight the points being raised. The central problem, from this perspective, is the representation problem—the construction of appropriate descriptions or depictions.

DESIGN VERSUS THEORY

The relation between theory and practice is of central concern to several chapters of this volume, particularly those of Wright (Chapter 4), Duffy (Chapter 6), Carter (Chapter 7), and Kern (Chapter 13). As is well known, there is a voluminous and thriving literature on the processes of comprehension and pro- duction of both oral language and written texts. That research is devoted to constructing a general yet detailed model of the primary structures and pro- cedures involved in using language; and most models, certainly the one I dis- cussed in the preceding, differentiate at least two and sometimes three major constituents. Such an analysis may be elaborated as a *theory* of comprehension. But all of the chapters in this volume agree that such a theory cannot be taken as a program for *designing* usable texts. As Wright (Chapter 4), Smillie (Chapter 10), Sticht (Chapter 12), and others argue, *theory* cannot be equated with *design*. Wright (1978) asks, "What is it that after many years of research so little progress has been made in the development of specifications for designing writ- ten communications so that they are easily understood?" (p. 254). There are at least two answers. The first is that we were naive to believe that they would. To show this, I would like to make a brief detour through the domains of *theories* of reading and *design* for teaching reading, where this exact problem has risen.

Theories of reading and research on reading processing have reached the state of a fine art, the same art roughly as the field of language comprehension. The theoretical and empirical issues are interesting and challenging, and we have every reason to expect that added research will yield increased understanding of both the nature of literacy and of learning to read. But what about the design problem—for example, the problem of designing reading programs that will successfully teach children to read?

Helen Popp (1975) reviewed the overwhelming wealth of reading programs developed by publishers to teach reading. Textbooks, and especially the graded reading-series, have improved gradually since Comenius introduced them into the common (public) schools in the seventeenth century. All of them have evolved to meet a small set of criteria—controlled levels of difficulty, appropri- ate subject matter, accompanying reference books, appropriate accompanying activities, and the inevitable workbooks. Texts, including reading series, are a highly evolved technology that, over time, have become quite well adapted to the needs and demands on the child, the teacher, and the classroom. And they have taken the form they now possess, not particularly because of Comenius's education theory or, for that matter, Piaget's or Bruner's, but because they represent workable solutions to a number of practical constraints. Anderson and Armbruster's (Chapter 8), Frase, Macdonald, and Keenan's (Chapter 5), Horn's (Chapter 9), and Smillie's (Chapter 10) programs are particularly practically oriented and are similarly independent of psychological theory. Theory tends to follow rather than lead such programs.

Design considerations rather than theory have led to the development of many different reading series, all of which are quite good if quite similar. Further, the more revolutionary a reading series is claimed to be, the less likely it is to be good. What is more, the reading theories that attempt to rationalize the particular virtues of various reading series are largely trivial. Series vary in matters of taste more than in matters of substance. Textbooks, including reading series, represent the accumulation of practical experience in the form of an evolved technology of design, and although we may hope that future discoveries in human cognition will substantially alter our conception of the practical art of pedagogy, the contributions of cognitive psychology to date have been modest.

While all reading series succeed in the same way, they also fail in the same way. In that they are mass produced for the general audience, they fail to address the particular child in the personal, direct way that speech does; that is, there is no way for it to address the particular PW of the individual child. There is no possibility of the text "speaking" to the child and the child speaking back and, in the process, negotiating the meanings of the expressions or the particular Ms involved, a process of particular importance to young children and for speakers of nonstandard dialects and of divergent social experience. The preparation of a different early reader for each child, with the child's help, is a form of individualization that, despite its advocacy by such reformers as Sylvia Ashton-Warner and Sybil Marshall, has not been widely adopted. The reason is that individualized texts would be neither profitable for publishers nor labor-saving for teachers. Without genuine individualization (not the spurious individualization achieved by ability groupings), the best primers in the world cannot alter the one dominant feature that differentiates printed text from oral, conversational utterances, namely, that the linguistic conventions employed and the PWs specified are lodged unalterably in the text itself. As Socrates argued, if you ask a text what it means, it merely repeats itself. The text makes no rhetorical allowances for the individual scanning of it, and the child will have to come to understand that text; unlike speech, neither the code nor the content is negotiable.

But now the relation, or perhaps the nonrelation, between scientific *theories* of the linguistic processes related to reading of texts and the applied arts of pedagogical design of text is shown clearly. Reading series, as exemplars of the process of design, appear to be the product of an effective technology. Thus, design addresses the task of developing a technology to achieve a particular range of effects. There may eventually evolve a theory of design, but I doubt if design will depend highly upon such a theory. More importantly, the technologies developed to achieve a practical effect via design are not the same as theories of the psychological processes involved. And, what is worse, it is not clear how the two are related.

But the second answer to the questions of the relation between theory and design is more optimistic. It derives from the analysis of the relation between practical know-how and theoretical conceptual knowledge that has been described by Elting Morrison's (1974), analysis of the history of American technology, *From Know-How to Nowhere*. He shows that it has only been in the 1900s that theoretically derived scientific knowledge has come to affect practical know-how. The practical knowledge acquired through experience in the context of practical action, a powerful form of competence, has gradually been superseded by the development of theoretical derived principles for which technology realizations were then sought, and then only for some areas of technology. Until the early part of the twentieth century, if a technical problem arose, one called upon the person of experience; in the latter part of this century, industry has called, rather, upon the scientist. While that shift has not occurred in the social sciences, we may be approaching the time when scientific theories have useful implications for problems of textual and pedagogic design.

There appears to be an enormous gap between educational theory and education practice. And this gap is not, as it was described in the 1970s, the result of the failure to apply theory to practice. Rather, we have, side by side, a thriving research enterprise and a sophisticated applied technology. We have two things evolving in parallel, one extremely ancient—pedagogical procedures linked to technological devices—and one quite recent—the construction of scientific theory. And it may simply be the case that the research has not yet outstripped, or, perhaps more correctly, caught up with, practical knowledge. Yet that does not make the enterprise worthless—we may yet outstrip practical knowledge.

In the meantime, what is the relation between these two forms of knowledge— the practical and the scientific, between theory and design? The primary, immediate use of theoretical knowledge is both to try to understand the structure of that practical knowledge and more helpfully to criticize that practical knowledge on the basis of theoretical, empirical, and even ideological grounds, a proposal similar to that offered by Wright (1978). But the responsibility for the development and execution of actual workable programs remains, thus far, firmly in the hands of the practitioners, not the theorists.

Design, I believe, is in relatively good hands. There is already an impressive tradition in publishing, illustrating, editing, and so on, that is relatively successful at least for producing reading series and textbooks, and there is now a group of researchers who are devoted to improving the structure of the language of such texts and of contextualizing the structure of language in terms of the reader's prior knowledge. We may be cautiously optimistic about the productivity of the interface between these divergent forms of activity.

REFERENCES

Bransford, J. D., & Franks, J. J. (1971). The abstraction of linguistic ideas. *Cognitive Psychology, 2,* 331–350.

Cajal, Ramon Y. (1937). In E. H. Craigie & J. Cano (Trans.), *Recollections of my life.* Cambridge, MA: MIT Press.

Gombrich, E. (1974). The visual image. In D. R. Olson (Ed.), *Media and symbols: The forms of expression, communication and education.* The 73rd Yearbook of the National Society for the Study of Education. Chicago: University of Chicago Press.

Morrison, E. (1974). *From know-how to nowhere.* Oxford: Blackwell.

Olson, D. R. (1977). From utterance to text: The bias of language in speech and writing. *Harvard Educational Review, 47,* 257–281.

Olson, D. R., & Hildyard, A. (1983). Literacy and the comprehension of literal meaning. In F. Coulmas (Ed.), *Writing in focus.* The Hague: Mouton.

Olson, D. R., Torrance, N. & Hildyard, A. (eds.) (1984). *Literacy, language and learning.* New York: Cambridge University Press.

Paris, S. G. (1975). Integration and inference in children's comprehension and memory. In F. Restle, R. M. Shiffrin, N. J. Castellan, H. R. Lindman, & D. B. Pisoni (Eds.), *Cognitive theory, Vol. 1.* Hillsdale, NJ: Erlbaum.

Pope, A. (1711/1966). An essay on criticism. In W. K. Wimsatt (Ed.), *Alexander Pope: Selected poetry and prose.* Toronto: Holt. (Reprinted 1966).

Popp, H. M. (1975). Current practices in the teaching of beginning reading. In J. B. Carroll & J. S. Chall (Eds.), *Toward a literate society,* (pp. 101–146). New York: McGraw-Hill.

Winograd, T. (1980). What does it mean to understand language? *Cognitive Science, 4,* 209–241.

Wright, P. (1978). Feeding the information eaters: Suggestions for integrating pure and applied research on language comprehension. *Instructional Science, 7,* 249–312.

PART II

Authoring, Editing, and the Production Process

CHAPTER 2

The Author: Help or Stumbling Block on the Road to Designing Usable Texts?

Elizabeth Orna

INTRODUCTION

This chapter presents five simple propositions about producing usable text and uses them to make a case for specific practical action. The propositions assume the author is potentially, if not always actually, a thinking entity in control of what he or she writes, well informed on the range of possibilities for presenting information and on the principles that have emerged from research, fully in control of the choice of means of expression, and free to make his or her own decisions about how and when to apply them.

The propositions state (I) if the author does not get it right, no one else can put it right. In addition, (II) the author's putting it right is a necessary but not a sufficient condition for the final product being usable. The next proposition is that (III) the main problems faced by authors relate to thinking and the organization of ideas. Although authors may need help with these problems, they should be wary of printed advice because (IV) much of the advice at present given to authors in texts on writing and communication is irrelevant to the main problems and can actually obscure them. However, (V) the necessary skills and ways of thinking can be learned by authors. Before discussing the propositions, the chapter first proposes a definition of usable text.

WHAT IS USABLE TEXT?

It is tempting to define usable text in terms of what users should be able to do as a result of reading it: if, after reading, they can understand or do certain things

19

successfully that they had not been to understand or do before, that should prove that the text was usable. Usability is not, however, an all-or-nothing concept; there are degrees of it, and a text can be fairly easy, very difficult, or nearly impossible for the would-be users to make use of. Nor is a text a work of nature; it is a human creation. So the definition of usable text must also take into account the contribution of the makers of the text to making it usable and manageable, and the interaction between their efforts and those of the user.

The following definition may be more suitable for our purposes. A *usable text* is one that allows a successful transaction to take place between user and maker. In this transaction the user's initial unsatisfactory state of knowledge (which is what makes him or her a user in the first place) is transformed, by gaining access to knowledge that the maker has structured to meet the user's needs, into a better

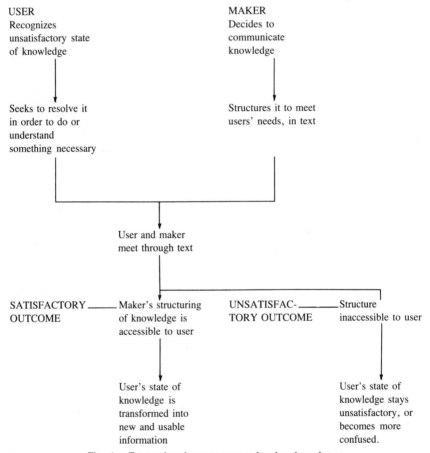

Fig. 1.   Transactions between user and maker through text.

organized one. As a result, the user becomes master of new information that he or she can manage and apply for his or her own purposes.[1]

Figure 1 represents the interactions involved between the user and maker—it makes the point that the two parties are separated in space and time and meet only through the medium of the text.

PRODUCING USABLE TEXT: FIVE PROPOSITIONS

This definition refers to the *maker* of the text as one party to the transaction; in fact, of course, the maker is a compound entity, comprising all the people who take part in the process of making the text that reaches the user: publisher, author, editor, designer, illustrator, typesetter, platemaker, printer, and so forth. However, although the author is one among many in this process, the definition, with its emphasis on knowledge and its structuring to meet user needs, makes the main argument for the first of my propositions:

Proposition I
If the author does not get it right, no one else can put it right.

Authors hold the key in the transaction with users because they have the knowledge that potential users need in order to do or know something that is of use to them. The way the author puts knowledge into words is the main factor that determines whether in the end the text will be usable. The author is responsible for the first structuring of knowledge, on which all succeeding transformations are carried out.

Good editing and design can work wonders to sharpen text, and to bring out basic structure that the author has managed to obscure, but if the basic material is hopelessly wrong for its purposes, no amount of skilled interpretation and re-organization will rectify it.

The author's responsibility is thus the heaviest one, and too often authors do not rise to it, but sink ingloriously beneath it. If we can find out why authors fail, we are on the right path to being able to do something to help them to succeed. If we can do that, it should make the work of those who produce their text more rewarding, the users will employ their time more profitably, and the whole business will be a great deal more economic than it is at present.

---

[1]This definition owes something to Brookes (1980) definition of information as "that which mediates all our interactions both between ourselves and between each of us and our environment" (p. 20). Wright (1980) defines usability in terms of the cognitive activities involved when people use documents, and proposes that research to analyse these activities can lead to improved decisions by those who make informative text about how to present it. (p. 185)

There are three main groups of reasons for an author's failure to make text fully usable by the intended readers. The first group is related to the author's state of knowledge of the subject. Here there are two possible cases. Authors can be so immersed in the subject and so at home in it that they cannot see what it looks like from the outside to people with less knowledge. This leads to elliptical writing, and to logical jumps that are easy for the author, but that make chasms into which readers can fall, never to emerge.

Other authors, far from being completely at ease in their subject, have gaps or confused areas in their knowledge. These are not bad enough to be a serious hindrance in their day-to-day use of it, but when it comes to writing, the gaps of knowledge cause blurring whenever the writer approaches them. The fact that the author is on unsure ground is often signalled by confused and illogical sentence construction, which mirrors the conceptual ambiguities.

The second set of reasons for authors' failure lies in inadequate knowledge of both the users and the use of the text. This may be solely the author's responsibility; on the other hand, the author may be in some measure a victim of inadequate thinking and/or a poor brief (or outline) from those who commission the text.

However it comes about, the results of imperfect knowledge of users and use show themselves in such things as (1) omission of necessary content and inclusion of irrelevant content; (2) structure and sequence that do not match the approach that users will need to take, given their state of knowledge; (3) methods of presenting information that are not readily accessible to the users; or (4) a level of writing that does not fit the reading skills of the users.

The third group of reasons for failure lies in the author's lack of appreciation of the professional skills involved. Authors who are professionals in their own field of knowledge but amateurs in writing (a frequent situation with informative texts) often fail to realize the difficulty and intensity of the work required in transforming their own expert knowledge into writing that others can understand and make their own. The worst case is when authors combine high regard for their own brand of professional knowledge with near-contempt for that required by the writer. Authors with this attitude are often disastrously overconfident of their ability to get it all down on paper in a short space of time; they do not realize until too late that very few people are able, as Wason (1980) puts it, "to do two incompatible things at the same time: say something, and say it in the most acceptable way" (p. 132).

Authors can also present insoluble problems to those who take over their text for the next stages of its transformation because of their ignorance of the production process. It can lead them to present heavily amended typescript, without appreciating the delays and errors in typesetting it will cause; and to assume that proofs can be treated as a first draft and amended at will. It can mean that they permit themselves inconsistencies in headings and numbering, in the use of terms, and between what they say in one place and what they say in another—not realizing that this imposes additional editorial work (assuming that a competent editor is employed—and that in itself is a dangerous assumption). It can lead to their giving no thought to the visual organization of their text, and so leaving it to the mercy of either a designer who has not been properly briefed (assuming that one is employed), or of whatever the typesetter sees fit to do with it. The days have long gone when Moxon (1683/1958) could advise the compositor to be "ambitious as well to make the meaning of his *Author* intelligent to the *Reader,* as to make his work shew graceful to the *Eye* and pleasant in Reading" (p. 211) and to "read his *Copy* with consideration: that so he may get himself into the meaning of the Author . . . " (p. 212). Typesetters do not come like that any more.

Proposition II
The author's getting it right is a necessary but not a sufficient condition for the final product being usable.

The production of usable text depends on more people than just the author, and even if the author does get it right, there is plenty of scope for others to get it wrong.

Figure 2 represents the stages of transformation from the first ideas for a text through to publication—one sequence as it should be, the other as it often is and should not be. The form is evidently an oversimplification of what happens in real life, but the purpose is to show the difference between two possible courses of events.

The first four stages are mainly the responsibility of authors and of anyone else who initiates the development of texts. But there are many more, and it is only if all stages of transformation are linked by mutual understanding of the purposes among the people responsible that the processes will be integrated and mutually reinforcing, instead of being, as too often they are, fragmented. Without mutual understanding at each stage, effort is wasted and ideas are lost; with it, the original intentions can emerge and be brought to life, with their full potential realized.

The other thing to be said about this series is that the people at the initiating end—including authors, editors, and designers—should be the main decision makers, who define the field in which those responsible for the later stages apply their skills, who secure everyone's commitment to the same understanding of the purposes of the text, and who coordinate the various activities that go into the making of the final text.

This is very different from what usually happens. Authors are often discouraged from contact with editors and designers, or do not know how to use such contact if it is offered; editors are restricted to a narrow application of a set of house rules; and designers are brought in late in the day and expected to work at a superficial decorative level rather than to be concerned with what the content

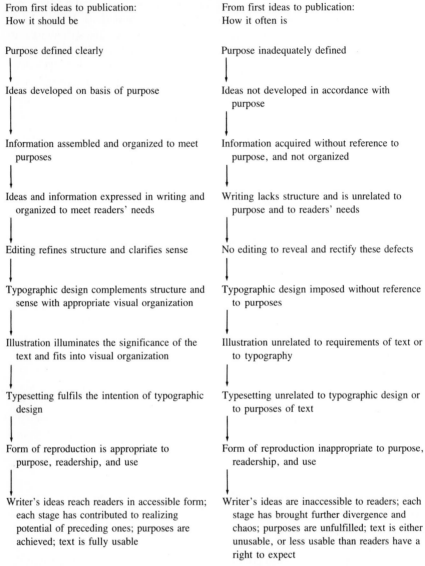

From first ideas to publication: How it should be	From first ideas to publication: How it often is
Purpose defined clearly	Purpose inadequately defined
Ideas developed on basis of purpose	Ideas not developed in accordance with purpose
Information assembled and organized to meet purposes	Information acquired without reference to purpose, and not organized
Ideas and information expressed in writing and organized to meet readers' needs	Writing lacks structure and is unrelated to purpose and to readers' needs
Editing refines structure and clarifies sense	No editing to reveal and rectify these defects
Typographic design complements structure and sense with appropriate visual organization	Typographic design imposed without reference to purposes
Illustration illuminates the significance of the text and fits into visual organization	Illustration unrelated to requirements of text or to typography
Typesetting fulfils the intention of typographic design	Typesetting unrelated to typographic design or to purposes of text
Form of reproduction is appropriate to purpose, readership, and use	Form of reproduction inappropriate to purpose, readership, and use
Writer's ideas reach readers in accessible form; each stage has contributed to realizing potential of preceding ones; purposes are achieved; text is fully usable	Writer's ideas are inaccessible to readers; each stage has brought further divergence and chaos; purposes are unfulfilled; text is either unusable, or less usable than readers have a right to expect

Fig. 2.   Stages of transformation.

means (an expectation in which many still concur). By default, control often finishes up in funny places—instead of decisions being made by the originators, in terms of rational objectives, they are made by people at the other end of the chain, who are not in a position to know anything about the purposes.

That is a traditional kind of mess, which has been common for a long time. There are nastier dangers upon us now, however. Changes in the technology of origination and reproduction of text can give those who are wholly unacquainted with the skills necessary for controlling the technology the power of being their own editors, designers, typesetters, and printers. For example, word processors may be linked with computer phototypesetting, and so the editorial and design phases can be completely bypassed. In the face of this real danger, both self-preservation and the readers' interests demand that authors, editors, and designers understand one another's professional contribution to the production of text. By understanding and making common cause, they have a chance of gaining more control over the originating end of the process of conveying information in print. If they can manage this, they can help to ensure that developments in information technology become the intelligently employed servant of the communication of information, rather than its ignorant and capricious master. (These questions are discussed by Orna and Stevens (1985) in a text designed to help raise awareness of the issues involved in the presentation of information, among those who find themselves engaged in that activity without adequate preparation.)

So much for the power structure. It is time to turn to the specific problems with which authors need to concern themselves if they are to contribute positively to the production of usable text.

Proposition III

The main problems for authors relate to thinking and the organization of ideas, and if those problems are resolved, the problems of writing become much more manageable.

It seems to be a fairly general experience that if purposes are clearly defined and information logically organized as it is gathered, the writing will more or less take care of itself when the time comes. If, on the other hand, the purposes have not been defined, and the information has been jumbled into a disorganized heap, it is almost impossible to impose logical structure when the time comes for writing: the writer is simultaneously contending with the problem of organization and that of getting information into words, and one interferes with the other.

The capacity of authors for defining the purpose of their writing and for managing the information they have to handle varies greatly. The author can acquire some ways of thinking about problems, which appear to lead to greater control by the author and to better transactions between author and reader. The emphasis in the discussion that follows is on ways of thinking, rather than on techniques that can be applied by rote; though acquiring ways of thinking will usually lead to writers cultivating certain skills and choosing to adopt certain techniques as an aid to applying the ways of thinking.

Defining Purposes

The first responsibility of the writer is to know the answers to certain key questions:

1. Who are the intended readers?
2. How will they use what is written for them?
3. What information do they need in order to make use of it?
4. From what sources should the information be assembled?
5. What is the time limit on the writing?
6. How long will what is written remain valid?
7. Who has to read and comment on the draft?

Developing a Structure

The answers can help the author to develop a provisional framework—a metaphorical set of pigeonholes into which information can be posted as it is acquired. The structure will almost certainly need to be modified more than once, but it is infinitely easier to make stepwise changes than to move straight from chaos to perfect order.

Finding and Controlling Information

While authors nearly always start off with knowledge of the subject on which they are to write, they usually need to acquire extra information from outside their own resources. In some cases it is in fact their task to apply their existing expertise in order to master some specific new topic and report on it for the benefit of others. This is often so with professional staff in industry or commerce who have to identify facts and problems and recommend solutions.

Authors need to develop their own personal methods for information management, which will be those with which they feel most comfortable. They need, first, to create physical means of storing information as it is gathered, in the place where it is needed, so that it is assigned to its place in the provisional conceptual structure.

In many situations, information can be gathered in discrete bits that can be assigned straight to their place in a framework. Often, however, this is impossible, and means have to be found for disentangling the relevant pieces of information from some other structure to get them to their rightful place. This requires the author to be skilled in note taking from written sources and from the spoken word. It also puts a premium on information-seeking skills, ranging from knowing one's way around library catalogues and abstracting and indexing services, to formulating questions for postal or interview surveys. These skills are unfortunately not as common as they ought to be—educational systems are often strong on teaching people how to answer questions, but none too keen on teaching them how to ask them!

Stibic (1982) offers many valuable and ingenious suggestions on ways in which writers can use modern information technology, especially word processing, to control and organize information.

Making Good Use of Time

The management of time is another essential but generally neglected skill of those who have to write in the course of their work, though time is usually the most important constraint they have to work with. Authors need to be able to estimate how long they need for each stage of the process. They have to learn the rule that *everything takes longer than you expect* and that the excess of actual over expected time is in direct proportion to the number of people involved. They need to allow time for reflection between the planning and drafting stages of their work, and between drafting and reviewing, because this is a creative process in which the subject may be out of their conscious thoughts but is being worked on by some organizing force below the conscious level. They also need to allow as much time as possible for the writing stage, because it is fatiguing for most people to write intensively for more than one or two hours at a time, and quality quickly drops when tiredness sets in.

Making Information Accessible

The author needs to acquire a range of ways in which information can be made accessible to the user. Structure takes first place; the author should look at the chosen structure in relation to what he or she knows of the readers and the ways in which they will want to use the information, and should ask such questions as: Does the chosen sequence fit the likely knowledge, experience, and approach of the readers? Does it flow logically from a starting point related to their experience, through stages that are clearly linked to one another? Does it present at the right point the information needed for understanding what comes later? Does it refer forward and backward to other related information necessary to give the reader the whole picture? Can the reader who needs a view of the whole subject easily find one? Are there convenient breaks in the text where progress so far can be reviewed?

Structure requires signposting—the devices that can be used to give the reader an overall view of what the text contains and to provide detailed guidance through and among different areas. If the readership is likely to be diverse, with varying needs (as is often the case with instructional texts, for instance), then signposting different routes through it so as to meet these different needs is necessary too. Unfortunately, few authors seem to appreciate how much help readers need from them, and those who do often choose ineffective means of giving the help.

The ineffectiveness often lies in *over*coding information to the extent that readers are confused rather than helped. Users of an aircraft manual produced some years ago, for example, were expected to contend with a three-part numbering system within chapters, in which the numbers were codes standing for subject matter. Thus, in order to find their way about the manual, users had first to learn what subjects were associated with numbers standing in first, second, or third position in the system. Not only that, instead of pages being numbered in the normal sequential way, sets of pages were assigned to given subjects, so that, for example, within any chapter, the pages relating to trouble shooting on the equipment or assembly dealt with in the chapter started at 201, and those on maintenance at 301.

The British viewdata system, Prestel, was in its early stages inspired by a similar misguided wish to impart to numbers more significance than they should be called on to carry. There was an attempt, fortunately soon abandoned under the pressure of constantly increasing input of information, to relate subjects to certain digits, both in page numbers and in the numerical codes used to link them with the next level down the hierarchy—for example, 5 was linked with business information. In this case, happily, it is doubtful if users of the system ever noticed the ingenuity that was being exercised on their behalf.

Making Information Manageable

Many access and guidance devices have the additional function of helping to make the information that the writer presents manageable by the reader. There are other aspects of this problem, however, that are more directly related to the ways in which people's minds work and in which they learn. Writers should remember that, by virtue of having gone through all the stages of assembling information and reflecting on it, they have the advantage of the reader in every way.

Authors should also remember that readers come to what the writer offers with their own predisposition of mind, their own experience, and their own expectation of what they are going to get from reading. Though human beings are essentially social and survive only by communication, the human mind is nonetheless an imperfect instrument when it comes to grasping what others are trying to tell it. This is partly because it is not a blank piece of paper but an active entity that tries to make sense of everything it meets, in the best way it can, in the light of what it already knows and of what is close and immediate to it. This is a double-edged quality from the point of view of those who seek to transmit ideas in writing; there is the danger that what the writer knows to be irrelevant or marginal will be seized by the reader as central because it happens to fit an existing mental "set." On the other hand, if the writer can hit on the reader's existing pattern of knowledge and ways of thinking, these can be the starting point for a journey that they can take together.

Waite (1982), in a useful brief review of research on "making information easy to use," sums up this requirement as knowing "how our customers process the information we write'' and making information ''as familiar and predictable'' to them as possible, using the ''terms, concepts, and problem-solving approaches'' that they use (p. 123).

The human mind is also often reluctant to move its mental furniture around to accommodate new ideas; it gets tired in following another mind along a new path, and no matter how motivated to follow is liable to wander off into irrelevant tracks. There are, of course, differences in the degree of effort the writer needs to make to help the reader; the task is easiest when the writer is presenting information to readers in a field they know well and are strongly interested in (as in trade, technical or hobby magazines) and hardest when readers have to be introduced to unfamiliar information or to new ways of looking at the familiar.

Apart from putting themselves intellectually in the place of the reader, authors must also learn to consider readers' feelings. Not all reading of informative material is done in situations where the mind can be applied calmly and rationally to the job. Examination instructions are read by few people with utter calm. Many official forms are approached by those who have to fill them in with feelings of anxiety or even acute distress, as Vernon (1980) has pointed out in a review of official forms and leaflets. He also draws attention to another characteristic of many readers that can cause them to approach informative text with apprehension—a reading ability that does not match the tasks set by much of what the average citizen needs to be able to read, understand, and act on.

A Repertoire of Methods for Presenting Information

In order to make their texts accessible to and manageable by readers, authors need to be able to draw on a repertoire of methods for presenting information. They need to be aware of research findings on such issues as the presentation of instructions, ways of helping readers choose the appropriate course of action, ways of making different information elements recognizable, and the use of tables. Besides knowing the options, they should also be able to relate them to both the use to which the information is to be put and the readers who will be using it.

Figure 3 suggests some of the options and tries to relate them to the readership and the readers' approach. There are many possibilities, and perhaps it is wrong to try to condense them into the formality of a matrix, but it offers a starting point for thinking.

Transforming Information into Writing

If the preliminary thinking and decision making have been thorough, and the writer has had adequate time for reflection, there is really little to be said about writing. The author will set about writing with a well-prepared mind, knowing clearly how the information is going to be presented, and therefore free to give full attention to the problems pertaining only to writing. The transition from the

Use	Readership	Useful forms of presentation	Inappropriate
Assess facts relevant to problems, take decisions, act on them; reading can be scanning, selective, or straight through	Managers, executives, professional staff; high level of education	Initial summary of findings; summaries at ends of sections; technical data in appendixes	Combined presentation of technical data and main findings
Gain initial grasp of subject; reading can be selective or straight through; information likely to be applied in study or work context; may involve note taking	Students, young people, employed adults; various educational levels	Highly organized presentation; checklists; questionnaires; recapitulations; simple tables and diagrams; examples for individual working; cross references; signposting of alternative reading paths; direct address; short paragraphs	Long verbal expositions; complex sentence structure; impersonal address
Deepen, extend, and revise knowledge; reading can be selective or straight through, following various paths; information likely to be applied in study or work context; may involve note taking	Adults with some knowledge of subject, who perceive need for more; medium to high educational level	Highly organized presentation; outline of topics treated to allow revision and access at points relevant to readers' state of knowledge; signposting of alternative reading paths; checklists; tables and diagrams; examples	Long verbal expositions; unstructured presentation
Find specific items of information; scanning followed by intensive reading; may involve note taking	Adults—general public or employees; various educational levels	Clear signposting; short sentences; lists; simple tables; codes to identify different types of information; standardization of information elements and of sequence	Variations in form of presentation; complex tables; codes that are difficult to remember or to distinguish

Purpose	→ Readership	→ Ways of presenting	→ Variations
Keep up-to-date with developments in subjects where readers already have knowledge and interest; scanning, selective or straight through reading	Adults—professional workers, amateurs; various educational levels	Standardization of sequence in which material is presented, and of recurring elements of information; cross references	Variations that are not demanded by the nature of the material itself
Find something of potential use or comply with legal requirements; reading may be accompanied by stress	Adults—general public; various educational levels	Definitions of terms; brief statements; simple tables; lists; simple flow diagrams; logical trees; clear visual signposting; informal and friendly style	Long verbal expositions; complex sentence structure; impersonal address; official jargon; complex tables
Carry out operations, tasks, procedures; reading likely to be intensive, sometimes with stress, sometimes in difficult conditions	Adults—general public or employees; various levels of education	Explicit and positive instructions; lists of short sentences; direct address; sequence of instructions in correct order; visual emphasis on attention points; illustrations	Long verbal expositions; instructions in passive rather than active form
Learn more of something that has already attracted interest; motivation to read can be high; pleasure in reading anticipated	Adults, young people—general public; various educational levels	Simple structure; integration of text and illustrations; informal address; definitions of unfamiliar technical terms	Long verbal expositions; complex sentence structure; technical jargon

Fig. 3. Ways of presenting information, related to readership and to use.

just-mentioned activities to writing a final draft will be just one step more in a logical process that will in any case have involved quite a lot of putting pen to paper.

Learning the skills of variation in sentence structure, choice of words, and punctuation will come more easily once the problems of thinking and organization are under control, and authors are more likely to take pleasure in developing those skills when they have got to that point. These are also the skill areas where shortcomings are more readily put right by good editing, though one would still prefer that the author got them right! By contrast, deficiencies in preliminary thinking and organizing of ideas either cannot be rectified at all, or cost an enormous amount of time and still give a botched result.

Critical Review of Text

There is one other skill that authors need: that of subjecting text to critical review and applying to it tests of logic, consistency, clarity, and appropriateness. Authors should be able to apply tests of this kind to their own work, and to modify their text, if necessary, in the light of what they find before it goes under the scrutiny of anyone else. It is important that they should be able to do this, because, by virtue of knowing the subject matter and the stages of their own thinking about it, they can bring to bear insights that nobody else can.

Critically reviewing their own text brings authors onto part of the editor's territory. The meeting place between author and editor is often a no-go area, full of mines and booby traps. An author's ignorance of the editor's true role can lead to the suspicion that the editor is a superfluous persons seeking to justify his or her existence by tampering with text and asking silly, if not impertinent, questions. The situation is not made easier by the fact that this is a pretty fair description of what some editors do, out of ignorance of their real job and from a lack of training or aptitude for it.

The editor's real job consists in

1. Understanding the author's intentions, preferably by means of direct dialogue
2. Disengaging the conceptual structure of the text from whatever will interfere with its being fully usable by the readers
3. Bringing to bear a wider knowledge of possible ways of presenting information than authors usually dispose of
4. Helping to bring together the author and those responsible for the visual organization of the text (typographer and illustrator) so that the author's meaning is reinforced by every aspect of visual presentation, instead of—as too often happens—being either obscured or contradicted by it, and
5. Coordinating all the transactions involved in the transformation of the original text into its final published form, and at each stage mediating between the specialisms and ensuring that each stage of transformation contributes to meeting the purposes of the text and the needs of its users.

If the author understands this role of the editor (and if the editor actually fulfills it), then a constructive association of mutual professional respect can develop, from which both benefit. If this can really happen—and my own experience shows that it can, at any rate on occasion—then, instead of hard edges and uncultivated wastes between the specialisms in which understanding of the purpose of text runs into the sand, the boundaries come closer and start to merge; each specialism retains its identity, but the identity is enriched by the fact that each recognizes and is capable of talking on equal terms with the others.

Proposition IV
Much of the advice at present given to authors in texts on writing and communication is irrelevant to the main problems and can actually obscure them.

Nearly all the ideas I have been advancing can be found in many of the existing texts on technical or scientific writing or on report writing. Yet the majority of those texts do not themselves meet the criteria of usability as defined at the beginning of this chapter, that is, promoting a transaction in which the users' knowledge becomes better organized, with the result that they become masters of new information that they can manage and apply for their own purposes. And a lot of them do not even live up to their own principles for organization and presentation.

It may be, of course, that no text can help writers to become more competent at their job—as some would indeed maintain. But if so, what is so special about texts for authors? Maybe no text can help anyone to do anything. In which case this book was an expensive mistake!

This judgment of the worth of texts designed to help authors has to be a subjective one—I know of no experimental work on their effectiveness, which is a pity, because it would be well worth doing, though difficult to design. In looking at the texts (a sample ranging from the mid-1940s to the present), I asked questions like these:

1. Is the advice given to writers capable of being followed, and if followed is it likely to result in usable text?
2. Is the organization logical?
3. Is the information accessible and manageable for the intended readers?
4. Is the activity of writing related to the other processes of transformation that follow it?

To take the worst case first, texts that obscure the problems and tend to mislead the reader, either by giving downright awful advice or by stating worthy principles but giving no hint of how to put them into practice.

Tichy (1966) characterizes this lot as the "Write-Good-Quick-and-Easy" school, whose members "promote one remedy for all writers and for all faults in writing—a magic average number of words for sentences, avoiding long words, beginning every paper with a statement of the problems, using only one organi-

zation, 3 or 5 or 7 (choose your own magic number) commandments''.
Here is a perfectly fatuous piece of advice for technical writers.

> Mental analysis of a technical problem becomes a useful exercise whenever there is half
> an hour or so to spare, for clear thinking always precedes clear writing. . . . There are
> always subjects to analyse near at hand. For instance when travelling in a railway
> carriage, some of the time might be spent in considering, say, the problems of train
> lighting. It is surprising what can be conjured up from the writer's angle without any
> precise knowledge of the systems employed. (Baker, 1961)

Surprising no doubt, but useful . . . ?

Then there is the article which also encourages writers to use their traveling
time profitably, in this case by imaging ideas and concepts—by imagining, for
example, that the car in front of them is a giant submarine. The intended result of
this curious exercise is that the writers should impress top management with their
written reports.

This following excerpt has some positive rules for readability—perhaps fortunately the author does not give much advice on how to carry them into practice:

> (a) Ensure that you start on a high point of interest. . . .
> (b) Other points of interest must be introduced every 500 words
> (c) Avoid using mathematical formulae or detailed statistical tables in the main body of
>   the report
> (d) Finish on a high point which almost leaves the reader breathless.(Bentley, 1976)

This writer also seems to think that the ''fog index,'' which is designed to predict
the readability of text, was invented by one ''Fogg'' (possibly to fill in the odd
moments while going round the world in 80 days).

Then there are the texts on writing that are strong on good principles, but short
on telling the reader how to get to the end result: ''Make every word do its job.
Carry no passengers—but enlist a good crew.'' The picture of the author pacing
the deck, reviewing candidate words and taking on a crew of likely fellows is an
engaging one, but some advice on principles of selecting applicants would not
come amiss.

More rules for writing—this time for ''Making the paper interesting,'' for
which purpose the reader is daringly advised to make ''judicious use of some of
the devices of the journalist'' that may serve—''without breach of propriety''
you will be relieved to know—''to give a scientific or technical paper an attractive and interesting style'':

> Make the paper as easy as possible for the reader to comprehend.
> Emphasize the new and the unusual.
> Precede every dull passage by a stimulating introduction.
> Introduce striking or unexpected statements, contrasts, and paradoxes.
> Ask provocative questions.
> Let the reader feel that he is doing his own thinking, not merely following.
> Stimulate the imagination and give him a sense of achievement. (Trelease, 1958)

to quote out of context, and most of the writers who
some attempt to tell their readers how to follow
the attempt by their own weakness in organiza-
of methods of presentation, and by sheer incapacity
aders are expected to cope with concepts that cannot
thout definitions that have not yet been presented, or
hey cannot do without knowledge that is presented later
ack structural signposting; others have too much (United
o this). One very good text, well constructed and full of
excellent and usable advice based on long teaching experience, makes itself
unnecessarily difficult to approach by being heavily peppered with very complex
hierarchical numeric coding.

Some authors appear to know of no means of exposition other than paragraph
after paragraph of continuous prose, unbroken by any subheading. Example
material, one of the most essential elements in texts of this kind, often fails to
make the point that it is introduced to illustrate. One sometimes suspects that
authors have a mixed bag of old examples that are brought out to serve all
purposes.

The choice of techniques of presentation is often eccentric. A writer who has
the worthy aim of helping engineers to compose paragraphs that can be read and
understood in approximately 30 seconds takes as his chosen tool of instruction a
checklist whose wording makes it clear that it is for *retrospective* application.
The questions are all sensible, but they are all of the kind: Have all the relevant
facts been included? Is a topic sentence used that contains a topic phrase at the
beginning? This kind of reviewing checklist could not be used directly by readers
as a help to composition; they would have to unpick it and transform it into a set
of reminders they could use in planning their writing—and by definition this
ability is unlikely to be developed in them.

While writers often exhort their readers to be adventurous in their choice of
verbal and visual means of presenting information, most of them show little sign
of being equipped to practice what they preach. The different elements of text,
such as lists, examples, or sequences of instructions, are often inadequately
distinguished. And alas, some of those that have good content and conceptual
structure are undone by the visual illiteracies perpetrated on them—one must
assume without the author's being able to do anything about it. This kind of text,
which is mainly intended for self-instruction, particularly needs careful visual
structure that reinforces conceptual structure—but it does not often get it! Publishers claim that they cannot afford to pay typographers to design anything but
the book jacket and frontmatter—and if they can keep on selling their books
without skilled design, even if thereby the readers are deprived of much of the
help they could get—what is going to make them do differently?

Finally, to end this catalog of what makes texts on writing unusable, writing is
nearly always treated in them as if it were an isolated self-standing activity.

While consideration is sometimes given to the circumstances in which authors are briefed to write, and the relationships to their superiors in organizations, there is hardly any attention to what happens to a text after it has left the author's hands. The editor's role is hardly mentioned, nor yet the work of typographers and illustrators and how the author can help them to apply their skills to the best advantage. There is no useful information about typesetting and production processes (which today are much less far removed from the author than they used to be) and how they affect the author and how the author can take advantage of them.

Proposition V
The necessary skills and ways of thinking can be learned by authors.

One of the main problems lies in reaching those who need to learn the necessary skills and ways of thinking. The majority of informative texts are probably published by organizations and firms, rather than by conventional publishing houses; brochures, leaflets, and manuals, in the nature of things, never come near conventional publishers; many reports on research or on assignments are self-published by organizations, and so are many instructional texts. The majority of the people who write them are, with the exception of those described as technical authors, not recruited as authors; writing informative texts is just one aspect (and quite possibly an unforeseen one) of the job they do. So the target population for training is scattered, isolated, and difficult to find.

Defining what the authors of informative texts need to learn if they are to contribute toward producing usable texts is perhaps a less intractable problem. They need to learn how

1. To define or to elicit from others, the purposes of what they have to write
2. To find out the characteristics of the intended readers and the conditions under which they will use the text
3. To establish what information is needed and how to locate sources for it
4. To acquire and manage information
5. To plan and structure the information in the light of knowledge of purposes, users, and use
6. To manage the time available for writing
7. To master a repertoire of methods of presenting information and to be able to choose the ones that best fit purpose, users, and use
8. To develop confidence in handling language and a range of ways of using it
9. To develop critical and analytical skills for reviewing what they write
10. To understand the contributions of other professionals who work on the transformation of text—especially editors and designers—and to be able to work constructively with them

11. To appreciate the range of options for typesetting and production and to take account of the constraints they impose and of the advantages they can offer.

The underlying *aim,* as distinct from the specific learning objectives, is to give the authors of informative text a *generalizable* range of knowledge, and *transferable* skills, under their own control, rather than a set of rules that are highly specific to a particular task. To meet these aims and objectives, a learning program would have to consider the following topics:

1. Locating sources of printed information—what librarians call subject bibliography
2. Methods of designing questions for eliciting information, including simple questionnaire design and survey methods
3. Interview techniques and interactive skills
4. Methods of observing and analyzing the performance of tasks
5. Cognitive and affective aspects of reading
6. The psychology of learning, including the influence of age and cultural background.
7. The results of research on information-handling, and on the accessibility of various forms of presentation of information
8. The range of means available for managing the use of language: sentence structures; forms of verbs; vocabulary alternatives; the results of research on the accessibility of different forms of verbal presentation to different groups of readers
9. The work roles of editors, typographers and illustrators
10. The main contemporary options for typesetting, reproduction, and finishing, and their advantages and constraints from the writer's point of view
11. Methods of analyzing text content and testing for internal consistency
12. Techniques of proof reading and indexing.

The implications of many of the items in this list of skills and knowledge are considered by Wright (1981), who identifies five sets of skills that technical writers need:

1. Analysis of how readers will use the document
2. Use of language
3. Use of graphic and typographic presentation to make the structure of the text accessible to readers
4. Interpretation of research relating to the design of information
5. Management of the document production process. (p. 10)

Finally, how would one present this content in order to make it usable by the people we are aiming at, so that they can make it their own in the shortest possible time and apply it effectively in their work?

As a general principle, it should be carefully phased in small manageable stages, in the proper sequence, with plenty of opportunity for practice on a small scale, and planned and monitored application in the actual work environment.

Thus, as well as formal instruction and lectures, a course would include a lot of graded exercise and projects. These would be designed to introduce students to the skills they need, and to give practice in exercising them—starting from small, closely defined tasks, and developing to larger projects that they themselves would mainly define, control and monitor.

Some of the things one might do, taking them in the sequence of the learning objectives, would include the following:

1. Identify gaps and points that need clarifying in a preliminary brief.
2. Role-play interviewing a "client" to clarify and confirm a final brief.
3. Consider ways to find out about users and use of a text.
4. Formulate questions and interview a sample of users.
5. Observe the conditions in which text will be used, and analyze tasks performed by users.
6. Devise practical exercises in searching for documentary information.
7. Plan systems for storing and retrieving information that will be used in writing texts and try them out.
8. Plan timetables for writing and test them in practice.
9. Organize given information elements to form a logical structure for a given purpose.
10. Define one's own list of elements on the basis of a detailed brief and plan a structure for them.
11. Practice choosing appropriate methods of presentation for given users and use and apply them.
12. Evaluate text written in various ways for its fitness for various readerships and uses.
13. Identify linguistic elements that characterize written text.
14. Present the same information in various ways to fit different specified users and use.
15. Prepare briefs for designers and illustrators.

A final component of a course would be what might be called "practical appreciation sessions"—discussion with the specialists who take over the author's text, seeing them at work, and listening to their comments as they work on the decisions they have to make and the methods they use. This could include the following:

1. Work with professional editors on the analysis of the students' own texts.
2. See how designers and illustrators tackle their work on texts and learn from them the help they need from authors.
3. Get to know the available modern technology and how it affects the author's work, for example, in matching methods of presentation to the technology of typesetting and production, and the economic implications of different methods of typesetting for correcting proofs.

Since this chapter was originally written, I have had the opportunity of trying out some of these ideas for course design in practice, in two different settings for people from two very different backgrounds.

The first group consists of first-year students of visual communication at Ravensbourne College of Art and Design, who take a one-week course on "Writing to Inform" as part of their "fundamental studies". The course starts with small-scale exercises designed to introduce them to such skills as

1. Deciding what information is needed to meet a defined purpose for specific readership
2. Identifying sources for the information
3. Developing ideas about appropriate presentation
4. Putting elements of information into a helpful sequence and selecting appropriate methods for presenting different elements
5. Analyzing informative text written by other people to determine what information it is seeking to communicate, how the writer has structured it, and how effectively the information is presented in relation to users and use.

The major part of the week is taken up with writing a short informative text to a detailed brief for an actual client who requires it for a real purpose (to date, projects have included leaflets for the education department of a museum, for a puppet center, for the British Broadcasting Corporation's Data Enquiry Service, and for the Intermediate Technology Development Group). The students are briefed by the client, and then work in groups on planning, drafting, editing, and preliminary designing of the text. At the end of the course each group makes a final presentation of their solution to the client, and submits a written report to him or her. The outcome is the selection by the client of one of the texts for actual publication, and the group then goes on to final revision of the text and finished design work, taking the whole project through to final production.

The combination of practice in some of the essential skills of informative writing with immediate application on a real job for a real client, whereby they can bring together their own special skills in graphic design with the new ones of presenting information in writing, seems to have a stimulating effect, both immediately and, for some students, in the long-term.[2]

The other group with whom these ideas have been tried out in practice is drawn from information professionals—librarians and information scientists who, like many other professionals, find themselves required in the course of their work to take responsibility for writing, editing, designing or producing informative texts. Courses for them have been run during 1983, as part of a new program of professional development in the presentation of information, under the auspices of the Association for Information Management. The strengths of this group are precisely in the areas where the other group is least sure of

[2]The ideas underlying the course are discussed in Orna (1983).

themselves, and vice versa. The information professionals are strong in handling and structuring information but desperately in need of help in matters of visual presentation, design, typography, and choice of methods of production.

One innovation with this group which seems to meet a need is the "clinic session," to which students are invited, if they wish, to bring examples of actual informative text for which they have been responsible. They are able to have individual one-to-one discussion with specialists in writing, design, and editing. The opportunity to discuss problems they have identified for themselves with someone who will listen and will use personal experience to suggest lines of action seems to help the students in seeing how to apply the generalized information given in the more formal parts of the course.

THE AUTHOR: HELP OR HINDRANCE?

The title of this chapter asks a question: Is the author a help or otherwise on the road to designing usable informative text? The thinking author, who knows how to plan and to handle information, and who has command of a range of methods for presenting information, is a real help to those who produce the text. Unfortunately, authors like this are in short supply, and there is a surplus of those who constitute a positive hindrance, with very expensive consequences. Their activities present problems to editors and designers, they shortchange their readers, and it is unlikely that they themselves get much enjoyment from their work.

Those who are a hindrance are often so because they have not been given the help they deserve in tackling an uncommonly difficult job, which is often not of their own choosing. I believe that such help can be given effectively, and that if it were given it could change the whole production of usable text and bring the control of the operation into its logical place. The fact that there are probably limits to the improvability of all the parties to the transaction—authors, readers, and texts—is no reason for not trying a variety of means for achieving what improvement *can* be made. There is room for it.

REFERENCES

Baker, C. (1961). *A guide to technical writing*. Pitman.
Bentley, T. J. (1976). *Report writing in business*. Institution of Cost and Management Accountants.
Brookes, B. C. (1980). Informatics as the fundamental social science. In F. Taylor (Ed.), *Proceedings of the 39th FID Congress, University of Edinburgh September 1978,* (pp 19–29). London: Aslib.
Moxon, J. (1683/1958). In H. Davis & H. Carter (Eds.), *Mechanick exercises on the whole art of printing*. London: Oxford University Press.
Orna, E. (1983). *Writing to inform.* Bromley: Ravensbourne College of Art and Design

Orna, E. & Stevens, G. (1985). *The presentation of information.*London. Aslib.

Stibic, V. (1982). *Tools of the mind—techniques and methods for intellectual work.*Amsterdam: North-Holland.

Tichy, H. J. (1966): *Effective writing for engineers, managers, scientists.* New York: Wiley.

Trelease, S. F. (1958).*How to write scientific and technical papers.* Baltimore: Williams and Wilkins.

Vernon, T. (1980). *Gobbledegook: A critical review of official forms and leaflets—and how to improve them.* London: National Consumer Council.

Waite, R. ((5–8 May 1982).) Making information easy to use: a summary of research. In *Proceedings of the 29th International Technical Communication Conference* Boston MA. pp E120–123

Wason, P. (1980). Specific thoughts on the writing process. In L. W. Gregg & E. R. Steinberg (Eds.). *Cognitive processes in writing.*New Jersey: Lawrence Earlbaum Associates, pp 129–137

Wright, P. (March 1981). Five skills technical writers need. IEEE Transactions on Professional Communication, Vol. PC-24, No. 1, pp 10–16

Wright, P. (1980). Usability: The criterion for designing written information. In P. A. Kolers, M. E. Wrolstad and H. Bouma (Eds.) *Processing of visible language* (Vol 2). New York: Plenum, pp 183–205

CHAPTER 3

Training Authors of Informative Documents

Daniel B. Felker
Janice C. Redish
Jane Peterson

INTRODUCTION

Our task in this chapter is to say something *useful* about training authors who write material of practical value to the real world. We draw upon our work in the Document Design Center where, since 1978, we have conducted research on the comprehension of meaningful written prose, applied this research in the development of actual documents used by large numbers of the general public, and trained authors who write in the real world of work to write usable and understandable documents.

We proceed by

1. Describing the authors we are talking about
2. Discussing what we know about the writing capabilities of these authors
3. Pointing out some of the major issues that influence what and how they write
4. Sharing what we know about training these authors.

Our discussion, of necessity, weaves together what we know from the research literature with what we have learned from grappling with practical reality. Cognitive psychology, human factors, educational psychology, psycholinguistics, typography, and readability contribute to a large body of research related to writing, reading, and creating comprehensible written prose (Felker, 1980). Although some of this research bears directly on what we discuss, other research is peripheral. For some of our needs, there is simply a void in research knowledge. Where we can, we ground our points in extant research; where we cannot, we offer informed opinion that is grounded in our own experiences.

Designing Usable Texts

WHO ARE THE AUTHORS?

Any sensible discussion about training authors requires first that we establish who the authors to be trained are. For present purposes, we are concerned with adult authors who write for adult audiences. As implied in other chapters of this book, these authors are found in many work settings—in government, business, the professions, or the military. Some of them routinely spend all day, every day writing; some write only once in a while. They write materials that are used within a single office or company, or they write for audiences across the country.

The writers who concern us here, and who come to the Document Design Center's training workshops, are white-collar writers. For the most part, they are well educated. They hold jobs that require college degrees, and many hold advanced or professional degrees. Most write a lot in their jobs, far more than they ever imagined that they would. Almost all are articulate speakers of English. Most are not trained as writers and they do not primarily identify themselves as writers. Most have had a formal academic course in writing in college, but it was taken a number of years ago. We think that our experience is probably typical. In a survey of 254 mid- and senior-level managers in business and professional occupations, more than half ($N = 139$) had had no training in writing beyond freshman composition (Aldrich, 1982). Moreover, Burhan's (1983) analysis of 263 American college catalogues, which revealed that only 1% of colleges require a writing course beyond freshman composition and 20% require none whatever, suggests no increase in the amount of college training in writing is likely.

Working writers do different kinds of writing. Some compose original writing. Others revise existing written text. Still others edit. Many do all three. Whatever they write, and wherever they work, the written products they finally generate have practical uses. Whether we call these written products informative documents, functional text, public documents, or some other name, they are written to inform a particular audience about something and to help the reader decide whether and how to act. Many different sorts of documents meet this description, including directions for putting a widget together, eligibility requirements for tuition aid, and insurance policies. These informative documents are not designed primarily to entertain, to be aesthetically pleasing, or to be newsworthy.

WHAT ARE THE WRITING CAPABILITIES
OF THESE AUTHORS?

This question can only be partially answered because much of the research to answer it has not been done. Extensive comparative profiles of backgrounds and abilities of writers in different companies and industries have yet to be systematically compiled. Nevertheless, empirical research suggests some characteristics of these authors. In addition, we have our impressions of what working authors can and cannot do, impressions that we have developed from several years of training a broad spectrum of these authors. Both sources of information provide insights for how to design useful training for this particular target group.

We can get a broad overview of some general writing characteristics of working authors from the few research studies that have been reported. Faigley and Miller (1982) have established the perhaps obvious fact that working authors vary in their ability to write well. The researchers surveyed more than 200 people who routinely write at work for a variety of companies and agencies in several southwestern cities. The survey results revealed that the quality and diversity of writing encountered in the workplace varies. Bad writing is common and can be due to any number of reasons, such as lack of organization, poor syntax, or excessive use of technical jargon.

Other studies have shown that the writers of many bureaucratic, legal, and military documents seldom meet the needs of their audiences. In a study by Flower, Hayes, and Swarts (1980), readers could not comprehend a federal regulation without restructuring and translating it. Charrow and Charrow (1979) showed that typical jurors often misunderstand written jury instructions—defeating the judge's purpose in giving the instructions. And Rose and colleagues (1981) concluded from their evaluation of the U.S. Army's Soldier's Manuals that they are full of polysyllabic technical terminology even though they are intended for low-ranking troops, many of whom did not finish high school. Obviously, the fact that bad writing is encountered does not preclude finding good writing on the job as well.

Indeed, typical working authors apparently possess some very sophisticated rhetorical knowledge. In an in-depth analysis of writing samples from 11 experienced writers working for a government agency, Odell and Goswami (1982) learned that these writers were quite sensitive to rhetorical context. That is, this group, who were not trained as writers, showed awareness of audience, self, and subject in their writing and were adroit at tailoring their writing to specific audiences. The Faigley and Miller (1982) survey provides evidence consistent with this finding. They found that many college-trained working authors have a sophisticated knowledge of the rhetorical demands of writing. Although most of these college-trained people are not aware of rhetorical theory per se, they often talk about writing in terms of subject matter and audience.

How do we explain the apparent contradictions between the analyses of documents and the studies of writers? Two points come to mind. First of all, in the studies by Odell and Goswami and by Faigley and Miller, we have only authors' reports of their sensitivity to audience and purpose. Neither study followed the writers' products to see if the rhetorical choices the authors made were successful. In the studies on regulations, jury instructions, and Soldier's Manuals, the researchers were looking at the success (or lack of success) of the product.

Second, Odell and Goswami looked at letters, memos, and reports on clients' visits—all very short documents. The author controls these documents from start to finish. The writer usually knows who the audience is. A regulation, manual, or technical report, on the other hand, is a much longer document. It has multiple and sometimes unknown audiences. It has multiple purposes, some of which may seem to the writer to contradict each other.

In working with authors in workshops and on projects to create or revise documents, we have found that they are aware of the importance of the audience, but have not thought about how their document does or does not meet the readers' needs. Most of the authors we train are only attuned to some of the purposes of their documents, not all.

Clearly, working authors in general have both strengths and weaknesses. Their knowledge about the demands of writing often exceeds their ability to perform— their ability to produce effective documents. Research has begun to investigate the performance of writers by comparing experienced writers with novice writers and by examining how different experienced writers work.

Flower and Hayes (1980) examined how novice writers and expert writers differ in representing the same rhetorical problem of writing for an audience of young teenage girls. As the subjects performed the writing task, they gave thinking-aloud protocols (a research technique based on the work of Newell & Simon, 1972). Their subjects included both expert writers (teachers of writing who had received fellowships to study writing) and novice writers (college students with writing problems). Flower and Hayes found that the expert writers made reference to the audience more than twice as often as novice writers, and that the experts spent much more time thinking about and commenting on the rhetorical problem. The expert writers also represented the rhetorical problem in much more breadth and depth. The conclusions were that experts interpret writing tasks differently than novices do and that experts solve a qualitatively different rhetorical problem.

Atlas (1979) compared the processes expert and novice writers use to generate ideas, organize the ideas into a framework, and translate the framework into text. The task consisted of writing a business letter to a carefully defined recipient for a specific purpose requiring tact. The writers were thus forced into a common rhetorical stance. The experts were 10 college graduates who were singled out as good writers by business and academic colleagues; the novices were 20 first-semester freshmen. Strong expert–novice differences were found. Experts were far more likely to generate plans before writing, add ideas to outlines, include more and broader ideas in their letters, and address the reader's concerns.

Other research has documented expert–novice differences in revising text. Faigley and Witte (1981) collected examples of revisions from six inexperienced students, six skilled students, and six expert adult writers. Analyses of the revisions showed that both the adult expert writers and the skilled student writers made similar and qualitatively better revisions than the inexperienced student-writers. The inexperienced students' changes were mainly surface changes whereas the other two writing groups made more meaningful changes. Overall, the inexperienced students made fewer revisions of all kinds.

Research thus suggests that novice and experienced writers differ, both in how they approach writing tasks and in what they produce. Differences are found whether text is being written or revised. But what about experienced writers? How do they differ in what they write or revise, or in how they approach writing? Research sheds some light on this group of working authors as well.

Stephens (1981) provides one view of experienced writers. She interviewed 30 writers in business and professional occupations in a study of how they write. One finding from her analysis was that writers approach writing differently: Some revise line by line as they write; some draft quickly, then review. An additional finding from this study was that working writers in general feel inadequate as writers. They think that their way of writing is the wrong way and that there are better and more efficient ways to write.

Gould (1980) studied working writers who were college graduates as they produced several business letters using different methods (e.g., writing, dictating). Authors devoted different proportions of total composition time to planning, writing, reviewing, and editing—with most time (65%) being devoted to planning. Good authors (judged good because their products received high ratings) spent similar amounts of time in these various activities. Good authors were also good across different writing tasks and methods, and poor authors were poor, regardless of task or method. Williams (1983) came to the same conclusion even though the "good" writers were college freshmen.

Experience does not equal excellence in revising text. Using the same protocol technique referred to earlier, Bond, Hayes, and Flower (1980) studied experienced writers revising text. They asked eight experienced government writers— four lawyers and four nonlawyers—to think aloud while they rewrote a portion of a Small Business Administration regulation for a general, nontechnical, reading audience. The revised versions of the regulation were then rated for understandability by students who knew nothing about the technical content. The revisions varied markedly in understandability, and the processes that writers used to develop their revisions also differed.

Writers who provided the most understandable versions read the original completely through before attempting any revision. They actively considered their audience. They made frequent use of generally effective writing principles (e.g., active voice). They were concerned with the spacing and overall appearance of the finished copy, and they reread their revisions. The poorer writers did not consider the audience and tended to make the revised version look and sound similar to the original. Faigley and Witte (1981) also found extreme diversity in how expert writers revise. Some revised whole pages at once; others plodded line by line. Some writers completed a second draft; others only pruned words.

Diversity among experienced adult writers is not limited to how they revise text. Berkenkotter (1981) found differences in how 10 experienced writers (all publishing academics) interpreted the same writing task. Recently published case studies of the composing habits of an experienced engineer (Selzer, 1983) and of a professional writer (Berkenkotter, 1983) reveal differences broad enough to suggest the existence of varied composing styles. Similarly broad differences have appeared in writers' descriptions of their own writing (Ede & Lunsford, 1983) and researchers have commented on the varied composing styles they have observed (e.g., Faigley & Witte, 1981). With continued research, we may be able to describe accurately several composing styles and determine their influence on document effectiveness. For now, we can state with certainty that experienced writers vary in *how* they compose and in *what* they do when they write.

It is in this area of what writers do—the various phases or subprocesses of writing—that we see differences in those we train. In writing informative documents, authors ideally define the context in which the document is to be used as well as its audience and purpose. Later, they review and edit, and after writing, test the document to make sure it is understandable to its intended audience. Frankly, it is our experience that not all working authors consider writing to be a multiphase process. Most will give at least lip service to the value of the prewriting phase, especially to defining the audience. Almost all working authors, however, draw a blank when it comes to the postwriting phase. The notion of trying out a newly written piece of material on a sample of the intended audience to see if they understand it is simply a foreign concept and untried technique for most. The material is considered sufficient as long as it passes the author's own review or the supervisor's review.

We recognize that not all writers dismiss empirical evaluation. Those who develop training and instructional materials for agencies that follow Instructional Systems Design principles use empirical procedures when conducting formative and summative evaluations. However, most of the authors who create insurance policies, loan agreements, government regulations, and application forms for social services have little experience with or interest in empirical procedures.

HOW DOES THE JOB SETTING INFLUENCE WHAT AND HOW THESE AUTHORS WRITE?

The designer of a training course aimed at working authors clearly also needs to know something about where these authors work. Why do they write as they do on the job? What parts of their jobs are really important to them? Is there any *real* job pressure for them to become better writers? Any number of realities in the job setting converge to shape what working authors write on the job, how they go about writing, and the value they place on improving their writing. We will look at some of these realities now to complete our discussion of what we know about these authors.

Perhaps the overriding reality of the job setting is the enormous influence it wields over what authors write and how they write in the workplace. The job setting provides constant reminders of "this is what we write" and models of "what we write looks like this and sounds like this." The working author is continually exposed to the writing standards of the job. Authors who have a distinctive style of writing will find it hard to maintain their flair when it conflicts with institutional notions of acceptable writing. It is easy and it is natural to conform. Evidence of this abounds. Lawyers write like lawyers and regulation writers write like regulation writers, even when they know that what they write is dry, lifeless, and vague. Most lawyers and most regulation writers did not always write like they now do.

Many writers work for large, hierarchically structured organizations—government, business, or military. This means that there are always some, and frequently many, different levels of review between the writer who writes or revises the original material and the person who has final approval. Much can happen to the material as it meanders from desk to desk through the labyrinth—paragraphs are dropped or added, pages are rearranged, words are struck out and new ones substituted, and so on. The original writer may never see the written material again until it is released for publication; he or she may barely recognize the material when it emerges.

A corollary reality that arises from organizational structure is that, in many job settings, individuals do not write documents—committees do. As Faigley and Miller (1982) found, it is common practice to "staff" writing assignments. Substantive experts (and there may be several), lawyers, analysts, and editors all contribute ideas, negotiate, write preliminary drafts, and compromise. Only when consensus is achieved (or the deadline arrives) does the committee's document start its way through the review and approval process. Writing by committee is not the best way of motivating authors to improve their writing.

Sometimes there is no stimulus to improve writing on the job. The written materials that are being produced are viewed as completely acceptable, either because of tradition, decree, or lack of outside pressure. Indeed, the perception that one ought to even consider change is remote. Writers write what they do because no one tells them not to.

The standards of good writing against which writers are judged vary, not only between companies, but sometimes even within a company. This was vividly demonstrated in a study reported by Hairston (1981). She presented 65 sentences that contained different errors of usage to over 100 professional people from various occupations. Each was asked to note whether the sentences bothered them "a lot," "a little," or "not at all." Most agreed that several specific errors of usage were serious (e.g., double negative), and most agreed that several other specific errors of usage were not bothersome (e.g., qualifier before the word *unique*—"very unique"). There was much disagreement, however, about whether many of the other errors of usage were bothersome (e.g., not setting off *however* with a comma). Some people were bothered a great deal by these errors, some a bit, and some not at all. A person judged to be a good writer in one company might be seen as deficient in another. Clearly, the specific standards applied at work will shape what is written.

WHAT DO WE KNOW ABOUT TRAINING WRITERS?

Our understanding of how to successfully train writers in work settings comes primarily from experience. We know of no experimental studies that compare different forms of training in clear writing nor any studies that have systematically monitored the writing of trainees for a specified period of time after training. In planning a training course for authors, we use four criteria to select the guidelines that we cover:

1. The guidelines and the examples should be relevant to the types of material these authors write.
2. At least some of the guidelines can be learned quickly so that authors are immediately reinforced by success.
3. The guidelines, when applied, should make a dramatic difference in the comprehensibility and also the appearance of the document.
4. Most of the guidelines should be supported by empirical research.

Readers who come to this chapter with a background in instructional research or instructional design will immediately recognize the behavioral principles underlying these criteria. Rather than spend time on the research basis of *how* we train authors, we concentrate on our fourth criterion—the research that supports *what* we teach.

Very little of the research that we cite in this section was done on documents of the types our authors write or in the settings in which they write. In some cases, we are extrapolating from research that was done in a laboratory setting on small segments of prose (words, sentences, or short, contrived passages written for experimental purposes). In others, we are extrapolating from work on writing stories, essays, or textbooks that have different audiences and purposes from the documents our authors are writing. Nonetheless, the research basis that we can cite for most of what we teach makes the guidelines compelling to authors (and helps them justify changes that they want to make against the resistance of supervisors and of other technical specialists).

Among other topics, we train authors to:

1. Organize for the reader, not the writer
2. Use context and informative headings to help readers find their way through the document
3. Write "scenarios" so that documents are performance oriented
4. Write sentences that do not overtax the reader's short-term memory
5. Use layout and typography to enhance comprehension rather than impede it; and
6. Use empirical evaluation techniques as guides to rewriting instead of readability formulas.

In an actual training session, of course, each of these topics has to be operationalized in specific guidelines with examples and practice.

ORGANIZING FOR THE READER

Our major goal in training is to teach authors to write reader-based, rather than writer-based, documents. Readers bring their own goals to informative documents. They likely use a "top-down" processing strategy (Bobrow & Brown, 1975) in which what they want from the document determines their approach to the document. Because most informative documents serve primarily as reference tools, a reader-based organization stresses ease of access and chunks information under headings that reflect the questions readers ask about the information.

USING CONTEXT AND INFORMATIVE HEADINGS

Informative documents, unfortunately, often lack any context-setting information for their readers. The title is often a string of nouns that the reader has to untangle in order to understand. What is a report with the following title about?

Flag Prairie Validation Prescribed Control
Burn Cultural Resource Reconnaissance

(That's really the name of a report. You can buy a copy if you want to read it.)

Titles are not the only problems. Instead of finding a context at the beginning of a document, readers are often dropped into the middle of critical information without any notion of where they are going or why they are going there. Compare the beginnings of the two regulations in Schemes 1 and 2; note how the marine radio example provides context for the reader and the other does not.

Instructional research has shown that beginning a text or a section of a text with an overview of what is coming helps students to remember the information that follows the overview. Hartley and Davies (1976) review much of this research. Psycholinguistic research has shown that a context as simple as an appropriate title can make a significant difference in readers' ability to recall the ideas in a passage (Bransford & Johnson, 1972).

Subpart CC — How To Use Your VHF Marine Radio

General

VHF Marine Rule 1
Who are these rules for?

These rules are for recreational boaters who have put VHF (Very High Frequency) marine radios on their boats. A VHF marine radio is a two-way radio for boaters. VHF marine radios operate on channels in the very high frequency band between 156 and 162 MHz.

VHF Marine Rule 2
What do these rules tell me?

Rules 3 through 9 tell you how to get a license for your radio. Rules 10 through 20 tell you how to operate your radio.

Scheme 1

PART 30—GENERAL GRANT REGULATIONS AND PROCEDURES

(Editor's note: 40 CFR 30 was replaced in its entirety by a new 40 CFR 30 on May 8, 1975, in 40 FR 20231.)

AUTHORITY: Sec. 20 and 23 of the Federal Insecticide, Fungicide, and Rodenticide Act, as amended (7 U.S.C. 135); (33 U.S.C. 1251; 42 U.S.C. 241, 242b, 243, 246, 300j-1, 300j-2, 300j-3; 1857, 1891, and 3251) et seq.

§ 30.100   Purpose.

This Subchapter establishes and codifies uniform policies and procedures for all grants awarded by the U.S. Environmental Protection Agency (EPA).

§ 30.101   Authority.

This Subchapter is promulgated by the Administrator of the Environmental Protection Agency pursuant to the authority conferred by Reorganization Plan No. 3 of 1970 and pursuant to the following statutes which authorize the award of assistance by the Environmental Protection Agency:

(a) Clean Water Act, as amended (33 U.S.C. §§ 1251 et seq.).

[43 FR 28484, June 30, 1978]

(b) The Clean Air Act, as amended (42 U.S.C. 1857 et seq.);

(c) The Solid Waste Disposal Act, as amended by the Resource Conservation and Recovery Act of 1976 (42 U.S.C. 6901 et seq.).

[42 FR 56050, October 20, 1977]

(d) The Safe Drinking Water Act (42 U.S.C. 300j-1, 300j-2, 300j-3);

(e) Section 301 et seq. of the Public Health Service Act, as amended (42 U.S.C. 241, 242b, 243, and 246);

(f) Sections 20 and 23 of the Federal Insecticide, Fungicide, and Rodenticide Act, as amended (7 U.S.C. 135); and

(g) Federal Grant and Cooperative Agreement Act of 1977 (41 U.S.C. 501); and

(h) Toxic Substances Control Act (15 U.S.C. 2601).

[43 FR 28484, June 30, 1978]

§ 30.105   Applicability and scope

(a) Parts 30 through 34 of this Subchapter contain policies and procedures which apply to all grants made by the Environmental Protection Agency and are designed to achieve maximum uniformity throughout the various grant programs of the Environmental Protection Agency and, where possible, consistency with other Federal agencies. These policies and procedures are mandatory with

Scheme 2

Hartley and Trueman (1982) showed that headings as statements or questions helped students to recall and to retrieve information from both familiar and unfamiliar text. In one of the few studies on legal documents, Swarts, Flower, and Hayes (1980) showed that headings as single nouns or short noun strings can mislead readers. Their subjects could neither correctly predict what information would follow the original headings nor match headings and text. The original headings in the regulation they were studying were nouns and phrases: "Definitions," "General Policy," "Requirements," "Procedure," and "Use of Advance Payment Funds." When they rewrote the headings to be more informative (e.g., "Setting Up the Bank Account"), subjects performed significantly better both in predicting what information would follow and in matching headings with text.

WRITING SCENARIOS

We believe that informative documents should be reader based. That is, they should be performance oriented. Informative documents should anticipate and answer questions the reader might have, they should help the reader find specific information in the document, and they should enable the reader to take appropriate action. However, most informative documents are writer based. That is, they are topic oriented. They are filled with definitions and facts, and they often obscure actions—who is doing what to whom.

Yet it is these actions that readers need in order to understand text. This was clearly shown in a study by Flower et al. (1980). They asked readers to give thinking-aloud protocols while reading part of a writer-based federal regulation. The readers most often actively converted the passive–nominal sentences into active–verbal sentences in order to understand the passage. They created "scenarios" in which human actors took actions in explicit circumstances. These researchers coined the phrase "scenario principle" to describe text that is "structured around a *human agent* performing *actions* in a particularized *situation*" (Flower et al., 1983, p. 42; emphasis in original).

The scenario principle has proven to be one of the easiest to teach trainees. The principle unites and explains several guidelines commonly suggested by style manuals, namely, use personal pronouns, write in the active voice, and use action verbs. The principle not only makes a passage easier to read but its effects are immediately visible to trainees. To see how the scenario principle works, compare these two versions of the same passage:

BEFORE

The Protocol Familiarization Period may be employed to run additional preliminary tests of the performance of the device. These tests may evaluate linearity, recovery, or any other feature not addressed in this document. The purpose of such preliminary acceptability tests should be the early discovery of any serious problems with the device. If such problems are encountered, the manufacturer should be contacted to determine the cause of error. No final judgment as to the acceptability of the device should be made from such limited tests.

AFTER

While practicing the experiment, you can also test other features of the equipment, such as linearity or recovery. Use these tests to see if there are any serious problems with the equipment. If you find any problems, contact the manufacturer to find out what is causing the problem. Don't decide if the equipment is acceptable solely on the basis of these limited, preliminary tests.

WRITING SENTENCES THAT DO NOT OVERTAX
SHORT-TERM MEMORY

Another major reason why readers cannot understand typical documents is that the sentence structures overtax the cognitive capacity of short-term memory. Research studies in cognitive psychology and psycholinguistics point to several sources of difficulty, each of which suggests a guideline for a training course in clear writing. We give only a few here.

Sentence length, in itself, can be a problem when we consider legal documents that have 150 or more words in a single sentence. These sentences clearly violate the "magic number 7, plus or minus 2" (Miller, 1956), which according to Miller is the number of chunks of information a human can hold in short-term memory at one time.

However, a sentence does not have to be long to tax the reader's short-term memory. Propositional density (the number and organization of ideas) is more important than the number of words (Kintsch & Kozminsky, 1977). Even in sentences of reasonable length, grammatical structure can create comprehension problems. For example, sentences with extra phrases at the beginning (left-branching) and sentences with extra phrases in the middle (center-embedded) are more difficult to understand than sentences with extra phrases tacked onto the end (right-branching). Many studies support this finding (Fodor, Bever, & Garrett, 1974; Hakes & Cairns, 1970; Larkin & Burns, 1977; Miller & Isard, 1964). We teach trainees to make sentences right-branching or to put the extra phrases into a second sentence.

Another example of a syntactic structure that often overtaxes cognitive capacity is the conditional (if/then) sentence. Technical manuals, many regulations, and most forms include many examples. Complex conditional sentences are often very difficult for readers to understand. Holland and Rose (1981) found that, after a brief initial practice session, people could assign themselves to the proper condition more quickly and more accurately from an algorithm (a pictorial flowchart) than from the single prose sentence. For some trainees working on technical manuals, algorithms may be the appropriate solution to this particular syntactic problem. Other solutions that work well are to list the conditions using typographic cues or to write the parts of the condition as separate prose statements (Wright & Reid, 1973).

USING LAYOUT AND TYPOGRAPHY TO ENHANCE COMPREHENSION

In deciding what to teach authors about layout and typography, perhaps even more than in selecting writing guidelines, we are careful to choose guidelines that trainees can use, that make a dramatic difference in their documents, and that are easy to learn. Authors do not see themselves as designers; they are not interested in a lengthy session on design. Good design decisions, however, can make a tremendous difference in how comprehensible and useful a text is. Therefore, our goal is to help authors work well with designers. We cover the basic vocabulary of design and a few simple, research-supported guidelines. Tinker (1963, 1965) has done much of the early research in this area, and Hartley (1978, 1981) has summarized much of it.

One useful technique is to set off headings and other important information by placement and highlighting. Considerable research supports the notion that typographic cues for highlighting can help readers find or remember information (Foster & Coles, 1977, on boldface; Crouse & Idstein, 1972, on underlining; Jenkins & Bailey, 1964, on underlining and color). Research has also shown that combining too many highlighting techniques impedes comprehension (Glynn & DiVesta, 1979).

Two other key typographic guidelines for prose writers concern line length and the use of all capital letters. A line length of 50 to 70 characters is easiest for the eye to scan (Tinker, 1965). This usually means printing two columns to a page. The outline of a capital letter is not as distinctive as the outline of a lowercase letter. Therefore, text in all capitals takes longer to read (Tinker, 1963). It also takes up more space in a typed document. Moreover, all capitals are not as effective as boldface for highlighting (Foster & Coles, 1977).

Figures 1 and 2 show the dramatic difference an author can make in a text by using just these few design guidelines.

USING EMPIRICAL EVALUATION TECHNIQUES

The last topic we want to mention briefly in this chapter on training authors is evaluation. In putting together a training course for authors, we realize that there are some points the trainees are going to learn and apply immediately (e.g., the

FEDERAL INSURED STUDENT LOAN PROGRAM

The Federal Insured Student Loan Program (FISLP) enables students to borrow directly from qualified lending institutions to pay for their costs of attending eligible postsecondary educational institutions. The loans are made at the discretion of the lenders. Such loans are insured by the Federal Government.

Terms and Conditions of Loans

A student may apply for a loan if enrolled or accepted for enrollment on at least a half-time basis in an eligible institution. A student may borrow up to $2,500 per academic year as an undergraduate or vocational student. The total amount a student may have outstanding while an undergraduate is $7,500. The aggregate limit for graduate or professional study, including loans made at the undergraduate level is $15,000. The ANNUAL PERCENTAGE RATE on such loans cannot be more than 7%.

Most students are eligible for a Federal interest subsidy whereby the Federal Government, rather than the student, pays the interest on the student's outstanding loan during the time the student is in school, during a "grace" period (consisting of 9 to 12 months after the student has left school), and during any authorized deferment of repayment. There is no family income requirement for the Federal interest subsidy. In order to qualify for this interest subsidy, the law requires that the student must provide the lender with a statement from the school indicating the student's estimated cost of attendance and other financial assistance which has been awarded the student. The portion of the loan application to be completed by the school includes this required information. Students attending foreign schools which refuse to complete the school portion of the student loan application may still apply for loans, but will have to pay their own interest throughout the life of the loan.

Fig. 1.   Information for students applying for federal loans.

scenario principle). There are others that they begin to think about in the class and later find themselves using regularly (e.g., techniques for organizing reference documents). There are others that we have to put in a category we might call raising consciousness. Trainees think about them, but seldom, if ever, use them. Evaluation fits into this last category.

Many working authors have heard of readability formulas and are charmed by their apparent objectivity and ease of use. However, there is now consistent research evidence *against* using readability formulas as measures of success in writing and in rewriting technical and legal documents for adult audiences (see Duffy, Chapter 6, this volume).

Charrow and Charrow (1979) found that there was no correlation between improvement in comprehension scores on their rewritten jury instructions and the readability scores of the instructions. Kern (1979) in reviewing readability research in the military found very little consistency in the predictions made by different formulas. He also found that the formulas could not make very precise predictions of the reading levels of military texts. Duffy and Kabance (1982) recently tested the effects of rewriting reading passages to readability guidelines and concluded that rewriting to improve the readability score of a passage will not necessarily produce a more comprehensible text.

We can usually convince authors that readability formulas are not particularly useful measures of successful writing. For instance, showing them that the nonsensical poem "Jabberwocky" gets an almost perfect score from the most commonly used readability formula helps get the point across. It is harder to convince authors of the value of more suitable empirical evaluation techniques.

We are realistic enough to know that authors who are lawyers, English majors, MBAs, and from other nonscientific, nontechnical fields will have a limited grasp of the potential of data-driven empirical evaluation. The typical 3–5 day

Basic Grant Application Form 1981-82 School Year

You can use the form in this booklet to apply for a Basic Educational Opportunity Grant (Basic Grant) for the 1981-82 school year (July 1, 1981-June 30, 1982). Basic Grants are awarded to students who need money for their education after high school. A Basic Grant is not a loan, so you don't have to repay it.

Your need for a Basic Grant will be figured out by the Basic Grant Program, using a formula established by law. In 1981-82, the amount of a Basic Grant will be between $200 and $1,900. The actual dollar amount of your Basic Grant depends on:

—your eligibility index
—whether you are a full-time or part-time student
—how much it costs to go to your college
—how long you will be enrolled between July 1, 1981 and June 30, 1982.

The instructions in this booklet will answer most of your questions about the Basic Grant Program. If you still have questions after you have read the instructions, talk to your high school counselor or the financial aid administrator at the college you want to attend.

Who can get a Basic Grant?

To get a Basic Grant, you must be:

—a U.S. citizen or an eligible noncitizen
—an undergraduate student who does not yet have a Bachelor's degree
—going to college at least half-time
—enrolled in a college that takes part in the Basic Grant Program

If you meet all of these requirements, you may be eligible to get a Basic Grant award.

I've already filled out a different student aid form. Do I have to fill out this one too?

Maybe not. There are other forms that you can use to apply for a Basic Grant and other student aid:

—Family Financial Statement (FFS)
—Financial Aid Form (FAF)
—Pennsylvania Higher Education Assistance Agency (PHEAA) Form
—Student Aid Application for California (SAAC).

Each of these forms has a box for you to check if you want to apply for a Basic Grant. If you checked that box, you have already applied for a Basic Grant and you don't need to fill out this form.

What if I want to apply only for a Basic Grant?

If you plan to apply **only** for a Basic Grant, you should use the form in this booklet, not one of the other forms. If won't cost you anything to apply only for a Basic Grant.

What happens after I mail in this form?

Within six weeks after you mail your form, we will send you a Student Eligibility Report (SER). On the SER there will be a number called an eligibility index. We figure this number from the information you give us on your application. It helps us decide whether you can get a grant—and if so, how much. The lower the number, the higher the award.

Be sure to read all the instructions that come with the SER. They will tell you what to do next to get a Basic Grant.

If you do **not** get a SER in six weeks, write to:

Basic Grants
P.O. Box 92864
Los Angeles, CA 90009

Give your name, address, social security number, and date of birth, and ask for another copy of your SER. If your address has changed since you sent in your application, be sure to give us your new address.

What if my financial situation changes?

The Basic Grant Application Form asks mostly about income and expenses for 1980. If your financial situation has recently changed for the worse, you may be able to fill out a Special Condition Form. That form asks mostly about the income and expenses you expect to have in 1981. Read page 8 of this booklet to find out more about the Special Condition Form.

Deadline: March 15, 1982

We must receive your application by March 15, 1982. However, you should apply as early as possible because mailing in your application is only the first step to getting a Basic Grant. There are other deadlines that you will have to meet.

Fig. 2.   Information for students applying for federal grants.

training workshops designed for working authors do not provide enough time to transform them into researchers even if they were philosophically sympathetic to the empirical approach. We do try to introduce them to the merits of the concept of field testing—of taking the document to its intended users to see if it accomplishes what it is supposed to. In the process, we introduce them to empirical techniques that are feasible for nonscientists, such as paraphrase protocols, comprehension tests, and usability analysis.

WHAT RESEARCH IS NEEDED?

What we know about training authors to produce informative documents—and what we have presented in this chapter—is based partially on our experience and partially on research. We, like other document designers and trainers, have learned a great deal in the past 5 years about informative documents and those who produce them. However, much empirical study remains to be done. We can suggest at least three areas for further fruitful research.

One area of needed research involves the content of training programs—the guidelines that we and other trainers teach writers to use. Many of these guidelines are based in research from disparate fields. Although some of the guidelines (e.g., use active voice, use personal pronouns) have been tested in informative documents, many have not. And the guidelines that have been tested have only been tested with one or two types of documents (e.g., regulations, warranties, or insurance policies). What is needed is research that tests combinations of guidelines and that can answer questions like these:

> Do some combinations of guidelines make a greater difference in the comprehensibility and usability of informative documents than other combinations?
> Do specific combinations of guidelines have the same effects on different types of documents?

In short, we need to know more about the make-up of effective informative documents, and the evidence needs to be gathered in the context of real-world writing.

A second area of needed research centers on the authors themselves and the processes they use while drafting their own work or reviewing and editing the work of others. Research into the composing processes of writers is relatively recent, and little of it focuses on working adult writers. In particular, we need research on the processes of people who write complex documents. Do writers who produce usable policy statements, regulations, or instructions have similar composing processes? Are the processes needed to draft effective documents the same whether the product is a letter, memo, loan agreement, or technical manual? Are the strategies for effectively editing a manual or warranty the same as those needed to write one?

The third area of needed research involves follow-up studies to determine the effects of training on authors when they return to their workplaces. One set of questions focuses on what the authors learned:

> Do authors really learn enough from short training courses to be able to apply what was taught?
>
> How long do they retain this knowledge? 1 month after training? 6 months?

If writers do learn what is taught in a training course, are they permitted to apply this learning in their work setting? This raises a set of questions about the work setting:

1. What is the employer's stance toward writing?
2. How do internal review systems work?
3. Are authors rewarded or punished for writing differently?
4. Are some changes more acceptable than others?
5. How does the level of acceptability vary? by the type of document? by the type of organization that employs these authors? by the supervisor's personal preferences?

Research in these areas is important for a very simple but compelling reason. Thousands of informative documents will continue to be written in the real world every year. And these documents will continue to affect the lives and well-being of large numbers of people. Any research that can help writers write documents to better meet people's needs is research that contributes both to human knowledge and to social goals.

REFERENCES

Aldrich, P. (1982). Adult writers: Some factors that interfere with effective writing. *The Technical Writing Teacher, 9,* 128–132.

Atlas, M. *Addressing an audience: A study of expert-novice differences in writing* (Document Design Project Technical Report No. 3). Pittsburgh, PA: Carnegie-Mellon University.

Berkenkotter, C. (1981). Understanding a writer's awareness of audience. *College Composition and Communication, 32,* 388–399.

Berkenkotter, C. (1983). Decisions and revisions: The planning strategies of a publishing writer. *College Composition and Communication, 34,* 156–169.

Bobrow, R., & Brown, J. (1975). Systematic understanding: Synthesis, analysis and contingent knowledge in specialized understanding systems. In D. Bobrow & A. Collins (Eds.), *Representation and understanding: Studies in cognitive science.* New York: Academic Press.

Bond, S., Hayes, J., & Flower, L. (1980). *Translating the law into common language: A protocol study* (Document Design Project Technical Report No. 8). Pittsburgh, PA: Carnegie-Mellon University.

Brandsford, J., & Johnson, M. (1972). Contextual prerequisites for understanding: Some investigations of comprehension and recall. *Journal of Verbal Learning and Verbal Behavior, 11,* 717–726.

Burhans, C. (1983). The teaching of writing and the knowledge gap. *College English, 45,* 639–656.

Charrow, R., & Charrow, V. (1979). Making legal language understandable: Psycholinguistic study of jury instructions. *Columbia Law Review, 79,* 1306–1374.

Crouse, J., & Idstein, P. (1972). Effects of encoding cues on prose learning. *Journal of Educational Psychology, 63,* 309–313.

Duffy, T., & Kabance, P. (1982). Testing a readable writing approach to text revision. *Journal of Educational Psychology, 74,* 733–748.

Ede, L., & Lunsford, A. (1983). Why write . . . together? *Rhetoric Review, 1,* 151–157.

Faigley, L., & Miller, P. (1982). What we learn from writing on the job. *College English, 44,* 557–569.

Faigley, L., & Witte, S. (1981). Analyzing revision. *College Composition and Communication, 32,* 400–414.

Felker, D. (Ed.), (1980). *Document design: A review of the relevant research.* Washington, DC: American Institutes for Research.

Flower, L., & Hayes, J. (1980). The cognition of discovery: Defining a rhetorical problem. *College Composition and Communication, 31,* 21–32.

Flower, L., Hayes, J., & Swarts, H. (1983). Revising functional documents: The scenario principle. In P. Anderson, R. Brockmann, & C. Miller (Eds.), *New essays in technical and scientific communication: Research, theory, practice* (pp. 41–58). Farmingdale, NY: Baywood Publishing Company, Inc.

Fodor, J., Bever, T., & Garrett, M. (1974). *The psychology of language: An introduction to psycholinguistics and generative grammar.* New York: McGraw-Hill.

Foster, J., & Coles, P. (1977). An experimental study of typographical cueing in printed text. *Ergonomics, 20,* 57–66.

Glynn, S., & DiVesta, F. (1979). Control of prose processing via instructional and typographic cues. *Journal of Educational Psychology, 71,* 595–603.

Gould, J. (1980). Experiments on composing letters: Some facts, some myths, and some observations. In L. Gregg & E. Steinberg (Eds.), *Cognitive processes in writing.* Hillsdale, NJ: Erlbaum.

Hairston, M. (1981). Not all errors are created equal: Nonacademic readers in the professions respond to lapses in usage. *College English, 43,* 794–806.

Hakes, D., & Cairns, H. (1970). Sentence comprehension and relative pronouns. *Perception and Psychophysics, 8,* 5–8.

Hartley, J. (1978). *Designing instructional text.* New York, NY: Nichols.

Hartley, J. (1981). Eighty ways of improving instructional text. *IEEE Transactions on Professional Communication, 24,* 17–27.

Hartley, J., & Davies, I. (1976). Preinstructional strategies: The role of pretests, behavioral objectives, overviews, and advance organizers. *Review of Educational Research, 46,* 239–265.

Hartley, J., & Trueman, M. (1982, March). *Headings in text: Issues and data.* Paper presented at Annual Meeting of American Educational Research Association, New York.

Holland, V., & Rose, A. (1981). *A comparison of prose and algorithms for presenting complex instructions* (Document Design Project Technical Report No. 17). Washington, DC: American Institutes for Research.

Jenkins, J., & Bailey, V. (1964). Cue selection and mediated transfer in paired-associate learning. *Journal of Experimental Psychology, 67,* 101–102.

Kern, R. (1979). *Usefulness of readability formulas for achieving Army readability objectives:*

Research and state-of-the-art applied to the Army's problem. Fort Benjamin Harrison, IN: Technical Advisory Service, Army Research Institute.

Kintsch, W., & Kozminsky, E. (1977). Summarizing stories after reading and listening. *Journal of Educational Psychology, 69,* 491–499.

Larkin, W., & Burns, D. (1977). Sentence comprehension and memory for embedded structures. *Memory and Cognition, 5,* 17–22.

Miller, G. (1956). The magical number seven, plus or minus two: Some limits on our capacity for processing information. *Psychological Review, 63,* 81–97.

Miller, G., & Isard, S. (1964). Free recall of self-embedded English sentences. *Information and Control, 7,* 292–303.

Newell, A., & Simon, H. (1972). *Human problem solving.* Englewood Cliffs, NJ: Prentice-Hall.

Odell, L., & Goswami, D. (1982). Writing in a non-academic setting. *Research in the Teaching of English, 16,* 201–223.

Rose, A., Shettel, H., Wheaton, G., Bolin, S., & Barba, M. (1981, February). *Evaluating the effectiveness of soldier's manuals: A field study* (AIR Final Report, Contract No. MDA 903-78-C-2033, Army Research Institute). Washington, DC: American Institutes for Research.

Selzer, J. (1983). The composing processes of an engineer. *College Composition and Communication, 34,* 178–187.

Stephens, R. (1981). Variations in composing style. *Journal of Advanced Composition, 1-2,* 45–52.

Swarts, H., Flower, L., & Hayes, J. (1980). *How headings in documents can mislead readers* (Document Design Project Technical Report No. 9). Pittsburgh, PA: Carnegie-Mellon University.

Tinker, M. (1963). *Legibility of print.* Ames, IA: Iowa State University.

Tinker, M. (1965). *Bases for effective reading.* Minneapolis, MN: University of Minnesota Press.

Williams, J. (1983). Covert language behavior during writing. *Research in the Teaching of English 17,* 301–312.

Wright, P., & Reid, F. (1973). Written information: Some alternatives to prose for expressing the outcomes of complex contingencies. *Journal of Applied Pyschology, 57,* 160–166.

CHAPTER 4

Editing: Policies and Processes

PATRICIA WRIGHT

INTRODUCTION: WHY BOTHER WITH EDITING?

One of the most important reasons for a concern with editing is that editors stand between the writer and the reader. In general this is a desirable intervention because authors do not necessarily choose the clearest way of expressing their thoughts, nor even feel obliged always to say what they mean (see Chapter 2 in the present volume by Orna and Chapter 3 by Felker, Redish, and Peterson). The catalyst of editorial mediation is often the crucial factor that enables the final communication to be successful.

Nevertheless, editorial intervention is not always advantageous. Editorial policies such as "guidelines for authors" may function as boundary constraints limiting the forms of expression available to authors. At times these limitations may extend to the content itself, for example, when editors invite work on certain topics and discourage it on other subjects.

Of course, there are several different kinds of editor, from managing editors to copy editors. This diversity serves to emphasize that a published text is essentially the product of a team effort and that the author is by no means responsible for all the features that may enhance or detract from the usability of the final publication. The views of publishers, printers, and marketing experts may all have played a part in shaping various facets of the text—from the provision of a picture on the dust jacket to the omission of an index at the end of the book.

If editing were simply a matter of making and adhering to policy decisions, then changing such decisions (e.g., in order to improve the usability of texts) might require nothing more than evidence that such changes were desirable. However, numerous editorial decisions are concerned with the author's verbiage. Here editing requires fine judgment about content, style, and presentation. Relatively little seems to be known about the cognitive processes mediating such

63

DESIGNING USABLE TEXTS

editing skills. Later in this chapter I review some preliminary studies of editing processes, but first let us consider the ways in which editorial policy on content, style, and presentation can have important consequences for readers.

The editors of learned journals usually define their own fields of interest. However, the distinction between content and style is not always clear-cut. The overlap is illustrated in the following quotation from the first paragraph of the statement of "Publishing and Editorial Policy for NSPI Manuscripts Selected for Publication." (NSPI is the American-based National Society for Performance and Instruction.) The original had no typographic distinction, but as reproduced here, certain phrases have been italicized to draw attention to the extent to which editorial policy may intervene between author and reader:

> Manuscripts selected for publication will be edited to comply to space and style requirements and may be *edited to emphasize aspects of content.* Authors are responsible for the accuracy of their manuscript and their *opinions are respected and expressed where appropriate in the judgment of the NSPI.* The elements of grammar, spelling, manner of expression, punctuation and the like are the sole province of NSPI editors

Editorial influences on presentation affect page layout, number of subheadings, location of illustrations, biases for or against using illustrations, and so on. Not only editorial policy but also other aspects of the way the text is produced may curtail an author's presentation options. This is easily seen by considering briefly how the new information technologies may influence the preparation of texts.

NEW TECHNOLOGIES MAY CHANGE EDITORIAL FUNCTIONS

There are many ways in which the use of sophisticated word-processing systems can provide support for some of the routine editorial functions (Frase, Keenan, & Dever, 1980; Lefrere, Waller, & Whalley, 1980). Robinson (1981) provides useful illustrations of how problems of hyphenation at the ends of lines can be dealt with much more satisfactorily using computer-based editing techniques. Word-processing systems can now assist editing by globally checking such text characteristics as spelling and sentence structure. In the future the techniques of artificial intelligence may assist writers in the thematic construction of their material (Lefrere, 1982). (See Chapter 5 in the present volume by Frase, Macdonald, and Keenan for a discussion of the AT&T WRITERS' WORKBENCH program.)

With many word-processing systems the final product remains print on paper, but increasingly it becomes necessary to evaluate the future of the printed word relative to other communication media (e.g., Hills, 1980). Some car maintenance manuals have already been issued as videocassettes. The economic argument that printed educational texts may be replaced by laser-disc technologies (Blunden, 1981) obviously widens and enriches the presentation options available to authors. New editorial skills may also be required.

While some new developments offer enhanced communication facilities, with other new developments the trend appears to be in the reverse direction. For example, if texts are printed on demand from some computerized database, then presentation options may be severely curtailed. This is even more true at present when publications are provided as soft-copy displays on interactive visual display units, that is, "electronic journals" (Senders, 1977; Shackel, 1982). Perhaps if electronic journals are presented on microcomputers, then color may become a conventional way of denoting some of the facets that are at present indicated by typographic distinctions within the text. For example, instead of using an italic font to emphasize particular phrases perhaps, on a CRT screen, highlighting the phrase by reversing the color of text and background may be appropriate. Editorial guidance to authors working in these new media may be of the utmost importance because the electronic medium allows direct transmission from writer to reader without the civilizing effects of editorial intervention.

A reduction in editorial processing for electronic texts is not inevitable. Shackel (1982) has pointed out that the electronic medium permits readers to pass comments on the text directly to authors. Moreover, authors can easily make any changes that they feel are necessary as a result of such feedback. Lefrere (1981, 1982) has discussed many aspects of how editorial functions may change for the editors of electronic journals.

Technological developments have also reduced the editorial control of some printed texts. The use of in-house printing facilities seems to be on the increase, both for journals and for texts of conference proceedings. Again this has implications for the usablity of the text because many of the typographic options available with traditional printing procedures will not be possible on more limited production systems. For example, when journals are prepared from camera-ready copy provided by the author (e.g., the Journal of Research Communication Studies), the text may be composed on a typewriter; the typewriter's uniform letter spacing is not as easy to read as the proportional spacing of most typeset material. But perhaps most serious of all is the risk that these amateur production systems may bypass the writer's interaction with editorial expertise that could improve the quality of the text.

It would be useful to know more about the nature of editorial expertise and the impact it has on the usability of a text. Can editorial skills be made explicit so that they can be readily acquired by others, and in particular by writers themselves? Hayes and Flower (1980) have discussed some of editing processes that writers apply to their own draft manuscripts as they write. Galbraith (1980) has suggested that when reviewing their own text, authors can find it difficult to maintain the distinction between the goal of what they wanted to say and the goal of understanding what they have actually written. Bartlett (1982) has reported that writers are much less likely to notice ambiguities in their own texts than in material written by others.

The new communication technologies may add urgency to finding ways of improving authors' abilities to edit their own texts. An understanding of the strengths and weaknesses of the present editorial systems would be valuable if we are to preserve the vital editorial functions when these are transformed by the new technologies.

EDITORIAL POLICY AND USABLE TEXTS

What are the factors that make a text usable? In one sense there are many factors, ranging from legibility to the adequacy of the content. For simplicity it may be helpful to follow Wright (1980) in subdividing readers' interaction with technical material into at least three stages: locating relevant material, interpreting it, and applying the newly, acquired knowledge. Various design factors contribute to the usability of the material at each of these stages. Waller (1979) has discussed in detail the ways in which different access structures can allow readers to locate specific information easily. Research by psycholinguists has explored some of the cognitive processes that mediate comprehension. The predominant concern of these researchers has been with the effects of alternative linguistic structures. Yet in many texts the reader's problems of understanding extend beyond this. The readers of a research report may be confident that they have understood the meaning of the text in the results section. They may also feel sure of the meaning of an accompanying graph. However, difficulties sometimes arise when these two meanings do not appear to be compatible. Therefore a third component of usability concerns the reader's problems in applying the information from the texts. Often a critical determinant of whether the information can be successfully applied will be the context within which the reader interpreted the text.

Appeals to context have often been criticized for being vague and imprecise. Clark and Carlson (1981) have provided a detailed classification of some of the factors found under this umbrella term in the research literature. Nevertheless, the term *context* is used here deliberately because of its breadth of scope. There seems to be no other term that adequately describes the user's need to relate an understanding for a particular portion of a text both to other information within the text and to a much wider body of knowledge within which that information must be used (e.g., knowledge about the physical environment when the reader of a set of operating instructions must relate the meaning of the text to the appliance itself). The surrounding text and the reader's more general knowledge of the world are clearly very different kinds of context, and it may be a mistake to use the same label for both (Barnard & Hammond, 1982). (See Chapter 1 by Olson in the present volume for a discussion of the difficulties in anticipating a reader's knowledge of the world and the possible writing strategies for address-ing this problem.) Nevertheless, for our present purposes it is sufficient to note that, if a text is to be usable, readers must be able to do more than locate the information they need. They must also understand the writer's intended mean-ing. Furthermore, that understanding must be adequate for whatever subsequent action is necessary.

What determines editorial policy? The difficulties arising from writers having conflicting goals while editing has already been mentioned, but editors too may be seeking to satisfy a variety of criteria of which usability may be only one. For editors, much more than authors, aesthetic criteria can be important and can sometimes conflict with usability criteria. For example, it was probably on aesthetic grounds that an editor chose to separate the figure and legend of a graph within a journal publication. The page layout was a three-column format, the figure appeared at the bottom of the first column, and the caption was printed at the bottom of the third column (Marcel, 1978). In one sense the aesthetic balance of the page looked fine, the text forming the shape of a capital T. There just was a slight problem of usability as readers worked their way down the first column and encountered an unexplained graph.

Possibly one way of reducing the risk of editorial decisions detracting from the usability of a text might be to encourage greater interaction between editors and authors. A text production system does not necessarily work well if the manu-script travels only from writer to editor and thence onto the reader.

Some of the problems editors face in coping with the conflicting demands made upon them have been discussed by Heap (1980). When addressing the Institute of Scientific and Technical Communicators in London, Heap pointed out that, even within the restricted domain of published periodicals, editors do not all share the same objectives. For example, the editors of academic journals are primarily concerned with maintaining the quality of the content of that journal because these journals have archival status. In contrast, the editors of those periodicals that are sold by bookstores often have as their primary objective the capturing and entertaining of the reader. Yet a third category of periodicals is the trade journal, which is financed entirely by the advertising it contains. Heap points out that for such publications the editor's major criterion must be to satisfy, not the reader, but the advertiser. If the reader wants any change in these journals, particularly any change that might either reduce the advertising space or that might increase the cost of the publication, then it is very unlikely that the advertisers will be willing to agree to the implementation of such changes. If the advertisers withdraw their support, the periodical ceases to exist. With system constraints this strong is there any room for considering usability?

What is true for periodicals is equally true for other kinds of texts. For example, the educational publishers' main objective is to sell their texts. They will therefore require that editors conform to the conventions that seem related to the saleability of the publication. Hence the choice of print size, the use of justified right-hand margins, the selection of illustrative materials, and even the choice of softback and hardback binding are all geared to the marketing of the finished publication. This strategy is undoubtedly successful.

Another example of how criteria other than usability are applied to publications can be seen in coffee-table books. These are glossy productions that appear to sell mainly on their pictorial merits. They are bought by people who either like to give them away as presents or who like to have them about the house as conversation pieces. The notion that readers may want to use the books is clearly far down the editor's list of priorities when decisions are made about the format of such a book. So it should not come as a surprise to find that it is very difficult to use the table of contents in a text such as *The British Isles* (Smart & Gibbon, 1978). Editors have not catered to readers who may wish to locate a specific section of the book. Many pages do not have legible page numbers (presumably lest this spoil the illustrations). It appears that the book's intended use was for browsing rather than for information retrieval.

Surprisingly, the low priority afforded to broad-based usability criteria can also be true of educational texts. When selecting a textbook for pupils or students, the teacher's main criteria are likely to be the content of the text and its price. If the editor and publisher are aware that the book is being sold primarily on the contents, then again there is very little incentive for them to worry about whether readers will be able to find, understand, and apply what they read. Indeed the price consideration may militate against providing features such as detailed indexes.

Financial considerations often need to have a high priority in editorial decision-making. This can result in several aspects of editorial policy risking conflict with usability criteria. The ways in which space-saving policies are implemented serve as an illustration of this conflict. The need for concise expression in publications such as academic journals is clear to see because the journal subscription list will support only a given number of published pages. Therefore to be attractive to a wide readership, as many research reports as possible need to be fitted within the available space. Yet Wason (1962) demonstrated that readers found it much more difficult to understand prose that was a tightly condensed version of an original text. So once more usability and economic criteria are in conflict, and there may be no readily available compromise.

Another potential conflict concerns the stylistic objectives that editors adopt. Consider, for example, the proceedings of international conferences. Such proceedings often end up in the form of a multiauthored book in which the editors seek to strive for a uniformity of style that reduces the individual stylistic differences among the conference contributors. Such editorial changes are often made in the name of usability. For example, when an editor imposes a uniform nationalistic style of expression, be it American English or British English, then readers may find this helpful. Editorial policy about uniformity of length from different contributors may be much less helpful to readers. The problems of having authors condense their contributions has already been mentioned. One ingenious solution arrived at by an editor, who was embarrassed by one chapter being considerably longer than that of most of the other contributions to his text, was to lift out the middle section of the offending chapter and publish it separately within the same volume (Hills, 1980). Thus there was no overall saving of space in the final publication, only an apparent uniformity in the lengths of chapters within the volume. Whether this editorial policy helped readers is hard to say. Yet the editorial view of space allocation is one of the most important constraints on the usability of text.

Perhaps one of the few areas in which usability is actually being accorded high priority in the criteria that published documents must reach, is the area of industrial manuals. Here the law appears to be increasingly on the side of the reader. If readers misinterpret some element of the documentation and as a result misuse a piece of apparatus and so cause loss or damage to themselves or to others, the law is increasingly taking the view that the ultimate responsibility lies with those who provided that written information. Here at least it would seem that there is a growing concensus that the usability of the document really matters.

A similar increase in concerned awareness exists with regard to government publications (e.g., Anonymous, 1982; Rayner, 1982). There is a vociferous element within the consumer-oriented public who are demanding that as taxpayers they have a right to be provided with information by government departments, and furthermore that the information provided must be in a form that they as readers can use (e.g., Cutts and Maher, 1980; Vernon, 1980). The authors of technical materials may often be hampered by their own specialist knowledge from understanding what the reader needs to be told. As a consequence, the contribution of editorial skills in applying concepts such as quality control to the domain of document design may be increasingly important.

EDITORIAL POLICIES AS HOUSE RULES

The guidance to which many editors turn is enshrined in a list of do's and don'ts that are generally referred to as editorial house rules. These can be formulated at a variety of levels, ranging from the general to the specific. At the higher, more global level, the editor of a scholarly journal may be seeking to assess whether the author is making a new contribution to existing knowledge, or whether that contribution is appropriate to a particular publication. At the lower, more detailed level, the editor may be seeking to ensure that the text follows certain stylistic conventions (e.g., the use of various levels of headings or the format for references).

The strict application of the lower-level house rules are designed to bring consistency and order into a publication. Although consistency and order will generally make a positive contribution to the usability of a text, some house rules may detract from the facility with which readers interact with the text. For example, some journals require authors to cite references within the text as numbers rather than as names and dates. This practice is probably motivated by the space that it saves. There are various typographic ways of implementing such a space-saving strategy. The *British Medical Journal* uses superscripts, whereas the *Transactions of the Institute of Electrical and Electronic Engineers on Professional Communication* uses numbers within square brackets on the line of text. Although saving space, this kind of referencing system detracts from the usability of the text because readers can have no idea whether the quoted source is familiar or not unless they interrupt their reading to consult the reference list and decode the numbers.

Usually the numbering in the text runs sequentially and the final bibliographic listing maintains this ordering. Because the list itself has no visual ordering, it is very difficult for readers to scan the list for new references. Hartley (1981a) has argued that reference lists are most usable when organized alphabetically with the date given both alongside the author's name and adjacent to the bibliographic source. Editorial policy rarely permits, far less encourages, such redundancy.

If superscripts are used in the text to denote referenced sources, this increases the problems facing the typist who has to repeatedly pause to realign the text. Worst of all, if the author finds that one early reference has been accidentally omitted from the numbering system, it becomes necessary to change every reference number throughout the text. Usability was scarcely in anyone's mind when the editorial policy of adopting this system of referencing was decided upon, although it does bring consistency and order to the publication. Clearly such criteria may be necessary but are not sufficient.

Even house rules that generally facilitate usability can cause problems if they are implemented without thought as to their appropriateness. The house rules of one academic journal stipulated that the order of mention of the experimental treatments within the procedure section should correspond to the order in which the results of these treatments were presented subsequently. This is obviously a sensible convention most of the time, but there may be instances in which usability requires two different orders. For example, the results section may be easier to digest if the data are tabulated in rank order. It may not be practicable to explain the treatments in this order if they are derived by various manipulations from a common "text." Making the procedure section usable necessitates starting with an explanation of this core material that formed one of the experimental treatments. Unfortunately this core treatment gave neither the best nor the worst performance so the author presented the data in the results section in an "inconsistent" order. The editor intervened and the house rules won. In the table of results the ordering of the data was rearranged to make the table arguably less usable because the trend across treatments was no longer apparent (Wright & Barnard, 1975). Perhaps interested readers chose to reconstruct the more meaningful ordering of the results and wondered why the authors did not bother to be that helpful in the first place.

These examples of relatively low-level guidelines, the sort of rules that any well-trained computer could follow, are simply specific examples of the plethora of advice that is available to authors and editors on how to create successful written communications (e.g., Flesch, 1960; Gowers, 1954; Hartley, 1981b). In mathematical form the advice turns itself into readability formulas, and many such formulas exist (Klare 1976; see also Chapter 6 by Duffy in the present volume). Nevertheless, in spite of the abundance of guidelines and advice, all examples of this approach suffer from at least four major weaknesses.

First, because there will be many lawful exceptions to these rules, their unintelligent application can be counterproductive. As was illustrated in the preceding example they can have the effect of reducing the usability of the text rather than enhancing it.

Second, these low-level guidelines seldom deal with the thematic organization of the text. There are times when the reader's bewilderment arises not so much because of the difficulty in understanding *what* the writer is saying in a specific sentence but in understanding *how* this sentence relates to those that precede and follow it.

Third, and perhaps most seriously, there will never be sets of rules that can guarantee to detect and remove specific ambiguities from a text. In some documents it may be much more important to know that the critical information will be correctly interpreted (e.g., that the reader of a manual will fit the safety valve the correct way round) than to know that on average most of the text can be read and understood by the average 9-year-old.

The fourth disadvantage of low-level guidelines arises simply because of their quantity. When the list of guidelines becomes too long, authors or editors have difficulty remembering the advice. Hartley has extended his list of guidelines from 50 to 80 (Hartley & Burnhill, 1977; Hartley, 1981b). Why stop there? The specification of the standards that military documentation must reach took 35 pages to print (e.g., DOD-STD-1685 (SH) 10 October 1978). These may not be the best example of a usable set of guidelines. At a conference during 1980 I met one military contractor whose technical writing department had spent 3 days trying to unravel the specification they were told to work to before they could begin to think about trying to produce any documentation. The use of numerous detailed house rules seems to be an expensive way of seeking to ensure that texts are designed to be usable. So it is worth exploring alternative approaches, such as the more general guidelines concerned with principles rather than details.

The Impracticalities of High-level Guidelines

General principles such as "write clearly" or "avoid ambiguity" are not going to be troubled by the exceptions that pervade low-level house rules. The problem with high-level guidelines is knowing how to instantiate them at the level of textual detail. There are several instances in which editors have made serious attempts to enhance the usability of some information ("enhancing usability" being a high-level guideline), which nevertheless resulted in texts that caused readers difficulties. For example, there is a textbook in which three changes in typographic font were used to distinguish chapter headings from main and subordinate headings within the chapter, and these typographic cues were carried through into the numbering system of the contents page. This resulted in a vertical column of page numbers that appeared to waiver in depth as one viewed it, the larger and bolder numbers appearing closer to the reader than the other numbers, (e.g., Rumelhart, 1977). The editorial decision appeared well motivated from considerations of consistency with the text and a desire to provide a rich cueing system for the reader; but at the level of detailed instantiation, other factors (such as the total gestalt of the column of numbers) became of overriding importance.

A similar problem arose in another index that listed in three columns the names of authors, the titles of books, and the names of those who had reviewed books for that journal. The editor realized that it was difficult to predict whether readers would access information in the table by author, by title, or by reviewer. So to help readers, each column was separately alphabeticized. The related entries across the three columns were denoted by alphanumeric codes. Unfortunately readers' expectations that the related elements would be on the same horizontal line led them to make many mistakes when using the index, even though they understood that this was an unusual arrangement (Wright & Threlfall, 1980). So an editor's good intentions to follow the spirit of high-level guidelines may not be enough to create an adequate text.

A leaflet giving safety advice on the use of a stepladder warned "Do not drop things off the ladder." Undoubtedly sound advice. The problem is knowing how to comply with it. Many high-level guidelines seem to encounter this problem. Exhortations to think of the reader are all very well, but unless the advice becomes programmatic in some sense it is not easy to follow. Suggestions have been made elsewhere about how to analyze the reader's interaction with text in order to motivate editorial decisions about the choice of content, its sequencing, and its presentation (e.g., Wright, 1980). Similarly, suggestions have been made elsewhere about how to use empirical techniques for finding out about readers' knowledge and expectations (e.g., Wright, 1979). There is not space to amplify these suggestions here. The important point is that, if high-level house rules are to be of any value to editors, then these guidelines must be accompanied by details concerning how the objectives specified in the rules can be achieved.

This discussion of high- and low-level guidelines has intentionally characterized the extremes of the continuum. Obviously there is a lot of middle ground that may avoid some of the dilemmas arising at the extremities. For example, the Information Mapping system developed by Horn (1976) requires writers and editors to apply their intelligence to the writing task by considering at least certain elements of the thematic structure, and it provides the writers with a training program for achieving this skill. It therefore differs from a simple, low-level listing of do's and don'ts and is more programmatic than most high-level advice. Nevertheless, any system that advocates a rigid presentation format may be adopting a style that is more appropriate for some classes of communication than for others (Hartley, 1982).

One thing that high- and low-level guidelines share is that editorial success relies on knowing how to apply the rules. This raises issues about how editors edit; that is, how do they identify trouble spots in text and recognize the corrective action to take. The next section explores some of the processes involved in editing.

SOME PRELIMINARY STUDIES OF EDITING PROCESSES

The data from five small investigations, all relating to editing processes, are reported in this section. Most of these experiments were carried out with the cooperation of volunteers from the general public. Upon first consideration, these people might seem to be an inappropriate population for such an investigation. However, it is important to note that many editors both in industry and in academic fields—particularly editors of academic publications such as learned journals and conference proceedings—are often members of the general public in that they have received no special training in editorial work. Journal editors may be appointed either because of their high academic standing as researchers or because of their known ability as administrators. Similarly, design engineers may be acting as editors of technical documents because of their specialized knowledge of the subject matter. Perhaps the tacit assumption often made is that, just as it is believed that anyone can write well if they really try, so too anybody who was well educated could act as an editor if they were prepared to give the time and trouble to the job. The data from the following studies may raise doubts about the validity of these assumptions.

This series of five experiments starts by looking at peoples' ability to make fairly global judgments about a short text. Subsequent studies explore how adequately people can detect specific trouble-spots within a text. The final investigation concerns peoples' sensitivity to styles of expression and also their awareness of the changing acceptability of alternative linguistic styles. In this respect the studies shift their focus from the macro- to the microdecisions that editors make.

In terms of the underlying cognitive processes on which editing depends, the present experiments seek to explore the issue of whether inappropriate editing is the result of a failure of knowledge (e.g., not knowing that certain sentence structures are difficult for readers to understand) or a failure to recognize where this knowledge can be appropriately applied. Such a distinction has practical implications for the kinds of training that might be most useful to editors.

EXPERIMENT 1: PEOPLES' GLOBAL ASSESSMENT OF TEXT

It seems a common everyday experience that we know when a piece of writing is successful, and we are even more aware when it is unsuccessful. We perhaps take it for granted that others will agree with our judgments, but as Steinberg (1980) has pointed out, "Each of us 'knows' a good bit about how to write . . . but . . . many of our peers 'know' not only a variety of similar truths, but even a variety of truths that flatly contradict ours" (p. 158). This point has been empirically underlined by Klare (1981), who reports wide discrepancies in the guidelines formulated for good writing by 15 different authorities. Therefore this series of preliminary investigations of editing processes starts by examining whether discrepancies arise only at the micro-level of dealing with specific sentences, or whether they also exist at the level of a global evaluation of the adequacy of a text.

In order to see whether people agreed with each other when making global judgments, our editors were presented with three typewritten accounts of how to play the game draughts and three accounts explaining how to play snakes and ladders. These texts were selected from a number that had been written on a previous occasion by members of the Applied Psychology Unit's volunteer panel. The basis of the selection was simply that the texts appeared to be stylistically dissimilar. Table 1 shows some of the physical characteristics of the texts such as number of words and number of sentences that they contained. The order in which the texts were presented varied among editors.

Forty-two people gave marks out of ten to each of the six texts. Three sets of marks were given, providing separate estimates for comprehension, content, and style. As the lower half of Table 1 shows, the three measures appeared to be highly correlated for each text. Therefore the analysis was carried out on the total score that each text received. An analysis of agreement among the editorial ratings showed that there was a significant concensus within the group as a whole

Table 1

Experiment 1: Global Assessments of Text

Text	Snakes and Ladders			Draughts		
	S1	S2	S3	D1	D2	D3
Characteristics						
Length in words	56	112	134	161	167	227
Length in sentences	1	8	7	5	8	7
Words per sentence	56	14	19	32	21	32
Results of overall assessment (marks out of 10)						
Content	3.0	8.1	6.1	8.0	6.5	7.2
Comprehension	3.5	8.0	6.0	7.7	6.7	5.8
Style	3.1	7.4	5.5	7.4	7.0	5.5
Mean score	3.2	7.8	5.9	7.7	6.7	6.2

(the Kendall Coefficient of Concordance, $w = 0.488$, $\chi^2 = 102.48$, $df = 5$, $p < .001$, two-tailed). This implies that people agree in their assessment of the overall merit of a text. But individual differences were apparent when each editor's rank ordering was correlated with the group's mean rank order. Given that there are only six texts, a correlation coefficient of .77 is significant at the 5% level on a one-tailed test. However only 21 (i.e., 50%) of the editors had individual rank orderings of the texts that correlated this highly with the overall group mean assessment. Figure 1, which gives the frequency distribution of various levels of correlation obtained by the different editors, shows that many

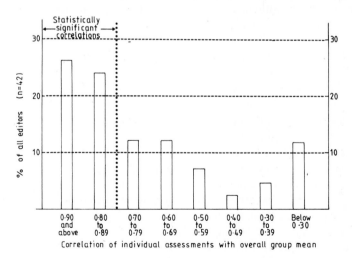

Fig. 1.   Agreement among editors making global assessments of six texts about board games.

people were forming judgments that differed markedly from those of the group average.

It is possible that the editors who were out of step with the majority of their colleagues nevertheless formed an internally consistent subgroup. Therefore the editors were split into two subgroups: those people with rank order correlations of .77 and above (Consistent group, $n = 21$) and those with rank order correlations of .6 and below (Inconsistent group, $n = 13$). By definition there was considerable agreement within the Consistent group, although the mean ordering of texts by this group differed slightly from the average of all editors. For the Consistent group the mean rank ordering of texts from good to bad was S2, D1, D2, S3, D3, S1. (This ordering is based on the total of the marks given for content, comprehension, and style.)

As expected, the mean rank ordering of texts by the Inconsistent group is different. From good to bad the order was D3, D1, D2, S2, S3, S1. Correlating each individual's rankings with the mean order of the Inconsistent group gave a significant correlation for only 5 of the 13 editors. In fact, the concensus within the group was strong only for text S1, which 10 of the 13 editors gave marks that ranked it as sixth and one editor made it fifth, that is, there were only two discrepant judgments about this text. For all other texts there were four, five, or six people who gave the text a score that caused it to fall, within their own rank ordering, outside ± 1 of the group mean rankings. On average for all texts except S1, 37% of the Inconsistent group differed from the mean rank assigned to the text by ± 1 rank position. It therefore seems appropriate to conclude that the Inconsistent group did not form an alternative, cohesive subgroup.

Because the rankings analyzed in the preceding paragraph were derived from raw scores, it is possible to ask a variety of other questions about the differences between the Consistent and the Inconsistent subgroups. For example, did one set of editors tend to be more lenient? Did the groups differ in the relative importance attached to the factors of content, presentation, and style? Further analysis of the data revealed no significant differences between the two subgroups in either of these respects. (Pooling across texts, the average mark out of 10 given for content was 6.5 for the Consistent group, 6.4 for the Inconsistent group; for comprehension, 6.4 for Consistent, 6.0 for Inconsistent; for style, the mean of both groups was 6.0).

Table 2 shows how the pooled scores for content, comprehension, and style were distributed across texts within each group of editors. Here it can be seen that the largest difference in the scores given by the two groups relates to texts S2 and D3. The Consistent group considered S2 to be much better than D3. (Each of the 21 editors gave S2 higher marks than D3.) Within the Inconsistent group only 2 of the 13 editors gave S2 higher marks than D3, whereas 10 editors reversed this trend and gave D3 higher marks than S2. It has not yet been possible to specify the reason for this discrepancy, but text S2 was the only one that departed

Table 2

Average Scores Given to Each Text by Subgroups of Editors

| | Subgroups of editors | | |
Text	Consistent ($n = 21$)	Inconsistent ($n = 13$)	Difference between subgroups
S2	8.9	6.3	2.6
D1	7.8	7.2	0.6
D2	7.4	6.7	0.7
S3	5.6	6.1	−0.5
D3	5.2	7.6	−2.4
S1	3.0	3.2	−0.2

from paragraph style and presented the information as a numbered list. The Consistent group clearly thought that this was a good idea whereas the Inconsistent group did not. This raises questions about the ability of untrained editors to make well-formed judgments about the typographic presentation of written information.

The conclusion suggested by this first study is that although there is considerable agreement among some people about what constitutes a good text and which texts are deficient, there can also be marked differences of opinion among people when they are making global assessments of a text. The materials used in this first experiment were entirely verbal (i.e., there were no numeric, algebraic, or pictorial elements) and presentation was predominantly in paragraph style. It is not clear whether agreement among judges would increase or decrease if judgments were made about other sorts of materials where presentation factors are much more critical, for example, application forms.

EXPERIMENT 2: GLOBAL ASSESSMENT OF FORMS

This study was carried out in collaboration with Philip Barnard and Penelope Wilcox. Each of five local authority forms were given to 59 people. These were genuine forms that had been issued to the public by a local authority in the United Kingdom. The presentation order of the forms varied for different people, and within the available testing period, some people did not manage to complete their assessment of all five forms. The number of people assessing each form is shown in Table 3.

Several techniques were used for obtaining judgments about the relative merits of the forms. First, each form was divided into small sections that were numbered. A section might be a question, a paragraph in the notes section, or a column heading in a table. Each editor was asked to go through the form and

Table 3
Assessment of Five Local Authority Forms

Measurement	Forms				
	A	B	C	D	E
Total items on form	70	59	59	66	67
Total editorial assessors	52	54	49	52	50
Detailed evaluation					
% Items on form rated as "easy"	90	81	83	64	76
Presentation (% editors rating as "good")					
Instructions	88	79	82	62	76
Legibility	90	89	86	71	36
Answer space	84	91	90	71	50
Global assessment					
Mean "exam" score	85	86	86	76	63
% Editors saying form is "good"	62	52	61	35	18

decide how easy or difficult they thought each numbered section would be for an applicant to understand. They recorded these decisions on an answer sheet by circling a number between 1 and 6 for each of the listed items. Circling 1 meant that the item was very easy and 6 meant that it was very difficult to understand. After having gone through the form in this detailed way, people were then asked to assess various design and presentation factors. They did this by ticking one of six multiple-choice alternative statements in answer to each of four assessment questions. The first assessment was of the print on the form. Editors were told, "Sometimes statements, words, or questions are printed in a way that makes it uncomfortable or difficult to read. Please tick the statement below that comes closest to your own opinion of the printing on this form." The second assessment concerned the ease of understanding the instructions on the form. The third assessment was of the adequacy of the answer space. Here the editors were told, "Application forms need to have blank spaces for the applicants' answers. Sometimes people find there is not enough room for their own answer, or they may at first be uncertain where to write." Finally, the editors made an overall judgment about the design of the form. Here they were told, "Pretend that you are judging a contest for forms designers, how many marks out of 20 would you give the designer of this form? You should take into account the way in which the questions were phrased as well as the general layout of the form."

The results of these four assessments are shown in Table 3, where it can be seen that form D was thought to have the worst instructions, whereas form E received the poorest rating for legibility and adequacy of answer space. Statistical analysis indicated that forms A, B, and C were judged to be significantly better ($p < .01$) than forms D and E on all five measures (detailed evaluation, the three presentation factors, the global assessment). Forms D and E differed significantly ($p < .01$) on judgments of legibility, answer space, and the global assessment. Correlating the global assessment scores with the various presentation factors showed that there was a significant relation with both legibility and answer space (Spearman's $r = .97$, $p < .05$ for each measure) but not with comprehension scores of items on the forms (Spearman's $r = .57$, n.s.).

The figures in Table 3 suggest a higher degree of consistency among the editors than had been apparent in Experiment 1. For example, the ratings of the three presentation factors show very high agreement in the judgments of forms A, B, and C; on average 87% of those assessing these forms considered them to warrant one of the two highest category ratings. Consistency dropped as the forms became poorer; on average 68% of the editors agreed about the presentation factors on form D and 63% agreed about form E. Nevertheless, consistency among the 31 editors was significant both for the detailed evaluation of presentation factors ($w = 0.202$, $\chi^2 = 25.1$, $df = 4$, $p < .001$) and for the global assessment ($w = 0.291$, $\chi^2 = 40.4$, $df = 4$, $p < .001$).

Adopting the analysis procedure used in Experiment 1 and looking at individual correlations with the group mean revealed the existence of two subgroups, each showing significant concordance within their own subgroup on the various editorial assessments. For example, on the detailed evaluations 11 people had a high correlation with the group mean ($w = 0.744$, $\chi^2 = 32.7$, $df = 4$, $p < .001$), and 15 people had a low correlation ($w = 0.126$, $\chi^2 = 15.6$, $df = 4$, $p < .01$); on the global assessment scores 6 people had high correlations ($w = 0.735$, $\chi^2 = 17.6$, $df = 4$, $p < .001$), and 11 people had low correlations ($w = 0.164$, $\chi^2 = 7.22$, $df = 4$, $p < .05$). Closer inspection showed that the assessments of the two groups differed substantially for only one of the forms, which in the group having a high correlation was ranked as second best but in the group having a low correlation was ranked as lowest of the five forms. The only other differences between the groups were a tendency for the high group to be less lenient and to differentiate more among the forms than the low group.

Two points come out of this study. One is a methodological one that has relevance to the evaluation of draft documents. People's ratings of the elements within a form (and presumably other texts) can be used to pinpoint trouble-spots within the text. In the present study it was possible, from averaging the ratings given to the various individual numbered elements on the form, to obtain a profile of those elements that many people felt to be unsatisfactory. Such a technique can indicate where revision is necessary.

The second point arising from this study concerns the subgroup of editors who were not able to make such discriminations. These people who had trouble detecting the inadequacy of specific elements also found themselves out of step with the remainder of the group when making global assessments of the various aspects of a form. From this data it is not possible to say whether the performance of these out-of-step editors is due to their not knowing what to look for or simply not recognizing where their knowledge should be applied. This issue is taken up in Experiment 3.

EXPERIMENT 3: DETAILED REVISION OF A TEXT

One of the ways of exploring whether editors who have difficulty in editing do so because of inadequate knowledge or for other reasons is to compare the effects of providing editors with certain kinds of guidelines and seeing how this affects their editing performance. If the problem is a lack of knowledge, then performance should be improved by guidelines. However, if the difficulty comes from the application of knowledge that people already have, then guidelines may not help. The results of this comparison will also have implications for the training of editors.

A carefully prepared typescript of about 340 words explaining how to wire an electric plug was presented to 28 people. Within this text there were three typographic slips and eight aspects of sentence style which it was thought, on the basis of psycholinguistic research, that editors might choose to change if given the opportunity. The original text, which had been typed double-spaced on paper with the longer side vertical, was photographically reduced to half-size so that it fitted onto the left-hand side of a sheet of paper having the longer side horizontal, leaving the right-hand side of the page blank. The editors were instructed to read through the explanation and then underline any part of the text that they felt could be changed in some way to make it easier for the reader to understand. Editors were asked to use the left-hand margin to number each underlining they made, and then on the right-hand side of the page to indicate what changes they felt would help the reader, such as suggesting an alternative wording to that given in the typescript where they felt this was appropriate. Editors were also invited to make any other comments on the writing style or the layout of the information that they felt might improve it. They were given no specific guidance on the changes they should make.

Another group of 31 volunteers were given the same text and the same instructions but with an accompanying sheet headed "Suggestions for improving text." This sheet contained six recommendations, each stated as a general principle and also illustrated by a bad example plus a revision, as follows:

1. Try to get rid of stacked adjectives.
   e.g., Instead of "the microprocessor-based data acquisition system,"

   Try   "the system for data acquisition based on microprocessors".

2. Try to have the main clause first in a sentence.
    e.g. Instead of "Unless it rains we will go to the theatre",
        Try   "We will go to the theatre unless it rains".
3. Try to avoid interrupting the main clauses. Use two sentences if necessary.
    e.g. Instead of "The tiger which had escaped from the zoo hid in the
                supermarket",
        Try   "The tiger escaped from the Zoo. It hid in the supermarket".
4. Try to avoid passive verbs. Mention the actor or agent first in a sentence.
    e.g. Instead of "The photographs were taken by the boy scouts",
        Try   "The boy scouts took the photographs".
5. Try to avoid long forms of words when shorter forms could be used.
    e.g. Instead of "Scholars found that identification of the plant was difficult".
        Try   "Scholars found it difficult to identify the plant".
6. Try to get rid of ambiguities, even if it means using more words.
    e.g. Instead of "The old man the boats",
        Try   "The old people are manning the boats".

A summary of the main characteristics of both groups' editorial performance is given in Table 4. The groups did not differ in their ability to detect typographic slips. However, of the 8 intended lapses in style the group working alone corrected only 1.8, whereas the group given the example sheet corrected 3.1. This difference between the groups is of borderline significance ($\chi^2 = 2.90, p < .05$, on a one-tailed test). The groups also differed with respect to the total number of changes they made to the text. The effect of the example sheet was to increase the total number of changes from an average per editor of 4.5 to an average of 8.8. This difference was statistically significant ($\chi^2 = 7.36, p < .01$, two-tailed test). Such an increase appears consistent with the view that some editors may lack certain kinds of knowledge. When the guidelines provide them with this knowledge, they seem able to apply it to the text.

Experiments 1 and 2 raised the issue of how consistently editorial views agreed with each other. This issue can be examined for the present data by looking at the points within the text where editorial changes were being proposed. Figure 2 shows the percentage of editors in each group recommending a

Table 4

Editorial Corrections to the Text on Wiring a Plug

Editorial corrections	Editing alone	Editing with guidelines
Typographic errors (max = 3)	1.1	0.9
Intended changes (max = 8)	1.8	3.1
Total changes	4.5	8.8

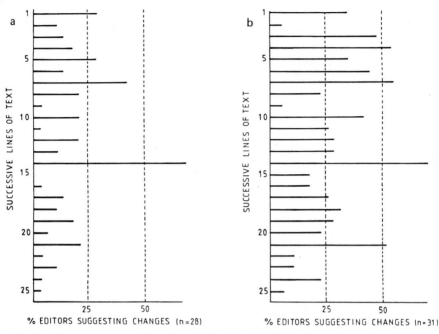

Fig. 2.   Consensus among editors about the location of desirable changes to a text: (a) without guidelines (b) with guidelines.

change to a particular line of text. The data shown in Figure 2 actually overestimate the agreement among editors because not all changes on the same line were necessarily related to the same element within the text.

When people were editing without the example sheet, Figure 2 shows that there was very little agreement in the location of editorial changes. Only on line 14 did more than 50% of the group agree that a change should be made. Only on three other lines (lines 1, 5, 7) did as many as 25% of the group agree that a change should be made. Because Table 3 has shown that, on average, people made four or five changes to the text, Figure 2 suggests that diversity rather than consistency seems to characterize these editorial decisions. On 24 of the total 25 lines of text at least one person felt that a change should be made somewhere.

If *consistency* is taken to mean that at least half the group agreed, then Figure 2 shows that one effect of the guidelines was to increase the consistency within the group. There were now four lines of text on which more than 50% of the group agreed that a change should be made (lines 4, 7, 14, 21). For a further 11 lines there was now agreement among more than 25% of the group. However, this increase in consistency may be more apparent than real. When guidelines were provided there was an overall increase in the number of changes being made. On average, people now made eight or nine changes to the text. Figure 2 shows that these changes are still distributed across all 25 lines of text.

An overall similarity in the pattern of changes made by both groups might imply that the guidelines had no specific effects on the detection of particular infelicities of style, but only a general effect on encouraging editorial intervention. This lack of specificity is well illustrated by noting that the first principle on the sheet of guidelines recommended eliminating stacked adjectives. Line 17 of the text contained this sentence: "The green and yellow, striped, plastic-coated earth wire." Although with the guidelines there was an increase in the number of people suggesting changes to line 17, considerably more than half the group having guidelines did nothing to the text at this point.

In addition to analyzing the location of the editorial changes, we also examined what sorts of changes people suggested. Here the differences in the performance of the two groups were more striking. The changes made were categorized in three ways. Some changes were major structural alterations to the syntax of the sentence. Some changes were simply suggestions to delete certain information from the original text. The third category of changes includes small changes to specific lexical items and the insertion of new material (e.g., new phrases). These were changes that did not disrupt the original sentence style. Table 5 shows how the example sheet affected these three classes of changes that the editors were proposing.

The group provided with guidelines made significantly more changes that structurally affected the syntax of the sentences ($\chi^2 = 12.4$, $p < .001$, two-tailed). This group also recommended significantly more deletions although there had been nothing on the example sheet to suggest that this was a desirable option ($\chi^2 = 6.35$, $p < .02$, two-tailed). The two groups did not differ statistically in the frequency with which they made the smaller changes ($\chi^2 = 0.35$).

One implication from these data is that editing skills seem very malleable. Editors readily shift the criterion that they are applying to a text. Reading just six examples of alternative sentence styles was enough to produce a shift in willingness to intervene. Nevertheless, people made changes to the text, such as dele-

Table 5

Analysis of Total Changes Made to Text on Wiring a Plug

Kind of change	Editing alone	Editing with guidelines
Sentence restructured	1.3	3.2
Deletions	0.8	2.4
Miscellaneous	2.4	3.2
	4.5	8.8

tions, that were not directly related to the examples they had been given. It is unclear why such a generalized effect on editing performance occurred, but it presumably contributes to the low consistency within the group. Therefore the present data do not support the conclusion that guidelines operate by supplementing knowledge deficits. These data do not satisfactorily resolve the issue of whether poor editing performance is the result of a lack of relevant knowledge or a failure to recognize those situations in which the knowledge should be applied, but they do suggest (e.g., in the failure to apply Principle 1 to Line 17) that perceptual and/or recognition problems are an important contributory factor.

The observation that people with guidelines were suggesting more changes does not necessarily imply that they were functioning more adequately as editors. Undoubtedly some of the changes being proposed would actually be detrimental to the reader. Sometimes the new information being suggested was factually wrong or ambiguous—as when reference was made to the "top" of an electrical plug. It has not yet been possible to assess the adequacy of the editorial changes proposed for these texts.

It is perhaps appropriate to pause and ask whether the variability noted among the editors in this experiment is typical of that which would be found in the real world. Obviously there are few authors who would have the benefit of so many editorial opinions about their text; nevertheless, those of us who frequently wear out our friends by asking for their comments are familiar with the phenomenon of different readers tending to complain about different facets of the text. Hartley (1984) has reported receiving some diverse editorial comments about a text he circulated to nine colleagues. The only time I have tried a similar exercise it became possible to predict the professional affiliations of the readers (designers or psychologists) from the tenor of their comments, but even within professional groupings there was considerable variety of opinion. Hartley suggested that, in spite of the diversity, most of the comments he received were helpful. My own experience has been similar. So perhaps the emphasis on consistency in these studies is somewhat out of place. Of practical importance would be evidence as to whether the changes being suggested are right or wrong, in the sense of whether they would help or hinder the reader's comprehension.

In the next experiment people's preference for one of two linguistic styles of communication was directly related to the time taken to read each expression. As well as validating editorial decisions such a study continues to pursue the issue of whether poor editorial performance is due to lack of knowledge or lack of awareness about where to apply this knowledge. Whereas in Experiment 3 the guidelines were an attempt to supplement the editors' knowledge, in the next experiment both alternative styles of communication were brought to the editors' notice, thereby seeking to facilitate the recognition processes. Differences among editors in their performance would therefore seem attributable to differences in knowledge.

EXPERIMENT 4: THE RELATION BETWEEN PREFERENCE
FOR LINGUISTIC STYLES AND COMPREHENSION
OF THESE STYLES

Forty-nine people were presented with 36 pairs of typewritten sentences, 6 pairs to a page. To the right of each sentence pair was a five-category analog scale, with one end of the scale labeled "Sentence (a) very much easier" and the other end labeled "Sentence (b) very much easier". The middle category was labeled "no difference." The 36 pairs of sentences represented contrasts within six sentence styles: sentences with nominalizations, sentences with relative clauses, sentences with adverbial clauses, sentences with either active or passive verbs, sentences with stacked adjectives, and garden path sentences. Examples of the contrasts are shown in Table 6. The (a) or (b) allocation within pairs was counterbalanced. One instance of each sentence style occurred on every page, but the order of these sentences varied between pages. The order of the pages varied among editors.

The following instructions appeared at the top of every page: "Often there are different ways of saying the same thing. It may be easier for readers to understand some versions than others. Please put a cross on the line beside each pair of sentences to indicate which of the two sentences you think readers would find easier."

Another 46 people read each of the sentences when it was projected as a photographic transparency of white typescript against a blue background. In

Table 6

Examples of the Sentence Pairs Used in Experiment 4

Nominalizations
(a) The tenants wanted a reduction in the charge for electricity.
(b) The tenants wanted the charge for electricity to be reduced.
Relative clauses
(a) The pond which had frozen yesterday was melted by the bonfire.
(b) The pond had frozen yesterday. It was melted by the bonfire.
Adverbial clauses
(a) The student copied the critical diagrams before returning the book.
(b) Before returning the book the student copied the critical diagrams.
Active/passive verbs
(a) The government forces soon pursued the retreating guerrillas.
(b) The retreating guerrillas were soon pursued by the government forces.
Stacked adjectives
(a) The gamekeeper preferred to make wildlife television documentaries.
(b) The gamekeeper preferred to make television documentaries about wildlife.
Garden path
(a) Instead of increasing the price as a result of the budget had fallen.
(b) The price had fallen instead of increasing as a result of the budget.

order to measure comprehension times, these people were asked to press a button if they thought that the sentence made sense. Intermingled with the sentences that the preference raters had seen were a comparable number of ''silly sentences'' (such as ''The glacier which was 1000 years old was frozen by the sun''). In this task the latency of the button presses in response to sentences correctly thought to be sensible should indicate the time taken to read and understand those sentences. Therefore these reading times afford an independent measure of ease of comprehension and so provide a criterion against which to judge the editorial preferences expressed by the other group. The data from only the first three of the sentence styles given in Table 6 are reported in detail.

Nominalization

There are many nouns that are derived from verbs. For example, *invitation* is derived from the verb *invite*. Psycholinguistic research suggests that people find it easier to understand the verb form than the derived nominalization (e.g., Briem & Loewenthal, 1968). The data on editorial judgments collected in Experiment 4 also reflected a preference for the verb form. The first analysis was carried out by pooling across the six pairs of sentences and examining the frequency with which ratings fell into categories 1 and 2 (preference for verb form) and the frequency with which these ratings fell into categories 4 and 5 (preference for nominalization). This analysis indicated that 48% of the ratings expressed a preference for the verb form, only 26% of the ratings expressed a preference for the nominalized form, and 26% were indifferent (rating category 3). The reading times were also in the expected direction. Sentences containing the verb forms took on average 4.9 seconds to read compared with 5.6 seconds taken for sentences having the nominalized form. On average 40 of the 46 readers were faster when reading the verb form sentences than when reading the sentences containing nominalizations, ($p < .01$, two-tailed).

Although this pattern of data was expected on the basis of psycholinguistic literature, such a summary statement masks the considerable variability found among the six sentence pairs. This variation is shown more clearly in Table 7, both for preference data and for reading times. Table 7 suggests that, when people were in greatest agreement in preferring the verb form (sentences A, B, C, D), there was also the greatest reading difference obtained between the verb form and its corresponding nominalization. Nevertheless, the variation among the sentences shown in Table 7 must caution against any simplistic generalizations from the psycholinguistic literature. Perhaps with frequency of usage, some nouns such as *reduction* and *investment* may no longer function as derivatives but as lexical terms in their own right. The present data seems to support the suggestion that editorial judgments may be more valid than the rote application of simplistic guidelines.

Table 7
Performance with Nominalization

Sentence	Subjects' preference (%)		Reading times (sec)		Speed advantage of verb (sec)
	Verb form	Nominalization	Verb form	Nominalization	
A	71.4	16.3	6.17	7.24	1.07
B	69.4	8.2	4.55	5.27	0.72
C	53.1	10.2	5.20	6.09	0.89
D	46.9	32.7	4.57	5.37	0.80
E	24.5	38.7	4.48	4.91	0.43
F	22.4	46.9	4.79	4.82	0.03
Mean	48.0	25.5	4.96	5.62	

Relative Clauses

It is often said that one of the characteristics of poor writing is that the sentences become too long (e.g., Flesch, 1960). Nevertheless, there are times when long sentences can be easier for readers to understand and remember than a series of very short sentences (e.g., Bransford & Franks, 1971). As always there may be problems in making safe generalizations about sentence length. One of the difficulties with the materials used in laboratory studies can be that the resulting short sentences are devoid of a strong thematic structure. A sequence of ideas expressed in short sentences such as

"The dog chased the ball.
The ball was spotted.
The dog was black.
The chasing was noisy."

contains a continual shift in focus that may be particularly difficult for the reader to adjust to. In contrast many sentences containing subordinate relative clauses may be capable of being reformulated as two separate sentences without there being a shift in topic or any marked discrepancy in the thematic structure of the text. For example, the sentence "The carpet was woven by craftsmen who had learned their trade in China" can be rephrased as two sentences: "The carpet was woven by craftsmen. They had learned their trade in China." The comparison of these two alternatives might seem to be a fairer evaluation of whether people find it easier to comprehend short rather than long sentences. Four of the six sentence pairs made this comparison. The remaining two pairs contrasted the preference for a subordinate clause early in an active sentence versus the same clause late in a passive sentence, and vice versa.

From the subgroup of four pairs it was found that editorial judgments were in favor of the longer sentence containing the relative clause (58% in favor) compared with the two-sentence version (18% in favor), with 23% of the editorial decisions indifferent to the two alternatives. The reading times were in the same direction as the preference ratings. The relative clause sentences took on average 5.6 seconds while those expressed as two sentences took on average 6.0 seconds to read. A difference in reading speed in this direction was shown by 35 of the 46 readers ($p < .01$, two-tailed).

Table 8 shows the performance on each of the four pairs of sentences. Unlike the previous data for nominalizations, the strength of the preference bias seems unrelated to the reading speed advantage. However, these data do suggest that, even when thematic continuity is maintained, people find it easier to understand one slightly longer sentence than two short ones.

In the two pairs of sentences in which both clause position and voice of the verb were varied, there was a strong preference for the active verb (when the subordinate clause was related to the agent, 42.9% preferred the active and 28.6% the passive; when the subordinate clause was related to the patient, 40.8% preferred the active and 26.5% the passive). However, the anticipated speed advantage for active sentences was only obtained when the subordinate clause referred to the agent (4.42 seconds for the active voice, 5.54 seconds for the passive) not when the subordinate clause referred to the patient (4.22 seconds for the active voice, 4.21 seconds for the passive). These data might suggest that editorial preferences were influenced by one set of factors (perhaps verb form), whereas reading comprehension was more influenced by other factors (perhaps clause location). The effects of clause location will be seen more clearly from considering adverbial clauses because these can occur at several positions within a sentence without requiring any change in the words.

Adverbial Clauses

Consider the following three sentences:
1. *In absent-minded fashion* the cyclist pedaled along the footpath.
2. The cyclist pedaled *in absent-minded fashion* along the footpath.
3. The cyclist pedaled along the footpath *in absent-minded fashion*.

All the preceding sentences contain the same words and so are exactly the same length, but in sentence (2) the adverbial clause interrupts the main clause. Psycholinguists have suggested that they may be costly to some comprehension processes (e.g., Yngve, 1960). Table 9 shows the editorial judgments made about each of these sentence styles, together with the time taken to read each style of sentence.

The data from editorial preferences appear clear. People preferred sentences having the adverbial clause in the middle of the sentence; 62% of the judgments expressed a bias for this sentence style. In contrast, the reading time indicated that sentences in which the adverbial clause came either early or in the middle were

Table 8
Performance with Subordinate Noun Clauses

	Subjects' preference (%)		Reading times (sec)		Speed advantage of relative clause (sec)
Sentence pair	Relative clause	Two sentences	Relative clause	Two sentences	
A	67.3	18.4	6.36	7.17	0.81
B	59.2	12.2	5.25	5.66	0.41
C	53.1	10.2	5.03	5.16	0.13
D	53.1	32.7	5.78	6.15	0.37
Mean	58.2	18.4	5.61	6.03	

read significantly faster than those sentences in which the adverbial clause came at the end (Wilcoxon tests on 24 subjects who made no errors in judging whether the sentences made sense, gave T values of 68 and 78; for both, $p < .05$, two-tailed). Consequently there is a discrepancy between editorial bias against sentences in which the adverbial clause came at the beginning and the speed with which readers could understand such sentences.

It is difficult to account for this discrepancy solely on the basis of the present data because several possibilities exist. Such discrepancies may reflect ambiguities inherent in the tasks themselves. Perhaps, for some other kinds of comprehension, it may be a handicap to have the adverbial clause early in the sentence. For the reading task in this experiment, people needed only to decide whether or not the sentence made sense. When people were expressing their editorial preferences for certain styles of sentence, the sentences were presented outside a clear communication context. Therefore those judgments may either have been very global, in the sense of responding to a broad range of communicative tasks, or may have been narrow but focused on reading contexts that were different from the comprehension task used in the experiment. Undoubtedly

Table 9
Performance with Adverbial Clauses[a]

Occurrence of clause in sentence	Subjects' preference for position of adverbial clause (%)	Mean reading time (sec)
Middle	62(a)	5.49(x)
Late	28(b)	5.28(x)
Early	21(b)	5.79(y)

[a]Cells having the same letter are not significantly different.

studies of single isolated sentences pose many such problems (Wright, 1978). Nevertheless the present data emphasize that editorial judgments about preferred forms of expression may not always correspond to the reader's relative ease of comprehension. Similar observations have been made about editorial assessments of spatial arrangement on forms (Wright, 1981).

Before leaving these data, it should be noted that within the test procedure used in this experiment it was not possible fully to counterbalance for all variations in sentence content across the three adverbial clauses. Nevertheless, because every content occurred in two of the three sentence styles, it seems unlikely that such a confounding factor would account for the obtained performance. Indeed such confounding might be expected to increase the agreement among editors. Tables 8 and 9 show that rarely did two-thirds of the editors agree about which of a pair of sentences would be the easiest to understand.

Since the experimental procedure used in Experiment 4 has reduced the recognition problem for editors, these data tend to suggest that as editors the people taking part in the study may have lacked specific knowledge that would have been useful to them in editing tasks. One facet of language that makes it difficult for people to acquire adequate knowledge about styles of expression is that the database is continually changing. That is to say, peoples' notions about linguistic style, about what is good grammar, even about the acceptability of certain words or phrases, is continually changing. Experiment 5 explored peoples' sensitivity to such changes.

EXPERIMENT 5: "CORRECT" STYLE AS SEEN BY AMATEUR AND PROFESSIONAL WRITERS

In 1979 Christopher Turk of the University of Wales circulated to British members of the Institute of Scientific and Technical Communicators a 21-item questionnaire. In this questionnaire he asked readers to indicate whether they felt that certain styles of expression were unacceptable, in the sense that the expression might cause them to pause when reading. The results from this questionnaire are summarized in Turk (1980). Because the readership addressed by Turk were professional technical writers, it seemed interesting to compare his data with that of a similar study carried out on our amateur population. The contrast between the performance of the professional writers and the amateurs gives some indication of whether professional technical writers were in the vanguard of linguistic change or tended to be fighting a rearguard action for the maintenance of the language "as it ought to be."

Two slightly different editorial procedures were given to two groups of amateur editors. In one procedure, 43 people were required simply to put a tick or cross beside each sentence to indicate whether they thought it was alright or there was something wrong with it. This resembles Turk's questionnaire. In the other procedure 49 editors were invited to suggest an alternative phrasing for any sentence with which they felt unhappy. One editor's data were excluded from the analysis because no revisions were suggested. Table 10 summarizes the results obtained for some of the expressions that were used in the two Cambridge studies, together with the data obtained by Turk. Perhaps the most striking characteristic of the data is the lack of agreement *within* both the professional and amateur groups. If *consistency* is defined as 75% agreement within the group, then only 5 of the 11 expressions met this criterion among the professionals and only 4 among the amateurs having the most similar procedure. Furthermore, there appears a complete lack of correspondence between the "consistent" judgments of these two editorial groups. The professionals rejected A–D and accepted K, whereas the amateurs rejected only G and accepted D, F, and J.

Table 10 shows that for many expressions, the general public seemed much more willing to accept current vernacular usage than did the professional technical authors who responded to Turk's questionnaire. This difference between the amateur and professional editors does not seem to be entirely due to the amateurs being too lenient or unwilling to reject sentence styles that they felt were unacceptable. For 7 of the 21 items, the amateurs in both procedures had lower acceptances than in Turk's sample.

When the amateur editors were asked to suggest alternative expressions, their revisions showed that the unacceptability of the sentence was sometimes related to something other than the expression that was the focus of Turk's study.

Table 10

Percentage of Editors Accepting Various Expressions

Expression	Professionals (n = 160) Turk's data	Amateurs, no revision (n = 43)	Amateurs and revision (n = 48) Raw	Corrected[a]
A. Very exploited	5	19	23	31
B. Comprises of	8	49	58	63
C. Seat only has	10	51	46	46
D. To try and	24	78	76	85
E. Different to	33	56	38	56
F. To reliably convert	48	91	73	75
G. Less failures	53	19	31	73
H. Between five	58	73	65	86
I. Control, whose fr.	69	37	46	81
J. Data is	70	77	63	94
K. Might . . . if . . . are	82	57	70	93

[a]The corrected scores assume that the expression was acceptable if the editor's revision shows that the reason for rejecting the sentence was other than the particular expression of interest.

Table 11

The Effect of Age on People's Willingness
to Accept Variations in Linguistic Expression

Age range	n	Mean number expressions rejected (max = 21)
When no revision required		
19–34	10	8
35–49	16	12
50–64	17	11
When revision required		
19–34	12	11
35–49	14	10
50–64	22	10

Consequently the figures shown in columns 2 and 3 of Table 10 (included for comparability with Turk's study) actually underestimate people's willingness to accept the semantic and syntactic forms given at the left of the table. This willingness to accept deviant phrases is consistent with the previous suggestion of a knowledge deficit on the part of the amateur editors.

One factor that might influence people's willingness to accept certain linguistic changes could be their age. The 91 amateurs spanned the age range from 19 to 64. Yet, as Table 11 shows, there appeared to be no systematic relation between age and people's tendency to reject certain forms of linguistic expression.

CONCLUDING COMMENTS ON EDITING PROCESSES AND POLICIES

The preceding five experiments serve only as a very preliminary exploration of editing processes; nevertheless, they highlight three facets of the cognitive skills involved. It appears that knowledge deficits may not be easily remedied by written guidelines (Experiment 3). It appears that preferences for linguistic expression may not correspond to the styles of language that readers find easier to understand (Experiment 4). But above all it appears that there are considerable individual differences among people both in the quantity and in the quality of their editorial decisions (Experiments 1 and 2).

These studies were carried out with the help of members of the general public, and there was some evidence that the editorial decisions of professional communicators would be different from those of the amateurs (Experiment 5). Nevertheless, there are two important reasons for an interest in the editing abilities of nonprofessionals. One that has already been mentioned is the involvement of amateurs in editorial roles for various scholarly publications. The second is that the revision of a draft text is an integral part of all successful writing. While agreeing with Galbraith (1980) that there are specific problems for writers revising their own manuscripts, some of these difficulties were avoided in the present studies by requiring people to revise texts produced by someone else. The results are not very encouraging and offer scant support for the notion that such revisions improve the quality of a text or its usability.

Although there are few studies of the editorial decisions made by authors with respect to their own writing, there are even fewer still that relate to authors' evaluation of graphic and illustrative materials that may be part of the text. Nothing seems to be known about what prompts an author to abandon prose for some other form of expression. Surprisingly few amateur writers appear to introduce illustrations spontaneously, even when describing the rules of a board game such as draughts. When collecting the materials for use in Experiment 1, volunteers from the general public were invited to write out the rules of a board game in a way that would be suitable for inclusion in the box lid of that game. Approximately 1 hour later, photocopies of their own texts were returned to each author, and they were invited to make editorial changes and particularly to consider the uses of sketches or diagrams. Of the 15 editors who wrote about draughts, 7 chose to provide no illustration, and 3 provided inadequate illustrations (e.g., just an empty board); only 5 attempted to provide useful illustrations (e.g., about setting up the board or moving certain pieces during the game), and several of these illustrations would not have been clear to someone who was unfamiliar with the game.

A similar pattern of inadequate illustrations was obtained with those who wrote about Snakes and Ladders or Ludo. Of 14 editors, 6 chose not to include any illustrations. Of the 8 who did, none included an illustration of how a piece would move if it alighted on different parts of the board. The closest anyone came was a verbally explained arrow alongside a snake or ladder.

It is possible that those who chose not to use illustrations had been very successful with their verbal descriptions. However, this assumption did not seem warranted. Verbal descriptions of the legitimate moves in draughts sometimes became very complicated reading. So part of the problem when revising a text may lie in people's expectations about the adequacy, perhaps even desirability, of a paragraph style of communication. It was noted in Experiment 1 that opinions were sharply divided on the single text that departed from a paragraph style by providing a numbered listing of the procedural steps for playing Snakes and Ladders. Perhaps this preference for paragraphs arises from the way written composition is taught in schools. For technical materials, in which the concept of usability is much more relevant, different writing and editing techniques may be called for.

We began by exploring some aspects of editorial policy and noted that such policies were diverse and required sensitive application if they were to enhance the usability of texts. From a brief exploration of some editing processes we have found that many individuals would have difficulty operating in an editorial role because their decisions differed from the majority opinion. One explanation for the variability might be that different people are looking for different things within the text. There may well be cognitive limitations on people's ability to monitor several aspects of the text simultaneously. Recognizing this need to read a passage more than once may be among the techniques that professional editors acquire. Studies of experienced editors might indicate many more special procedures that could be incorporated into training schemes so that more authors could acquire editorial skills.

Obviously many questions remain unanswered by the studies reported here. Given the involvement of editorial processes in revising one's own writing, it is tempting to ask if it is only good writers who can function as good editors. Certainly it seems inconceivable that a poor writer could be a good editor, but the converse is not a logical necessity. Further explorations of such questions are currently in progress.

ACKNOWLEDGMENTS

Thanks are due to the editors of the present volume for their numerous helpful comments on an earlier draft of this chapter. Their generous donation of both time and talents was much appreciated. I would also like to record my indebtedness to Mrs. Susan Threlfall for help with the analysis of Experiments 1, 3, 4, and 5 and to Dr. Philip Barnard and Ms. Penny Wilcox for their collaboration in Experiment 2.

REFERENCES

Anonymous (1982). *Administrative forms in government.* Cmnd. 8504. London: Her Majesty's Stationery Office.

Barnard, P., & Hammond, N. (1982, September). Usability and its multiple determination for the occasional user of interactive systems. *Proceedings of the 6th International Conference on Computer Communication,* London.

Bartlett, E. J. (1982). Learning to revise: Some component processes. In M. Nystrand (Ed.), *What writers know: The language, process and structure of written discourse.* New York: Academic Press.

Blunden, B. (1981). Computer aids in publishing. In E. Tham (Ed.), *Computer Graphics Manual* (pp. 79–90). London: NordMedia.

Bransford, J. D., & Franks, J. J. (1971). The abstraction of linguistic ideas. *Cognitive Psychology, 2,* 331–350.

Briem, J., & Lowenthal, K. (1968). Immediate recall of nominalizations and adjectivalizations. *Psychonomic Science, 11,* 209.

Clark, H., & Carlson, T. B. (1981). Context for comprehension. In J. B. Long & A. D. Baddeley (Eds.), *Attention and performance IX* (pp. 313–330). Hillsdale, NJ: Erlbaum.

Cutts, M., & Maher, C. (1980). *Writing plain English*. Salford, UK: Plain English Campaign. (Also British Library Report No. 5591)

Flesch, R. (1960). *How to write, speak and think more effectively*. New York: Harper & Row.

Frase, L. T., Keenan, S. A., & Dever, J. J. (1980). Human performance in computer aided writing and documentation. In P. A. Kolers, M. E. Wrolstad, & H. Bouma (Eds.), *Processing of visible language 2*. New York: Plenum.

Galbraith, D. (1980). The effect of conflicting goals on writing: A case study. *Visible Language, 14*, 364–175.

Gowers, E. (1954). *The complete plain words*. London: Her Majesty's Stationery Office.

Hartley, J. (1981a). Sequencing the elements in references. *Applied Ergonomics, 12*, 7–12.

Hartley, J. (1981b). Eighty ways of improving instructional text. *IEEE Transactions on Professional Communication, 24*, 17–27.

Hartley, J. (1982). Information mapping: a critique. *Information Design Journal, 3*, 51–58.

Hartley, J. (1984). The role of colleagues and text-editing programs in improving text. *IEEE Transactions on Professional Communication, PC-27*, 42–44.

Hartley, J., & Burnhill, P. (1977). Fifty guide-lines for improving instructional text. *Programmed Learning and Educational Technology, 14*, 65–73.

Hayes, J. R., & Flower, L. S. (1980). Identifying the organization of writing processes. In L. W. Gregg & E. R. Steinberg (Eds.), *Cognitive processes in writing*. Hillsdale, NJ: Erlbaum.

Heap, H. R. (1980, October). *What technical communication means in magazine publishing*. Paper presented to the Institute of Scientific and Technical Communications, London.

Horn, R. E. (1976). *How to write information mapping*. Lexington, MA: Information Resources.

Hills, P. J. (Ed.) (1980). *The future of the printed word: The impact and implications of the new communications technology*. London: Pinter.

Klare, G. R. (1976). A second look at the validity of readability formulae. *Journal of Reading Behavior, 8*, 129–152.

Klare, G. R. (1981). *Practical aspects of readability*. Open University, Milton Keynes: Institute of Educational Technology.

Lefrere, P. (1981). Editors' roles in on-line journals. *Journal of Research Communication Studies, 3*, 157–167.

Lefrere, P. (1982). Beyond word-processing: Human and artificial intelligence in document preparation and use. In P. J. Hills (Ed.), *Trends in information transfer*. London: Pinter.

Lefrere, P., Waller, R. H., & Whalley, P. (1980). Expert systems in educational technology? In L. Evans & R. Winterburn (Eds.), *Aspects of educational technology XIV* (pp. 338–343). London: Hogan Page.

Marcel, A. J. (1978). Unconscious reading. *Visible Language, 12*, 391–404.

Rayner, D. (1982). *Review of administrative forms: Report to the Prime Minister*. London: Management and Personnel Office, Whitehall.

Robinson, P. (1981). Production of graphic arts text. In E. Tham (Ed.), *Computer Graphics Manual*. London: NordMedia.

Rumelhart, D. E. (1977). *Introduction to human information processing*. New York: Wiley.

Senders, J. (1977). An on-line journal. *The Information Scientist, 11*, 3–9.

Shackel, B. (1982). The BLEND system: Programme for the study of some electronic journals. *Ergonomics, 25*, 269–284.

Smart, T., & Gibbon, D. (1978). *The British Isles*. Surrey, UK: Colour Library International.

Steinberg, E. R. (1980). A garden of opportunities and a thicket of dangers. In L. W. Gregg & E. R. Steinberg (Eds.), *Cognitive processes in writing*. Hillsdale, NJ: Erlbaum.

Turk, C. (1980). Attitudes to English usage. *The Communicator of Scientific and Technical Information, 42,* 8–12.

Vernon, T. (1980). *Gobbledegook.* London: National Consumer Council.

Waller, R. H. (1979). Typographic access structures for educational texts. In P. A. Kolers, M. E. Wrolstad, & H. Bouma (Eds.), *Processing of visible language 1.* New York: Plenum.

Wason, P. (1962). The retention of material presented through precis. *Journal of Communication, 12,* 36–43.

Wright, P. (1978). Feeding the information eaters: Suggestions for integrating pure and applied research on language comprehension. *Instructional Science, 7,* 249–312.

Wright, P. (1979). The quality control of document design. *Information Design Journal, 1,* 33–42.

Wright, P. (1980). Usability: The criterion for designing written information. In P. A. Kolers, M. E. Wrolstad, & H. Bouma (Eds.), *Processing of Visible Language, 2.* New York: Plenum.

Wright, P. (1981). Informed design for forms. *Information Design Journal, 2,* 151–178.

Wright, P., & Barnard, P. (1975). Effects of 'more than' and 'less than' decisions on the use of numerical tables. *Journal of Applied Psychology, 60,* 606–611.

Wright, P., & Threlfall, S. (1980). Readers' expectations about format influence the usability of an index. *Journal of Research Communication Studies, 2,* 99–106.

Yngve, V. H. (1960). A model and an hypothesis for language structure. *Proceedings of the American Philosophical Society, 104,* 444–466.

CHAPTER 5

Intuitions, Algorithms, and a Science of Text Design

LAWRENCE T. FRASE
NINA H. MACDONALD
STACEY A. KEENAN

THE INCREASING COMPLEXITY OF COMMUNICATIONS

As society has become more complex, so has reading. There is broad concern about our ability to use written materials as they become more complex and numerous and as they change form. A few hundred years ago the primary purpose of public documents was to transmit community morals; then, remembering what one read was the main literacy demand (Resnick, 1979). Today, all of us are required to maintain records, and to retrieve, interpret, and integrate documents, just to pay taxes. Even the most common legal documents can be a challenge. State and federal governments have legislated standards for readability to protect consumers. "Plain language" legislation, passed by six states, allows courts to rewrite texts that are unclear (Battison, 1981).

Reading at work is especially affected. In the 1970s a professional had to read 30 documents a day to keep up with the field (Chapanis, 1971). Today that figure has more than doubled, and technological change has compounded the problem. The Naval Air Systems Command, for instance, supplies technical manuals for 135 aircraft. There are over 25,000 manuals, totaling 3 million pages. In 1950 the manuals for one aircraft contained fewer than 2000 pages; today the manuals for one aircraft contain nearly 300,000 pages (Muller, 1976).

Not only has the amount of information changed, but its form as well. Computers have altered the form of information from the familiar page to small packets of information displayed on a screen. These bits and pieces of information, propelled by satellite, stream round the globe ignoring geographic and national boundaries. Indeed, literacy has entered a new age.

NEED FOR A MULTIDISCIPLINARY
APPROACH TO TEXT DESIGN

A new age requires new approaches. We have learned much about reading, and research on text design and writing is beginning to solidify. How can we integrate this knowledge with the skills needed to design effective written communications? Our understandings are scattered in behavioral theories, task analyses, intuitions of design experts, and new technologies. The complexity of integrating these sources of expertise to produce a text is a challenge that must eventually stimulate advances in language research, design, and development.

Now, however, we need a focus to bring together knowledge from different disciplines; and we need a technology, not only to force mathematical or algorithmic expression of design principles, but to carry through complex chains of decisions and actions involved in producing usable text. A focus for multidisciplinary efforts can be found in specific design problems; for instance, how to determine the optimal physical dimensions for a text display. A technology can be found in computer applications; for instance, programs that generate different text styles and formats and evaluate their cognitive consequences.

PSYCHOLOGY AND TEXT DESIGN

Until recently, document technology has consisted of two parallel, but separate, lines of work. The first line of work consists of experimental research on what makes text easy or hard to understand. This work, reflected in psychological and linguistic research, includes studies of the effects of text format, wording, and graphic displays (Hartley, 1981). Behavioral science, especially research on human information processing and cognitive processes, reveals cognitive activities that support learning, retention, and use of written materials. In this research we can discern weaknesses and strengths of human information processing that text designs might support. For instance, inference activities depend on grouping related information together. Text format can be used to bring together or separate related items and thus facilitate or inhibit reasoning (Frase, 1973).

The second line of work includes intuitive or prescriptive bases for writing and text design. This involves the expertise of text and graphics designers (Ferguson, 1977), such as technical editors and layout specialists, as well as rhetorical traditions that specify writing standards (Lanham, 1979). For instance, how to array information to improve grouping is the province of design, so we consult design experts for creative ways to rearrange information. Exemplary tabular and graphic displays can thus provide a context and testing ground for psychological theories about the processes involved in visual search and detection (Macdonald-Ross, 1977). In this way the all-too-common assumption that we do fundamental research, and then transfer findings to applied questions, is turned about; practical design problems focus the issues studied in the laboratory.

Unfortunately, text researchers and designers have not always worked closely together. Psychological theories of what makes a document difficult to understand often seem oversimplified to designers, and designers' intuitions and prescriptions often seem vague to researchers. Designers have been concerned with engineering good documents, while researchers have been trying to understand problems of text comprehension. However, both knowledge bases, one derived from experimental research and the other from nonexperimental sources, have provided useful guidelines for effective text design. As discussed in the following, common ground for sharing across these disciplines is growing.

COMPUTER AIDS

The use of computers for language analysis is helping to integrate knowledge from research and design areas. Work by Cherry (1980, 1982), for instance, shows how language analysis, such as assigning parts of speech to words, can be done reasonably accurately by computer. Models of decision processes used by experts have been incorporated into programs that make design recommendations; for example, recommendations for the most suitable column width to use for a particular text (see section on format design aids), or recommendations about the mechanics and style of a text (see section on language analysis aids). Knowledge-based expert systems (Duda & Gaschnig, 1981), developed by researchers in artificial intelligence, provide additional ways of expressing, in computer-readable language, expertise derived from different disciplines. The creation of a common language and environment for sharing and testing knowledge from different domains is an important consequence of computer applications.

In the next two sections of this chapter we give examples of computer applications in the areas of text formatting and language analysis. These applications include programs that model cognitive outcomes and programs that assess text style. In the section on text formatting, we explore the problem of deciding how long the lines of a text should be. This problem is explored as much as an example of how one might conduct informal design experiments on a computer as for its practical consequences. The section on language analysis aids then expands the concept of text patterns to include features that characterize difficult or undesirable text styles. These patterns include misspellings, awkward phrases, overly complex sentences, passive constructions, and punctuation errors. The result is a set of programs that deliver detailed editorial comments about text features. Uses and limitations of these programs are discussed in the final section of this chapter.

COMPUTER-AIDED FORMAT DESIGN

Introduction

Computers can make design decisions regarding the format of text. To do this, the computer needs two models: first, a cognitive model of the information-processing demands of different linguistic features; second, a model of text features that can be changed. Using these models, it is possible to develop computer-based projections of the demands that a document will make on a reader when it is designed in different ways.

We are most concerned with using the computer to help us think about design problems. Our approach yields solutions to specific design questions without the need to rely on vague general principles. Recommendations are based on the linguistic features of a specific text. In this section, we illustrate this approach with a computer program that determined the best line length for individual texts based on the occurrence of meaningful units of information, or "chunks," on text lines.

Problem

The question of how long a line of text should be is important to those responsible for putting words and ideas into printed form. Expert designers are aware that the arrangement of words on a page is important for comprehension and artistic effect. Concern for the cognitive consequences of typographic formats raises questions about what the most effective typesize or number of columns might be. Design journals, such as *Visible Language,* report empirical research on typographic forms. But the research findings have not resolved questions about multiple-column formats and line length.

People process complex information by segmenting and grouping related items together. Cognitive segmentation occurs at gross levels—for instance, in discriminating buildings from the sky—but finer discriminations occur in segmenting episodes in a film (Carroll & Bever, 1976) or in the processing of symbolic materials. In reading aloud, for instance, readers pause at the boundaries of words that form meaningful units of information. Some writing systems include special markers for these boundaries (Gelb, 1952), and early literary works, only spoken before print became generally available, contained special marks indicating breath pauses. These marks evolved from theatrical breath-pause markers into markers that set off the boundaries of major thought units (Treip, 1970). Poetry often reinforces cognitive boundaries typographically by starting a new line when a new unit of thought begins. Thompson completed a redesign of the Washburn College Bible based on his segmentation of the text into "natural and proper" breaks in prose (Grumbach, 1979). As the following example shows, Thompson's design resembles poetry, each line containing one, or a few, phrases.

> In the beginning
> God created the heaven and the earth.
> And the earth was without form, and void;
> and darkness was upon the face of the deep.
> And the Spirit of God
> moved upon the face of the waters.

So a variety of sources, theoretical and applied, suggest that grouping or segmentation of information constitutes an important event for reading and for cognition in general.

Ordinary text obscures meaningful units by running them together, perhaps several on a line, or by separating words that belong in the same unit. Sensitive to these undesirable effects, Thompson created the design for the Bible shown in the example. Research confirms these design intuitions; studies show that, if each line of a text contains only one meaningful segment, memory, reading speed, and problem solving are improved (see Frase & Schwartz, 1979). In this chapter we refer to these meaningful units as chunks (see Simon, 1974).

One goal for the design of written material is to present text in a way that simplifies the reader's cognitive processing. Formatting text with a single meaningful chunk on each line is one effective way of doing this; however, this is not generally done. Chunks vary greatly in length and most are short, hence putting one on each line results in much white (unused) space.

Ordinarily, text is formatted in a uniform line length. Line length affects the probability of a reader's obtaining exactly one chunk on a line; a very short line length prevents complete chunks from fitting on one line, and a very long line length might contain several chunks. Unless all the chunks in a text are of equal length (an unlikely occurrence), no line length will result in the ideal case of one chunk on each line. But we might expect that some line lengths will yield a higher percentage of single chunks on a line than others. In addition, the best line length should differ according to the readability level of a text. For instance, as words and sentences become more difficult and longer, more space is needed to express an idea. Our aim in this study was to explore computer recommendations for text line length, and to determine whether those recommendations correspond to human judgment and recommendations derived from previous research findings.

PROCEDURE

Texts

We used 60 text passages of easy, medium, and difficult readability levels. As measured by the Kincaid readability formula, the easy text passages averaged fourth-grade reading level, the medium passages were at the tenth-grade reading level, and the difficult passages were of eighteenth-grade reading level. The texts were each about 150 words long.

Each passage was segmented into meaningful chunks of information by a human. Segmentation was also done by computer. (See Hartley, 1981, for an example of output.) The computer segmentation algorithm was based on an analysis of the boundaries used by humans in segmenting text into meaningful chunks. There was high agreement among five human judges that the chunks originally marked by another person represented meaningful units of information, and there was also high agreement between human and computer segmentations of the text (90% of the boundaries were the same).

Cognitive Model

Here we describe a simple model of the occurrence of meaningful chunks on lines. In ordinary text, chunks are arranged haphazardly. Various outcomes are possible within each line; for instance, some lines contain several chunks, others contain only parts of a chunk. In our study we classified lines into four categories:

1. Exactly one chunk
2. No complete chunk (called particles in Figure 1)
3. Two or more chunks, with or without chunk particles (called overloads in Figure 1)
4. One chunk, plus chunk particles (called other in Figure 1).

Our model considers one chunk on a line the optimal condition for efficient reading. Multiple chunks (overloads) require the reader to break lines into meaningful segments, and chunk parts (particles) require the reader to assemble components, broken by the typographic design, into meaningful groups. Both of these, chunk overloads and chunk particles, are undesirable design outcomes. The remaining possibility, a chunk and particles on a line, although not optimal, seems somewhere between a particle and an overload in undesirable cognitive consequences. Of course, one might assign different weightings to chunks, particles, and combinations of chunks and particles. The success of different weightings in predicting reading outcomes could have useful theoretical implications. However, for simplicity, in the following discussion we weight particles and overloads equally, and assume that measurements of these two (equally undesirable) outcomes are sufficient to judge the suitability of a text design.

Format Model

After segmentation into chunks, each passage was formatted by the computer into line lengths ranging from 5 to 75 characters. Five or 10 characters on a line approximates a "vertical" typography, which uses only one word on each line. Coleman and Hahn (1966) showed that reading efficiency deteriorated when they used a vertical typography of one word per line. In keeping with this finding, our cognitive model categorizes one word on a line as a chunk particle—an undesirable outcome. A line length of 25 corresponds to the line length used in two-column formats such as those found in *McCall's* magazine. A line length of about 66 characters is often used for business letters and single-column memoranda.

Computer Analysis

We programmed the computer to classify each line of formatted text (with the chunks marked) into one of the four categories of our cognitive model. Then it calculated the percentage of lines in each category for each text. The computer analyzed each of the 60 passages, at each of 15 line length formats, thereby performing 900 analyses. The result of the analysis indicates the best line length for each text passage.

RESULTS

Figure 1 shows the percentages of lines in the easy readability passages that fall into each of the four categories of our cognitive model at each line length. As expected, at short line lengths almost all the lines are chunk particles. This percentage decreases rapidly as line length increases. Chunk overloads seldom occur at short line lengths but increase rapidly with line length. There are few instances of a single chunk on a line at any line length.

Chunk particles and overloads are undesirable outcomes. If we assume that both are equally undesirable, then these undesirable outcomes can be minimized by formatting text at the line length at which the sum of particles and overloads is the least. This concept is illustrated in Figure 2, which plots the percentages of undesirable outcomes for the easy readability passages. The best line length for the easy passages as a group was 44 characters. But note that, because lines were forced to have the same length, as is commonly done in text production, at all line lengths there was a high percentage of undesirable outcomes. The best design, at 44 characters per line, resulted in about 75% undesirable outcomes.

The chunk characteristics of text vary across readability levels. The mean chunk lengths (measured in characters) were shortest for easy text and longest for difficult text. The mean best line lengths for passages in different readability groups were also significantly different: 44, 50, and 56 characters for the easy,

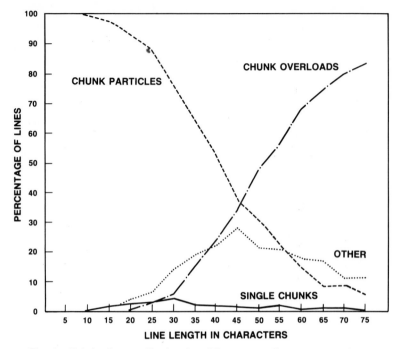

Fig. 1.   Relation between line length and line contents (for easy passages).

medium, and difficult groups, respectively. However, there was much variability within readability groups. For example, one easy passage had the fewest undesirable outcomes at a line length of 75 characters. This was very different from the average best line length for easy passages of 44 characters. Also, texts varied dramatically in whether improvements would result from reformatting. For some texts the line shown in Figure 2 was flat; that is, an equal number of unfavorable outcomes resulted regardless of line length. Hence our results illustrate why the design of a text format must be determined by the language characteristics of the individual text rather than by group norms.

The data suggest that line lengths between 40 and 60 characters are suitable for most texts, which agrees with human preference data (Tinker, 1963). But such general rules, as our analysis shows, apply only roughly to a particular text.

CONCLUSIONS

Our studies show that we can do better than to rely on general design rules. The best line length for a text can be selected by a computer with an appropriate text and cognitive model. With flexibility one could adopt a format that places

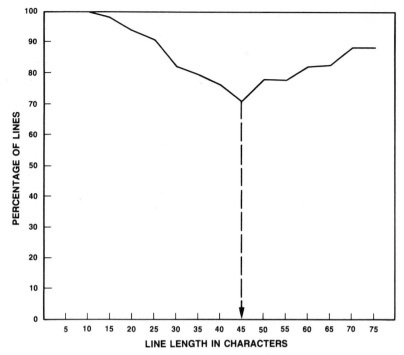

Fig. 2.   Undesirable outcomes for easy passages as a function of line length.

one chunk on a line. This is the ideal. Poets and master designers aside, such a format will not be popular, for economic reasons. It would roughly double the amount of paper used.

The typographic feature we worked with was line length, which can easily be varied using a computer. Other text features, such as point size, font, type style, and hyphenation, might also be explored in studies like this. In short, we propose a form of computer-aided, cognitively based, text design.

COMPUTER-AIDED LANGUAGE ANALYSIS

INTRODUCTION

Not everyone worries about line length, because we seldom have control over the length of lines beyond a ragged versus justified right margin. Line length is primarily a typographer's issue. However, we are all concerned about the quality of what we read and what we write. Computers will be widely used to aid writing if they can help evaluate the quality of a text and provide guidance for improving it. Indeed, availability of such programs could dramatically affect what writing skills are emphasized in the schools and how those skills are taught.

Writing instruction has a long tradition, stretching back over 2000 years. The knowledge base for writing is rich and diverse, almost distractingly so. A review of the relevant literature shows considerable agreement in coverage—standards for grammar and word usage, and long lists of principles for clear writing and clear thinking. Major topics for writing courses usually include the author's purpose, audience orientation, content coverage, organization, style, punctuation, and other mechanics. Recent psychological studies of writing (Gregg & Steinberg, 1980) make use of these traditional categories, and they either confirm or elaborate them. Hence the rich knowledge available in the writing literature provides a consensus for building programs that use generally accepted standards.

In addition to identifying standards for writing, the technology of writing instruction has also advanced. Instructional techniques, once strongly declarative and hortatory, have begun to emphasize procedural description. Students are taught to recognize patterns that reflect faulty constructions, and they are taught procedures to remedy those faults. Instead of broad guides for clear word use or sentence construction, students are now told to count items, such as the number of simple sentences, or to underline forms of "to be" and then simplify where underlining was done (Flower, 1981; Lanham, 1979). The more precisely these patterns and actions are described, the easier it becomes to realize detection and correction procedures in computer programs. Insightful process analyses of writing—for instance, in papers by Hayes and Flower (1980) and Collins and Gentner (1980)—can help shape effective language analysis programs.

PROGRAMS

Emphasis on procedural descriptions has important implications for automated text design. Several language analysis programs have been developed that capitalize on the consistencies in our language rules and on the procedural approaches to analysis of writing. These programs extend considerably beyond the more common word-processor spelling checkers and correctors. EPISTLE is a business office system still in the developmental stages at IBM (Heidorn, Jensen, Miller, Byrd, & Chodorow; 1982). The system is designed to facilitate the handling of intercomputer communication in automated offices. It will abstract incoming mail and will correct grammatical errors in outgoing mail. JOURNALISM is a program developed at the University of Michigan (Bishop, 1975); it provides proofreading assistance. Also, if specific knowledge about an article is entered, JOURNALISM will comment on its organization and content. Another program, CRES, was developed by the U.S. Navy (Kincaid, Aagard, O'Hara, & Cottrell, 1981) to analyze the readability of text and to flag uncommon or misspelled words and long sentences. It can also suggest simple replacements for difficult words and phrases. Finally, at AT&T Bell Laboratories we have developed a text analysis system, the UNIX[1] WRITER'S WORKBENCH[2] Software (Macdonald, Frase, Gingrich, & Keenan; 1982), which is a broad array of programs designed to analyze prose and suggest changes. The AT&T programs are outlined in the following, and they are described at length in other papers (Cherry, 1982; Frase, 1983; Macdonald, 1983). The WRITER'S WORK-BENCH software is in widespread use within the Bell System (see Gingrich, 1983, for program trials within the Bell System), with thousands of users on many machines in AT&T Bell Laboratories, and it has been used by the English Department at Colorado State University to teach composition to college students each semester (Cherry, Fox, Frase, Keenan, & Macdonald, 1983; Frase, 1983; Macdonald, 1983). The programs are commercially available through AT&T Technologies for use on the UNIX operating system.

Users of the WRITER'S WORKBENCH system may either compose their text on-line, using one of the editing systems available on the UNIX system, or they may write off-line and then have clerical staff enter the draft. We have found that writers use both approaches, though with experience they often prefer on-line writing. Once the text is stored in the computer, the author or editor simply issues a one-word command along with the file name to run one of the programs. A summary of the programs is shown in Table 1. Thus if the author typed "abst proposal" the program "abst" would be run on the file named "proposal." The output from this program would be the percentage of total text words that are on its list of highly abstract words. The programs know about special text formatting commands that control headings and lists, so these can be ignored or included in calculating readability and other measures.

The WRITER'S WORKBENCH programs focus on three major areas: (1) proofreading, (2) stylistic analysis, and (3) on-line reference information about English usage. The "parts," "style," and "diction" programs, developed by Cherry (1980, 1982), are the basis for other programs in the WRITER'S WORKBENCH system. "Parts" assigns grammatical parts of speech to words in a text. "Style" provides statistics on many text variables. For instance, it reports four different readability calculations, tabulates parts of speech, and reports the percentage of complex sentences. "Prose," on the other hand, uses statistics from "style" to produce ordinary-language commentary on an author's writing. Given this feedback, the author can then make text changes, or go to information files for help with various aspects of writing. (See the "punctrules" and "worduse" commands in Table 1.)

Many programs can be altered by typing an option (a letter appended to a

---

[1]UNIX is a trademark of AT&T Bell Laboratories.
[2]WRITER'S WORKBENCH is a trademark of AT&T Technologies.

Table 1

Selected WRITER'S WORKBENCH Programs

Program names[a]	Description
Analyses	
abst	Evaluates text abstractness
match	Collates styles of different texts
parts	Assigns grammatical parts of speech
sexist	Finds sexist phrases and suggests changes
style	Summarizes stylistic features
syl	Prints words of selected syllable length
topic	Suggests topics, keywords
parts	Assigns grammatical parts of speech
wwb	Runs proofreading and stylistic analysis
proofr	Gives proofreading comments
diction	Finds awkward phrases and suggests changes
double	Detects repeated typings of words
punct	Checks punctuation
spellwwb	Checks spelling, using spelldict
prose	Gives extended editorial comments
style	Summarizes stylistic features
parts	Assigns grammatical parts of speech
Explanations	
prosestand	Prints standards used to evaluate text
punctrules	Explains punctuation rules
worduse	Explains frequently misused words
wwbaid	Describes programs and how to use them
wwbhelp	Gives information about commands and functions
Environmental tailoring	
dictadd	Adds phrases to user specified dictionaries
spelladd	Adds words to spelldict dictionary
mkstand	Builds standards for prose from user documents
User-specified dictionaries	
ddict	Personal list of awkward phrases
sexdict	Personal list of sexist terms
spelldict	Personal list of correct spellings

[a]Indented commands are automatically run by the less-indented commands that precede them.

command) to restrict or expand the output. For instance, the output of the "prose" program can be reduced to a few summary lines by requesting a short version using the -s option.

An author can request other analyses and print sentences that have certain characteristics—for instance, sentences that exceed a certain length, or are passive, or are above a selected readability level. In addition, an author can compare features of a text with statistics derived from texts supplied by the program developers, or created from a set of documents supplied by the author. These features have obvious instructional applications.

CONCLUSIONS

The WRITER'S WORKBENCH programs are a rich information resource for the review and revision stages of writing. Information can be obtained easily and rapidly. Various features of the programs can be tailored to suit the needs of an author; for instance, a text can be evaluated against technical or training materials.

The programs have been tried in different settings by thousands of authors. Comments, obtained from user questionnaires, suggest that the programs may have indirect effects on writing. The programs encourage careful analysis of one's writing; therefore, features may be detected that go beyond the patterns used by the programs. Indirect effects of these aids are confirmed by data collected in college composition courses (Smith, 1983), where it was found that students who used the programs revised their writing spontaneously more than students who did not use the programs.

However, these language analysis aids are not perfect. They address only a portion of the topics that make up a complete analysis of text. Important writing processes, such as planning the content and organization of a composition, are only weakly addressed. Currently the programs emphasize analysis of written products, and not the processes of writing. Useful additions might include means for keeping records of changes to drafts, and information summarizing changes in readability and word use, as a paper progresses in its development.

The programs concentrate on prose material, but many documents consist of semi-prose, such as procedural directions, and include displays, such as tables, which are ignored during program analysis. Our ability to assess the difficulty of graphic materials is not well developed, and it would be useful to attempt measures of other than just text material. In addition, at the risk of increasing the complexity of the system, information files could be expanded to include additional help and useful literary resources such as exemplary texts and bibliographies. We anticipate the day when language analysis tools and on-line library resources will be easily accessible to all students.

SUMMARY AND IMPLICATIONS

In this chapter we described two computer applications to text design; one used a cognitive model of reading to evaluate text format and the other used English-language standards to help evaluate style and mechanics.

In the section on format design aids we described a computer analysis of the cognitive effects of different line lengths (using 60 texts of varying readability). Following recommendations from psychological research and design experts, we defined an optimal line as a line that includes only one phrase. We were then able to determine by computer, for different standard text designs and for each text, the percentage of lines that contained several phrases or just parts of phrases. This allowed us to find a line length for every text that minimized undesirable outcomes, and hence to obtain a visual picture of cognitive demands as text format is altered. Our analysis was based on evaluation of 900 text designs, which would be difficult without the aid of computers. Results showed that the content of different texts forces a different recommendation for line length depending on text features. For instance, two texts on the same subject may require different line lengths depending on word length and variability, or other factors. Experiments show the inefficiency of standard text formats, and our computer recommendations were consistent with human preference data. We have shown that when text is appropriately segmented people read 18% faster than with ordinary text (Frase & Schwartz, 1979), and recently Grist (1982) has shown that children read and recall better with texts formatted according to our computer recommendations than with standard formats.

In the section on language analysis aids we described the WRITER'S WORK-BENCH programs, which evaluate a variety of stylistic patterns. The programs are used by many people with positive results, and they have many applications that we have not pursued. Management can use such computer measures to track changes in documents over time and to evaluate the quality of products. The programs can also provide detailed feedback to writers on the characteristics of their texts and how they depart from characteristics of literary giants, or of whatever standard we wish to employ. We find from personal experience that using these tools alters writing; hence our programs have educational consequences in addition to helping resolve problems in document design.

Language analysis programs are limited. They are limited by the text features they can recognize and by our understanding of the relation of text features to reading difficulty. For instance, we have no program to recognize when content is missing, nor can the programs "understand" the subject and object of a sentence as humans would. Nevertheless, the richness and variety of feedback delivered by the programs is a considerable aid.

The development of a science of text design depends on putting complex assumptions into algorithms so others can understand them and computers can use them. Our perspective on this problem suggests that, through technology, designers and researchers will inevitably draw closer together.

REFERENCES

Battison, R. (Ed.) Plain language laws. (1981). In *Simply Stated* (Newsletter of the Document Design Center, Vol. 18, p. 1). Washington, DC: American Institutes for Research.

Bishop, R. L. (1975). The Journalism programs: Help for the weary writer. *Creative Computing, 1,* 28–30.

Carroll, J. M., & Bever, T. G. (1976). Segmentation in cinema perception. *Science, 191,* 1053–1055.

Chapanis, A. (1971). Prelude to 2001: Explorations in human communication. *American Psychologist, 26,* 949–961.

Cherry, L. L. (1980). PARTS—A system for assigning word classes to English text (Computing Science Tech. Rep. No. 81). Murray Hill, NJ: Bell Laboratories.

Cherry, L. L. (1982). Writing tools. *IEEE Transactions on Communication, COM-30*(1), 100–105.

Cherry, L. L., Fox, M. L., Frase, L. T., Keenan, S. A., & Macdonald, N. H. (1983, May/June). Computer aids for text analysis. *Bell Laboratories Record,* 10–16.

Coleman, E. B., & Hahn, S. C. (1966). Failure to improve readability with a vertical typography. *Journal of Applied Psychology, 50,* 434–436.

Collins, A., & Gentner, D. (1980). A framework for a cognitive theory of writing. In L. W. Gregg & E. R. Steinberg (Eds.), *Cognitive processes in writing.* Hillsdale, NJ: Erlbaum.

Duda, R. O., & Gaschnig, J. G. (1981). Knowledge-based expert systems come of age. *Byte, 6,* 238–281.

Ferguson, E. S. (1977). The mind's eye: Nonverbal thought in technology, *Science, 4306,* 827–836.

Flower, L. (1981). *Problem-solving strategies for writing.* New York: Harcourt.

Frase, L. T. (1973). Integration of written text. *Journal of Educational Psychology, 65,* 252–261.

Frase, L. T. (1983). The UNIX Writer's Workbench Software: Philosophy. *Bell System Technical Journal, 62* (No. 6, Part 3), 1883–1890.

Frase, L. T., & Schwartz, B. J. (1979). Typographical cues that facilitate comprehension. *Journal of Educational Psychology, 71,* 197–206.

Gelb, T. J. (1952). *A study of writing.* Chicago: University of Chicago Press.

Gingrich, P. S. (1983). The UNIX Writer's Workbench Software: Results of a field study. *Bell System Technical Journal, 62* (No. 6, Part 3), 1909–1921.

Gregg, L. W., & Steinberg, E. R. (1980). *Cognitive processes in writing.* Hillsdale, NJ: Erlbaum.

Grist, S. (1982). *Effect of discourse segmentation on comprehension and reading rate of eighth grade children.* Dissertation, Rutgers University.

Grumbach, D. (1979). A handsome, poetic new design is wrought for the Great Book. *Smithsonian, 10,* 72–81.

Hartley, J. (1981). Eighty ways of improving instructional text. *IEEE Transactions on Professional Communication, PC–24,* 17–27.

Hayes, J. R., & Flower, L. (1980). Identifying the organization of writing processes. In L. W. Gregg & E. R. Steinberg (Eds.), *Cognitive processes in writing.* Hillsdale, NJ: Erlbaum.

Heidorn, G. E., Jensen, K., Miller, L. A., Byrd, R. J., & Chodorow, M. S. (1982). The EPISTLE text-critiquing system. *IBM Systems Journal, 21,* 305–326.

Kincaid, J. P., Aagard, J. A., O'Hara, J. W., & Cottrell, L. K. (1981). Computer readability editing system. *IEEE Transactions on Professional Communication, PC–24,* 38–41.

Lanham, R. A. (1979). *Revising prose.* New York: Scribner's.

Macdonald, N. H. (1983). The UNIX Writer's Workbench Software: Rationale and design. *Bell System Technical Journal, 62* (No. 6 Part 3), 1891–1908.

Macdonald, N. H., Frase, L. T., Gingrich, P. S., & Keenan, S. A. (1982). The Writer's Workbench: Computer aids for text analysis. *IEEE Transactions on Communication, COM–30(1)*, 105–110.

Macdonald-Ross, M. (1977). Graphics in text. In L. S. Shulman (Ed.), *Review of Research in Education*. Itasca, IL: Peacock.

Muller, W. G. (1976). Useability research in the navy. In T.G. Sticht & D. Welty- Zapf (Eds.), *Reading and readability research in the Armed Services*. Alexandria, VA: Human Resources Research Organization.

Resnick, D. P. (1979, May). *Social environments for text: An historical view of literacy, literacy standards, and the textbook*. Paper presented at The textbook in American Education Conference, Library of Congress, Washington, DC.

Simon, H. A. (1974). How big is a chunk? *Science, 183*, 482–488.

Smith, C. R. (1983, March). *Writer's Workbench: Applications in the classroom*. In K. Kiefer (Chair), Papers presented at The Computer in the Classroom 34th Annual Meeting of the Conference on College Composition and Communication, Detroit.

Tinker, M. A. (1963). *Legibility of print*. Ames, IO: Iowa State University Press.

Treip, M. (1970). *Milton's punctuation and changing English usage, 1582–1676*. London: Methuen.

CHAPTER 6

Readability Formulas: What's the Use?*

Thomas M. Duffy

INTRODUCTION

Since the late 1970s, perhaps beginning with President Carter's comments on bureaucratic paperwork in one of his fireside chats, there has been a resurgence in the public demand for plain English in our books and documents. The strength of this movement can be seen in the increasing number of state legislatures imposing legal requirements for plain English in public documents and contracts (Pressman, 1979). Plain English has been given additional legal status through court decisions upholding the liability of manufacturers for ensuring that instructions accompanying their products can be easily understood (Wright, Chapter 4, this volume). Very few people would disagree with the basic goals of the plain English movement. The problem is how to produce documents that are easy to use and understand. What is plain English? How do we write and design texts in plain English (Charrow, 1979)? How do we identify whether a text will or will not be plain English for its intended audience? Writing and design strategies that prove effective often conflict with the conventional wisdom expressed in guidelines (Charrow, 1979; Davison, Kantor, Hannah, Hermon, Lutz, & Salzillo, 1980). The myriad of writing guidelines that have received general acceptance often conflict with each other (Klare, n.d.). Judges, including expert writers, cannot reliably judge the comprehensibility of text or graphics (Wright, this volume; Carver, 1974).

There has been widespread application of readability formulas as a tool for defining plain English in the production of texts as well as in judging existing

---

*The views expressed in this paper are those of the author and do not necessarily reflect the views of the U.S. Navy or the federal government.

Designing Usable Texts

documents. There are numerous reasons why readability formulas have been selected to fulfill this defining role. Foremost among these reasons is that the formulas are objective and therefore can be used as legal and contractual criteria. Thus most state legislatures have relied on a readability criterion for judging the plain English of consumer documents. Similarly the military is increasingly requiring readability formulas as a criterion in contracts to produce technical manuals. A second reason for the popularity of readability formulas is that the simple counting characteristic of most have made them readily adaptable to computer application. Therefore the rapid expansion of the computer-based editing and authoring systems has carried with it the increased availability and utilization of readability formula (Frase, 1980; Kincaid, Aagard, O'Hara, & Cotrell, 1981). Even without computerization, however, the ease of calculation and the apparent simplicity of interpreting a score have made the use of these formulas a popular and inexpensive technique for attempting to control the comprehensibility of text (Davison, et al., 1980; Duffy & Kabance, 1982).

This chapter examines the logic and the research support for the primary applications of readability formulas in evaluating and producing texts. While there have been frequent cautions and criticisms in the literature about the over-extension of readability formulas, these papers usually end by suggesting that readability formula can be useful if properly applied (Klare, 1981; Holland, 1981). The conclusion that I draw from this review is that there are few if any proper applications of existing readability formulas that are of practical use. The context for this review is military applications of readability formulas. The military is a closed, minisociety in which all of the various uses of texts and documents are represented—contracts, education, training, reference, job use, and so on—and readability formulas have been increasingly invoked in preparing and evaluating most of these materials (Duffy & Kabance, 1982).

Because of the strong technological base of the military systems, the use of printed text is not only more pervasive than in the society as a whole, but text is also a more critical component of daily life. It is the primary means of transmitting technical information to millions of personnel distributed worldwide in relatively small groups. Because of the criticality of texts, the military has made especially strong efforts to ensure their usability. This has included both research support (Curran, 1980; Sticht & Welty-Zapf, 1976) and support in the development of production and design systems (Sulit & Fuller, 1976). Thus the military provides a manageable context in which the design and use of texts are emphasized in both research and application. Within this context we are more readily able to see the rationale for the use of readability formulas, the feasibility of various alternatives to readability, and the broader issue of the need to control the quality of text.

In the next section I present a brief overview of the volume and importance of texts—particularly technical manuals (TMs)—in the military, the various usability issues in evaluating the texts, and, in particular, the use of readability in that evaluation. I then examine in detail the logic and support for the various applications of readability formulas. Finally, alternatives to traditional readability formulas are presented.

MILITARY TEXTS

In the U.S. Navy alone there are over 4500 courses offered each year. These courses range in length from a few days to over a year. The courses include traditional classroom lecture as well as self-paced (with and without instructor assistance) delivery, and the content spans the range from highly technical subjects to general education. The Navy prepares texts, or contracts for the preparation of text, for all of these courses. There are also advancement-in-rate manuals for each level of expertise in each of the Navy's 76 areas of specialization that an individual must study in preparation for advancement exams. The other services have similar text requirements; but in all cases the text system that is far and away the largest and the most critical is the TM system. The TMs serve as the primary, and often the only, documentation for the operation and maintenance of all of the military systems and equipments. They are primarily job manuals. However, the manuals are also the primary text in most advanced training programs and must also be studied as part of the qualification for certification on the particular equipment.

Most TMs are prepared under contract by civilian organizations that have a publications division. In the case of new equipment it is generally the manufacturer of the equipment. The volume of TM text is of gargantuan proportions. The Navy had an estimated 25 million pages of TM documentation in 1978 and was adding or revising 400,000 pages yearly (Sulit & Fuller, 1976). Across the services there are 131,000 aviation maintenance manuals alone, containing an estimated 13 million pages (General Accounting Office, 1979). The documentation system is not only voluminous but it is costly. In 1978 the Air Force estimated that it spent $70 million per year to add new manuals or revise existing ones (General Accounting Office, 1979). Today the per page development cost is estimated at $250 for a standard manual and up to four times that for user-oriented manuals.

Obviously the military services did not begin with such a vast inventory of manuals. Rather, the volume of documentation grew as the varieties and technological sophistication of the equipment increased. For example, when the Cougar aircraft was introduced in 1950, only 1800 pages were required to document the entire operation and maintenance system. By 1975 the figure had grown

14,000% to 260,000 pages for the F-14 fighter (Muller, 1976). In 1984, one million pages are projected for the B1 bomber.

Usability

Given the growing volume and criticality of text materials, major programs have been instituted to ensure that both training text and technical manuals will be maximally usable (Sulit & Fuller, 1976). In this work four major components of usability are considered: access, accuracy, completeness, and comprehensibility. By access we mean the ease with which the technician can find his way to the particular page or section required for the job task. Ease of access is largely a function of the overall organization and indexing of the manual. A most dramatic example of poor access was described in a General Accounting Office report (1979). They found that to isolate and repair one particular C-141 radar malfunction required that the technician refer to 165 pages in eight documents and look at 41 different places in those documents. Once the technician accesses the relevant section, it is essential that all the information required for the job be present and accurate. However, even if all the information is accurately presented it will be of little use if it is not presented in a clear and understandable manner, that is, if it is not comprehensible.

In the military programs, as well as in text design efforts in general, specifying criteria and procedures for ensuring comprehensibility have proved most elusive. In large measure, this is because comprehensibility is the only usability factor that is inextricably tied to the interaction of the reader with the text. The comprehensibility of any particular text will vary as a function of the reading skill, the graphic interpretive skill, and the technical knowledge of the reader, as well as with a variety of transient situational variables. Ideally the judgment of whether or not a text is comprehensible would therefore depend on a reader test, that is, the ability of a sample of readers to do a variety of job tasks using the text. Indeed, when military texts are prepared under contract, the requirement for acceptance almost always includes just such a test (Duffy, in press). However, the actual evaluation is seldom carried out because of the expense and logistics involved. As an alternative, the military has turned increasingly to the use of readability formulas.

Readability formulas have received wide application as a standard and specification in the production of texts as well as to determine if existing texts are usable. These two uses correspond to the prediction and production functions described by Klare (1976, 1979). Klare (1979) has argued that readability formulas, while not ideal, are considerably better than other available instruments and have proved to be excellent tools for prediction in many situations. He further argues that several formulas have sufficient validity to be effective tools in guiding production. In the following sections I discuss the readability formulas as a tool for prediction and for production.

READABILITY AND PREDICTION

THE OBJECTIVE OF PREDICTION

The prediction of readable writing refers to the use of a formula to accurately predict comprehension scores for a large number of different passages (Klare, 1976). But what is an "accurate" prediction? In a weak sense a formula is accurate if it can rank order texts in terms of difficulty. That is, we can use the formula to predict that text A will be more difficult to comprehend than text B. There is no suggestion that the readers will be able to adequately comprehend either text. The skill of the reader is not referenced except for the implicit assumption that texts A and B are read by the same individuals. This use of the formula is extremely limited because it does not indicate the degree of difficulty an individual will have in comprehending either text.

Accurate prediction in the strong sense, and in the vast majority of uses, refers to the prediction of the specific level of reading skill that will be required to comprehend the text. It is not simply that text A is easier to comprehend than text B, but that the text will be comprehended by a reader at a particular reading level. In this strong sense of prediction the readability formula score is referenced to another measure that scales the ability of the reader, that is, there is a comparison of indexes of text and reader. For example, Dale and Chall (1948) state that the reading grade level (RGL) score from their formula indicates the reading grade at which a book or article can be read with understanding. It is in this strong predictive sense that formulas have been most often used. Biersner (1975), using a readability formula, found Navy texts were written at an average of 14th RGL and assumed that this was too difficult for the average reader in the Navy who is at the 10th RGL. Duffy and Nugent (1978); Mockovak (1974); Carver (1974); and Caylor, Sticht, Fox, and Ford (1973) all compared the readability formula scores of military texts to the reading skills of the readers to determine if there was a "literacy gap" that could affect job performance or learning. That is, was the formula RGL score for the text higher than the reading test RGL of the users? They found significant numbers of individuals with a literacy gap, as defined by such a score comparison, and concluded that such a gap will likely affect the ability to effectively use the text. However, as we shall see, these types of readability comparisons are of questionable validity and are likely to lead to very misleading conclusions.

Kern (1979) has argued effectively that existing readability formulas are unsuitable for achieving the objective of matching the comprehensibility (or read-ability) of the text to the reader. His argument is based on an analysis of the absolute errors in the prediction of cloze comprehension when military-based formulas are applied to other military texts. Errors ranging up to 9 grade levels were obtained when the readability formula scores for passages from military texts (other than the ones on which the formula was based) were compared to the tested cloze comprehension. The error in prediction far exceeded the standard error value for the formulas, which is about 1.6 grade levels. Thus these for-mulas (the FORCAST and Kincaid-Flesch formulas) are ineffective for exact prediction of cloze comprehension even under conditions in which generality of the formula should be high. Kern's (1979) findings are damning of existing readability formulas. However, the regression analyses on which the formulas are based involved no more than 20 sets of scores (20 passages). The error reported by Kern could be greatly reduced by larger and more divergent sampling techniques in the formula development procedure.

REQUIREMENTS FOR VALID PREDICTION

Our argument extends beyond Kern's error analysis, in that we contend that the formulas as presently conceived cannot be used, in principle, to predict the reading comprehension skills required to use a text on the job or in training. Exact prediction is impossible simple because the task being predicted, that is, the task used in the development of the formula, is grossly different from the practical tasks for which texts and documents are used. This is not simply a "radical empiricist" viewpoint. The readability formula index is related to a wide variety of indexes of comprehension and a wide variety of comprehension tasks. Indeed, one could only wish that other experimentally obtained rela-tionships would generalize as widely as has the readability work. However, it is not the general rank-order relationship that is of concern; nor is this the use to which the formula is typically put. The concern is the use of the formula to make exact predictions of reading requirements without adequately considering the effects of deviations from the conditions of development upon the accuracy of that exact prediction.

DEVELOPING A FORMULA

Consider the procedure for developing a formula (Caylor et al., 1973; Kin-caid, Fishburne, Rogers, & Chissom, 1975). First, comprehension of a set of passages is tested using a sample of readers with known reading skill. Each passage is then given an RGL score based on the RGL level of the readers who comprehend the passages. Next, a variety of physical features of each passage are counted, for example, number of prepositions, letters per word, syllables per word, words per sentence, phrases per sentence, number of nouns, and so on. An assessment is made of the extent to which variations across passages in each of the physical features is related to variations in comprehension. Finally, the most strongly related physical features are entered onto a regression analysis to develop the best linear prediction of the comprehension score for the passages. Most researchers find that a word factor (e.g., number of syllables per word) and a sentence factor (e.g., number of words per sentence) together yield the best prediction of the comprehension score (Entin & Klare, 1978). Thus most readability formulas are of the form:

$$RGL = a + b \text{ (word measure)} + c \text{ (sentence measure)}.$$

The expected RGL requirement is a function of a constant a plus the weighted sum of the word and sentence factors.

Why Are There New Formulas?

Klare (1979) has counted over 100 different readability formulas. Given they all follow this same general development strategy, why is there a need for so many formulas? In some cases the alternative formulas offer a choice between simplicity of application (a few, easily counted predictors) and accuracy of prediction (all predictors necessary to achieve the highest multiple correlation). However, most formulas are developed because the authors feel that the existing formulas will not generalize to some particular situation of interest (Klare, 1963). That is, the concern is whether the existing formula will be accurate for the particular application because the conditions of reading being predicted are generally different from the conditions of development. Invariably the focus is on either the similarity of the readers or the similarity of the passages in development and application (Klare 1979; Redish, 1979). Thus new formulas are developed based on a sampling from more appropriate universes of readers and texts.

Just such an issue led each of the military services to develop their own readability formulas (Caylor et al., 1973; Kincaid et al., 1975; Smith & Kincaid, 1960). The formulas were developed because it was felt that existing formulas like the Dale–Chall (1948) and Flesch (1948) Reading Ease, which were based on children readers and children's textbooks, would not accurately predict the requirements of a military technician reading a technical text. The appropriateness of word and sentence factors as predictors was not questioned nor was the comprehension criterion (though the latter was changed by necessity). Rather it was the value of the intercept and the weights in the basic formula. In fact, Kincaid et al. (1975) considered themselves simply to be recalculating three existing formulas using Navy men and materials. Kincaid et al. (1975) felt that the existing school-based formulas predicted too high a reading skill requirement. There were two reasons for this assumption. First, long technical words in a technical text are familiar to the technical reader but are nonetheless scored as difficult in the school-based formulas. Thus establishing new norms using military text should result in a lowering of the weight b given to the word length factor. Second, because of the difference in world knowledge, the adult with an RGL of 9.0 on a standard reading test will (it is thought) actually comprehend more in the technical text than the child with the same RGL (see Curran, 1980). The effect of establishing new norms using military readers would thus be to decrease the size of the intercept a in the basic readability formula.

It should be clear from the preceding discussion that new formulas were developed with the intent of increasing accuracy of prediction in the strong sense, that is, the score resulting from the application of the formula could be referenced to the skill required of the reader. New formulas would not be required if the goal was simply to rank order the difficulty of the texts. The military formulas and the school-based formulas are highly correlated. Caylor *et al.* (1973) obtained co-relation coefficients of .94 and .92 between the Army's FORCAST formula and the Dale–Chall and Flesch Reading Ease formulas, respectively. Thus the readability relationships generalize, and the rank ordering of technical text difficulty could be done as well with a school-based formula as with the new military formulas. Indeed, Klare and Smart (1973) found a formula based on children highly effective in predicting the relative difficulty of military correspondence texts.

The formulas were developed to make exact grade-level predictions of reading requirements, and that is how they have been used. Most of the literacy gap research discussed previously (Biersner, 1975; Caylor *et al.*, 1973; Duffy & Nugent, 1978) used the military-based formula. In this research the formulas were used to predict reading skill requirements regardless of whether the text was for use on-the-job, for correspondence training, for classroom instruction, or for self-study. For some reason it has been assumed that, because the formulas are based on military men and materials, we can predict the exact (within the standard error of estimate) RGL the reader must have to comprehend the text regardless of the comprehension task or the situation in which it is carried out. In generalizing readability formulas we have forgotten half of the development particulars. The development of a formula involves not only a particular set of people reading a particular set of passages but also the assessment of a particular type of comprehension under particular reading conditions. In the same way that there have been reservations in generalizing to different readers and to different passages, so there must be concern about generalizing to different comprehension tasks and reading conditions.

Failure to Define the Situational Factors

Klare (1963), in discussing the limitations of readability formulas, states that they do not measure the effects of the purpose or motivation in reading nor the effects of the format, of the typography, or of the content on comprehension. It is quite true that a readability formula does not measure these variables; they were not varied in the formula development procedure. However, the passages used must have had some format and the reader some purpose. The time for reading and the nature of the questions had to be specified. That is, the developer, although not manipulating these variables, had to fix them at some value. In using the formula our prediction of comprehension will be in error to the extent that we violate the assumptions of the developer. These situational variables are no less important in specifying the limits for generalizing a formula than is the consideration of the particular text and readers used in the development.

Consider the variety of situational factors and how they affect performance. In developing the formula the readers are subjects in an experiment and thus not very well motivated. Suppose, however, that we told these individuals that their promotion depended on their comprehension score. Scores would zoom up, and, given a fixed comprehension criterion, the resulting readability formula would predict all texts to be much easier. If we want to predict reading skill requirements for texts used in studying for promotion just such motivational instructions should be given; that is, if accurate prediction is the objective. Similarly, giving two or three readings of the text, as occurs in typical studying, will result in higher scores and, if the criterion for comprehension is fixed, predictions of higher readability. Using the typeface found in some military texts instead of a typewritten version would reduce comprehension, if reading time were restricted.

Reading time is also an obvious variable that will affect comprehension scores. Klare (1976, 1979) has stated that readability formulas are not predictive when reading time is unlimited. However, his focus is on the relative difficulty of materials, that is, the weak prediction. If we want to predict the level of reading skill required to achieve a specific level of comprehension (e.g., 75% correct on a factual, multiple-choice test), then the accuracy of our predictions (e.g., the prediction that a ninth-grade reading skill is required) will depend on the time allowed for reading when the formula was developed as well as the time allowed in the situation for which the prediction is being made. Obviously, a given formula cannot predict the particular reading skill required to comprehend a book irrespective of whether the reading time allowance is 100, 200, or 300 words per minute.

These situational factors can have a major effect on the resulting formula prediction of an RGL requirement. Yet it is highly unlikely that more than a small minority of the situational factors in development will match the situational factors in application. Thus it would be inappropriate to make exact predictions using the formula.

Failure to Define the Comprehension Task

Of even greater significance than the situational variables is the definition of comprehension used in developing formulas. The grade-level score from a formula is not the grade level required for some amorphous, universal comprehension. It is the grade level required to accomplish a very specific comprehension task to a very specific criterion level. If we wish to predict the skill requirement for a different reading task, then the effects of that change on performance must be known and accounted for in the readability formula. Failure to do so must lead to spurious predictions.

Consider the measures of comprehension in the military formulas. Kincaid *et al.* (1975) assigned comprehension scores to passages based on a combination of performance on a cloze test and performance on the Gates–MacGinitie reading test (Gates & MacGinitie, 1965). Specifically, an individual was said to comprehend a passage if he or she scored 35% or more on a cloze test of that passage. The reading grade level required for comprehension of the passage was then determined by first categorizing the readers into RGL categories, that is, readers between RGLs of 8.5 to 9.4, 9.5 to 10.4, and so on, based on the Gates–MacGinitie testing. Then each group was examined to determine if 50% or more of the readers in that group comprehended that passage, that is, scored 35% on the cloze. The passage was assigned the RGL of the lowest Gates–MacGinitie RGL group meeting the criterion. Caylor *et al.* (1973) used an identical procedure but a different reading test in developing the Army's readability formula. In sum, if a text has a 10.0 RGL score on the Kincaid–Flesch formula (Kincaid *et al.*, 1975), it means that at least 50% of the readers with a 10.0 RGL or higher on the Gates–MacGinitie test may be expected to score at least 35% on a cloze test of the text. What does this have to do with the skill required in reading to do a job or reading to pass a test?

Compare this reading criterion with the definition of comprehension in a self-study course, comprehension is defined as a score of 100% on a closed-book, multiple-choice test taken after the student has spent no more than the allotted number of hours or days studying the chapter and receiving information clarifying the text when requested. In correspondence courses there is a different criterion, and it is generally an open-book test. In advanced training open-book tests are generally used, and there are lecture supplements. How is a tenth-grade readability score based on 35% cloze comprehension to be interpreted in judging the appropriateness of a text for the readers who have these actual comprehension requirements? One might argue that because our concern is the comprehensibility of the text we cannot have lecture supplements in developing the criteria. But if the formula is to be used to predict comprehension skill requirements under those circumstances, it is of little use to develop a formula to predict the skill requirement needed to understand when reading in isolation.

In fact, the comprehension measure and criterion are quite arbitrary. Why not score synonyms correct on the cloze test instead of requiring the exact word that was deleted? The correlation would not change but the predicted comprehensibility of the passages would. Requiring 50% instead of 75% of the people in an

RGL category to demonstrate comprehension sounds like a minor and rather arbitrary decision. Who could say what is the "proper" criterion? Yet such a decision could result in a three or four grade-level change in prediction using the resulting formula. Since all decisions in establishing the comprehension criterion are arbitrary, the resulting prediction of a comprehension requirement must also be arbitrary (again, in the absolute sense). But, it would seem that because the prediction is in terms of a reading grade level there is some assumption of a real-world reference.

A CASE STUDY

We all recognize the difficulty in interpreting an RGL score in terms of comprehension skills, especially when it is for an adult reader. Yet, we all "know" what a 10th-grade reader is like—even an adult 10th-grade reader. Similarly we all know what a 10th-grade text looks like. Although the formulas may be based on arbitrary decisions, they "seem" to predict accurately. Nonsense! The arbitrariness of the readability formula score can perhaps most clearly be illustrated by an examination of the assumptions and errors in establishing the comprehension criterion for the Army FORCAST (Caylor *et al.*, 1973) and Navy Kincaid–Flesch (Kincaid *et al.*, 1975) formulas.

As discussed previously, a 35% cloze criterion was used in both the Army and the Navy work based on the assumption that 35% cloze was equivalent to a 70% multiple-choice score. This equivalency is based on the authors' interpretations of two reports on the relationship of multiple-choice and cloze testing (Bormuth, 1967; Rankin & Culhane, 1969). There are two problems with this criterion: first, if it were equivalent to a 70% multiple-choice score it would be too stringent; second, if anything, the criterion relates to a much lower multiple-choice score. A 70% multiple-choice comprehension score on a passage is taken by reading teachers to indicate that the reader is at the "instructional level" in attempting to comprehend the passage, that is, the reader cannot adequately comprehend the passage without assistance (Entin & Klare, 1978). This obviously is an inadequate match of reader and text if the text is to be used on the job or in independent study. For military use we want the readers to be able to independently read and comprehend the text. Reading teachers consider a 90% multiple-choice comprehension score to reflect this self-study criterion (Entin & Klare, 1978), which according to Bormuth (1967) equates to a 50% cloze score. Thus military readability formulas should have been based on a 50% cloze criterion instead of a 35% cloze if the authors wanted the formulas to predict the reading skill required to work independently with the text.

If the instructional level of comprehension was the goal of prediction in the military formulas, even this goal was not achieved. This is because the second problem with the criterion is that a 35% cloze score does not equate to a 70%

multiple-choice score. As Klare (1979) points out, the findings of Bormuth (1967) and of Rankin and Culhane (1969) have been misinterpreted in developing both the FORCAST and Kincaid–Flesch formulas; they found a 40% cloze equated to a 70% multiple-choice. Klare (1979) estimates that the 35% cloze equates to only a 50% multiple-choice score. Thus both Kincaid *et al.* (1975) and Caylor *et al.* (1973) set the comprehension criterion well below the instructional level of reading and even below the "frustration" level, that is, the level at which a reader will get frustrated and quit reading. If readability formula scores predicted accurately, then the matching of readers and texts by using these military formulas throughout the services would result in frustration in reading and rejection of all the texts by the readers. Obviously, if the scores had any absolute meaning, the Kincaid–Flesch and FORCAST formulas would have to be withdrawn and renormed (normative values would be redetermined). The failure to withdraw and renorm the formula reflects a recognition of the arbitrariness of the scores.

VALID PREDICTIONS

Because of the arbitrary value of readability scores, the formulas have very limited practical use. Two uses come to mind. First, the formula may be used to select between alternative texts for the same or similar groups. The aim may be to select the easiest of several existing texts or, if the texts are to be revised, it may be used to select the most difficult materials so that they may be the first ones submitted for revision. Note that this application does not predict which text will be acceptable. All of the texts may be incomprehensible or they may be easily comprehended by the intended audience.

Second, the readability formula score could be used as a variable in relating text comprehension to other variables. For example, Klare and Smart (1973) found the readability score of military correspondence course texts correlated .75 with course attrition, suggesting that difficulties in comprehension of the text contributed to attrition. Other work has included readability as an independent variable in factorial experiments on text comprehension (Klare, 1979). In all valid applications, however, the concern is relative—not absolute—difficulty.

READABILITY AND PRODUCTION

In prediction the readability formula is used to assess already written material. The attempt is to identify text *in use* that will be difficult to comprehend. In production the readability formula score is a standard that is set prior to writing. Obviously readability formulas are of much greater value if they can be used in the production stage to ensure comprehensible text from the outset. Formulas are used in two ways in the production system. First, a readability formula score is identified to the writer and editor as the criterion for comprehensible text (see Curran, 1977; Davison and Cantor, 1982; Department of the Air Force, 1977; Department of the Army, 1978; Kern, 1979; Pressman, 1979). Typically the formula score is the only criterion for comprehensible text. The second production use of the formula is in providing readability feedback or guidance to the writer as he or she writes each paragraph (Curran, 1977; Klare, 1979). Computer editing systems are virtually all equipped with subroutines to calculate readability (Frase, 1980; Frase, Macdonald, & Keenan, Chapter 5, this volume; Kincaid *et al.*, 1981). Thus as the writer enters the text he or she is given immediate feedback on word and sentence length or difficulty and, in some cases, is provided with alternative "simpler" words.

READABILITY AS A CRITERION

Meeting a minimum readability formula score may be a legally imposed criterion in text development. This is the case with many military contracts for the preparation of technical manuals. Also, an increasing number of states have legal requirements that consumer contracts meet a readability standard. Rather than a legal requirement, a readability standard may be an in-house requirement of the publisher; this is the case with many publishers of school texts. Regardless of the source of the requirement, a specific formula score is specified as the criterion and upon completion of a draft the formula is applied to samples of the text to ensure that the criterion was met. From our discussion about prediction it should be clear that formulas as they presently exist cannot be used to set such a specific grade level. However, can the formula be used in production to achieve if not an exact grade level then at least more comprehensible, that is, simpler materials? There is general agreement that many military texts are written very poorly and are difficult if not impossible to comprehend. Biersner (1975) found the readability formula scores for Navy rate training manuals to be, on the average, at the 14th-grade level. Would writing these materials to a 9th-grade criterion improve the comprehensibility?

If a formula is to be used as a production criterion then the formula must be put on the side until the text is written or revised. As Klare (1979) points out, all experts in the area of readability agree that it is ineffective to write to formula, that is, to change only those variables indexed by the formula without regard to whether or not the change would make the materials easier to understand. The formula criterion must be achieved using clear writing techniques. Klare (1979, pp. 82–83) provides a step-by-step procedure for what he considers to be the proper use of readability formulas in production: (1) Apply a formula to see if a piece of writing is likely to be readable to intended readers. (2) If the readability index suggests it is, and if other requirements for good writing have been met, stop there. Keep in mind, in other words, that while a poor index value predicts poor writing, a good index value by itself need not mean good writing. (3) If the readability index suggests the piece of writing is not likely to be readable to intended readers, put the formula aside so as not to be tempted to "write to formula." (4) Rewrite the material, trying to discover and change those parts likely to cause trouble. Use the formula information only as a guide to where to begin. (5) Apply the formula again to see if the piece of writing is now more likely to be readable to intended readers. (6) If it is, and other requirements for good writing are met, stop there. (7) If it is not, repeat steps 3, 4, and 5 until an appropriate readability index is achieved.

Klare's procedure raises two questions: (1) Can the writer put the criterion "on the side"? (2) What are clear writing techniques that will both improve comprehensibility and reduce the formula score? One might expect that a writer will be more able to ignore the formula while writing, to the extent that other comprehension criterion are available. For example, in newspaper and magazine writing the real comprehension criterion is readership. If an individual's writing does not attract readers he or she will be fired even if his or her articles achieve a low formula score. An individual in this situation would be foolhardy to write to the formula. But what of the military or industrial writer writing under a contract that includes as the only criterion for text comprehensibility the achievement of a specific readability formula score? One might expect this writer to prepare what he or she considers to be a complete and accurate text that is comprehensible. If the formula score disagrees with that judgment of comprehensibility and the formula is the only comprehensibility criterion for acceptance, then the writer is very likely to write to the formula. The tendency will increase to the extent that budgetary constraints are severe and the individual's job depends on meeting tight production schedules, both of which are common circumstances in the production of technical text (Caird, 1975; Duffy, in press). In addition, and most obviously, a writer will write to the formula to the extent that he or she finds it difficult to otherwise achieve the readability criterion. Hooke, DeLeo, and Slaughter (1979) report that Air Force writers find it extremely difficult to achieve readability scores below 10.0 RGL. In sum, it is likely that technical writers will, in a significant number of instances, write to the formula if it is possible to do so.

READABILITY FEEDBACK

The second use of readability formulas in the production process has been as feedback to the technical writer on the expected difficulty of a segment of text. Of course, it is essential that the formula score not be the criterion, but simply serve as guidance to the writer as to whether or not the particular paragraph will be comprenended. The goal in this application of the formula is to achieve comprehensible text in the first draft and thus save the time and cost of revision. In this section I examine the validity requirements and evidence for the use of readability formulas as feedback devices. The basic conclusions are (1) the validity of the formula depends on the validity of readable writing guidelines; (2) individual guidelines have not, and maybe cannot, be validated; and (3) readable writing approaches have only marginal effects of comprehension.

Although the formula score is only a guide, it is, in another sense, a criterion because the writers, if they use the formula as a guide, will continue their revision until the formula score predicts an acceptable level of comprehension. Thus the formula in its use as a guideline will be applied to a passage after each revision. If the formula is to be effective as a guide then the formula score must have a consistent meaning, that is, a consistent relationship to comprehension, across the successive applications. This can only be the case if the revision effort has the same effect on both the readibility formula score and comprehension, that is, the linear regression does not change. The validity of the formula as a guideline therefore depends on identifying and applying readable writing guidelines that result in a lowered readability formula score *and* increased comprehension. The guidelines basically will serve as the causal link between readability and comprehension.

Since even the most complex formula is restricted to the measurement of sentence and word characteristics, the guidelines must address the simplification of words and sentences. In his *Manual for Readable Writing* Klare (1975) describes the process of making writing more readable as "changing words" and "changing sentences" to make them easier to understand. Graphics, format, and organization, although important to comprehension, are not a part of readable writing. Therefore if the writer is using the formula as feedback, then graphics and format are irrelevant to the revision process. If graphics are added, for example, the formula score would not change. Therefore the writer would either have to assume comprehension was unaffected or discard the formula and look for a new index of expected comprehension.

Not only does the formula guide the writer away from graphics and format, but changing the graphics and format would invalidate the predictions from the formula if those changes resulted in improved comprehension. That is, the comprehension score would change (theoretically) but the readability score would not. Thus the formula would not even provide a relative index of difficulty from one revision to the next.

READABLE WRITING GUIDELINES

There are innumerable style manuals available that recommend a variety of techniques for improving comprehension. Included in the recommendations are techniques for readable writing, that is, simplifying words and sentences. Klare

(1963, 1979) and Flesch (1949) specifically address readable writing and present guidelines that they propose will improve both readability and comprehension. The vocabulary recommendations include the manipulation of word dimensions like familiarity, concreteness, and association value, and the manipulation of grammatical class, for example, increasing the proportion of function words and avoiding nominalizations. Sentence recommendations include using active sentences with minimum embedding. It can be easily demonstrated that following these guidelines will improve most readability formula scores because active sentences tend to be short sentences and familiar words are primarily short, one-syllable words. However, the guidelines must improve comprehension as well as readability, and here the evidence is not so clear.

There has been very little research on the effects of these variables on text comprehension, and hence the guideline recommendations are based on verbal learning research findings (Klare, 1975). However, the verbal learning research is on the learning of word and sentence lists and the verbatim recall or recognition of those lists. We know surprisingly little of the generalization of list-learning research to text comprehension (Goetz, 1975). Where tests have been carried out, the generalizations have been difficult to specify (Reder, 1978). Klare (1976) was able to identify only 36 studies since the mid-1940s that evaluated the effects of readable writing techniques on text comprehension. Even in many of these studies, the readable writing variables were confounded with other variables making a valid evaluation impossible. In the extreme the readability comparison was between passages from different books. Klare (1976) reports that there was ''evidence of an attempt'' to control content in only 11 of 27 studies. In some of the controlled studies, however, the text revision still involved considerably more than the application of readable writing guidelines. For example, Hiller's (1974) simplification of a 1200-word mathematics passage increased the length by 18% and included the addition of a concrete example. Feldman (1964) controlled content but passage length increased by 40%. Obviously more than sentence and word simplification was involved.

Vocabulary

Very few of the studies reviewed by Klare (1976) or published subsequently have evaluated specific readable writing guidelines. The research that has been carried out, however, has failed, in the main, to find any effects of practical significance due to applying the guidelines. Nolte (1937) in one of the earliest studies simplified passages using the requirement that all words be on a fourth-grade vocabulary list. Although an extensive test program was carried out, no effect on comprehension could be demonstrated. Duffy and Kabance (1982) also used vocabulary lists to simplify passages. Although 25% of the content words in eight passages were changed, effects of practical significance were obtained only under very specific conditions and in only one of four experiments. Tuinman and

Brady (1973) held the passages constant across conditions but "simplified" by teaching the unfamiliar vocabulary to the students in a series of sessions extending over a week. Although the instruction improved vocabulary knowledge by 20%, there was no effect on comprehension.

Sentences

A similar lack of significance has resulted when sentence variables have been manipulated. Duffy and Kabance (1982) revised passages using a rule that every sentence must be a simple sentence with no more than one adverbial or prepositional phrase. As a result, sentence length was halved, from 20 to 10 words per sentence, yet in a series of four experiments no comprehension effects were obtained. Coleman (1962) varied the average sentence length of a passage from 16 to 39 words by applying Flesch's (1949) readable writing guidelines for sentences. While the manipulation resulted in statistically significant comprehension effects, the effects were meager and of little practical significance. Coleman (1962) concluded that shortening sentences may not be an effective readable writing strategy. In a post hoc analysis he examined three simplification strategies. Breaking a compound sentence joined by "and" into two sentences had no effect on comprehension. Raising clause fragments (e.g., participle, gerund, and infinitive phrases) in a complex sentence to the status of a full sentence resulted in only marginally significant improvement in comprehension. Only breaking sentences joined by coordinate conjunctions other than *and* resulted in an improvement in comprehension that is likely to be reliable.

A General Writing Approach

The research reviewed thus far has focused on the evaluation of either specific vocabulary or specific sentence simplification guidelines. The findings have failed to support the validity of the revision strategies as a means of improving comprehension. However, it has been argued that the readable writing approach cannot be validated by the separate validation of individual guidelines (Klare, 1976; Nolte, 1937). Indeed, Klare (1976) has suggested that the manipulation cannot even be restricted to just vocabulary or to just sentence simplification. The argument is that the individual application of guidelines will result in awkward, stilted writing, counteracting the effect of simplification. Thus it is argued that the validity test must involve the application of a general or broad-based readable writing approach that involves simplifying both sentences and words.

Developing and validating a general readable writing approach is fraught with difficulties. A general approach consists of a series of individual guidelines. Yet, because individual guidelines cannot be validated, there is no empirical way of determining which guidelines to include. An intuitive approach does not seem to be effective either because across existing style manuals there is little agreement and frequent contradiction in the writing guidelines proposed (Klare, n.d.).

Without the ability to validate individual guidelines in some way, it is quite likely that a general writing approach will include particular guidance that is ineffective (e.g., Coleman, 1962) or even detrimental (e.g., Pearson, 1974–1975) to comprehension. Thus a significant part of a revision effort based on such a general approach could be counterproductive. The general approach also breaks down in that a writer does not apply a general approach, but rather individual guidelines in a general approach. What guidance is the writer to be given regarding the mix of guideline applications required to be effective in improving comprehension. Suppose, for example, in simplifying sentences the writer finds it easiest to break up complex sentences and thus uses primarily this approach. Or the writer may feel that vocabulary cannot be simplified and hence restricts his or her simplification efforts to sentences. In both cases a general readable writing approach was used as applicable in the best judgment of the writer. The readability formula score (and hence the writer's feedback) would indicate improvement, yet it is doubtful whether either effort would result in improved comprehension (Coleman, 1962; Klare, 1976).

Inconsistencies such as these may account for the fact that even when a general readable writing approach is used the effects are weak at best. Klare (1976) judged findings from readable writing evaluations on the basis of statistical significance and concluded that readability makes a difference, sometimes. We must add that readability makes a practical difference, seldom. Kincaid and Delionbach (1973), in one of the statistically significant studies, rewrote passages from a military maintenance manual to be read by the 8th, 12th, and 16th RGL. The 8-grade manipulation resulted in an increase of only 7 percentage points on a multiple-choice comprehension test. There was no difference in performance between the 8th- and 12th-grade versions. Similarly, Klare, Mabry, and Gustafson (1955) obtained a statistically significant 8% improvement in multiple-choice performance when a 16+ grade-level version of a military maintenance passage was simplified to the 7th–8th grade level. A middle version was not significantly different from either of the extreme versions. One might argue that a reliable 7–8% gain in performance is of practical significance. However, the gain is quite small (1% per grade level) relative to the effort required to make an 8-grade-level or greater reduction in a readability formula score. Additionally, extreme simplifications of 8 grade levels will seldom be required and thus the improvements in comprehension would be of even less significance.

A Research Model

In both the Klare et al. (1955) and Kincaid and Delionbach (1973) studies, as well as in most of the other readable writing studies, neither the motivation nor the reading skill of the readers was assessed or controlled. Klare has argued that the failure to control such variables may account for the many weak and nonsignificant effects. Klare (1976) has presented a model of the reading situation as it applies to readability in which it is argued that the failure to control these and other variables may account for the many weak and nonsignificant effects. Basically, if readers are well motivated and have sufficient reading time, they will be able to work their way through a text regardless of style difficulty. Similarly, if the reader is already very familiar with the topic or if the readability scores for both versions of a passage are neither above nor below the reading skill of the üsers, we can scarcely expect the manipulation of the text to have more than a minimal effect on comprehension. Fass and Schumacher (1978) have extended Klare's model to include the readers' processing activity as a critical intervening variable. They propose that difficult text requires more elaborate or deeper processing than simple text. If the reader can and does engage in appropriate processing activities, then the effects of simplification will be negated. Their argument is in the context of the learning of a lengthy passage, but the argument may be expected to apply to any comprehension task requiring inference or long-term memory. Many of the variables in Klare's (1976) model (e.g., motivation, background knowledge, and reading time) can be interpreted in terms of their effect on processing activity.

Two studies carefully attended to the variables identified in Klare's model, yet failed to offer any support for readability formula as a production guideline. One of the studies (Duffy and Kabance, 1982), however, yielded some evidence that the degree of information processing required is a relevant variable in determining the effectiveness of simplifying text. In both studies the manipulation of readability failed to facilitate comprehension. Kniffen, Stevenson, Klare, Entin, Slaughter, and Hooke (1979) manipulated the literacy gap—the difference between the readability score for the materials and the reading skill score for the readers. Two different 5000-word samples of technical text were rewritten to the 8, 10, 12, and 14 RGL using Klare's (1975) *Manual for Readable Writing*. These materials were then administered to military personnel with skills at the 8th and 10th RGL as necessary to create literacy gap conditions of 0, −2, and −4 RGL. In addition, reading time was manipulated allowing for an overall reading rate of approximately 85, 130, or 175 words per minute. A very carefully constructed multiple-choice test was administered after reading. In the first analysis, performance on each passage was analyzed separately. Neither the literacy gap effect nor the interaction of literacy gap with reading time was significant in either analysis. In a subsequent combined analysis the literacy gap did produce a statistically significant effect. Comprehension test performance improved by five percentage points, hardly an effect of practical significance. Even in the overall analysis, the literacy gap did not interact with reading time, thus failing to support the hypothesis that restricted reading time will enhance readability effects.

Duffy and Kabance (1982) simplified the eight passages in the Nelson–Denny (1960) Reading Test using a restricted vocabulary list (generally words at or below the fourth-grade level) and a syntactic complexity limitation described earlier. Thus both sentences and vocabulary were simplified using fundamental readable writing strategies. In all revisions every attempt was made to maintain a smooth writing style. The result of the manipulation was a reduction of average Kincaid–Flesch (Kincaid *et al.*, 1975) readability from the 11.5 grade level to the 5.5 grade level.

In carrying out our tests with these passages, we used a very low motivation context. The readers were Navy recruits in the midst of basic training. No special incentive was provided for good performance, the testing was unrelated to their basic training, and they knew that their performance scores would be confidential. Thus the conditions of motivation were such as to maximize the effects of the readability manipulation. We gave a reading skill pretest to all the recruits so that the interaction of reader skill level and change in readability could be evaluated. Because recruit reading varies from less than a 7th-grade skill level to the college level, a wide range of literacy gaps were evaluated in the interaction. Across experiments we manipulated the comprehension test (cloze vs. multiple-choice), reading time, and memory requirement. Basically, we attempted to address, either within or between experiments, every one of the major variables called out by Klare (1976) as moderators of the comprehension effect of readable writing manipulations. Yet across all experiments, the only readability effect of practical significance was simplifying vocabulary for low-ability readers when memory was required. In all other conditions across all the experiments we failed to find practical effects on any of the readable writing manipulations. There was no trend toward a readability effect with decreasing reading skill or reading time. Even in the memory experiment the effects were not consistent with readability predictions. The vocabulary simplification that resulted in improved comprehension actually produced the smallest change in readability score. Simplifying both vocabulary and syntax consistently failed to facilitate comprehension. Thus the findings offer no support of a readability formula as a feedback device for predicting the effects of simplification. The fact, however, that the simplification effect was only obtained when the task involved a significant memory component offers some support for Fass and Schumacher's (1978) proposal that the effectiveness of simplification will depend on the processing demands of the task.

Summary

The findings of Duffy and Kabance (1982) along with Kniffen *et al.* (1979) present a strong case against the readable writing approach to revision and hence against the use of a readability formula as a feedback device for the writer. We rewrote using fundamental readable writing techniques. Kniffen *et al.* (1979) used a readable writing style manual. In both cases conditions were optimal for the readability improvements to facilitate comprehension. Yet in both cases the manipulations, with one exception, resulted in no effect or, at best, marginal effect on comprehension. If the revision approach does not produce large comprehension effects under these ideal testing conditions, then there must be little expectation for the approach to be effective in practical application. The findings of Duffy and Kabance (1982), in fact, suggest that some readable writing techniques will not be effective in improving comprehension under any circumstances. The effectiveness of other simplification strategies will depend on the reading requirements and reading conditions.

ALTERNATIVES TO EXISTING READABILITY FORMULAS

The popularity of readability in both prediction and production indicates that there is a need, or at least a perceived need, for some low-cost, easy-to-apply method for assessing the comprehensibility of text. Therefore, it will do us no good to simply point out that readability formulas are inadequate for the task. It is too often the case that the researcher tells the practitioner what he or she should not do without presenting acceptable options. Because there is a need, the practitioner will use the best technique that is available. Without other options, this means the continued use of readability formulas. The "best" it should be remembered does not mean simply the most effective but rather the most cost-effective. Thus if we are to aid the practitioner and end the widespread misapplication of readability formulas, we must offer alternatives for which the increased effectiveness is not outweighed by the increased cost (Duffy, 1981). In concluding this Chapter I briefly examine the alternatives to existing readability formulas for achieving this quality control objective.

PREDICTION

In prediction, the goal is to identify whether or not a particular audience will be able to successfully use a text in a particular comprehension task. That is, we want to match the audience and the text given a particular comprehension objective. It would seem that there are only two alternatives for accomplishing this task—direct assessment or the use of prediction devices.

The direct assessment approach is really no different than the tryouts called for in summative and formative evaluation (Briggs, 1977; Redish, Felker, and Rose, 1981). The text is given to a sample of the audience, and comprehension is either tested directly or specific judgments as to comprehensibility are solicited. The approach however is not as straightforward as it might appear. There are numerous methodological issues involved: test item validity, representative sampling of the audience, sampling of the text, establishing a test context representative of the actual context of use, and so on. These issues would have to be resolved in each and every application resulting in the potential of a lengthy and complex evaluation that simply would not be feasible in most of the instances in which prediction is required. In addition to the complexity, there is the potential for exorbitant costs not only in supporting the evaluation but also in bringing the audience sample and the text together. It was to avoid just these complexities and costs that readability formulas were developed and used in the first place.

If we do not use direct assessment, then we must look to the development of readability formulas that will properly predict the skill required to comprehend a text. How then are we to modify the readability prediction approach? Existing readability formulas have come under considerable criticism because the predictor variables included in the formulas are not the underlying factors that cause variations in comprehension (Davison and Kantor, 1982; Miller and Kintsch, 1980). Thus Miller and Kintsch (1980) have attempted to develop a formula that reflects the coherence between propositions. Amiran and Jones (1982) propose a new definition of readability, based on the structure, texture, and information density of the text. Rubin (1981), meanwhile, proposes that the formulas must take into account how arguments are presented, what inferences must be made by the reader, the use of examples and other high level text characteristics.

Notice that all of these new or proposed readability formulas call for the identification of additional measures of the structure of the prose. Thus, in this approach better readability prediction is to be obtained by including prose structure variables that are the determinants of variation in prose comprehension. However, the particular strength of existing readability formulas has been that they do an excellent job of accounting for variations in the difficulty of prose (Bormouth, 1969). Identification of causative factors is not required for prediction. Prediction requires the identification of variables that account for, not necessarily those that cause, variation in performance. Indeed, inclusion of the causative factors would probably contribute little to the accuracy of prediction (McGinitie & Tretiak, 1971)! These approaches should not be considered new definitions of readability, if readability is the use of formulas for prediction. The identification of these causative variables is central to the writing and revision process, and thus these text factors rightfully reflect a new approach to instruction on effective text writing, an approach that reflects the growth in our knowledge of the cognitive processes involved in comprehension (Gagne & Bell, 1981; Duffy, 1981).

A readability approach, called the "degrees of reading power" (DRP) (The College Board, 1980), which involves both reading tests and a readability formula, has been proposed as providing a comprehensive system for matching readers with texts. The DRP readability formula is based on the readability formula developed by Bormouth in 1969. Like the formulas that have been the focus of this chapter, the Bormouth formula uses word and sentence measures to predict cloze comprehension scores on 100 to 150 word passages. The only modification of the Bormouth formula for use in the DRP system has been a change in scale so that possible DRP readability scores range between 15 and 100. The DRP readability formula, then, is comparable in development methodology and format to the traditional readability formulas discussed earlier.

The DRP readability formula is only one half of the DRP system. The other half is a reading test that uses a cloze-like testing procedure on paragraphs with known DRP readability scores. The competency of an individual is assessed in terms of the level of passage difficulty, measured in DRP readability units, on which successful performance is demonstrated. Thus the reading ability score is in DRP units rather than grade level. The combination of the readability formula and the reading test is described as a system for providing a "direct link . . . between individual student ability scores and the text readability values" (The College Board, 1980, p. 2) The system is promoted as a mechanism for selecting textbooks that the students will be able to comprehend.

Unfortunately, the DRP system, while very thorough in development, does not represent a new approach to matching people and texts. The DRP–Bormouth formula predicts the expected cloze test score on a passage. The Kincaid–Flesch formula predicts the reading test score required to obtain a specified level of cloze comprehension on a passage. The DRP system links to the ability of the individual by determining the ability of the individual to comprehend passages at particular DRP levels. The Kincaid–Flesch formula could be linked to the ability of the individual by simply testing the individual with the same reading test that was used in the development of the formula. In essence, the Kincaid–Flesch approach brings a reading test into the development of the readability formula, whereas the DRP system brings the readability formula into the development of the reading test. While there might be psychometric advantages to the DRP approach, the DRP system suffers the same conceptual problems as have been discussed for other formulas earlier in this chapter.

What, then, would be an appropriate prediction system? The purpose of the prediction system is to represent direct testing. For example, for the selection of school texts, we are attempting to predict whether or not students will be able to use their texts effectively in the classroom setting. In order to have an effective predictive device we must be certain that the criterion performance is properly assessed and that the environmental variables that produce variation in performance are properly represented. Because the intent is exact prediction we require different formulas for different comprehension tasks: locating information, low-level inference, integrating information, and so forth. While the criterion is the probability of successfully completing the particular comprehension task, the predictor variables must capture the variance in the environment that affects success. These factors include people variables (reading ability, background knowledge), text variables (prose, graphics, and format characteristics) and task variables (time to read, lecture, or other external support).

Of course there are an unlimited number of environmental variables and an unlimited number of comprehension tasks. The logic permits virtually an infinite number of formulas and an infinite number of predictor variables. However, the formulas are empirical devices and the proportion of variance in comprehension that can be captured determine the limits. At a minimum, however, we have to represent the major classes of environmental variables: text, people, and task. Thus far, the only consideration in both the design of the criterion test and in identifying the predictor variables has been the characteristics of the prose.

Consider the development of such a formula for self-study texts. The unit of analysis would not be a 200-word passage but rather the unit that is tested— probably the chapter. The comprehension score would simply be the score obtained on the regularly administered test. If the test items are considered inadequate in quality or number, additional items could be generated and administered as a second test. Next the ability of the test takers would be indexed. In a typical readability formula, reading ability is taken into account in determining the criterion, for example, 50% of the readers at a particular RGL score 35% on the comprehension test. In the proposed procedure reading ability would be a predictor variable, that is, comprehension is predicted for the particular text–reader combination. Next, physical attributes of the chapter would be indexed. Because a whole chapter is the basic unit, we can go beyond word and sentence factors and include various format and graphic factors. Data of this type would be collected on 30 or more texts—remembering that the use and the context of the use must be similar in each instance. Finally, a regression analysis is carried out and a prediction function is generated of the form:

$$P(\text{comprehension}) = a + b(\text{reading skill}) + c(\text{subject matter knowledge})$$
$$+ d(\text{prose factor}) + e(\text{format factor}) + f(\text{graphic factors})$$

Using this function we could thus analyze a text and predict the level of comprehension by an individual with a particular reading skill and background knowledge. If we are selecting a text for beginning students reading at the ninth-grade level, these predictor values would be entered along with the text values. If an expected comprehension score of .80 is obtained, the teacher would probably select the book. It must be remembered, however, that the formula must have been validated. Such a readability effort would, of course, require a tremendous amount of effort and therefore would not be carried out unless there was a high volume of text to be evaluated. The situation that is most obvious is textbook selection in the schools. The effort could be supported by a cross-district cooperative effort or by the textbook publishers. The other obvious situation is the military with the massive number of technical manuals we have been discussing throughout this chapter.

In actually carrying out the development of a formula as we just described, there will, of course, be a considerable number of psychometric issues involved in defining and measuring the variables. We would also expect there to be other variables added. For example, the format variable may be composed of several independent variables. Even after all of these issues are addressed and hopefully resolved the formula still may not be effective. The cognitive and information-processing variables involved in the real-world interaction of a reader with a text may involve too many complex interactions and may not be subject to any simplified scaling approach of the sort described (Bruce, Rubin, & Starr, 1981). If this is in fact true and the error variance cannot be accounted for, then the readability prediction effort should be abandoned. After all, the readability formula is an empirical tool, not a theoretical construct. If real-world variations in comprehension cannot be predicted with sufficient accuracy, it serves little purpose to turn to accurate predictions in artificial situations.

A potential alternative to the readability approach is the use of judges to evaluate comprehensibility. However, there is serious question as to whether even this approach will work. Wright (Chapter 4, this volume) and Carver (1974) found that untrained judges cannot reliably rate the comprehensibility of text. Furthermore, Carver met with only limited success in training journalism students to rate the comprehensibility of texts even when they were provided a set of standards for judging. Even experienced writers disagree and contradict each other in their specification of rules for comprehensible writing (Klare, n.d.). Perhaps a new kind of expertise could be trained. As I discuss in the next section, an expert representative of the reader, and thus an expert judge of comprehensibility, would be a welcome addition to the publication effort (see Macdonald-Ross & Waller, 1976). However, this type of expert judge would not be easily exportable to the field application at a particular school. Clearly, new research efforts are required to meet this need of the practitioner to match readers and text.

PRODUCING COMPREHENSIBLE TEXT

Guidelines

There are four basic strategies for controlling the comprehensibility of text in the production process: providing guidelines, imposing regulations, training personnel, and changing the management philosophy and process. We have discussed readability formulas as guidelines and as regulations and found them to be inadequate. We would argue that guidelines and regulations in general will be ineffective when relied upon as the primary control strategy. Guidelines at best can provide the novice with general strategies for preparing a document. Thus new authors of academic textbooks might find guidelines to be useful (Kirschner, 1981). However, except for the authors, everyone involved in the publication effort, for example, editors, illustrators, and typographers, is a professional. In the vast majority of writing efforts even the writers are professionals, for example, the writers for industrial and military manuals, newspapers, magazines, and

even many types of educational text material (see, e.g., Davison *et al.,* 1980 and
Carter, Chapter 7, this volume). Because the guidelines are simply statements of
expert knowledge, we would expect them to be of little help to the expert. At best
they could be used as a checklist for the expert to use in reviewing options. The
inadequacies of guidelines for experts becomes apparent when one considers the
simplicity of most guidelines. Professional authors know they should use concrete and familiar words, define new words when they are introduced, use simple
sentences, use illustrations to emphasize points, ensure that the main points are
not hidden, and so on. It will do us no good to provide such guidance. We must
focus on strategies for enabling or encouraging the author to prepare text consistent with his or her professional knowledge; we must get the author to do what
he or she knows should be done.

Regulations

Imposing regulations is one way to try to force the professional to meet desired
standards. A regulation is simply the imposition of a guideline as a requirement
rather than a suggestion. The objective of the regulation is quality control and
product uniformity. All publication houses have regulations in the form of house
rules under which the editor, author, typographer, and illustrator operate. All
military manuals prepared under contract must meet detailed contractual regulations known as specifications. These specifications include statements on writing
and illustrations and in many instances will include a readability formula score
requirement. If the regulation is to be specified in a contract or other legal
document, then it must also be phrased in such a way that it is objective and
measurable. An extreme example of the imposition of regulations to obtain a
comprehensible document is the Department of Defense's (1978) preparation of
a specification for comprehensibility. This is a 40+ page document in which all
the various guidelines for writing and illustrating are presented as objective,
measurable, and therefore contractually enforceable rules.

Within a large publication effort, the imposition of regulations is a necessary
condition for obtaining effective documents. Regulations provide for uniformity
in the design and style of the document, and they indicate the comprehension
issues and desired approach in producing a comprehensible text. However, no
matter how extensive and detailed they are, regulations are not sufficient for
producing a comprehensible document. A guideline imposed as regulation pre-
sumes that writing and illustrating are algorithmic processes. Although this may
be true, we are a long way from specifying the algorithms. Effective writing and
design is still very much of an art; we simply do not have an understanding of the
complex interactions among the myriad of linguistic, semantic, and perceptual
factors determining comprehension at any one time. The writing and formatting
of a particular sentence or preparation of a particular illustration depends on the
surrounding visual and semantic context. Because of this we find that when we

try to follow guidelines or regulations, the exception is very often the rule and failure to make the exception reduces the comprehensibility of the text.

The regulation may provide guidance but the expertise of the writer is required to determine the appropriateness of the guideline in the particular instance, to fine-tune the application, and to resolve the conflicts between the requirements of the multiple regulations that may apply in a particular instance. The shortcomings of the regulation approach to controlling comprehensibility can best be illustrated by the continuing difficulties the military services are experiencing with their manuals despite the extensive imposition of specifications (General Accounting Office, 1979). See Duffy (in press; 1981) and Wright (1981, this volume) for further discussion of the shortcomings of the regulation and guideline approach to obtaining comprehensible writing and design.

Computer-aided editing and authoring systems (e.g., Frase, 1980), like written regulations, require the algorithmic description of design applications and therefore have the same shortcomings. That is, the computer-aiding can only be suggestive and the applicability in a particular instance will depend on expert judgment. The advantages of computer-aiding are not in controlling the writing or design but in reducing the effort required for production. The computer systems can significantly aid the author and improve the comprehensibility of the document by providing options and checks at appropriate times that the author can respond to effortlessly. Computer-aiding can provide significant savings in labor as, for example, in formatting, in carrying out copyediting routines, or in readjusting text to accommodate a change in format or text. By making it easy to try out alternatives, the computer-aiding may also encourage the author–illustrator to explore alternative phrasings and formatting, which in turn could result in significant improvements in the document. Finally, the computer authoring can serve as a useful memory aid, ensuring that the author does not forget to attend to particular formatting and writing style requirements. Thus the computer may indicate that the sentence may be too complex or that a listing appears to have occurred and the author may want to exercise the list format option. These aids should substantially improve the quality of the document. However, once again, the aiding cannot replace but must work with expert judgment.

Training

The third alternative is to train the members of the publication team. Obviously, in the case of professionals, a typical training course in, for example, technical writing will be of little use. However, training in related disciplines can be utilized to provide a new orientation as well as new skills in writing and design. Writers may not appreciate the difficulty the reader will have with their text, they may view other issues as more important to the writing and design of the document, or they simply may not know how to assess the requirements of the user (Wright, this volume). Thus training in educational technology could provide the proper viewpoint as well as the ability to revise a text to make it more comprehensible and educationally sound. Carter (this volume) found just such an approach with editors to be very effective in improving the quality of correspondence texts.

The Transformer

The provision of appropriate training courses should be part and parcel of a redesign of the publication system so that the there is an agreed-upon primary objective of producing easily usable documents. That is, even an appropriate training program will be of minimal effectiveness if the publication system has primary goals that are not consistent with the user orientation, for example, the goal of sales. Competing goals or objectives is in fact a primary block to the development of usable texts especially in the production of military texts (Duffy, 1981; Wright, this volume). There are quality assurance systems in production; however, the goal of these systems is technical accuracy and completeness for technical materials and aesthetics for more general educational materials. Macdonald-Ross and Waller (1976) have argued that another quality assurance system is required that ensures that the document is in a form that the reader can understand. They call this activity the transformer process in that the message of the writer–illustrator is transformed into a user-oriented document. The "transformer office" would review the document at each stage of development with the sole focus of the comprehensibility and ease of use for the intended audience. In practice such an office would have sufficient authority to assure that the required changes are made despite the cost and time requirements. We would propose that a system resembling the transformer is a requirement for the production of comprehensible, plain English documents.

REFERENCES

Amiran, M., & Jones, B. F. (1982). Toward a new definition of readability. *Educational Psychologist, 17,* 13–30.

Biersner, R. J. (1975, May). *Reading grade levels of Navy rate training manuals and nonresident career courses* (CNET Rep. 2-75). Pensacola, FL: Chief of Naval Education and Training.

Bormuth, J. R. (1967). Comparable cloze and multiple-choice comprehension test scores. *Journal of Reading, 10,* 291–299.

Bormouth, J. R. (1969, March). *Development of readability analyses* (Contract # OEG-3-7-070053-0326). Washington, DC: U.S. Office of Education.

Briggs, L. J. (Ed.). (1977) Instructional design: Principles and applications. Englewood Cliffs, NJ: Educational Technology Publications.

Bruce, B., Rubin, L., & Starr, L. (1981, August). *Why readability formulas fail* (Reading Education report No. 28). Champaign, IL: Center for the Study of Reading.

Caird, H. G. (1975, May). *Publication cost management* (Anthology Series No. 3). Washington, DC: Society for Technical Communication.

Carver, R. P. (1974, September). *Measuring the reading difficulty levels of Navy Training manuals* (Tech. Rep.). Washington, DC: Office of Naval Research. (NTIS No. AD 780 448/7).

Carver, R. P. (1974b, October). *Measuring the reading ability levels of Navy personnel* (Tech. Rep.). Washington, DC: Office of Naval Research.

Caylor, J. S., Sticht, T. G., Fox, L. C., & Ford, J. P. (1973, March). *Methodologies for determining reading requirements of military occupational specialties* (HumRRO Tech. Rep. 73–5). Presidio of Monterey, CA: Human Resources Research Organization. (NTIS No. AD 758 872)

Charrow, V. (1979, December). *What is "plain English" anyway?* Washington, DC: American Institue for Research.

Coleman, E. B. (1962). Improving comprehensibility by shortening sentences. *Journal of Applied Psychology, 46,* 131–134.

College Board, The. (1980). *Degrees of reading power: Readability report.* New York: The College Board.

Curran, T. E. (1977, June). *Survey of technical manual readability and comprehensibility* (Tech. Rep. 77–37). San Diego, CA: Navy Personnel Research and Development Center. (NTIS No. AD A042 335)

Curran, T. E. (1980, March). *Tri-service literacy and readability: Workshop proceedings* (NPRDC SR 80-12). San Diego, CA: Navy Personnel Research and Development Center. (NTIS No. AD A083 04310)

Dale, E., & Chall, J. S. (1948). A formula for predicting readability. *Educational Research Bulletin, 11,* 37–54.

Davidson, A., & Cantor, R. (1982). On the failure of readability formulas to define readable texts: A case study from adaptations. *Reading Research Quarterly, 17,* 187–208.

Davison, A., Kantor, R., Hannah, J., Hermon, G., Lutz, R., & Salzillo, R. (1980, March). *Limitations of readability formulas in guiding applications of texts* (Tech. Rep. 162). Champaign, IL: Center for the Study of Reading. (ERIC No. ED 184 090)

Department of Defense. (1978, October). *Comprehensibility standards for technical manuals (metric)* (DOD-STD-1685 (SH)). Washington, DC: Department of Defense.

Department of the Air Force. (1977, March). *Publication Management: Writing Understandable Publications* (HQ Operating Instruction 5.2). Washington, DC: Headquarters U.S. Air Force.

Department of the Army. (1978, December). *Improving the readability of Army publications* (DA Circular 310-9). Washington, DC: Department of the Army.

Duffy, T. M. (1980, November). *Industrial manuals: A matter of priorities* In David Jonassen (Ed.) *The technology of text* (Vol. 2). Englewood Cliffs, NJ: Educational Technology Publication. In press.

Duffy, T. M. (1981). Organizing and utilizing document design options. *Information Design Journal. 2-4,* 256–266.

Duffy, T. M., & Kabance, P. (1982). Testing a readable writing approach to text revision. *Journal of Educational Psychology, 74,* 733–548.

Duffy, T. M., & Nugent, W. (1978, April). *Reading Skill Levels in the Navy* (NPRDC SR 78-19). San Diego, CA: Navy Personnel Research and Development Center. (NTIS No. AD A054 859/4)

Entin, E. B., & Klare, G. R. (1978). Some inter-relationships of readability, cloze, and multiple-choice scores on a reading comprehension test. *Journal of Reading Behavior, 10,* 417–436.

Fass, W., & Schumacher, G. M. (1978). Effects of motivation, subject activity, and readability on the retention of prose materials. *Journal of Educational Psychology, 70,* 803–807.

Flesch, R. F. (1948). A new readability yardstick. *Journal of Applied Psychology, 32,* 221–233.

Flesch, R. F. (1949). *The art of readable writing.* New York: Harper.

Feldman, M. E. (1964). *The effects of learning by programmed and text format at three levels of difficulty* Unpublished dissertation, Cornell University.

Frase, L. (1980, April). *Computer aids for text editing and design.* Symposium presented at the annual meeting of the American Educational Research Association, Boston, Ma.

Gagne, E., & Bell, M. (1981). The use of cognitive psychology in the development and evaluation of textbooks. *Educational Psychologist, 16,* 83–100.

Gates, A. I., & MacGinite, W. H. (1965). *Gates-MacGinite reading tests, Survey D.,* New York: Teachers College Press.

General Accounting Office. (1979, July). *Improved Management of Maintenance Manuals Needed in DOD* (LCD-79-105). Washington, DC: U.S. General Accounting Office.

Goetz, E. T. (1975, November). *Sentences in lists and in connected discourse* (Tech. Rep. 3). Urbana-Champaign, IL: Laboratory for Cognitive Studies in Education. (ERIC No. ED 134927)

Hiller, J. H. (1974). Learning from prose text: Effects of readability level, inserted question difficulty, and individual differences. *Journal of Educational Psychology, 66,* 202–211.

Holland, V. M. (1981, May). *Psycholinguistic alternatives to readability formulas* (Tech. Rep. No. 12). Washington, DC: American Institute for Research.

Hooke, L., De Leo, J., & Slaughter, S. (1979). *Readability of Air Force publications: A criterion referenced evaluation* (AFHRL-TR-79-21). Brooks Air Force Base, TX: Air Force Human Resources Laboratory. (NTIS No. AD A075 237)

Kern, R. P. (1979). *Usefulness of readability formulas for achieving Army readability objectives: Research and state-of-the-art applied to the Army's problem.* Fort Benjamin Harrison, ID: Technical Advisory Service, U.S. Army Research Institute. (NTIS No. AD A086 408/2)

Kincaid, J. P., Aagard, J., O'Hara, J., & Cottrell, L. (1981, April). *Computer readability editing system* (Technical Note 4-81). Orlando, FL: Navy Training Analysis and Evaluation Ground.

Kincaid, J. P., & Delionbach, L. (1973). Validation of the automated readability index: A follow-up. *Human Factors, 15,* 17–20.

Kincaid, J. P., Fishburne, R. P., Rogers, & Chissom, B. S. (1975, February). *Derivation of new readability formulas (Automated Readability Index, Fog Count, and Flesch Reading Ease Formula) for Navy enlisted personnel* (Research Branch Rep. 8-75). Millington, TN: Naval Air Station. (NTIS No. A006 655/5)

Kirschner, P. (1981). *Manual for editors and authors.* Paper presented at the annual meeting of the American Education Research Association, Los Angeles, CA.

Klare, G. R. (1979). *Readability standards for Army-wide publications* (Evaluation Report 79-1). Fort Benjamin Harrison, IN: U.S. Army Administrative Center.

Klare, G. R. (Undated). *Some suggestions for clear writing found in fifteen sourcebooks.* Unpublished Manuscript, Ohio University. Athens, Ohio.

Klare, G. R. (1963). *The measurement of readability.* Ames, IO: Iowa State University Press.

Klare, G. R. (1975). *A manual for readable writing.* Glen Burnie, MD: REM Company (119A Roesler Road).

Klare, G. R. (1976). A second look at the validity of readability formulas. *Journal of Reading Behavior, 8,* 129–152.

Klare, G. (1981). Readability indices: Do they inform or misinform? *Information Design Journal. 2-4,* 251–255.

Klare, G. R., Mabry, J., & Gustafson, L. (1955). The relationship of style difficulty to immediate retention and to acceptability of technical material. *Journal of Educational Psychology, 46,* 287–295.

Klare, G. R., & Smart, K. (1973). Analysis of the readability level of selected USAFI instructional materials. *Journal of Educational Research, 67,* 176.

Kniffin, J. D., Stevenson, C. R., Klare, G. R., Entin, E., Slaughter, S., & Hooke, L. (1979, November). *Operational consequences of a literacy gap* (AFHRL-TR-79-22). Brooks Air Force Base, TX: Air Force Human Resources Laboratory. (NTIS No. AD A084 782/2)

Macdonald-Ross, M., & Waller, R. (1976). The Transformer. *The Penrose Annual, 69,* 141–152.

MacGinitie, W., & Tretiak, R. (1971). Sentence depth measures as predictors of reading difficulty. *Reading Research Quarterly, 6,* 364–377.

Miller, J., & Kintsch, W. (1980). Readability and recall of short passages: A theoretical analysis. *Journal of Experimental Psychology: Human Learning and Memory, 6,* 335–353.

Mockovak, W. G. (1974, December). *Literacy skills and requirements in Air Force Career ladders* (AFHRL-TR-74-90). Lowry, AFB, CO: Air Force Human Resources Laboratory.

Muller, W. (1976, September). Review of Navy research on the usability of technical manuals. In T. G. Sticht and D. Welty- Zapf (Eds.), *Reading and readability research in the Armed Services* (humR RO FR-WD-CA-76-4). Alexandria, VA: Human Resources Research Organization. (NTIS No. AD A034 730/2)

Nelson, M. J., & Denny, E. C. (1960). *The Nelson-Denny Reading Test* (Revised by J. J. Brown). Boston, MA: Houghton.

Nolte, K. F. (1937). Simplification on vocabulary and comprehension in reading. *Elementary English Review, 14,* 119–124.

Pearson, P. D. (1974/1975). The effects of grammatical complexity on children's comprehension, recall, and conception of certain semantic relations. *Reading Research Quarterly, 10,* 155–192.

Pressman, R. (1979, December). *Legislative and regulatory progress on the readability of insurance policies.* Washington, DC: American Institute for Research.

Rankin, E. F., & Culhane, J. W. (1969). Comparable cloze and multiple-choice comprehension test scores. *Journal of Reading, 13,* 193–198.

Reder, L. (1978, November). *Comprehension and retention of prose: A literature review* (Tech. Rep. No. 108). Champaign, IL: Center for the Study of Reading. (ERIC No. ED 165 114)

Redish, J. (1979, December). *Readability.* Washington, DC: American Institute for Research.

Redish, J., Felker, D., & Rose, A. (1981). Evaluating the effects of document design principles. *Information Design Journal. 2–4,* 236–243.

Smith, E. A., & Kincaid, J. P. (1960). Deprivation and validation of the Automated Readability Index for use with technical materials. *Human Factors, 12,* 457–464.

Sticht, T., & Welty-Zapf, D. (1976, September). *Reading and readability research in the Armed Forces* (HumRRO FR-WD-CA-76-4). Alexandria, VA: Human Resources Research Organization. (NTIS No. AD AO34 730/2)

Sulit, R. A., & Fuller, J. J. (1976, March). *Navy technical manual system (NTMS) program summary* (TM-186-76-1). Bethesda, MD: Naval Ship Research and Development Center.(NTIS No. AD A029 483/5

Tuinman, J. J., and Brady, M. E. (1973, December). *How does vocabulary account for variance on reading comprehension tests? A preliminary to an instructional analysis.* Presented at the annual meeting of the National Reading Conference, Houston, TX.

Wright, P. (1981). Informed design for forms. *Information Design Journal. 2-4,* 151–178.

CHAPTER 7

Lessons in Text Design from an Instructional Design Perspective

INTRODUCTION

It has been suggested that the ideal teaching instrument would be low cost, easily portable, amenable to random search, and usable in self-paced study. As we all know there is no device that better fits this description than a textbook. Even in a day when the electronic options for communication and learning are emerging at an accelerated rate, and those approaches involving videodisks, video cassette recorders, electronic text, and personal computers are touted as the wave of the future, it is still the case that books and other forms of print-based communication constitute the overwhelming means by which we preserve and communicate knowledge in our world. I believe this will continue to be true, at least until our computer and communications technology friends are able to produce a large-capacity personal computer and video playback combination that fits easily into one hand and costs a few dollars.

Thus, it is appropriate that we continue to address ourselves to the development and improvement of the means whereby we can design more usable and effective texts. Moreover, it is especially appropriate that this be done through a cooperative dialog involving representatives from both sides of the research and development (R & D) equation. Current practice in text design, as Orna (Chapter 2 in the present volume) and Wright (Chapter 4) have suggested, depends on a confluence of objective and subjective inputs from a variety of sources. In fact, in most instances of publishing, it is probably the subjective inputs of editors and designers that most often dominate in the text design process as they grapple with economic and schedule constraints in trying to meet productivity requirements. It would seem, then, that text design practitioners have at least as much to say

DESIGNING USABLE TEXTS

about the real problems of arranging words on pages in optimum configurations as text researchers do about the scientific and algorithmic processes that might someday be available to assist with this.

For example, Frase, Macdonald, and Keenan (Chapter 5 in the present volume) give an interesting and insightful analysis of the problems and promise inherent in the development of a science of text design. They point toward a day when computers will be able to analyze text and generate prescriptions for its improvement. Already there are programs available for this that can analyze various linguistic properties of text, describe grammatical errors of various kinds, and make a limited comparison of stylistic variables (see, e.g., the writer's workbench discussed in Chapter 5). However, while such microanalytic procedures are no doubt useful, they do not have the ability to deal with many of the larger concerns in any text development process. These concerns include the appropriateness and adequacy of the textual content for a given audience, purpose, and context configuration; the internal consistency and coherence of ideas; and the ability of the text to stimulate the reader's information-processing apparatus in a suitable manner. Only when a science of text design can inform us on these matters will it reach the level of generality needed to substantially enhance our ability to produce usable and effective printed materials.

I am also concerned about our ability to disseminate knowledge about text design. We already know how to do more than we are doing in this area. By that I mean there is already a large reservoir of knowledge produced over the past several decades through research on learning from textual materials that is relevant to the design of effective texts. But this knowledge has not been well put to use. Pick up any recently published journal, magazine, textbook, or reference manual. Anyone who knows a little of the literature on prose research or cognitive psychology can describe several ways to improve its usability and effectiveness given a reasonable understanding of the audience and purpose for the publication. Moreover, the suggested improvements will not need to be esoteric prescriptions from some recently published state-of-the-art review in psychology, but such suggestions as to provide more explicit organizational information or to reduce the abstractness of the information through better use of concrete descriptions and pictorial illustrations. The problem, then, is not always a matter of not knowing what makes a difference but of getting text designers to implement the things that are already known to make a difference.

I would like to highlight these and related issues in the context of the design of printed instructional materials for use in a distance learning context. I have chosen this context for two reasons. First, it is the one in which I have worked extensively and from which I am best able to draw examples. Second, to design materials for learning at a distance involves consideration of a broad range of design variables that encompass many if not most of those that might be encountered in designing other kinds of textual materials. It provides a nearly ideal vehicle for examining current knowledge and practice in text design and development.

The following section discusses several questions that must be answered before a text design activity of any kind can be undertaken. Next we look at some of the contributions learning research can make toward increasing the effectiveness of text designs. Finally, we examine a number of the elements that must be considered in the management of a text design process if we are to produce better texts.

PRECONDITIONS FOR THE DESIGN OF USABLE TEXTS

There are several nagging questions that come to mind when one considers the question of how to design usable and effective texts. Specifically, usable by whom, for what purpose, and under what conditions? A text design process must be informed by answers to these questions before it can even begin to produce suitable materials. At the International Correspondence Institute (ICI) we go through a formal analysis of these concerns as part of the development of a "course strategy." In a more general text development situation, we might label this a "text strategy." Such an analysis establishes the criteria by which it is possible to judge usability and effectiveness of the materials. Without this analysis there is little possibility that instructional materials will meet anyone's criteria.

AUDIENCE

The question of who will use the text is important because it cannot be assumed that textual materials designed for maximum usability by one group will necessarily be so for another. For example, I once had a student whose mother tongue was not English ask me for a clarification of a particular section of English-language text he had been reading. He had spent a considerable amount of time trying to decipher a particular paragraph and relate it to the main topic under discussion. The problem was that in this particular portion of text the author had embedded a joke to illustrate a point. Not recognizing this, the student was trying to approach the statement as a serious comment on the topic. Now, I have generally found that the occasional use of humor in a text is a welcome relief from the normally dry prose of academic writing. In fact, humor is often useful for enhancing the interestingness and concreteness of textual materials and, consequently, their usability and effectiveness. However, if the user lacks the linguistic skill or experience needed for correct understanding of humorous content, it may actually reduce usability and effectiveness.

No doubt there are many interactions between text and user characteristics that could be cited to illustrate the importance of having a clear definition of the target audience before implementing a text design. We encounter many of these at ICI because we produce materials for use in cross-cultural settings, but even within a given culture there are variations in educational and experiential background and intellectual functioning that should effect the way a text is designed—assumed reading ability not being the least of these. If we are to have a science of text design, it will need to specify under what conditions different characteristics of text work for audiences possessing different linguistic, educational, and intellectual backgrounds.

Moreover, if such knowledge is to become a routine feature in the development of textual materials in the real world of publishing, it will need to be captured in an algorithmic form, preferably in computer models, as Frase, Macdonald, and Keenan have suggested in Chapter 5 of this volume. But I think there is considerable work to do before that will happen. In the meantime, most of us who take seriously the need to tailor texts to audiences will have to rely on the pooled expertise, experience, and informed intuition of our writers, editors, and instructional designers for this purpose.

PURPOSE

Defining the purpose for a given publication may be even more critical than defining the audience. Printed materials are used for many purposes—to learn, for entertainment, to execute procedures related to work, as reference materials, and so on. Those things that make the text usable for one purpose may not do so for another. In fact, the usability-enhancing devices created under one assumption of purpose might actually interfere with usability for another purpose.

If I were designing a self-instructional cookbook, for instance, I would include statements of objectives, study questions and exercises, marginal cues and diagrams, flow charts, and algorithms. In other words, I would use all of the generally accepted educational paraphenalia that theory and experience suggest will facilitate the usability and instructional effectiveness of educational materials. But these same features would probably not be conducive to usability in a cookbook intended for reference. Quite the contrary, they would likely interfere with usefulness for this purpose.

I suspect that many of the failings of publishers to produce effective and usable texts have resulted from a confusion of purposes. Because it is expensive to duplicate materials in several forms for different purposes, publishers try to make do with single multipurpose publications. Technical manuals, for instance, which are best developed as reference materials for expert users, are often given double duty as training manuals. Even if this dual purpose is defined in the beginning, it may give rise to a hybrid that does not serve either need very well.

Unless purpose is given sharp focus for all involved in a text design and development project, it is unlikely that the resulting text will be optimally usable.

CONTEXT

Finally, a text design must be informed by an understanding of the context in which the materials are to be used. A reference manual designed for the hold of a ship, for instance, would require a different design configuration from one intended for use in an office. A cookbook with glossy, nonporous pages might be more usable than one printed on standard paper. Size and style of type, clarity of graphics, size of the text, type of paper, and so on, are all variables that might be affected by different user contexts. Unfortunately such matters are more often determined by economic constraints and marketing conditions than thoughtful analysis of the context of use.

At ICI we produce self-instructional materials for a distance learning system not unlike that employed by the British Open University, except in scale. Because our materials are studied in nearly a hundred different countries by individuals for whom English is often a second language, we have designed study guides that employ as many potentially facilitative educational devices as we can think of. Those people who run our production division have often commented that these devices significantly increase production time and cost compared to standard book formats. However, because ICI is a school and our study materials are designed for educational purposes, we are able to maintain strict adherence to these requirements. If the production and marketing concerns were the only ones being heard, it would be much harder to meet our educational effectiveness criteria.

Lest this all appear to be belaboring the obvious, let me hasten to add that these are exactly the kinds of issues that text designers routinely face. And they are the kinds of issues researchers must address in the development of new and better approaches to text design and development.

I have called the three factors—audience, purpose, and context—preconditions for text design because I believe it is only within the intersection of these that it makes much sense to talk about specific approaches to improving text usability.

CONTRIBUTIONS OF LEARNING RESEARCH TO TEXT DESIGN

Since the mid-1960s, the dominant focus in learning research, especially as it relates to learning from text, has shifted from behavioral to cognitive psychology. Greeno (1980) and Calfee (1981) have recently described this transition.

Nevertheless, we can find within the discipline of instructional-materials development a deep imprint of behavioral psychology. The emphasis on use of instructional objectives, a requirement for student response, and the provision of corrective feedback are all examples of this influence. Moreover, coupled with systems thinking, behavioral psychology has helped produce the overall approach to instructional development that characterizes most existing models. These models tend to emphasize the systematic prespecification of objectives, development and formative evaluation of the materials, and feedback and modification of instruction in an iterative process intended to provide empirical validation of instructional success.

More recently the influence of behavioral psychology has begun to give way to that of cognitive psychology. The main difference is the emphasis in cognitive psychology on knowledge structures within the mind, how these structures are built and maintained and their influence on subsequent learning. The learner is viewed as an active participant in learning who processes and manipulates the information presented to him or her.

I believe that the combined contributions of both behavioral and cognitive psychology have provided powerful tools for the development of effective textual materials. In fact, as I mentioned earlier, it seems we already know a lot more about how to design effective texts than we are commonly doing.

For instance, I believe the following observations can assume the status of general principles for the design of instructional materials:

1. Where reading is purposeful, orienting devices such as objectives, headings, key words, and advance organizers contribute to understanding, learning, and retention.

Orienting information in a text (material that informs the reader of the purpose, goals, and structure of the text) serves a number of purposes. The first is motivational. A carefully written introduction can arouse the readers' interest and curiosity by establishing a set of questions or posing problems in which the student might have interest. It should also inform the reader of the purpose for the materials and give him or her a reason to study them. Several of the ways in which this can be done include statements of questions to be answered in a text, a presentation of objectives, and the provision of a real-world application for the knowledge or skill to be acquired. It hardly seems worth stating that students are more likely to learn something that they can relate to their personal interests. However, it is not always obvious to students just how a given portion of text relates to their overall educational goals, particularly because students have often been subjected to training that more close suited their instructors' interests than their own. Although students can learn without an intent to do so, it makes much more sense to enlist their deliberate cooperation in the enterprise.

Besides the fairly obvious logical relationship between a student's perception of the purpose of a lesson and his or her motivation to learn, there is evidence that arousing curiosity regarding the content of instruction facilitates learning (Berlyne, 1954, 1960; Frick & Cofer, 1972.) Thus it would appear that a careful delineation of the purpose of a lesson coupled with an example of a real-world application should have positive effects on the student's motivation to learn.

A second important contribution of orienting material involves pointing out the general structure of the lesson content and relating it to the learner's previous knowledge. In general, this notion harkens back to the concept of an ''advance organizer'' proposed by Ausubel (1960). Although there is a continuing discussion of exactly what constitutes an advance organizer and under what circumstances they facilitate learning as Ausubel claims (e.g., Barnes & Clawson, 1975), the evidence seems to generally favor a conclusion that advance organizers are helpful (Mayer, 1979, 1983).

2. Concretizing and simplifying textual content through the use of examples, analogies, metaphors, verbal and visual illustrations, flowcharts, and algorithms facilitates understanding, learning, and retention.

One of the reasons textual materials are sometimes ineffective is that they are written at too high a level of abstraction. Readability formulas are useful in predicting learning from text because many of the variables that enter into them, such as word familiarity, number of syllables and sentence length are related to abstractness. It so happens that short words and active sentences tend to evoke concrete referents more often and more easily than long words and passive sentences.

The work of Paivio (1979) has amply demonstrated the facilitative effects of text that is concrete and gives rise to imagery as compared to abstract text. In colloquial wisdom ''a picture is worth a thousand words,'' and many learners have wished for that single picture as they struggle to derive meaning from a thousand or so words of abstract, jargon-saturated text. Often a few well-placed diagrams, drawings, or pictures will clarify a concept or procedure in a way no amount of additional prose could do (see, e.g., Parkhurst & Dwyer 1983).

On the other hand, even careful attempts to weave illustrative written material into text has its benefits. If a picture is worth a thousand words, a good concrete example is at least worth several hundred words of further definition and explanation (Merrell & Boutwell, 1973; Tennyson & Park, 1980). In fact, a carefully developed presentation that interposes examples and written and visual illustrations of one kind or another within the normally abstract propositional content of educational prose can go far toward bringing the meaning of things within the grasp of the average person. Moreover, if we take the trouble to reduce event sequences to flowcharts and algorithms, many people will be able to understand a communication who could not or would not do so on their own.

3. Causing the student to interact meaningfully with the text through activities designed to induce processing facilitates understanding, learning, and retention.

This is the area in which cognitive psychology has had its most substantial effect on instructional design. Early work in the behaviorist tradition tended to emphasize the importance of "active responding" without differentiations as to the nature of that responding. It was left to cognitive psychology to emphasize the role of different levels and kinds of processing activities. Basically, we know that individuals will only learn at a meaningful level when the information-processing requirements demand that they do so. If processing requirements are limited to a superficial, rote level, individuals will seldom spontaneously generalize to higher levels. Thus texts that have a teaching purpose must include activities that will assure that individuals engage in intellectual activities congruent with the teaching objectives. Moreover, if there is anything that research on questions inserted into the text teaches us, it is that we should not expect students to acquire knowledge, cognitive structures, or skills that have not been subjected to some sort of response requirement (Rickards & Denner, 1978; Rothkopf, 1966). In other words, learning comes about with some kind of intellectual work. Seldom will students know what kind of intellectual work is appropriate on their own, and even if they do they will seldom do it unless it is a requirement. It is the role of the instructional designer to build these requirements into the text.

SUMMARY

My intent in this section has been to highlight some of the principles derivable from learning research that are pertinent to the question of how to design effective texts. My point is not that we already know enough about text design, or that there is no need to continue to press toward a full-fledged science of text design, but that we already know a great deal that is not routinely made a part of the text development process except, perhaps, in the design of self-instructional materials. Here it is done because the purposes of the material could not be achieved otherwise. With self-instructional materials all the help you are going to give the reader–learner must be included, or you have lost your teaching opportunity.

I believe these same devices can be used profitably to design textual materials of other kinds, such as technical manuals and textbooks. To the degree that the designer of any kind of text actively seeks to aid the reader to seek out the intended meanings, represent them concretely in cognitive structure, and constructively relate them to other elements in the reader's existing cognitive structure, it should be a better text.

Now, the question is why we do not more often see these elements manifested in textbooks and other written materials. Probably it is because the people who usually write and edit these kinds of materials have little or no formal training in either cognitive or instructional psychology. In other words, these principles are known but not by the people who write and edit most of the texts we encounter on our bookshelves. And this same problem of knowledge diffusion will confront us as we learn even more and develop better approaches to text design. Ultimately, it is not what is known by the theorist but what is known by the practitioner that sets the limits on the transfer of knowledge into actual practice. Whether text design practitioners possess the aforementioned knowledge base is in part a management issue related to their backgrounds and the roles they are asked to play. This is the subject of the next section.

MANAGING A TEXT DESIGN PROCESS

In the previous section I reviewed several of the general principles of text design that could be more routinely used by text designers to produce effective texts. Below are described some of the things that might be done in managing a text production system to ensure that these principles are followed. In doing so I draw upon some of my experiences in directing the text development activities of ICI. Some of the characteristics of our system are as follows.

1. The role of the writer is limited to that of content expert.

When ICI first began to develop materials for distance education, we recruited academics with specialties in various subject matter areas, gave them a week-long crash course in instructional design, and turned them loose writing self-instructional guides to accompany standard textbooks. Our writers dutifully developed learning objectives, study exercises, and test items. Our editors were told to preserve as much of the writer's material and style as possible and to concentrate on matters of grammar and language usage. The editor's role was clearly secondary to that of the writer who was assumed to know not only what should be taught but how it should be taught. Because most of the writers were also teachers this did not seem to be such a bad assumption.

But it did not work very well. The courses we got were fine on the content side but generally weak on the instructional process side. In general, the materials were weak in all three of the areas described in the learning theory section of this chapter. The objectives, though written with the correct behavioral language, often bore little relationship to either the relevant content or the study exercises that were presumably intended to provide practice toward their mastery. Moreover, the content-testing interactions tended toward the "tell 'em and ask 'em what you told 'em" syndrome of early programmed instruction. There was little drive toward higher levels of cognitive processing. When an author did include a good higher-level exercise, the text often lacked sufficient information for a student to make an adequate response. In other words, we suffered all of the problems that most text designers suffer when the writers are responsible for both content and presentation.

To correct these problems we took another tack. We began to limit writers to the role of content expert. In fact, we even defined this as the contribution of ideas rather than specific word patterns, so as to give ourselves the liberty to engage in extensive rewriting of original material wherever necessary to achieve instructional goals. In short, we redefined the writer's role, weakened it considerably, and undertook an enlarged role for our own editorial–development staff. As a result we began to get far better instructional materials that better served our ends and at the same time pleased our writers because it tended to make them look better than they might have otherwise.

But in order to make this work we also had to change the role of our editor. This is what I discuss in the next section.

> 2. The editor's role is filled by persons with training in instructional theory and design.

Successful editors or developers of textual materials must have a fairly broad range of skills. They must possess a strong sensitivity to language including the technical skills of good writing. They need to know something of the subject being written about, although, obviously, less than the content expert. At least they need to know as much as the intended audience for the publication.

Finally, it is my belief that they need to know something about learning and cognition. They need to know how people process information and what makes a difference in their ability to do so when confronted with information presented in text. Also, they need to know how to induce appropriate text-processing behaviors on the part of readers.

Although one can never guarantee that readers will perform the intellectual processing activities a text designer builds into the materials, at least the activities should be included so the conscientious reader who actively wishes to pursue a learning objective will be given the best opportunity to acquire the intended knowledge or skills. This is why it is important to specify clearly beforehand the intentions for the text, especially if it is instructional text. This tells the readers what you hope to accomplish and allows them to also establish that as a personal goal if it suits their fancy. Instead of letting a writer who knows little about cognitive or instructional theory muddle through the development of text processing exercises, we expect the editor to take on this responsibility.

So instead of giving our writers a crash course in instructional development, we give our editors a course of somewhat greater substance and duration on the subject. We even change the job title from ''editor'' to ''instructional development specialist.'' For a while that title was more a promise than a reality, but over a period with careful on-the-job review of work products, and systematic feedback regarding needed improvement, the notion began to take hold. Our editor–developers were able to view themselves as the ones primarily responsible for taking the content given by the writer and molding it into an effective instructional instrument.

>   3. There is a continuous review–feedback process by an editorial
>   committee familiar with the entire curriculum under development.

The third major element in the process of managing our text production system is an aggressive review and feedback process. No one writer or editor has the general perspective needed to judge how his or her work relates to those being completed by different teams. To provide this perspective and to assure that each course fits appropriately in terms of content and intended outcomes with other courses related to it, we have constituted an editorial review committee comprised of the heads of the divisions responsible for the development of the instructional materials and the utilization of the developed curriculum. These reviewers judge the general instructional quality of the materials that have been developed and decide whether the materials adequately match the overall goals of the curriculum. Besides these general considerations, the committee will ask whether the objectives, content, and study exercises appear to be congruent in a way that will promote optimum learning, and whether the organization and logical flow of ideas seem appropriate. If a computer could do this review function, this would be ideal; but until computers are equipped for the task, someone must. Moreover, that someone must be sufficiently knowledgeable about the desirable characteristics of text to be able to provide meaningful feedback to writers and editors. It seems to me that, given the level of technology that currently exists in this area, it is only through a production–review process similar to the one I have described that we can expect to maintain adequate control over the quality of text designs in the world of publishing most practitioners inhabit.

CONCLUSION

How is it, then, that we can produce more usable and effective texts while we wait for the outcomes of research and theory to catch up to the problems of day-to-day text design? The basic premise of this chapter has been that we already know a great deal that can be applied to do a better job. We can do a better job in defining the who, why, and where issues for a text design project. We can do better at incorporating the existing knowledge base of cognitive and instructional psychology into our designs. And we can do better at defining the roles of those who produce texts and providing them with the expertise needed to fulfill their responsibilities.

These are not startling revelations, to be sure. In fact, in a sense, they seem to be sufficiently obvious that they might have even been left unsaid. But, if there is anything I have learned as I have become involved in the development side of the technology transfer equation, it is that sometimes we lose sight of the known in search of the unknown. Those who wish to push back the frontiers of linguistic knowledge need to remember that many of the deep unexplored mysteries that tempt their consideration are often little more than minor nuisances to those who have to write something every Monday morning. If the history of text research repeats that of instructional research, we will find that a large proportion of the variance associated with text usability and effectiveness will be captured by a relatively small number of variables, such as those I have described in this chapter. If so, the problem of producing usable written materials may have less to do with discovering a host of new principles than with learning to routinely apply those we already know.

REFERENCES

Ausubel, D. P. (1960). The use of advance organizers in learning and retention of meaningful verbal material. *Journal of Educational Psychology, 51*, 267–272.

Barnes, B. R., & Clawson, E. U. (1975). Do advance organizers facilitate learning? Recommendations for further research based on an analysis of 32 studies. *Review of Educational Research, 45*, 637–659.

Berlyne, D. (1954). An experimental study of human curiosity. *British Journal of Psychology, 45*, 256–265.

Berlyne, D. (1960). *Conflict, arousal and curiosity.* New York: McGraw-Hill.

Calfee, R. C. (1981). Cognitive psychology and educational practice. In D. Berliner (Ed.), *Review of research in education* (Vol. 9). Washington, DC: American Educational Research Association.

Frick, J. W., & Cofer, C. N. (1972). Berlyne's demonstration of epistemic curiosity: An experimental re-evaluation. *British Journal of Psychology, 63*, 221–228.

Greeno, J. G. (1980). Psychology of learning, 1960–1980: One participant's observations. *American Psychologist, 35*, 713–728.

Mayer, R. E. (1979). Can advance organizers influence meaningful learning, *Review of Educational Research, 49*, 371–383.

Mayer, R. E. (1983). Can you repeat that? Qualitative effects of repetition and advance organizers on learning from science prose. *Journal of Educational Psychology, 75*, 40–49.

Merrell, M. D., & Boutwell, R. C. (1973). Instructional development methodology and research. In F. N. Kerlinger (Ed.), *Review of research in education.* Itasca, IL: Peacock.

Paivio, A. (1979). *Imagery and verbal processes.* Hillsdale, NJ: Erlbaum.

Parkhurst, P. E., & Dwyer, F. M. (1983). An experimental assessment of students I.Q. level and their ability to profit from visualized instruction. *Journal of Instructional Psychology, 10*, 9–20.

Rickards, J. P., & Denner, P. R. (1978). Inserted questions as aids to reading text. *Instructional Science, 1*, 313–346.

Rothkopf, E. Z. (1966). Learning from written instructive material: An exploration of the control of inspection behavior by test-like events, *American Education Research Journal, 3*, 241–251.

Tennyson, R. D., & Park, O. (1980). The teaching of concepts: A review of instructional design research literature. *Review of Educational Research, 50*, 55–70.

PART III

Graphics and Design Alternatives

CHAPTER 8

Studying Strategies and Their Implications for Textbook Design*

THOMAS H. ANDERSON
BONNIE B. ARMBRUSTER

INTRODUCTION

Our main thesis is that the design of textbooks can (and, perhaps, should) affect how effectively students are able to read and comprehend the information in them. This thesis is not well founded on findings from our (or anyone else's) research program, but rather it is a conclusion that we reached when we merged our notions about how effective studying should proceed, and which properties of text seem to facilitate or impede comprehension. The merger of ideas from these two areas led us to speculate that there are preferred ways of designing textbooks.

The following textbook description gives a flavor of the ideal textbook that we have in mind.

This ideal textbook is being used in an introductory biology course as a means of conveying information about the structure and principles of biology to students who are relative novices in the discipline. The students are expected to read and learn from the textbook in order to successfully complete the course.

The preface to the textbook tells how the approach of this textbook compares to the approach used by other introductory textbooks in biology.

---

*The work upon which this publication is based was performed pursuant to Contract No. US NIE-C-400-76-0116 of the National Institute of Education, and Contract No. HD-06864 of the National Institute of Child Health and Human Development. It does not, however, necessarily reflect the views of those agencies.

The preface also gives the overall purpose and scope of the textbook by presenting a brief overview of how the major divisions of the textbook are related to each other. The introduction to the first division does the same for the chapters of the division, as does the introduction of Chapter 1 for the sections of that chapter. From the introduction to Chapter 1, the student could almost predict the title of the first section. Furthermore, the title suggests how the content of that section might generally be organized. As the student reads on, she finds that the section *is* organized as anticipated. In fact, for each heading, subheading, and topic sentence, the student is able to predict how the following text will be organized.

The text seems to flow naturally from idea to idea; ideas are clearly related to each other, with explicit connectives and referents. The text is "clean" and not littered with details and tangential information. The content does not seem too difficult, although occasionally new terms are carefully defined when they are needed to elaborate a concept. Text that presents particularly complicated ideas is supplemented by charts and diagrams. These usually help to clarify the relationships. Toward the end of the chapter the student notices that she has not been underlining or highlighting anything because the format of the chapter has made important information stand out. Furthermore, it has been very easy to take notes and/or make an outline. At the end of the chapter, the student finds a statement that provides a transition to the next chapter. And so the student proceeds through the textbook, always with a clear sense of where she is now, where she has been, and where she is going.

Next we describe some of the important dimensions of the studying process. Later we relate these dimensions to important properties of text.

IMPORTANT DIMENSIONS OF STUDYING

We have organized our thinking about studying research into two major components: research on state variables and on processing variables. This research is described in some detail by Anderson and Armbruster (1984) and only a brief overview of it follows. The *state variables* are those related to the status of the student and the to-be-studied material at the time of studying. Important student variables include knowledge of the criterion task (a test or other event to be performed after studying), knowledge of the content in the to-be-studied material, and motivation to read and learn from the text. Important text variables include the amount and complexity of content covered, organization or structure and other features that affect its comprehensibility. The *processing variables* are those involved in getting the information from the written page into the student's head. Processing variables include the initial focusing of attention, the subsequent encoding of the information attended to, and the retrieval of the information as required by the criterion task. As we see it, the outcomes of studying are a function of the interaction of state and processing variables.

Our review of research led us to some simple notions about the complex phenomenon of studying. First, regarding state variables, when the criterion tasks associated with studying are made explicit, as compared to remaining vague, students spend more time and effort reading the relevant segments of text, and learning outcomes generally improve. Second, regarding processing variables, when students know the nature of the criterion task as well as the type of relevant encoding activities in which to engage, their performance on the criterion task improves.

Also, there is some evidence of improved learning when students use techniques that help them process, in a nonsuperficial manner, virtually all of the ideas found in text. Examples of such techniques include certain types of outlining (Barton, 1930), mapping (Armbruster & Anderson, 1980), and networking (Dansereau, 1979). These techniques demand a trade-off, however, in that a lot of time and substantial amounts of effort are required to learn and employ them properly. Both of these commodities are at a premium for most students.

In the real world of studying and schooling, students must decide where to focus attention and how to process the information. Because the specific demands of these activities seem to change from course to course, textbook to textbook, and assignment to assignment, we conclude there is *no one best studying strategy*. Instead the students must rely on a higher-order process, currently called metacognition (see, for example, Baker and Brown, 1984), to help them make decisions about what studying activities to use.

AN ANALYSIS OF TEXTBOOKS

Recall for a moment that the basic thesis of this chapter suggests that the demands of studying have something to say about the design of textbooks. We believe this to be a tenable hypothesis because some of the research that has investigated the effects of text characteristics on learning outcomes offers some encouraging results.

What characteristics are we referring to? We refer to four general ones (structure, unity, coherence, and audience appropriateness) that helped to guide our thinking in an investigation of children's textbooks (Anderson, Armbruster, & Kantor, 1980; Kantor, Anderson, & Armbruster, 1983). Our investigation was prompted by the puzzling fact that textbooks, especially children's, were very poor sources of text that could be used to help train children how to study. At first we considered the situation to be simply a nuisance to us as teachers and researchers. Later we concluded that the poorly written text must be a problem for students also. Using that perspective, we analyzed many text segments and reported on two of them in Anderson, Armbruster, and Kantor (1980).

In the next section we define these factors, briefly discuss the research that lends support to our contention that they are prime variables that affect how well students can learn from text, and offer guidelines to authors–editors who prepare textbooks.

STRUCTURE

DEFINITION

Very simply, structure refers to the system of arrangement of ideas in text and the nature of the relationships connecting the ideas. The structure of text is determined by the author's purpose. This purpose can be thought of as a question the author is addressing. In other words, the form of the text follows its function.

We have found it useful to think of the structure or form of text in terms of text units and text frames, terms that are defined below.

The Text Unit

In many disciplines authors appear to be guided by a few basic purposes or questions. Table 1 presents some of these general purposes or questions and the name of the text structure corresponding to each. The text structures corresponding to these general purposes constitute the basic structural components or building blocks of content area text. We call these basic building blocks text units. Each text unit is typified by certain kinds of relationships, expressed as words (usually connectives) and phrases.

The Text Frame

Like the text unit, the text frame contains information that responds to a question (usually implicit). The structure of a text frame is different from that of a text unit in that the frame's structure is shaped in large part by the thinking patterns that are typical of the discipline (content area) being represented in the text. For example, biologists deal with the generic concepts of systems, structures, and processes. Sociologists work with concepts of cultures, groups, and societies. Physical geographers think in terms of climate, landforms, and geological processes. One obvious purpose of content-area text authors is to communicate specific instances of the generic concepts of their discipline. For example, the author of a biology textbook who wants to inform the reader about the digestive system has as a purpose the answer to the question, What is the digestive system?

Each of the generic concepts of a discipline has a set of features or attributes that are typically associated with the discipline. For example, typical features of

Table 1

Types of General Author Purposes and the Corresponding Text Structures

Examples of author purposes or questions		
Imperative form	Interrogative form	Structure
Define *A*.	What is *A*?	Description
Describe *A*.	Who is *A*?	
List the features, charac- teristics, and/or traits of *A*.	Where is *A*?	
Trace the development of *A*.	When did *A* occur (in rela- tionship to other events)?	Temporal sequences
Give the steps in *A*.		
Explain *A*.	Why did *A* happen?	Explanation
Explain the cause(s) of *A*.	How did *A* happen?	
Explain the effect(s) of *A*.	What are the causes, reasons for, effects, outcomes,	
Draw a conclusion about *A*.	and/or results of *A*?	
Predict what will happen to *A*.	What will be the effects, out- comes, and/or results of *A*?	
Hypothesize about the cause of *A*.		
Compare and contrast *A* and *B*.	How are *A* and *B* alike and/or different?	Compare–contrast
List the similarities and dif- ferences between *A* and *B*.		
Define and give examples of *A*.	What is *A*, and what are some examples of *A*?	Definition– examples
Explain the development of a problem and the solution(s) to the problem.	How did *A* get to be a prob- lem, and what is (are) its solutions?	Problem–solution

biological systems are location, component parts, and function. In communicating a specific instance of a generic concept, then, the author responds to implicit questions about the associated features: Where is the digestive system located? What are its component parts? What is the function of the digestive system?

The kind of text that informs the reader about an instance of a generic concept is what we call a *frame*. A frame is a rather complex, content-specific text structure. It has "slots" for the associated features of the generic concept. Each slot has a purpose or question associated with it. Table 2 presents examples of some science frames identified by Lunzer, Davies, and Greene (1980). The table gives the generic name of the frame, the generic purpose of the frame, and the questions associated with the attributes or slots of the frame.

Table 2

Several Frames and Their Corresponding Questions from Secondary Science Textbooks[a]

Frame	Purpose of frame	Question slots in the frame
1. Parts	To describe and explain structure or parts, for example, plant roots, teeth, and nervous system	Give the name of the part Describe its location Describe the part Explain the function of the part
2. Mechanisms	To describe and explain mechanisms such as the aneroid barometer and the bicycle pump	Give the name of the mechanism Explain how it works Explain its function Describe its location
3. Processes	To explain transformations over a period of time, such as the formation of limestone	Give the name of the process Describe when it takes place and its duration Describe its location Explain the function of the process
4. Scientific theory	To describe and explain patterns of thinking about observed phenomena in the world and tests of those patterns such as the theory of evolution and of spontaneous generation	Give the hypothesis, question, or problem Describe the theory Explain tests of its validity Describe the scientist(s) who work with it Explain applications of it

[a]Adapted from Lunzer et al., 1980.

One would expect, then, that an author responding to a question such as, What is photosynthesis? would use a process frame. The text responding to this question would contain answers to the following questions: What is the name of the process? Where is it located? How does the process work? What is the function of the process? There may be no particular order in which the author should address these questions, but a complete answer to the question, What is photosynthesis? should contain *at least* the answers to the question slots of the process frame. Note that some of the question slots can be answered with a single word or phrase (give the name of the function), while other question slots require a full text unit as a response (explain how the process works). Thus a frame is an amalgam of single-word or sentence-length responses and more extended, full-fledged text units.

THE TEXTBOOK HIERARCHY

A textbook is a hierarchical arrangement of text units and frames. The author begins with some very broad purposes or questions. The responses to these questions suggest other component questions. As each question gives rise to a new frame or text unit, the hierarchy expands.

Research Evidence

Structure is the text feature that has received the most attention in the research literature. From a fairly extensive body of research, we know that structure or organization influences the *amount* as well as the *kind* of knowledge acquired from reading. With respect to the *amount* of knowledge acquired, the conclusion is straightforward. Better organized text is better remembered. (See Goetz & Armbruster, 1980; Meyer, 1979; and Shimmerlik, 1978.) Furthermore, information provided to the reader about the organization or structure of the text can facilitate recall (Meyer, 1979). Such information can be provided in two ways. One way is through "signaling." Meyer (1979; Meyer & Rice, 1982) has defined signaling as information in text that emphasizes certain aspects of the semantic content or points out aspects of the discourse structure. Types of signaling include (1) explicit statements of the structure or organization; (2) preview or introductory statements, including titles; (3) summary statements; (4) pointer words and phrases, such as "an important point is . . ."; and (5) textual cues such as underlining, italics, and boldface. Another means of providing information about structure is through repeated, consistent use of a particular structure. Presumably in this way the reader learns the structure and comes to expect that ideas will be organized in that particular way.

Structure of text also affects the *kind* of knowledge acquired from reading by influencing the way information is stored. The better organized the text, the more highly integrated the memory representation is likely to be. Highly integrated memory representations enable learners to consider related facts simultaneously, a necessary condition for higher-order cognitive processes such as inferencing, summarizing, and decision making (Frase, 1972; Walker & Meyer, 1980).

In sum, the better the structure of the text, the more likely the reader is to remember the information and to engage in the higher-level cognitive processes that are usually considered to be the important outcomes of a learning situation.

Guidelines Related to Structure

1. The author's topic, purpose or question, and structure should be readily apparent to the reader from titles, headings, and/or topic sentences.

By simply skimming the text, the reader should be able to determine the author's specific topics, the purposes the author is addressing with respect to those topics, and the structure of the ensuing text. The reader should *not* have to guess at the author's intention from a title, heading, and/or topic sentence. The following illustrates this guideline:

Poor indication of purpose	Improved indication of purpose
(1) What Are the Chances? [Suggests a list of probabilities consequent to a set of conditions.]	An Explanation of Probability [Suggests the topic and an explanation structure.]
(2) How fast are impulses? [Suggests a number.]	How do impulses travel? [Suggests a process or explanation structure.]
(3) Finland is East of Sweden [Suggests a true or false verification.]	Finland: Climate and Geography [Suggests a frame or descriptive structure.]
(4) New Genetic Types and Agriculture [The use of *and* in this heading leaves the relationship between genetic types and agriculture vague. The author's purpose could be to describe both new genetic types and agriculture, to compare and contrast new genetic types and agriculture, or to explain some uncertain relationship between new genetic types and agriculture.]	The Effect of New Genetic Types on Agriculture [Suggests an explanation structure with an emphasis on effect.]
(5) Chicago's suburbs grew and grew. [The author's purpose could be to give examples of suburbs that grew, to explain the causes of the growth of suburbs, or to explain the effects of the growth of Chicago's suburbs.]	Chicago's suburbs grew for many reasons. [Suggests an explanation structure with an emphasis on causes.]

2. The actual structure of the text should match the author's purpose as implied by titles, headings, and topic sentences.

The following excerpt illustrates a mismatch between title and text structure. Instead of tracing and elaborating on the decision-making process or, perhaps, where else they might go, the author chose to do something else.

The Pilgrims Decide to Go to America

Finally the Pilgrim leaders said, "Why don't we go to America? Part of America is claimed by England. There we shall be able to educate our children in English ways. And we shall be able to worship in our own way."

The Pilgrims began to make plans. How could they get to America? They were hardworking and thrifty people, but they were not rich. They could not afford to buy supplies and hire a ship and crew.

The next example illustrates a close correspondence between titles and text structure.

Vision Explained

Light rays coming from an object pass through the cornea, enter the pupil, and reach the lens. The lens bends the light rays, which then form an image on the retina. This image is formed in the same way that a camera lens forms an image on film. The image on the retina produces impulses that reach the brain by way of the optic nerve. When the impulse arrives at the special area of the cerebrum that controls vision, we become aware that we see something.

3. Text frames used repeatedly throughout the textbook should have a consistent structure.

The reader can learn to form expectations about content and structure if frames are used consistently. An example of a text in which frames are used consistently is one that organizes information about Latin American countries in the following parallel fashion: location, history, climate and landforms, natural resources, economy, and people. An example of a consistent use of a frame in a biology textbook would be one that presented information on all systems of the human body (respiratory, circulatory, etc.) in the following form: general functions of the system; component parts of the system along with the process that occurs in or as a result of each part; and comparisons–contrasts of the comparable system in other organisms.

COHERENCE

DEFINITION

Coherence means "a sticking together." With reference to text, coherence refers to how smoothly the ideas are woven together. In a coherent discourse, the relationships among ideas must be clear enough so that there is a logical connection or "flow of meaning" from one idea to the next. Compared to an incoherent discourse, a coherent discourse makes it easier for the reader to perceive the message as an integrated unit.

Coherence operates at both global and local levels; that is, at the level of the whole text as well as at the level of individual sentences. At the global level, a text is coherent to the extent that it facilitates the integration of high-level ideas across the entire discourse. Features that might contribute to global coherence include titles and visual displays or diagrams.

At the local level, features related to coherence help the reader integrate the information within and between sentences. One important local feature is connectives or phrases that function conjunctively. These include linguistic connectives that make explicit the temporal, causal, spatial, or conditional relationships between propositions (Halliday & Hasan, 1976).

RESEARCH EVIDENCE

With respect to *global coherence,* the research indicates that titles can have an important effect on comprehension (Anderson, Spiro, & Anderson, 1978; Bransford & Johnson, 1972; Dansereau, Brooks, Spurlin, & Holley, 1979; Schallert, 1976). In addition, visual displays, diagrams, and charts can facilitate comprehension presumably because of their ability to portray the "big picture" at a single glance; that is, these elements lend coherence to the content (Gropper, 1970; Holliday, 1975; Holliday, 1976; Holliday, Brunner, & Donais, 1977; Holliday & Harvey, 1976).

Research relating to *local coherence* has demonstrated that an explicit use of connectives (rather than a statement that requires the reader to infer the connective) facilitates learning (Katz & Brent, 1968; Marshall & Glock, 1978–1979; Pearson, 1974–1975). Other research related to local coherence has indicated that repeated references and concepts that help to carry meaning across sentence boundaries can decrease reading time and increase recall of text as an integrated unit. (See Goetz & Armbruster, 1980, for a review of this literature.)

In sum, features of text contributing to both global and local coherence appear to help readers comprehend and recall the text as a structured, integrated unit.

GUIDELINES RELATED TO COHERENCE

1. Relationships among ideas should be explicitly stated.

As discussed in Anderson, Armbruster, and Kantor (1980), the use of short, simple sentences can often obscure the meaning of relationships. Readers are then forced to infer those relationships from their own knowledge. If the reader has the relevant background knowledge, comprehension is possible, but it requires more effort than it would if the relationships were explicitly stated. If the reader does *not* have the appropriate background knowledge, the intended meaning will be lost.

The following paragraph is an example of a text in which many of the connectives indicating relationships are missing and left to be inferred.

> In the evening, the light fades. Photosynthesis slows down. The amount of carbon dioxide in the air space builds up again. This buildup of carbon dioxide makes the guard cells relax. The openings are closed.

The following paragraph represents an attempt to improve the coherence of the text by making the relationships more explicit.

> What happens to these processes in the evening? The fading light of evening causes photosynthesis to slow down. Respiration, however, does not depend on light and thus continues to produce carbon dioxide. The carbon dioxide in the air spaces builds up again, which makes the guard cells closes the leaf openings. Consequently, the leaf openings close in the evening as photosynthesis slows down.

2. Referents should be clear.

The comprehension of certain words and phrases in text requires that the reader have knowledge of other ideas to which the words and phrases refer. Helping the reader keep these referents straight is a prime responsibility of the author. Several types of words and phrases that require explicit referents are discussed.

Obscure *pronoun references* are common in textbooks. The following excerpt illustrates a confusing use of the pronoun *they*. We are still not certain whether *they* refers to "the people from the North" or "the Bronze Age people"!

> The people from the North learned from the Bronze Age people. They were skilled workers and traders. They made fine tools and jewelry from metals. They traded their beautiful cloth and pottery to peoples around the Mediterranean. They kept records of their trade on clay tablets.

Quantifiers (e.g., *some, many, few*) pose other potential reference problems. First, authors may omit the noun or noun phrase being quantified so that the reader has to infer it. Second, the intended quantity may be unclear, so that the reader does not have a good idea about the size of the object being referenced.

Problems with pronoun references and quantifiers are illustrated in the following excerpt. We suspect that readers may become confused when encountering four quantifiers and the pronoun *they* repeated seven times in this short passage.

> ### Why Women Should Not Vote
>
> "A woman's place is in the home!" many men said. Politics would have a bad effect on women's characters, they said. Women would soon be neglecting their homes.
>
> Many said also that women's voting would cause arguments in the family. Arguments would weaken the family. Some believed that women were inferior to men by nature. They said that men were physically stronger and more intelligent than women. They said that women were too emotional. They were too excitable to vote wisely.
>
> Many people attacked the women who were working for suffrage. They said that they were unattractive. They said that they were unhappily married and only wanted attention.

A *definite noun phrase* (e.g., "He saw *the accident*") without a clear referent is also a potential reference problem. The proper use of the definite noun phrase is predicated on the assumption that both the author and reader know the specific instance referred to. Thus the sentence "He saw the accident" is unclear without prior mention of a specific accident.

A *verb phrase* may cause another reference problem. For example, consider the following sentences: "When an Indian shot an arrow, he hardly ever missed. If he did, he might have to go to bed without his supper." It is not too difficult for an adult reader to infer that "If he did" means "If an Indian missed his target." But a young reader might not understand which preceding verb phrase is referred to by the *did*.

Other potential reference problems include the following: (1) the use of *also, too,* and so on, when the preceding cases are uncertain; (2) the use of *but, however,* and so on, when it is not clear what is being contrasted or qualified.

> 3. In temporal sequences–processes and in explanations, the order of events should proceed in one direction only.

The sequencing of events should be unidirectional. The direction should generally proceed from earliest to latest in text for younger children. Young readers can become confused if the order of events in the text does not match the order of actual occurrence. For older readers, the direction may not be so critical. However, for most purposes, it would seem that the text should remain consistent and not skip around in time. Text that changes the time frame may send the reader on a wild-goose chase; the reader may be unwilling to put forth the effort to figure out the chronological or logical order behind the rhetorical order.

The following is an example of a text that changes time frame. The sentences have been numbered so that the commentary is easier to follow.

> [1]Adult female alligators make large cone-shaped nests from mud and compost. [2]The female lays from 15 to 100 eggs with leathery shells in the nest and then covers it. [3]The heat from both the sun and the decaying compost keeps the eggs warm. [4]The eggs hatch in about nine weeks. [5]Unlike other reptiles that hatch from eggs, baby alligators make sounds while they are still in the shell. [6]The mother then bites off the nest so the baby alligators can get out. [7]When first hatched, baby alligators are about 15 to 25 cm long.

Note the many shifts in the temporal sequence. The first four sentences are fine; they present the order of events from earliest to latest. The fifth sentence reverts back to when the baby alligators were still in the shell. The time frame for the sixth sentence is when the baby alligators are sufficiently mature to leave the nest. The final sentence returns to when the baby alligators were first hatched.

UNITY

DEFINITION

Unity refers to the degree to which the text addresses a single purpose. The author of a unified text has not strayed from the purpose by including irrelevant and distracting information.

RESEARCH EVIDENCE

A case for the importance of unity can be made more firmly on theoretical than empirical grounds. Central to the theoretical argument is the notion of a limited capacity, short-term memory that can hold only about five to nine items at once (Miller, 1956). As reading proceeds, new information must be integrated with the few propositions stored in short-term memory. The more disunified the text, the lower the probability of integration. Comprehension will probably slow down and possibly fail. Presumably the difficulties are compounded for poor and beginning readers. In sum, text that is not well unified can theoretically create comprehension problems, particularly for less skilled readers.

GUIDELINES

1. Each idea in the text unit or frame should contribute directly to the fulfillment of the author's purpose.

An idea that is not clearly contributing to the purpose but still merits inclusion should be indicated by using phrases such as "incidentally," "as an aside," or "in case you were wondering about." If there is a large number of irrelevant ideas, they should be edited out or they should form the basis of another text unit.

The following excerpt illustrates a text that includes information not contributing directly to the author's purpose. The first paragraph of this section traces the history of European settlement in the New World. The following excerpt starts with the second paragraph.

> [1]Dutch merchants in the Netherlands started a company. [2]They wanted to make money, too. [3]The Dutch colony sent people to the New World. [4]The people built a fort on a large island in the Hudson River. [5]They called it Fort Manhattan (man HAT n).
> [6]Many Indians lived near Fort Manhattan. [7]Indians were good hunters and trappers. [8]They knew how to find wild animals in the forests. [9]When an Indian shot an arrow, he hardly ever missed. [10]If he did, he might have to go to bed without his supper.
> [11]The Indians caught animals for their beautiful, soft furs. [12]The Dutch wanted the furs to sell in Europe. [13]The Dutch traded many things with the Indians. [14]Fort Manhattan became the center of the Dutch fur trade.

Apparently the author's purpose is to trace the history of Dutch settlement in America, including the establishment of the Dutch fur trade. The information about the Indians in sentences 6–10, particularly sentences 8–10, does not contribute to the fulfillment of this purpose. In place of sentences 6–12, we believe it would have been more appropriate to say something like "The Indians living near Fort Manhattan were expert at hunting and trapping fur-bearing animals. The Dutch settlers wanted to obtain the beautiful, soft furs in order to sell them to Europeans who were eager to buy them." Although these two sentences are longer than others in this excerpt, we feel they clarify the intended meaning of the passage better than the seven sentences they replace.

2. Entire text units that are only slightly related to the main flow of prose in the textbook should be somehow set aside, for example, in boxed-in areas or appendexes.

Examples of such text units are those that
1. teach skills that are necessary for understanding a later text unit (such as reading maps or finding directions using a compass)

2. relate content area ideas to knowledge with which students are already familiar
3. lend some authenticity to certain ideas in the text (such as excerpts from letters, diaries, notebooks, etc.)
4. describe the people and personalities involved in the content area
5. have high interest value because of their unusual and/or attractive features (e.g., including a unit about the Venus flytrap, a plant that feeds on animals, in a chapter about animals that feed on plants)

These adjunct text units can be a valuable resource to textbook authors, who can use the units in a variety of ways to improve the textbook quality without increasing the risk of making the basic prose more difficult to comprehend. Even when written clearly, the prose of many content area textbooks is brutally boring, and many students understandably shy away from reading them frequently or for long periods of time. The solution to the problem of how to make textbooks more enticing and fun to read lies not in the manipulation of the basic text units, but rather in the cleverness that authors and editors can use to discover and develop intrinsically motivating adjunct units.

In the following paragraph, the author's purpose (as inferred from the context) was to trace the development of events leading to the establishment of tobacco as an important cash crop in the colony of Virginia:

> The Indians grew tobacco which they smoked in pipes. Smoking was probably brought to England in the late 1500's. It quickly became popular. Historians are not sure who brought tobacco to England. Some think it was Sir Walter Raleigh. (He named Virginia in honor of Queen Elizabeth, "the Virgin Queen.")

The last three sentences do not clearly contribute to the author's purpose. The last sentence is particularly out of place. The use of parentheses helps somewhat to set the last sentence apart from the main message of the text. However, we would go a step further and recommend that the last three sentences be removed from the text or at least relegated to a box.

Incidentally, the sentence "Historians are not sure who brought tobacco to England" also violates the temporal order. The succession of events is "Smoking was brought to England"; then "Smoking became popular"; then *back to* "Smoking was brought to England" (in the form of the sentence "Historians are not sure who brought tobacco to England").

AUDIENCE APPROPRIATENESS

Definition

Audience appropriateness refers to the extent to which the text matches the reader's knowledge base—knowledge both of the content and of discourse features such as syntactic and rhetorical structures.

RESEARCH EVIDENCE

The research most directly related to audience appropriateness has been concerned with the effect of prior content knowledge on comprehension. It is quite clear from the literature that possession of relevant topic knowledge prior to reading strongly affects comprehension (e.g., Anderson, Reynolds, Schallert, & Goetz, 1977; Spilich, Vesonder, Chiesi, & Voss, 1979).

Another line of research related to the effect of prior knowledge on comprehension has focused on vocabulary, or word knowledge. In their review, Anderson and Freebody (1979) conclude from many studies that "word knowledge is strongly related to reading comprehension" (p. 2). A considerable body of research on readability also supports the preeminent role of word knowledge in reading comprehension (see Klare, 1974–1975 for a review).

In sum, the degree of the match between the text and the reader's knowledge appears to have strong effects on the comprehensibility of the text.

GUIDELINES

1. Taking into account the prior knowledge of the readers, enough relevant ideas should be included in the text to form a complete answer to the author's purpose or question.

The following example from a social studies textbook suffers from incompleteness.

> It took the invaders a long time to develop civilizations. They were much farther away than Greece from the old civilizations of the Fertile Crescent.
> Another reason was the land of Italy. A chain of mountains runs along the peninsula. On the eastern side, these mountains are rough and steep. There were no good harbors along the east coast. Few ships visited this coast.

The first paragraph needs to be expanded so that the relationship between time to develop civilizations and distance from existing civilizations is clarified. The second paragraph needs to be expanded to explain how and why the particular landforms of Italy retarded its development. The connection between landforms and development of civilization is probably not apparent to the young readers of this textbook.

2. Technical terms or other difficult vocabulary words should be introduced only if learning their meaning is an intrinsic part of learning the content. When such vocabulary is required, clear definitions should be provided.

In the following example, the technical phrase *responds to stimuli* is not defined and is not likely to be understood by the very young reader.

What Is a Cell Like?

A cell is made of living stuff. It can grow. It takes in food and changes the food into more living stuff. A cell combines food and oxygen to make energy for all the things it does. The living stuff in a cell responds to stimuli. It moves.

The next example illustrates a reasonable way to introduce, define, and then use a technical term in text. Note how and where the concept of relief is defined.

A plateau is an area of horizontal rock layers that has high relief. Relief is simply the difference between the highest and lowest points of a region. There is no fixed amount of relief for a plateau. As a rule, however, a plateau's relief is 1000 meters or more. Its high points may be well over 1000 meters above sea level. Its low points are the bottoms of its canyons and steep river valleys.

3. Analogies, metaphors, and other types of figurative language should be used only if their referents are well known by the reader.

Only familiar concepts can serve as referents for figurative language when the purpose of using the figurative language is to teach students about an unfamiliar concept. Otherwise the student is left with the difficult task of comparing one unknown, the referent, with yet another unknown, the concept to be learned.

The statement that ''haciendas are very similar to plantations in the southern part of the United States before the Civil War'' will have no meaning to readers unfamiliar with the characteristics of antebellum southern plantations. A potential comprehension problem is circumvented if the author presents a full comparison–contrast of the features of haciendas *and* antebellum southern plantations. However, if the author's intent was to describe haciendas, there is no need to introduce southern plantations at all.

An example of an analogy or model used appropriately is found in a sixth-grade textbook. The text is attempting to teach the concepts of repulsion, attraction, and static electricity. The students have just completed an exercise in which they (1) rubbed one balloon all over with wool and held it up to a wall and (2) rubbed two balloons all over with the wool, dangled the balloons from strings, and brought the two balloons close together.

In a first paragraph (not included), the author reminds the students what happens when they play with bar magnets—the two like poles push each other away (repulsion) and the unlike poles move toward each other (attraction). The second and third paragraphs make and explain the analogy between the movement of magnets and of balloons that were recently rubbed with wool.

In a way, the balloons you used acted as if they were bar magnets. You saw attraction and repulsion. The first balloon clung to the wall, as if the balloon and the wall were unlike poles of two magnets. In the second case, the two balloons repelled each other. They acted as if they were the like poles of two magnets.

But we should not confuse balloons with magnets. Balloons are not magnetized when they are rubbed with wool cloth. But some force must be at work. Some force had to hold the balloon to the wall, and some force had to cause the two balloons to repel each other. The force at work was static electricity.

CONCLUSION

We developed the notion that the demands of studying from text can be affected in beneficial ways by changing the characteristics of the text itself. To lend support to this notion, we presented some of the major dimensions of studying: clarifying the criteria for studying, focusing attention on the relevant text segments, and engaging in high payoff encoding activities. We merged these dimensions of studying with four qualities of text (structure, coherence, unity, and audience appropriateness) that, when characteristic of text, appear to affect how well students can read and understand it. Some of the reasons why we think high-quality text will help studying are listed in the following.

1. Criteria for studying will be clearer to students because
   a. The titles, headings and topic sentences help the student identify the questions that the text is answering.
2. Focusing attention will be easier because
   b. Each idea unit in the regular text is important, in that it contributes to an answer and/or a question.
   c. The idea units that have a high probability of being nonessential are clearly marked as such by being in a box.
   d. The hierarchical structure of the text and high degree of unity make it easy and efficient for students to locate a specific text unit. Entire chunks of irrelevant text can be easily identified and skipped over.
3. Encoding activities will be more efficient because
   a. The high degree of coherence, structure, and unity will enable the students to select and rapidly engage in a variety of activities to promote encoding such as outlining, mapping, underlining, and notetaking. Even the more time-consuming activities proceed very smoothly when using text with these characteristics.
   b. The hierarchical structure of the text encourages students to use a top-down, higher-level perspective when reading and organizing ideas from the text. This perspective is contrasted with a bottom-up one in which the students are not sure where the author is going, and must put the puzzle together in an inefficient, piecemeal fashion.

REFERENCES

Anderson, R. C., & Freebody, P. (1979, August). *Vocabulary knowledge and reading* (Reading Education Report No. 11). University of Illinois, Center for the Study of Reading.

Anderson, R. C., Reynolds, R. E., Schallert, D. L., & Goetz, E. T. (1977). Frameworks for comprehending discourse. *American Educational Research Journal, 14*, 367–381.

Anderson R. C., Spiro, R. J., & Anderson, M. C. (1978). Schemata as scaffolding for the representation of information in connected discourse. *American Education Research Journal, 15*, 433–450.

Anderson, T. H., & Armbruster, B. B. (1984). Studying. In P. D. Pearson (Ed.), *Handbook of Reading Research*. New York: Longman.

Anderson, T. H., Armbruster, B. B., & Kantor, R. N. (1980, August). *How clearly written are children's textbooks? Or, of bladderworts and alfa* (Reading Education Rep. No. 16). Urbana: University of Illinois, Center for the Study of Reading.

Armbruster, B. B., & Anderson, T. H. (1980, February). *The effects of mapping on the free recall of expository text* (Tech. Rep. No. 160), Urbana: University of Illinois, Center for the Study of Reading.

Baker, L., & Brown, A. L. (1984). Metacognition skills and reading. In P. D. Pearson (Ed.), *Handbook of reading research*. New York: Longman.

Barton, W. A. (1930). *Outlining as a study procedure*. New York: Teacher College, Columbia University.

Bransford, J. D., & Johnson, M. K. (1972). Contextual prerequisites for understanding: Some investigations of comprehension and recall. *Journal of Verbal Learning and Verbal Behavior, 11*, 717–726.

Dansereau, D. F. (1979). Development and evaluation of a learning strategy training program. *Journal of Educational Psychology, 71*, 64–73.

Dansereau, D. F., Brooks, L. W., Spurlin, J. E., & Holley, C. D. (1979). *Headings and outlines as processing aids for scientific text*. Manuscript submitted for publication.

Frase, L. T. (1972). Maintenance and control in the acquisition of knowledge from written materials. In J. B. Carroll & R. D. Freedle (Eds.), *Language comprehension and the acquisition of knowledge*. Washington, DC: Winston.

Goetz, E. T., & Armbruster, B. B. (1980). Psychological correlates of text structure. In R. J. Spiro, B. C. Bruce, & W. F. Brewer (Eds.), *Theoretical issues in reading comprehension: Perspectives from cognitive psychology, artificial intelligence, linguistics, and education*. Hillsdale, NJ: Erlbaum.

Gropper, G. L. (1970). The design of stimulus materials in response-oriented programs. *AV Communications Review, 18*, 129–159.

Halliday, M. A. K., & Hasan, R. (1976). *Cohesion in English*. London: Longman's.

Holliday, W. G. (1975). The effects of verbal and adjunct pictorial-verbal information in science instruction. *Journal of Research in Science Teaching, 12*, 77–83.

Holliday, W. G. (1976). Teaching verbal chains using flow diagrams and texts. *AV Communications Review, 24*, 63–78.

Holliday, W. G., Brunner, L. L., & Donais, E. L. (1977). Differential cognitive and affective responses for flow diagrams in science. *Journal of Research in Science Teaching, 14*, 129–138.

Holliday, W. G., & Harvey, D. A. (1976). Adjunct labeled drawings in teaching physics to junior high school students. *Journal of Research in Science Teaching, 13*, 37–43.

Katz, E., & Brent, S. (1968). Understanding connections. *Journal of Verbal Learning and Verbal Behavior, 7*, 501–509.

Klare, G. R. (1974–1975). Assessing readability. *Reading Research Quarterly, 10*, 62–102.

Lunzer, E., Davies, F., & Greene, T. (1980). *Reading for learning in science* (Schools Council Project Report). Nottingham, England: University of Nottingham, School of Education.

Marshall, N., & Glock, M. D. (1978–1979). Comprehension of connected discourse: A study into the relationship between the structure of text and information recalled. *Reading Research Quarterly, 16*, 10–56.

Meyer, B. J. F. (1979). *A selected review and discussion of basic research on prose comprehension* (Prose Learning Series: Research Rep. No. 4). Tempe: Arizona State University, Department of Educational Psychology.

Miller, G. A. (1956). The magical number seven, plus or minus two: Some limits on our capacity for processing information. *Psychological Review, 63,* 81–97.

Pearson, P. D. (1974–1975). The effects of grammatical complexity on children's comprehension, recall, and conception of certain semantic relations. *Reading Research Quarterly, 10,* 155–192.

Pearson, P. D., & Camperell, K. B. (1981). Comprehension of text structures. In J. T. Guthrie (Ed.), *Comprehension and teaching: Research reviews.* Newark, DE: International Reading Association.

Schallert, D. L. (1976). Improving memory for prose: The relationship between depth of processing and context. *Journal of Verbal Learning and Verbal Behavior, 15,* 621–632.

Shimmerlik, S. M. (1978). Organization theory and memory for prose: A review of the literature. *Review of Educational Research, 48,* 103–120.

Spilich, G. J., Vesonder, G. T., Chiesi, H. L., & Voss, J. F. (1979). Text processing of domain-related information for individuals with high and low domain knowledge. *Journal of Verbal Learning and Verbal Behavior, 18,* 275–290.

Walker, C. H., Meyer, B. J. F. (1980). Integrating information from text: An evaluation of current theories. *Review of Educational Research, 50,* 421–437.

CHAPTER 9

Results with Structured Writing Using the Information Mapping® Writing Service Standards

ROBERT E. HORN

Table of Contents

®Information Mapping is a registered trademark of Information Mapping, Inc.

DESIGNING USABLE TEXTS

Background

We have been experimenting with one approach to developing usable text since the mid-1960s.

Our approach to structured writing is called the Information Mapping® method.

Original Impetus: Access and Structure Problems

Our initial impetus was twofold:

- frustration with the enormous amounts of time spent trying to locate what we were after in instructional materials

- a dissatisfaction with the impreciseness of the language with which professionals described the process of technical writing

Goals of Our Research

The goals of the structured writing method that we developed are to

- *Provide quick, reliable access*—To enable readers to find what they are looking for easily and precisely

- *Facilitate learning*—To enable learners to use their own learning styles to read and remember the material with the maximum efficiency and effectiveness

- *Ease the writer's job*—To enable writers to

  - analyze and write a document quickly and effectively

  - interlink complete components

  - update documents efficiently

  - index reliably and quickly

- *Provide framework for design of computer-based storage and retrieval*—To give structure to knowledge bases of curriculum and reference materials

Guideposts: Synthesize Current Research

The guideposts we have used for our research have been quite straightforward:

There are a lot of good ideas, techniques, and learning sequences around, but nobody has put them all together in a systematic way.

We have concentrated on searching out and collecting the good ideas, and, especially, on the synthesis of them.

Focus on Content Typology

One of the major deficiencies in our present teaching–learning-information theory is the lack of a comprehensive typology of the components that we use to communicate new information to others. We have concentrated our efforts on such a classification system.

Gather Ideas From Diverse Disciplines

No one discipline is producing all of the good ideas. We have looked everywhere: psychology, general systems theory, computer science, philosophy, advertising, and magazine writing. All these sources have provided us with ideas and methods.

Make Learning Easier

The basic job is to produce written material that makes learning and reference work easier and quicker—and perhaps more pleasurable.

Research Began with Task Analysis

Our earlier research had lead us up an interesting path. We published an early synthesis of methodologies of task analysis (Horn, 1963a) in programmed instruction that pulled together diverse works from Gilbert (1962), Upton and Samson (1961), and Woolman (1962).

Branching Typology

Our procedures also resulted in a major study that suggested a typology of branching techniques (Horn, 1963b).

Further Work on Sequence and Question Typologies

We then turned our attention to methods of analyzing sequences (Basescu & Horn, 1964). The problem of sorting learning objectives and terminal frames (test questions) has resulted in a rather elegant system of sorting called "A Terminal Behavior Locator System" (Horn, 1966).

Connect with Other Taxonomies

Our research relates to much past and current research and theory. Perhaps none of this research would have been as far along as it is had it not been for the pioneering efforts of Bloom (1956) whose work in the taxonomy of educational objectives has inspired many later workers. Among these have been Miller (1962) who extended the specification of task analysis to many areas. Gagné (1964, 1965) has done a good deal of work in applying learning theory to questions of information materials design. Bruner (1960, 1966a, 1966b) has focused our attention on the structure of subject matter although he has not given us the formats for the structure.

Integrate Specific Work on Components

Our specific problems, people such as Woolman (1962) and Roder-burg, Cluck, and Murray (1964) have worked on prerequisites. Upton and Samson (1961) have done work in the classification and the subject matter tree formats. A number of people have developed decision tables (Dixon, 1964; U.S. Dept. of Air Force, 1965). Flow charting has been pointed by Berry (1964) and Gagné and his associates (1965). Carroll (1964) has focused our attention on the notion of concepts, and Gilbert (1962) has contributed much to the analysis and teaching designs for procedures. However, as we stated in 1967, few of these investigators have attempted to put together all of the lines of research and formats available.

Two Lines of Research

By 1967 we had developed two very promising lines of research. These will be discussed under the headings of maps and content analysis.

Maps: Early Definition

We gave the name ''maps'' to the whole class of diagrams, maps, tables, charts, flowcharts, trees, and graphs.

Information maps can be defined as ways of displaying information so that the arrangement of the information on the page reveals something about the structure or interrelationship inherent in that information.

The physical arrangements of the maps provide a special analogue to the connections and relationships of the information. While our understanding of maps has increased, the basic metaphor remains.

How Maps Portray Structure

What do information maps reveal about the structure of the information contained in them? Consider a few examples: A cycle chart shows the flow of cyclical process coming back to the starting place. Would it not be an advantage to a learner if all cycles were displayed in this fashion? If they were, learners could see at a glance that they were dealing with a cycle and see the identifiable parts of the cycle. A nonnumerical table lines up similar things in rows and columns. By its very structure it says ''compare and contrast these things.''

A tree structure divides things; that is, it graphically sorts them into their kinds. A prerequisite network shows the paths a learner must use in order to reach some learning objective. In each case there is a spatial analogue to some important structure that relates the information displayed.

Concentrate on Nonquantitative Maps

We concentrated our activities on these maps—especially on those maps that displayed nonquantitative information, that is, maps that contained words rather than numbers.

(Numerical maps and tables seem to be a well-understood technique whereas nonnumerical information mapping is still in its infancy.)

Better Than Regular Prose

We tried placing the same information in prose paragraphs and in information maps so as to be able to compare the differences in communication value. Our early explorations suggested that the maps were better more often than not.

We combined maps with programmed instruction-like questions and found them to be of great use as the information portion of the programmed instruction "frame." All of these things give us confidence that we are pursuing something very basic to learning processes.

Investigated Other Aspects of Text

Maps are not the only good techniques we have collected and attempted to mold into a writing technology, but they are a dominating one. Other aspects of this work included the integrating of research relating to indexes, tables of content, subheadings, questions, typography, and so forth.

Developed Content Analysis

While classifying kinds of terminal behavior questions (Horn, 1966), we found what we believe to be a very general method of subject matter classification.

Research in Taxonomy

This lead to work in a taxonomy of the content categories of text made for learning. The basics of which are shown in a diagram entitled "Basic Types of Maps."

Criteria for Content

The criteria we use in this work are that if we had a classification system for components, we should be able to sort any sentence or illustrative material of a given textbook, program, or other written material into categories. Conversely, given a subject matter, we ought to be able to specify what sentences should occur.

This is a tall order. But our research has advanced to the point where we have a working set of categories for an estimated 70–80% of all the sentences we encounter.

Combine Maps and Content Analysis Categories

It soon became apparent that the categories we were developing in our content analysis work were precisely the categories required to specify parts of the maps. Thus the two lines of research merged. Examination of maps has added categories that might otherwise have been over-looked. Using content analysis categories has resulted in new kinds of maps.

Paragraphs Inadequate as Grouping Tool

It was at this point that we began to recognize that trying to chunk information according to the rules of the rhetoric we learned in school did not work very well. Paragraphs are too fuzzily defined to be used to aid communication in modern, complex, technological and admin-istrative environments. All they provide is a slight visual break in the dense grey once in a while. We invented a new, much more carefully defined grouping of information that we called the Information Block.

Definition

The *Information Block* consists of a label and text and/or graphics of specific types.

Types

We have been working with several major types of Blocks and have a working typology of over 200 of them (independent of subject matter) for different kinds of documents. For instructional text we work with a group of approximately 40 Blocks that on the average help us sort 80% or more of the content of instructional manuals and procedures.

Fundamental Unit Independent of Subject Matter

We saw that we were dealing with very fundamental units—units that writers thought with and readers looked for. The idea that you can divide all information in many different subject matters into about 40 little chunks of information was an attractive notion.

Learner and Referencer Need Access to Structure

We found a key to better access through a carefully designed labeling system that reflected the structure of the information to the reader (learner, referencer, or browser).

Our goal was to show at all times the structure of the

- subject matter, and the

- document

This would permit the reader continuously to be oriented and to rapidly locate material.

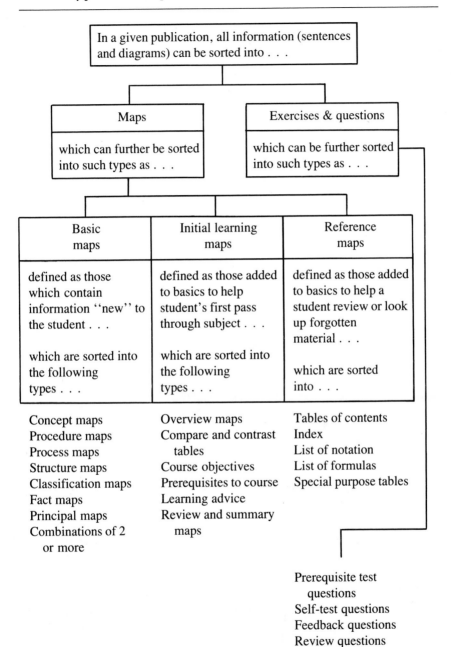

In a given publication, all information (sentences and diagrams) can be sorted into . . .

Maps

which can further be sorted into such types as . . .

Exercises & questions

which can be further sorted into such types as . . .

Basic maps	Initial learning maps	Reference maps
defined as those which contain information "new" to the student . . .	defined as those added to basics to help student's first pass through subject . . .	defined as those added to basics to help a student review or look up forgotten material . . .
which are sorted into the following types . . .	which are sorted into the following types . . .	which are sorted into . . .

Concept maps	Overview maps	Tables of contents
Procedure maps	Compare and contrast tables	Index
Process maps	Course objectives	List of notation
Structure maps	Prerequisites to course	List of formulas
Classification maps	Learning advice	Special purpose tables
Fact maps	Review and summary maps	
Principal maps		
Combinations of 2 or more		

Prerequisite test questions
Self-test questions
Feedback questions
Review questions
Practice questions
Structured exercises
Simulation exercises
Pretest questions
Posttest questions

NOTE: Each of the Basic Maps has specified types of blocks associated with it.

Block Labels Produce Easy Reference Access and Improve Learning

Research Shows Benefits of Labels	A series of major studies over the past 30 years supports the use of a consistent, carefully prepared labeling system to make access and learning easier and more cost-effective.
Humans Chunk Information	In one of the most fundamental and widely quoted papers in modern psychological research, Miller (1967) evaluated a large collection of perceptual and cognitive research and concluded that humans have a limited short-term memory that is about seven plus or minus two "chunks." The implication of this body of research is that writers should "predivide" information into these chunks. That is what our Information Blocks provide.
Chunking Aids Learning	Chunking of introductory information aids learning by calling learner's attention to important features (Gagné & Rhower 1969; Gagné, 1965).
Labeling Informs Learner of Nature of Task	Cuing (or labeling) aids learning by alerting learner to the nature of the learning task. Glaser (1965) has shown that cuing facilitates later recall. Hartley and Trueman's 1983 studies support this as well.
Advance Organizers Aid Learning	Ausubel (1960, 1963, 1964, 1968) has developed a logical and research-based case for showing that learning and long-term retention are facilitated by "organizers," which provide an "ideational scaffolding." He has amassed considerable experimental support for this idea.
Organization Aids Learning	The studies of Katona (1940) with college students pointed out the importance of organization for learning and retention.
	Underwood (1966) also surveyed the research on the organization of text to ease learning of verbal materials that supports this aspect of our approach.
Preview Aids Speed	Two researchers (de Leeuw & de Leeuw, 1965) found that previewing headings within a prose passage improves overall reading speed.
Facilitates Retention	Dooling and Lachman (1971) found that presence of a thematic title increased recall by 18%.

Helps Poorly Motivated

Poorly motivated subjects performed less well on poorly designed text (from standpoint of typography, layout, white space) than they did on a well-designed one (McLaughlin, 1966).

Subsequent Research Supports Labeled Blocks

Our conclusion based on the reading of this research was that labeled Blocks should be fundamental to the design of high-performance text. That is why we incorporated the labeled Block design into structured writing.

Subsequent research, which we describe later in this chapter, comparing our method to other methods, supports these conclusions (Jonnassen, 1979, Romiszowski, 1977, Soyster, 1980, Stelnicki, 1980, Stuart, 1979, Webber, 1979). References to earlier research may be found in the bibliography in Horn (1980).

Structured Writing

Definitions

Structure when applied to writing refers to different properties of the text that permit the structure of the subject matter and the text to be perceived by the reader.

Structured writing is writing that is relatively high in structure.

Structured writing using the standards of the Information Mapping® service refers to writing that is highly structured and meets these criteria:

- a method of analysis of subject matter content for different documents

- a specific set of principles and criteria to guide the writer's choices

- labeled Blocks (each with its own standards) to chunk information

- groups of Blocks that form into documents that are divided into maps (each with its own standards)

- Specified formatting for
  - texts, procedures, reference books, and manuals
  - reports, memos, and other administrative documents
  - computer displayed text
- specific graphic components (each with its own standards)
- specific guidelines on style, sentence length and type, and word choice (for different readers and user groups)

Examples   We provide examples of some pages from textbooks and procedure manuals used in industry in the following pages.

17.1.0 Nonregular and Regular Values of Variables

17.1.1 We will handle the situation of fixed increment data with a special command, the Input with Computed Clause Statement, that will permit the input of regular data in a compact form that is quicker to type than the normal input statement.

You should first have to distinguish between whether or not the data showed a regular pattern of intervals between the values, in other words, to distinguish between so-called nonregular data and regular data that has a data vector that progresses from some initial value with some fixed interval to another value, and then optionally from that to still other values by even increments.

Most measurements data do not exhibit regularities that are fixed intervals between values, so they are usually nonregular data. An example would be this vector: LABMEAS = .01, .09, .04, .3. Frequently time data will show regularities as, for example, when you collect samples of blood from a laboratory animal every hour on the hour, for which a time vector might be established called SAMPLEHRS and could be represented this way: 6, 7, 8, 9, 10.

Nonregular data values may *not* be inputted with the ''input with Computer Clause Statement.'' You must use the other input statement.

COMPARING	REGULAR DATA AND VALUES	NON-REGULAR DATA VALUES
Introduction	Some data have patterns. They progress by fixed increments.	Some data do not show any pattern of intervals between the values.
Definition	When the values of a data vector progress from some initial value with some fixed interval to another value, and then optionally from that to still other values by even increments, they are called *regular data*.	Data are called *nonregular* data when they have no systematic pattern of intervals between them.
Example one	Time data show frequent regularities. Samples of blood collected from a laboratory animal every hour on the hour might be called SAMPLEHRS and might look this way: SAMPLEHRS = 6, 7, 8, 9, 10	Most measurement data do not exhibit systematic regularities that are fixed intervals between values, so they are usually nonregular data. Here is an example: LABMEAS = .01, .09, .04, .3
Use this input statement	Input with Computed Clause Statement	Standard input statement
Comment	This statement permits you to input regular data in a very compact form and is much quicker to type than a normal input statement.	
Related maps	Input with Computed Input Statements, 23; Variables, 57; Clause, 75	

TRANSFERS

There are more and more requests for transfers as the company expands and the key work force adopts a more flexible lifestyle. The company supervisor is a key person in facilitating such transfers and in determining whether they would be in the best-interest of the company and the employees. This memorandum covers company policy that has been in effect for the past year and continues to be our policy. It outlines each supervisor's responsibilities when an employee under his or her supervision requests a transfer.

First, it is in the company's interest to retain employees who are performing satisfactorily, therefore, we will try to help employees to move to an area or job that they find more desirable. This is what you should do. When an employee comes to talk about a transfer or to request one, you should provide them with Form 742, Application for Transfer, and tell them to fill it out as soon as possible.

If the employee is applying for a new job and not just a new location and if there are any parts of the new job that you as the supervisor consider may disqualify the employee, then you should discuss with the employee those areas immediately. Remember, it is the company policy that if an employee wishes to be transferred, the company will make every effort to find a job acceptable to the employee. So you should not discourage any request for transfer, even if it would disturb the completion of projects or goals in your department.

At the bottom of the form, you should fill out the supervisor's comment. Be brief and to the point. When you have finished that, you should make a photocopy of the employee's latest Performance Evaluation and attach it to the form.

If the employee's current performance rating is unsatisfactory, then your signature and your immediate supervisor's signature on Part C of the form are required. If the current performance rating is outstanding, then attach a copy of any letters of commendation. If the current performance rating is satisfactory, you do not have to attach anything.

Send a copy of the blue copy of the form to the company Placement Bureau and a pink copy to your Departmental File. The yellow copy should be given to the employee.

HOW TO HANDLE TRANSFER REQUESTS

Introduction This procedure outlines each supervisor's responsibilities when an employee under your supervision requests a transfer.

Procedure table

STEP	ACTION
1	When employees request transfers, provide them with form 742, Application for Transfer.
2	Discuss with the employee any areas in the new job that you consider may disqualify the employee. Remember, it is our policy that if an employee wishes to be transferred, the company will make every effort to find a job acceptable to the employee. So you may in *no* way discourage a request for transfer.
3	At the bottom of the form, fill out the supervisor's comments.
4	Attach a copy of the latest Performance Evaluation.
5	<table><tr><td>IF the current performance rating is . . .</td><td>THEN</td></tr><tr><td>Unsatisfactory</td><td>Your signature and your immediate supervisor's signature on Part C of the form are required.</td></tr><tr><td>Outstanding</td><td>Attach a copy of the letter of recommendation.</td></tr></table>
6	<table><tr><td>Send this copy of the form</td><td>TO</td></tr><tr><td>Blue Copy</td><td>Placement Bureau</td></tr><tr><td>Pink Copy</td><td>Departmental File</td></tr><tr><td>Yellow Copy</td><td>Employee</td></tr></table>

Introduction

During the course of our work we realized that we consciously chose a set of values and assumptions that guided our approach to improving the communication process. I would like to share these values with you.

Less Work for Reader

Our principal value is clarity. We assume that this will produce less work for the reader in using our texts and manuals. We recognize that it is hard enough to do intellectual work without all of the impediments to communication that ordinary, relatively unstructured writing inflicts upon us.

Assume Reader Motivation

We have not attempted to incorporate systematically "motivational elements" to get people to read all of our materials. Some rhetorics, such as those that magazine writers use, try to get people to read the entire article. The value there is to get them to look at advertising on the page facing the text.

We assume that people in the business context have the motivation to read, learn, and explore. All we writers can do is discourage or encourage the reader's trust, depending on the way we design our text.

Individual Reader Unpredictable

We assume that we cannot predict what a particular reader will do in terms of how they will use the text. Some will be browsing through it. Others will scan quickly and skip large parts. Some will read from beginning to end carefully. Others will be using it for reference or relearning. Others will be looking for analysis of data. Therefore, we have to make trade-offs explicit so that readers can use the text for a variety of different purposes.

Cost-effectiveness

Businesses place a high premium on the cost-effectiveness of communication. Training time, time spent in meetings, and time spent preparing for decision making all cost money. Our overriding criteria is to make certain that the rules, standards, and procedures that we suggest meet high cost-effectiveness standards.

Explicit Rules Important

As we go through our various courses from elementary school through college, we collect in our heads a large variety of rules for writing. Many of these rules go back as far as the rhetoric that Aristotle made up for the Athenian courtroom. Because we are unlikely to stop people from carrying around rules in their head, we think they should have explicit ones and the best ones that research and analysis can provide.

Metalan-guage Needed	Writers need a shared vocabulary to identify and talk about composition. Our identification of the ''chunks'' of writing that we call Blocks and Maps give writers a metalanguage with which they can communicate about writing.
Theory Helps Practice	We are interested in theoretical explorations of writing only insofar as they help writers with the blank pieces of paper in front of them.
Task Analytic Driven	We assume that writing method based on analysis of the tasks used in job analysis will help the writer and the reader communicate. So we have routinely incorporated these into our methodology.

Principles of Structured Writing

Principles   We use the following principles for the design of the texts.

1. *Visible structure*   We believe the reader should be able to see instantly the structure of the subject matter and the documents.

2. *Pre-divided information*   We pre-divide all information into chunks of about three to five sentences plus or minus two.

3. *Labeling*   We give a descriptive label to every group of three to five sentences. We call this group of labeled sentences a Block.

4. *Assemble systematic hierarchy*   We give groups of seven plus or minus two Blocks a title and group them hierarchically.

5. *Relevance*   We make the contents of the Blocks relevant to the label. We permit no extraneous material in a Block. We require labels and titles to be relevant to the content of the Blocks they cover.

6. *Consistency*   Consistency of format, sentence titles, labels, and word choice enables readers to use the structure of a text with reliability.

7. *Establish criteria and standards*   We determine where specific criteria and standards should apply to groups of similar communications situations based on our research and that of others.

**Principles
(Continued)**

8. *Determine typologies*   We group Blocks, labels, Maps, and documents that have a similar purpose so that they can be treated together from the standpoint of the writer.

9. *Integrate graphics*   When a graphic communicates better than a word, we use the graphic. We integrate the graphic types into the collection of Blocks.

10. *Available detail*   We ensure that different types of readers and users with different purposes can have rapid access to the level of detail they want.

11. *Adaptability*   We ensure that the text can be used for initial learning (i.e., compatible with exercises and simulated applications) as well as for reference and browsing.

12. *Flexibility*   We incorporate new ideas and research findings into our framework continuously.

Standards: Their Goals and Use

Introduction

The industrial revolution is partially the result of standardization of material, methods, processes, and performance.

In large part, this is the result of a voluntary action of professions, countries, and managements recognizing the value of standardization.

**Aims of
Standards**

The aims of standardization in our work on structured writing are not different than aims of standardization in other industries.

As stated by Verman (1973) these aims are

(1) To achieve maximum overall economy in terms of:
     (a) cost,
     (b) human effort and . . .

(2) To ensure maximum convenience in use.
     It is this objective of standardization which leads to simplification, rationalization, interchangeability of parts and freezing of dimensions of components. . . .

**Aims of
Standards
(Continued)**

(3) To adopt the best possible solutions to recurring problems consistent with (1) and (2) above and taking into account all the available scientific knowledge and up-to-date technological developments.

This objective of standardization is aimed at facilitating design procedures and guiding the formulation of research and development programmes. It involves standardization of basic terminologies, codes of practice, model forms of contract and so on.

(4) To define requisite levels of quality in such a manner that practical evaluation of quality and its attainment are consistent with (1) and (2) above.

This aim leads to the standardization of sampling procedures, test methods, grading schemes and quality specifications in general.

Research on Components of Structured Writing

Introduction

Once we had developed the basic frameworks in our taxonomies and our formats, we could focus our attention on refining the different parts. Because we could always identify where they belonged and what kind of thing they were (i.e., what Block they belonged in), we could be far more certain of the standardized characteristics of our materials. This explicitness has aided us throughout our development of structured writing.

**Easy to
Incorporate
Other
Research**

This framework has also permitted us to incorporate the results of many other researcher's work.

For example, it has been quite easy to incorporate work on prerequisite charting, that is, the methods of portraying prerequisite hierarchies within a subject matter.

Introduction   Having come up with our taxonomies and principles, we developed standards for particular kinds of writing and subject matter and specific components.

Limits of space prevent me from going into all of the details.

Our analysis and standard making has been supported by brief empirical studies.

In the following material I simply sketch out some of the major areas of standards that we work with.

Block and Map Labels   Some of the important questions with Blocks and labels are

- are there different criteria for different kinds of labels?

- how are subject matter labels different from subject-matter-independent labels?

Relevance   How do we define relevance and hence implement our principle of putting only information regarding what has been labeled into the content of the Block?

Labels That Tell The Whole Story   What is the difference between a set of labels that attempt to provide a summary or precis of the entire paper as opposed to those labels that only define the function (e.g., definition or introduction)?

Types of Labels   What are the properties of different kinds of label forms such as

- Phrases

- Questions

- Newspaperlike headlines?

Hierarchical Sequencing Integrated with Prerequisites   To what degree can you separate a subject matter into different approaches to structure, for example, hierarchical and prerequisite?

What is the difference between the classificatory approach to subject matter that groups similar things together (as in a reference manual) with sequencing that depends on prerequisite structure (important to initial learning)?

Hierarchical Sequencing Integrated with Prerequisites (Continued)	How can these two be integrated? We have developed micro- and macrosequencing approaches based on our chunking method.
Interlinkages	How do we interlink subject matter such that prerequisites, similarities, and important connections can be indicated?
Learning and Reference	How do we distinguish between three major usages of text: • Initial learning • Reference • Browsing? How do we change the structuring of text to suit the needs of different users?
Paper- and Computer-based	To what degree do the constraints of storage and presentation within paper-based systems affect our design of text? What freedoms and constraints do we have using the computer for storage and presentation?
Transitions	How do we handle the functions of transitional phrases, words, sentences, and larger chunks?
Synonyms	Proliferating synonyms cause great difficulty in large files of information. How do we handle the question of synonyms?
Learner–reader Populations	Different readers have different reading levels and different styles. How do we write material that will be able to be used by a variety of different users?
Serialists and Holists	Pask and Scott (1972) and his associates have found that there are two different kinds of learners: holists and serialists. *Holists:* These learners, generally, scan a page in a variety of fashions reading only what they want.

**Serialists and
Holists
(Continued)**

They like to

- Open a book in the middle

- Flip around throughout the book

- Get the big picture

- Try problems from the end

Serialists: These learners start at the upper left-hand corner of page one and read along until they do not understand; then they go back and read the line over and over again until they do understand.

They do *not* like

- To have words thrown in that they do not understand

- Overviews very well because they always contain words that they do not understand

- To jump ahead and try to solve problems ahead of where they are.

How do we design text that will handle both types of learners?

Comment

These components are many and varied. Yet we attempt either in general standards or in project-specific guidelines to address explicitly each of the issues mentioned.

This list of questions only scratches the surface of the systematic work that has gone into the development of the Information Mapping approach to structured writing.

Questions about Specific Components

Introduction

After we divided our subject matter into a variety of different chunks, we had to develop standards for each of the chunks.

Comment

We cannot reproduce 400 pages of instructions, procedures, and standards here.

We can only indicate the kinds of problems that we faced and some of the general areas for which we have attempted to write standards and guidelines.

Definitions

One of the important Blocks on a concept map is the definition block.

How do you write definitions? Various observers have suggested 16–25 ways of writing a definition.

Do we write different definitions for different levels of population?

Examples

Among the questions that we address are

- How many examples need to be put in?
- What is the form of the example?
- What kind of nonexamples need to be put in?
- On which occasions do you need nonexamples?
- What should be the property of the nonexample?

Analogy

To what degree do we allow analogies to be just slipped in to our instructional prose?

Are we arguing from analogy, and are we labeling this clearly as an analogy?

Rules

To what degree do we simply present information as rules as opposed to presenting the reasons and perhaps the data that is involved?

Name (or Title) of the Map

Because we place a great value on the structure of information, each of the structures is named. Much like each subroutine of a computer program these topics have a distinct, unique name.

Some of the questions that *must* be considered include

- How do we name these chunks that we call Maps?
- What criteria should we use for selecting names?
- Should we have criteria for the name such as
  - Informative and functional
  - Not ambiguous, or
  - Cute or tricky?
- Where should we put the name?

Name (or Title) of the Map (Continued)	• What kind of distinctive typography should we use to facilitate access? • How are names different, depending upon the kind of subject matter you have; for example, how are the names of procedures different from the names of physical objects?
Priorities	If you have competing rule systems for different ways of labeling chunks of the subject matter, to what degree do you allow them to intermingle?
Standards for Words	To what degree are you going to require all technical terms to be defined? What should be the policies on jargon, slang, undefined terms, and undefined abbreviations? What style and tone should be used for different situations?
Standards for Sentences	How long should sentences be? What types of sentences are permitted, and which ones are not permitted? What kinds of formatting should we require for long lists of words, phrases, or sentences that are in a series?
Standards for Groups of Sentences	There are many standards that have to be set for groups of sentences. For example, we suggest that long bodies of text be broken up into smaller chunks. In fact, in many of our types of communications we are now recommending that there be a white space between each sentence. This permits, we believe, better scanning to occur.
Standards for Blocks	How are we to define and what are we to permit to be in a Block? Some of the questions that have been considered include the following: • May it be just one sentence? • May a Block contain several sentences?

Standards for Blocks (Continued)	• How many sentences may it contain?
	• May a Block be an elaborate diagram?
	• May a table be a Block?
	• May a list be a Block?
	• What do you do when your contents or subject matter gets too big for the existing chunk of information?

Comment	The reader can see that we address a great many questions of designing usable text in our guidelines and standards. Our approach has been to provide guidelines and standards where possible and defensible.

Result of Recent Research

Introduction	When we started working on structured writing 15 years ago, we surveyed the research on improving human communication and incorporated it into our design.
	Much of this research had to do with the components of structured writing.

Four Recent Theses	Recently four major dissertations were completed on the structured writing methods used in the Information Mapping® writing service.
	These four doctoral dissertations were done in three different countries: the United Kingdom, the Philippines, and the United States.

Two Other Studies	Two other important evaluation studies have been reported at conferences.

Populations	These studies were done with a variety of different students (high school and university and college students, adult learners, and clerical workers) ranging in low to high mental ability.

Compared With Prose or Programmed Instruction	All of the studies compared structured writing with some other method (either a conventional prose treatment or programmed instruction materials).

Compared Learning or Retrieval

Some of the studies compared two treatments from the standpoint of learning (errors and time), whereas other studies compared the ability of people to retrieve information from a document in joblike circumstances.

The latter test was done because we have pointed out that much of the learning that goes on in the business and industrial environment is relearning—that which requires the learner to go to a shelf of manuals, texts, or training materials and look up what they have forgotten or perhaps what they have never learned in the first place.

We have estimated that more than half of the learning that takes place in business and industry is of this type.

Summary Conclusions

All of these studies showed that structured writing was significantly superior to the more conventional methods in learning or reference or both.

We abstract these studies in the following table.

Summary of Recent Research on Structured Writing

INVESTIGATOR AND DATE	TYPE OF STUDY	VARIABLES	RESULTS	SUBJECTS
Stuart (1979)	Experimental	Structured writing versus conventional prose	Structured writing • resulted in better test performance in knowledge gain *and* • was preferred for readability, understandability, and acceptability	University students

INVESTIGATOR AND DATE	TYPE OF STUDY	VARIABLES	RESULTS	SUBJECTS
Stelnicki (1980)	Experimental	Structured writing versus conventional prose	Structured writing produced • higher gain scores for facts • high gain scores for learning concepts	Under-graduate college students
Jonnassen (1979)	Experimental	Structured writing versus programmed instruction	Structured writing provided a clear advantage in retrieving information from textual material	College seniors and graduate students
Webber (1979)	Evaluation	Structured writing versus conventional prose	With structured writing, training time was reduced by 50%, and subjects performed nearly twice as well on criterion tests.	Clerical workers
Romiszowski (1977)	Experimental	Structured writing versus conventional prose	With structured writing, subjects learned significantly more mathematics in less time.	High school adult learners

INVESTIGATOR AND DATE	TYPE OF STUDY	VARIABLES	RESULTS	SUBJECTS
Soyster (1980)	Experimental	Structured writing versus conventional prose	Subjects using instructional materials in structured writing achieved significantly higher levels of learning.	High school students ranging from low to high mental ability.

Webber (1979) Study

Introduction Naomi Webber of The Pacific Telephone Company reported on a result of an evaluation of a 2½-day course for clerical people on doing accounting coding tasks.

Her report, given at the convention of the National Society for Performance and Instruction in April 1979, indicated that learners using structured writing materials scored almost twice as well on the criterion test as did a similar group using programmed instruction texts (that had the characteristics of large amounts of text between questions).

Results *Initial Learning.* Learners using instructional material written according to the standards of the Information Mapping® writing service (MAP) scored almost twice as well on criterion tests as compared with a similar group using a programmed instruction (PI) text.

Training time. MAP learners took an average of 1 day in self-paced learning mode as compared with 2 days for PI students.

Attitude. Of the MAP learners, 80% felt the training was "fairly easy to easy" as compared with 60% of PI.

Of MAP learners, 95% felt "fairly well to well prepared and confident" at the end of training as compared with 44% of the PI learners.

Subjects   Clerical employees of the Pacific Telephone and Telegraph Company

Subject   Functional Accounting coding tasks
Matter

Other Results   "The performance level back on the job has been very good. We've seen them start out on the job making 85% accuracy to start out with, and within the month they're moving up into the 90's in on-the-job performance" (Weber, 1979).

Data

Factors/treatment	MAP	PI
Lesson test: average scores	95%	75%
Criterion test: average scores	91%	53%
Percentage of learners achieving 88% or above accuracy in • Lesson tests • Criterion tests	95% 83%	30% 0%
Course length	1 day	2 days

Comment   Webber did not describe controls or test instruments used in her study.

However, the study is significant in that it used real-world learners in real situations.

It is also important to note that it was a very large course—a more normal situation than many of the comparative learning studies we usually see.

Such studies are usually done on a small chapter or monograph of under 50 pages and take less than a couple of hours to work with.

We would expect structured writing to perform better the more material there was in the learning situation.

Importance
The importance of this study is obvious.

Marvin Sherman, a Cambridge (Massachusetts) office procedures and office automation specialist, has reported that 50–60% of the work done in an average office involves the correction of errors previously made.

Some of those errors, in fact a great many of them, are due to improper training and improper procedures.

Informal Research into Teachability and Uniformity

Introduction
One of the important questions that we need to face in having a comprehensive methodology of writing is, can we teach writers?

Other related questions include the following:

- How do we teach them with some assurance that our standards will be or can be followed by them?

- Would two or more of our trained writers deal with the same subject matter in a similar fashion?

- What implications does this have for the management of large writing teams?

We have done some informal experimentation with very encouraging results.

Experiment 1: Teaching
We teach several courses a month in writing procedures and instructional manuals.

In our classes we have an exercise that we give to every participant at about the third or fourth day of the course.

Time. The learners spend approximately 4–8 hours on this exercise.

Input. The input for this exercise is dialogue and drawings about how to run a piece of equipment (a printer from a data-processing system).

Expected Output. Seven maps all of the right type, right Blocks, and similar organization

Experiment 1: Teaching (Continued)

Results. We have never formally tabulated these in terms of a research methodology with strict criteria.

But we thoroughly edit the results of this test in each class.

We find approximately 80% or better congruity of answers of persons following the standards.

Implications. If we did a formal evaluation with judges scrambling the pages, and asked the judges to determine which person wrote which pages, we predict that the judges would be unable to tell who wrote which pages.

Second, the judges would find that 80% or more of the different treatments were almost identical with minor variations in wording.

Experiment 2: Inadvertent Experiment

Inadvertent experimental design. We taught a course here in England in 1973 at which Alexander Romiszowski attended.

Later, unknown to me, he developed a course in matrix algebra for business.

In the meantime, unknown to Romiszowski, I also wrote a course on matrix algebra.

About a year later he sent me a copy of his course.

Results. We found a remarkable similarity in choice of subject matter, division of the subject matter into Maps and Blocks and treatment of various Blocks.

We have never formally tabulated these results.

But I feel certain that judges would have been unable to tell from which of our two versions the pages came.

In other words, we could have scrambled the pages that Romiszowski and I each wrote and it would be impossible for a judge to tell from which version they came.

Conclusion

This illustrates that we can achieve a considerable uniformity and consistency of high-quality instruction using our methodology.

Future Research Should Focus on Variables

We have seen that research on our approach to structured writing yields improved communication, learning, and access.

Much needs to be done in the future.

In particular, future researchers should focus on finer-grain investigations of the variables we use.

Relearning and Review Need Investigation

Here are some of the important research questions:
How do we investigate "relearning" and how structured writing helps in looking up material?

What are the costs in "reinventing the wheel" because of poor access systems?

Decision-making Research

The executive reads large volumes of papers to make complex decisions.

How can structured writing improve the quality of the ordinary in-box?

I spoke recently with a manager from a large computer company who said that the company released a new piece of equipment every day.

That meant that the in-box of the sales person was filled with several inches of new product descriptions every day!

We need to do research in that environment.

Information-rich Environment

We are, many observers have said, in a time of information overload.

We need a considerable amount of experimentation and observation of the behavior of people operating in an "information-rich" environment.

Computer-based Handling

At Information Mapping, Inc., we have done some studies on computer-based handling of structured writing.

It has obvious uses in organization of large knowledge bases of text.

The next step is applications research.

Type of Readers

We are aware that structured writing has been used for a great many different kinds of readers and learners from elementary through postgraduate levels in education.

It has been used in industry for clerical workers and poor readers and for management, technical, and scientific people who have to process large amounts of information.

However, there is still a great deal of knowledge that needs to be obtained on the precise characteristics of different users.

Conclusion

Standards for Text

Most our writing is done in the real world of industrial training and writing.

We have developed a set of standards for our work in written communication that are based on the research available.

Our methodology permits the specification structuring and design of the basic parts of text that heretofore were only fuzzily described.

We feel that we have contributed to the process of standardization that Sen suggests (quoted by Verman, 1973) will provide a "stable basis essential to the growth and . . . consolidation of social, economic and technological attainments . . . so as to release creative energy for the search of higher and better values and systems."

We feel our research provides a wide jumping-off platform for future research on designing usable text.

REFERENCES

Ausubel, D. P. (1960). The use of advance organizers in the learning and retention of meaningful verbal material. *Journal of Educational Psychology, 51,* 267–272.

Ausubel, D. P. (1963). *The psychology of meaningful verbal learning.* New York: Grune & Straton.

Ausubel, D. P. (1964). Some psychological aspects of the structure of knowledge. In Phi Delta Kappa, *Education and the structure of knowledge.* Chicago: Rand-McNally.

Ausubel, D. P. (1968). *Educational psychology: A cognitive view.* New York: Holt.

Basecu, Bernard, & Horn, R. E. (1964, December). A response analysis system. *Programmed Instruction, IV.*(3).

Berry, Paul C. (1964). Pretending to have (or to be) a computer as a strategy in teaching. *Harvard Educational Review, 34,* 383–401.

Bloom, B. S. (Ed.) (1956). *Taxonomy of educational objectives, Handbook I: Cognitive domain.* New York, McKay.

Bruner, J. S. (1960). *The process of education,* New York, Vintage.

Bruner, J. S. (Ed.) (1966a). *Learning about learning: A conference report.* Washington, DC: U.S. Office of Education.

Bruner, J. S. (1966b). *Toward a theory of instruction.* Cambridge, Harvard University Press.

Carroll, John B. (1964). Words, meanings and concepts. *Harvard Educational Review, 34,* 178–202.

de Leeuw, H., & de Leeuw, E. (1965). *Read better, read faster.* Harmondsworth: Penguin.

Dixon, Paul (1964). Decision tables and their application. *Computers and Automation,* April, 14–19.

Dooling, E. S., & Lachman R. (1971). Effects of comprehension on retention of prose. *J. Experimental Psychology, 88,* 216–222.

Gagné, R. M. (1964). The implications of educational objectives for learning. In C. M. Lindvall, (Ed.), *Defining educational objectives* (pp. 37–46). University of Pittsburgh Press.

Gagné, R. M. (1965). *The conditions of learning.* New York, Holt.

Gagné, R. M., & Rhower, W. D. (1969). Instructional psychology. *Annual Review of Psychology, 20,* 381–418.

Gane, C. P., Horabin, I. S., & Lewis, B. N. (1966, April). Algorithms for decision making. In *The Proceedings of the Programmed Learning Conference,* Loughborough, England (pp. 481–502). London, Methuen.

Gilbert T. F. (1962, January). Mathetics: The technology of education. *The Journal of Mathetics, I*(1).

Glaser, R. (1965). *Training research and education.* New York: Wiley.

Hartley, J., & Trueman, M. (1983). The effect of headings in text on recall, search, and retrieval. *British Journal for Educational Psychology, 53,* 209–214.

Horn, R. E. (1963a). *Systematic task analysis.* New York, CPI Technical Memorandum Series.

Horn, R. E. (1963b). *A typology of branching technique.* New York, CPI Technical Memorandum Series.

Horn, R. E. (1966). A terminal behaviour locator system. *Programed Learning (United Kingdom),* February.

Horn, R. E. (1967). Information maps and computer-based learning and reference. *A research proposal for Hq Electronic Systems Division.* Bedford, MA: U.S. Air Force Systems Command.

Horn, R. E. (1980). *The research evidence about the Information Mapping® writing services approach to structured writing,* Lexington, MA.

Jonnassen, David H. (1979, February). *Recall and retrieval from mapped and programed text.* Paper presented to the AECT Convention, New Orleans, LA.

Katona, G. (1940). *Organizing and Memorizing.* New York: Columbia University Press.

McLaughlin, J. H. (1966). Comparing styles of presenting technical information. *Ergonomics, 9*(3), 257–259.

Miller, G. A. (1967). *The psychology of communication.* New York: Basic Books.

Miller, R. B. (1962). Analysis and Specification of Behavior for Training. *In* R. Glaser (Ed.), *Training research and education* (pp. 31–62). Pittsburgh: University of Pittsburgh Press.

Pask, G., & Scott, B. C. E. (1972). Learning strategies and individual competence. *International Journal Man Machine Studies, 4,* 217–253.

Roderburg, T. K., Cluck, H. D., Murray, G. R., Jr. (1964, November). *Preliminary research on the taxonomy of subject matter* Decision Sciences Laboratory, Electronic Systems Division, Air Force Systems Command, U.S. Air Force, L. G. Hanscom Field, Bedford, MA. Technical Documentary Report No. ESD-TDR-64-618 (Contract Nol AFI9 (628)-2407).

Romiszowski, Alexander J. (1977, June). *A study of individualized systems for mathematics instruction at the post secondary levels.* Unpublished Ph.D. Thesis, Loughborough University of Technology (U.K.).

Soyster, Thomas G. (1980). *A comparison of the effects of programmed instruction and the Information Mapping® method of instructional design on learning and retention of students with different mental abilities.* Unpublished Ed.D. Thesis, Temple University.

Stelnicki, Michael (1980). *The effects of information-mapped and standard text presentations with fact and concept levels of learning on low general ability adult learner cognition.* Unpublished Ed.D Thesis, Northern Illinois University.

Stuart, Teresa Habito (1979, October). *The effectiveness of Information Mapping® compared with the conventional paragraph in communicating technical information.* Unpublished Master's Thesis, University of the Philippines at Los Banos.

Underwood, B. J. (1966). *Experimental psychology.* New York: Appleton-Century-Crofts.

Upton, Albert, & Samson, R. W. (1961). *Creative analysis.* Whittier, College Press.

U.S. Department of the Air Force (1965, September). *The decision logic table technique* (Air Force Pamphlet, No. 5-1-1). Washington, DC.

Verman, Lal Chand (1973). *Standardization: A new discipline.* Hamden, CT: Archon Books.

Webber, Naomi (1979, April). *Some results of using the Information Mapping® writing service standards at Pacific Telephone Company.* Paper presented at National Society for Performance and Instruction, Washington, DC.

Woolman, Myron (1962). *The concept of the program lattice.* Washington, DC: The Institute of Educational Research.

CHAPTER 10

Design Strategies for Job Performance Aids

Robert J. Smillie

INTRODUCTION

Isaac Asimov (1969), the noted science fiction author, once wrote a story about two astronauts who were sent to some distant space station. Due to the restrictions of space travel, all the numerous pieces of sophisticated equipment required to establish and operate the station were sent unassembled, each with its own manual of instructions. After months of trying to understand the instructions that were perfectly clear to the writers of those instructions back on earth, the astronauts sent a message requesting assistance for assembling and repairing the equipment. Earth responded by sending a specially designed robot that could read and understand the complicated instructions and thus correctly assemble the equipment. When the rocket with the robot landed, the astronauts rushed over to it, removed a large container marked ''robot,'' opened it, and found 500 assorted parts and one $8\frac{1}{2} \times 11$ sheet of paper with blurred and ambiguous assembly instructions.

How many hours have been wasted on Christmas Eves and birthdays trying to assemble a bicycle or other toy from instructions that were difficult to understand? How much confusion has been caused by the photographs that are included in some instructions that show, for example, the lubrication points on a sewing machine or an automobile in which the locator arrows are obscured by some extraneous detail of the photo? How much frustration has been caused by the oft-used phrase in assembly and repair instructions, ''on models so equipped,'' when only a single set of instructions are prepared for multiple models? All of these examples illustrate how poorly instructions are generally written.

The problem of poorly written instructions is not new, and in fact, the solution is also not new. In the 1950s document designers recognized that the greatest portions of technical jobs, that is, maintaining and repairing various mechanical and electronic equipment, required procedural information. Previously individuals had received technical training by using manuals that contained mostly descriptive information. After training, time on the job (i.e., experience) was used to "discover" the best procedure for doing such technical tasks as checking, adjusting, servicing, removing, and replacing. Unfortunately, during this discovery period the individual performed many actions that were incorrect, and the overall time to complete specific tasks was unnecessarily long. Even if special ways of doing procedural tasks were emphasized during training, the individual had to rely on his or her memory on the job. In other words, there was a gap between the requirements of the job and the initial proficiency of the individual assigned to that job. Thus it was recognized that a well-designed set of procedural instructions that was highly prescriptive would aid job performance and would allow the newly trained individual to be able to do the procedural tasks without having to rely on memory or to discover his or her own procedure. This set of prescriptive procedures is called a job performance aid (JPA).

DEFINITION AND CHARACTERISTICS

While a JPA has been defined many ways, the definition used most often is, a JPA is a set of step-by-step instructions supported by illustrations. A typical example of a JPA is given in Figure 1. The name, job performance aid, evolved from the fact that, for specific job situations, instructional guidance is developed to aid the performance of that job or task. Other names include handbooks, job instructions, job aids, job guides, manuals, and checklists.

As already described, one way of performing specific tasks is to train for the tasks and try to recall from memory the exact way you were trained. Studies in cognitive psychology have shown that when individuals are required to remember something, it is easier to recall that something shortly after being exposed to it, that is, the longer the period of time between the training for a task and the performance of that task the harder it is to remember the exact training.

A major characteristic of the JPA is reliance upon short-term memory. JPAs provide on-the-job information through the use of detailed procedural instructions supported by explanatory illustrations. The individual only has to read the specific procedural step, look at the accompanying illustration, and then perform the required action and continue in this way until the task is completed.

A second characteristic of JPAs is that information is task oriented. Because JPAs are written for specific tasks, only the information needed to accomplish that task is provided. All extraneous information, for example, the purpose of a task, is deleted. The information relates only to the task for which the JPA was written. Prior to the presentation of the task steps, all the information necessary

Remove Air Cleaner Hose

4. Using blade screwdriver, loosen lower clamp screw (4).
5. Spread clamp (5) until it is loose.
6. Slide off air cleaner hose (6).

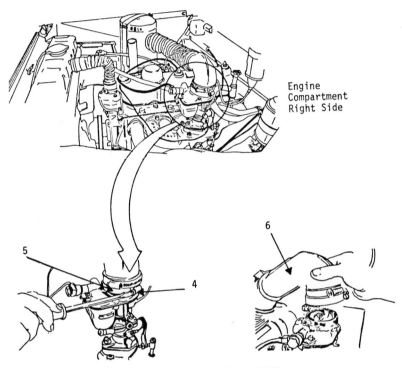

Engine
Compartment
Right Side

Fig. 1.   An example of a JPA (Shriver, 1975).

to start the specified task is also given. In this way, individuals are told what tools and materials they will need as they perform the task steps.

A third characteristic of a JPA is its focus on the user. Development of a JPA requires an understanding of the people who will be using the JPA in order to orient the task information to the capabilities of the user. For example, if the task requires the use of an adjustable wrench, the JPA designer has to determine if the user knows how to use the wrench. If not, some steps in the JPA will have to include "how-to" information on the use of an adjustable wrench. The JPA designer must understand the behaviors that will be used when the task is performed in order to develop information that reflects those behaviors.

JOB PERFORMANCE AID DEVELOPMENT

Systems Approach

As part of a systematic development process, JPAs have to be fully integrated with both the personnel and the equipment requirements. In the systems approach for design and development of a specific system, whether it is a weapons system or the development of a new automobile, the model delineating the elements and defining the developmental processes is the same, and is illustrated in Figure 2.

The initialization of the development process is more than defining the purpose for the new system or product. It must include function allocation and task analysis. In function allocation, the decisions are made as to what portions of the new system or product will be automatic or manual. Then decisions are based on human physical limitations and information-processing capabilities. For example, in the design of a new vehicle, technology may make it advantageous to automate the changing of gears, whereas the guidance and control may still rest with the operator. In the task analysis every task and function, in particular the ones performed by the human, have to be described in order to identify the personnel and equipment requirements. Task analysis is a technique developed by human factor psychologists to match the requirements of the job with the capabilities of the humans who will be expected to perform that job. For a more in-depth treatment of task analysis, the reader is referred to any general human factors text, for example, Meister and Rabideau (1965) or McCormick and Sanders (1982).

The important aspect of the personnel requirements is the user description. With this description the level of detail for the various technical data and training information can be developed. The user description identifies the intended users of the JPAs and has to address (1) job-relevant skills, knowledge, and experience, and (2) reading ability.

A user description should be developed for each category of people who will be required to operate or maintain the new system or product. This would be particularly difficult if the product is targeted for a wide range of consumers. The various trade-off points have to be identified. For example, a function identified in the task analysis as manual may, based upon the user description, have to be automated.

The equipment requirements should correlate with the personnel requirements. The functions originally designated as automatic may not be within the state of the art or may, for cost considerations, be considered inappropriate for automatic functions. Therefore, personnel requirements may have to reconsider additional functions that will be under manual control. On the other hand, the output of

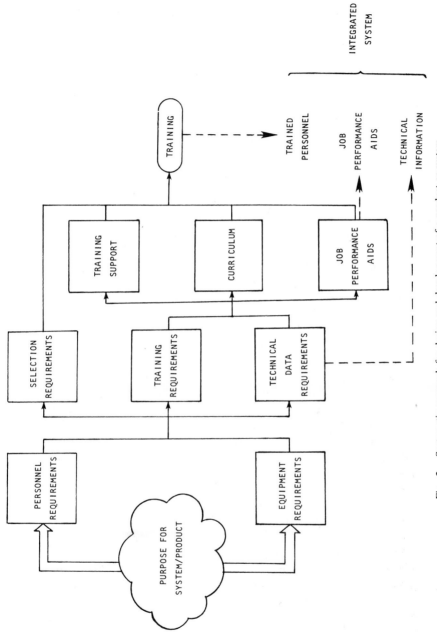

Fig. 2. Systematic approach for design and development of a product or system.

several manual functions may serve as an input to a piece of equipment, for example, a display, that can then be developed as an operator aid.

The completion of the task analysis will provide a complete listing of all tasks that have to be performed. Input from the personnel requirements and human–machine interface requirements will provide a listing of tasks that will have to be performed by the users. While technical data will have to be developed for all these tasks, the individual training requirements relating to these tasks will also have to be identified.

For the technical data requirements, all the information needed to adequately support training and on-the-job-performance is identified. Once the information is identified, the level of detail for the technical data has to be determined. As in the training requirements, in which a training–JPA trade-off must be made, the technical data development process also reflects a similar trade-off. Technical data that are going to serve as a base for training materials should be less detailed than the data that are going to be developed into stand-alone JPAs. Training implies learning the technical data to a certain criterion. On the other hand, the technical data for the same procedures, if relegated to a JPA, will require all the details necessary for successful completion. This does not imply that technical data learned in training will not be documented in adequate detail. On the contrary, technical data along with the source data used to develop training materials have to contain all the information that is required to accomplish all the identified tasks. The format of the data, however, will differ between training materials and JPAs.

Based on the training requirements, JPA–training trade-off ground rules have to be established to determine what should be put into JPAs. The trade-off rules determine what tasks the user has to perform with (1) training alone, (2) JPAs alone, and (3) both training and JPAs.

The trade-off ground rules are generated from consideration of what the operator, maintainer, or consumer has to do to operate and maintain the new system or product (task analysis) and what they are capable of doing (user description). While most assembly/disassembly tasks can be learned via training, it is uneconomical and relatively impossible to train consumers. In addition, for stressful situations, complete reliance on training (memory) could contribute to performance decrement. Thus, in determining the training/JPA trade-off ground rules, the following factors should be considered (adapted from Joyce, Chenzoff, Mulligan, & Mallory, 1973b).

1. **Ease of communication—learning versus book (JPA).** Put into training, tasks that are hard to communicate through words, for example, difficult adjustments. Put into JPAs, tasks that would benefit from the inclusion of illustrations, tables, graphs, flow charts, and so on.

2. **Criticality of the task.** Put into training, tasks in which the consequences of error are serious, for example, emergency procedures. Put into JPAs, tasks that require verification of readings and tolerances.

3. **Complexity of the task.** Put into training, tasks with difficult adjustments and procedures that can only be achieved through practice. Put into JPAs, tasks that require long and complex behavioral sequences and that are extremely costly to teach.

4. **Time required to perform the task.** Put into training, tasks with a response rate that do not permit reference to a printed instructions, for example, initial reaction to an emergency. Put into JPAs, tasks that are long and require attention to detail.

5. **Frequency of the task or similar tasks.** Put into training, tasks that are easy to learn through experience on the job, for example, day-to-day tasks. Put into JPAs, tasks that are rarely performed.

6. **Psychomotor component of the task.** Put into training, tasks that require extensive practice for acceptable performance, for example, vehicle operation. Put into JPAs, tasks in which reference to printed instructions are not disruptive to task performance.

7. **Cognitive component of the task.** Put into training, tasks that require evaluation of numerous existing conditions prior to making a decision. Put into JPAs, tasks in which binary fault trees can be developed into a decision aid.

8. **Equipment complexity and accessibility.** Put into training, tasks in which equipment is easily accessed. Put into JPAs, tasks that require detailed procedures to properly access equipment.

9. **Personnel constraints.** Put into training, tasks that require a team effort. Put into JPAs, only one- or two-man tasks.

10. **Consequences of improper task performance.** Put into training, tasks in which an occasional error will not damage equipment. Put into JPAs, tasks that require branching, for example, a diagnostic decision aid that lists failure mode symptoms.

It may be apparent that the application of one of these ground rules may conflict with another. Therefore, it is important not to apply these ground rules indiscriminately. Rather, each must be considered in the total context of tasks to be performed. Moreover, the application of these rules is only a preliminary step. During the actual design and development of the training curriculum and JPAs, the analyst may discover additional trade-offs that have to be made.

DEVELOPMENT PROCESS

After it has been determined what tasks will be learned through training and what tasks will be developed as JPAs, a behavioral task analysis is required for those JPAs that will be used as procedures.

The behavioral task analysis (see Shriver, 1975) lists each task element of a given task sequentially with each element analyzed in human performance terms. The delineation of the behavioral task analysis requires the analyst to identify and to describe exactly what the user will do. This requirement usually means that the analyst will have to either do the task himself or to observe another doing it. Each task element has to be carefully analyzed and described in detail. Along with each task element, the following should be described:

1. **Hardware interface.** What are the controls, displays, support equipment, and so on, the individual performing the task will encounter?
2. **Criticality.** What are the consequences of performing the task incorrectly?
3. **Cue.** What does the individual see, hear, smell, and feel to initiate the task?
4. **Response.** What action is required by the task performer when the task is initiated?
5. **Feedback.** What indication does the task performer have that the task element was completed correctly?
6. **Performance criteria.** What are the time and accuracy constraints of the task?
7. **References.** What was the source data used to generate the task element?

After the behavioral task analysis, the construction of the JPA begins, and decisions have to be made regarding the text and illustration requirement. When considering the format for the text, requirements have to be established for

1. Layout and size
2. Typeface and size
3. Borders
4. Page numbering scheme
5. Indexing
6. Method of tracking change pages
7. Placement of warnings, cautions, and notes
8. Paper stock
9. Binding method.

For illustrations, requirements have to be established for

1. Quality
2. Level of detail
3. Angle of view
4. Locator illustrations
5. Item enlargement
6. Exploded views
7. Call-outs.

The final step for JPA development is the validation and verification of the JPA. Once the JPA has been written, personnel representative of the intended users should perform the task on the equipment with no information other than that contained in the JPA. Successful performance will be an indication of the validity of the technical accuracy and intelligibility of the JPA. JPAs for tasks performed incorrectly must be corrected and revalidated. Verification differs from validation in that it requires the actual users in the user environment performing the task with the JPA. It can be thought of as the preliminary issue of the JPA because feedback from this field tryout should be used to produce the final product—a complete, accurate, understandable, and usable document.

The development of JPAs should be a planned systematic activity. Although developed for tasks in a military environment, two publications that provide specific guidance on systematic JPA development are Joyce, Chenzoff, Mulligan, and Mallory (1973a, 1973b). Joyce *et al.* (1973a) provides a military specification based upon behavioral research findings. Joyce *et al.* (1973b) is a handbook of detailed instructions for preparing JPAs according to the specification.

DESIGN STRATEGIES AND FORMATS

DESIGN STRATEGIES

Design strategies for JPAs have to focus on the purpose for which the JPA is developed. The passenger emergency information card on airlines is an attempt to convey a small amount of important information in a fully pictorial, attention-getting format. The purpose of this format is to present information that can be easily learned and recalled. The audience to which this information is directed varies widely in experience with this type of information and language ability. In addition, passengers generally have a short attention span and low motivation for an emergency that is very unlikely to occur. The resulting design strategy places heavy emphasis on illustrations over text because pictorial information is easy and quick to comprehend, and recall is superior. If there were a lot of emergency information and procedures to learn, a different strategy may have to be used. For example, airline pilots are trained and learn procedures for many types of emergencies. During the emergency only a narrative checklist is used to ensure all emergency actions are correctly executed.

In contrast a set of assembly instructions that are included with a new kitchen faucet usually includes illustrations with supplemental text keyed to each illustration that explains or amplifies the illustration. The purpose of this format is to describe desired behavior in enough detail to permit correct assembly. The audience for this information is more than likely totally unfamiliar with the information and will only use the information one time. Motivation, however, can be expected to be high; that is, the need to have the faucet work. Language is less of a problem, too, because users are more likely (when compared to airline travelers) to buy and use the product in the same area in which they live; that is, unless there was a serious marketing faux pas, the product information will be in the audience's language. The resulting design strategy is an illustration–text combination because resources, for example, tools and parts, have to be listed (text), part recognition is important (illustrations), caution and warnings have to be listed (text), and redundancy helps ensure correct assembly (illustrations with text). The problem, of course, is how does the JPA developer choose the correct design strategy?

The key to the well-designed JPA is the user. In an experiment comparing interpretations of sequences of pictorial instructions, Marcel and Barnard (1979) found that consideration of the task context alone will not necessarily provide a good design. The designer has to consider how the user will interact with a JPA. Specifically, the designer should try to anticipate, by actual user input, if possible, any questions or problems the user may have when using the JPA. Swaney, Janik, Bond, and Hayes (1981) found that good editing techniques were not effective unless the user was considered. In a series of experiments that used standard editing techniques to improve the comprehensibility of various documents, the authors found significant improvement only when reader protocols were used. The edited documents were rewritten after reader protocols were obtained to pinpoint comprehension difficulties. The importance of the user, that is, the target population, can not be overemphasized.

A primary characteristic of JPA development is the consistent focus of attention on the user in both the identification of information requirements and the formatting of that information. An optional format requires decisions concerning the mix of text and graphics, level of detail of both text and graphics, page layout, typeface, and writing style. Judgments on each of these issues must be based on a consideration of the user with the objective being the presentation of information in an unambiguous form for that user.

JPA FORMAT

The metric for format is the frame. In the paper medium, a frame consists of either a single page or two facing pages. Each frame has an integrated text and graphic field. Frames can be organized to have either the text support the illustrations or the illustrations support the text. Textual material is presented as discrete steps. And, although other formats are possible, the four most often used for standard operation, maintenance and assembly instructions, that is, proceduralized JPAs, are

1. Text and graphics are completely integrated (Figure 3).
2. The frame is divided vertically; text is presented on the left and graphics are given on the right. A similar version divides the frame horizontally with text on top and graphics on the bottom. Use of this format implies that the frame is approximately divided in half with both text and graphics always present (Figure 4).
3. Illustrations vary in size; the graphics are placed as required to support the

text (Figure 5). Depending on level of detail, use of this format is similar to the previous one.

4. Graphics are used sparingly with heavy text and only to illustrate areas unfamiliar to the user. Use of this format implies the writer has a fairly complete understanding of where the user may need clarification of the information presented in the text (Figure 6).

In these four formats, the level of detail, that is, how much information is enough, is a function of the audience characteristics, and, as such, has to be defined to meet the information requirements of that audience.

Troubleshooting JPAs, that is, information in which decisions have to be made to determine why something is malfunctioning, has been developed in a number of different formats. Functionally, however, the information is usually presented in either a table or chart format (Figure 7), or in a fault logic tree format (Figure 8). Usually, troubleshooting JPAs are less proceduralized than JPAs presented in the aformentioned four formats. The same formats, however, can be used to present proceduralized troubleshooting information. For example, Figure 9 uses the heavy text format to present a fault logic tree.

FORMAT VERSUS DESIGN STRATEGY

In tying format to design strategy it is important to realize that JPA formats can be categorized as either directive or deductive. With directive formats, all the information necessary to perform a task is included. In other words, it is assumed that the individual who is to perform the task knows no more about the task than the general population. For example, developing assembly instructions for a bicycle, the writer may assume that the user will understand how to use some basic hand tools. But to extend those assumptions to include an understanding of mechanics may result in providing a JPA that a large proportion of the population will not comprehend or, at the very least, become frustrated attempting to interpret what the writer had in mind. The format requirements for this example would also have to address the user's unfamiliarity with the product, which would necessitate the use of illustrations to clearly convey the intended meaning of the text. For a deductive format, however, the users are expected to know some information (by training and/or experience) about the task or product. For example, the development of a service manual for a new automobile is usually based on the premise that the individuals who will use the manual will be mechanics who are trained and experienced. Thus the manual writer does not have to go into great detail, with both text and illustrations, about the use of special tools or explain maintenance procedures common to all automobiles.

As a result of this dual categorization, two major design strategies emerge: directive formats are best for novice users, deductive formats are best for experienced users. To be effective for a wide range of users, however, more flexible

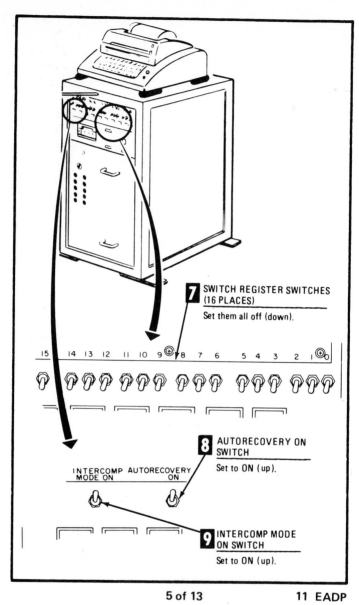

11 EADP

Fig. 3.   An example of a JPA with complete integration of text and graphics (Products produced under contract to the U.S. Navy Personnel Research and Development Center, EPICS Project Development Office, Code 52E, San Diego, CA 92152).

FRAME 5

REMOVE POWER SUPPLIES (Cont.):

NOTE: • If removing power supply A14, skip step 11 and go directly to step 12.
• If removing power supply A13, A15, or A16, skip step 12 and go directly to step 13.

11. Unscrew four screws, lockwashers, and washers (25) holding power supply (15, 16, 18) to plate (23). Remove power supply from plate.

12. Unscrew six Phillips screws, lockwashers, and washers (26) holding power supply (17) to mounting plate (23). Remove power supply from plate.

END OF REMOVE POWER SUPPLIES

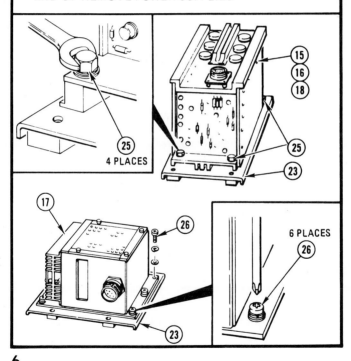

6

Fig. 4. An example of a JPA with text and graphics separated according to frame division.(Products produced under contract to the U.S. Navy Personnel Research and Development Center, EPICS Project Development Office, Code 52E, San Diego, CA 92152).

20. *Connect sensing hose (7) to elbow (6) and tighten jamnut (8).*

21. *Connect vent hose (4) to elbow (5) and tighten jamnut (9).*

22. *Connect fuel outlet hose (2) to reducer (1) and tighten.*

23. *Connect pad drain hoses (16 and 17) to T-fitting (18). Tighten jamnut (19).*

24. *Tighten fuel inlet hose (10).*

25. *Connect fuel enrichment hose (15) to check valve (14). Tighten jamnut (13).*

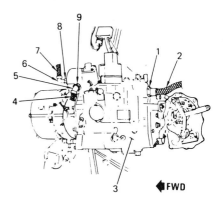

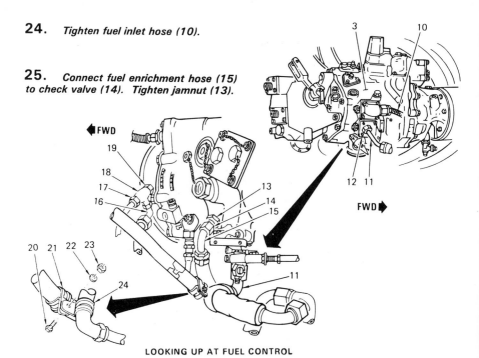

LOOKING UP AT FUEL CONTROL

Fig. 5. An example of a JPA with graphics placed, when required, to support text (Naval Air Systems Command, 1982).

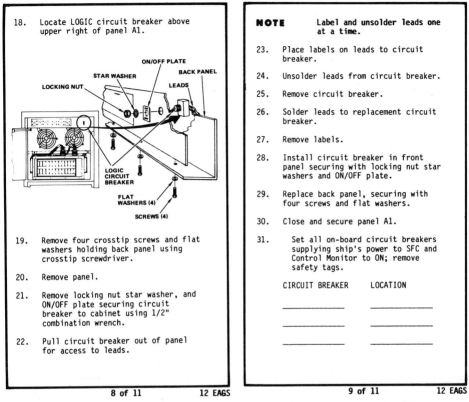

18. Locate LOGIC circuit breaker above upper right of panel A1.

19. Remove four crosstip screws and flat washers holding back panel using crosstip screwdriver.

20. Remove panel.

21. Remove locking nut star washer, and ON/OFF plate securing circuit breaker to cabinet using 1/2" combination wrench.

22. Pull circuit breaker out of panel for access to leads.

NOTE   Label and unsolder leads one at a time.

23. Place labels on leads to circuit breaker.

24. Unsolder leads from circuit breaker.

25. Remove circuit breaker.

26. Solder leads to replacement circuit breaker.

27. Remove labels.

28. Install circuit breaker in front panel securing with locking nut star washers and ON/OFF plate.

29. Replace back panel, securing with four screws and flat washers.

30. Close and secure panel A1.

31. Set all on-board circuit breakers supplying ship's power to SFC and Control Monitor to ON; remove safety tags.

CIRCUIT BREAKER	LOCATION
_____	_____
_____	_____
_____	_____

Fig. 6.   An example of a JPA in which text is emphasized and illustrations are used only to illustrate areas that might be unfamiliar to the user. (Products produced under contract to the U.S. Navy Personnel Research and Development Center, EPICS Project Development Office, Code 52E, San Diego, CA 92152).

design strategies are required, that is, strategies that address users at an intermediate level. One such strategy that has been used for troubleshooting is the hybrid JPA (Post & Price, 1972, 1973).

The hybrid JPA presents similar information at both a directive and deductive level. The purpose of the hybrid JPA is to enhance task performance by allowing individual flexibility in using the task information, that is, the inexperienced user can use the directive portion of the JPA and at the same time observe how the deductive portion of the JPA can be used to perform the same task. Such an approach is particularly useful in troubleshooting where there will be constant user interaction with the technical information. Figure 10 illustrates an example of a hybrid JPA in which the directive portion is a decision tree and the deductive portion a functional flow diagram.

Fault Indication	Trouble Isolation Data
1. RSC SYSTEM STATUS-GO light off and;	
a. RECEIVER light on alone	Refer to, Receiver Group Fault Directory, table 5-43
b. DIRECTOR light on alone	Refer to, Director Group Fault Directory, table 5-34
c. RADAR PROCESSOR light on alone	Refer to, RTDP Fault Directory, table 5-5
d. TRANSMITTER light on alone	Refer to, Transmitter Group Fault Directory, table 5-51
e. RADAR CONSOLE light on alone	Refer to, RSC Fault Directory, table 5-14
f. TV light on alone	Refer to, table 3-1, NAVORD OP 4053
g. FIRING CONSOLE light on alone	Refer to, FOC Fault Directory, table 5-59
h. COMPUTER COMPLEX light on with or without SYSTEM PERFORMANCE light	To determine if the fault is in the computer or SDC refer to NAVSEA OP 4004, table 9-1
i. SYSTEM PERFORMANCE light on	Refer to table 9-1 in NAVSEA OP 4004
2. RSC SYSTEM STATUS-GO light on and;	
a. Range/Range Rate indicator failure occurs	Refer to, SDC to RSC Analog Data Transfer procedure, paragraph 5-60
b. Director position indicators failure occurs	Refer to, SDC to RSC Analog Data Transfer procedure, paragraph 5-60
c. Indicator/logic failure occurs	Refer to, RSC Switch and Control Logic FID Off-Line Test procedure, paragraph 5-70

Fig. 7.   Table format used to present troubleshooting information (Naval Sea Systems Command, 1976).

A design strategy that incorporates hybrid JPAs is one that is sensitive to the motivation of the user. Specifically, the hybrid JPA provides the user with directive information to ensure task completion but allows the user to learn how to use the more abstract information in the deductive portion. Thus there are several advantages to using such a design strategy because

1. Inexperienced users can use the directive portion to complete tasks.
2. Experienced users can use the deductive portion to complete tasks.
3. Users at an intermediate level can use whatever portion or parts of the JPA that meets their information needs.
4. Inexperienced users can use the dual format to gradually learn the deductive troubleshooting process and become experienced users.

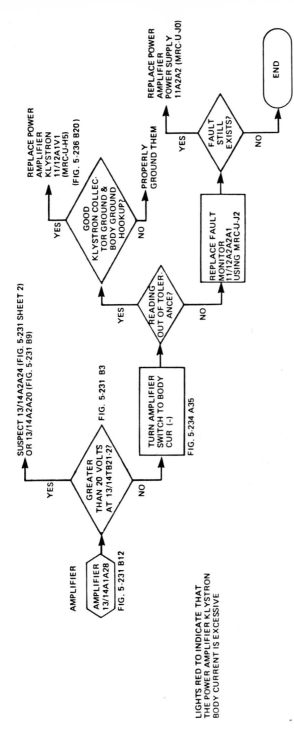

Fig. 8. An example of a fault logic tree JPA format. (Products produced under contract to the U.S. Navy Personnel Research and Development Center, EPICS Project Development Office, Code 52E, San Diego, CA 92152).

AT

21. Set HOT control to OFF. Disconnect Pressure Gauge.

22. Shut OFF gas to WH-1.

23. Shut OFF water supply.

24. Set HOT control to ON. Allow pressure to bleed off.
    Set HOT control to OFF.

25. Disconnect P-2 from WH-1. Connect Pressure Gauge to WH-1 outlet.

26. Turn water supply ON. Check that the Pressure Gauge indicates
    between 59.9 and 60.1 PSI. If not, go to Step 33.

27. Shut OFF water supply. Disconnect Pressure Gauge from WH-1.
    Reconnect P-2 to WH-1.

28. Disconnect P-2 from V-1. Connect Pressure Gauge to P-2.

29. Turn ON water supply. Check that Pressure Gauge indicates between
    59.9 and 60.1 PSI. If not, go to Step 31.

30. Shut OFF water supply. Disconnect Pressure Gauge. Replace V-1
    and go to Step 32.

31. Shut OFF water supply. Disconnect Pressure Gauge. Replace P-2
    and go to Step 32.

32. Reconnect P-2 and V-1. Turn water supply ON, go to Step 1.

CAUTION

33. Shut OFF water supply. Replace WH-1. Be sure to reconnect P-2
    before turning water supply ON.

34. Turn Water supply ON. Go to Step 1.

Fig. 9. Text format used to present fault logic tree type information (Joyce, Chenzoff, Mulligan, & Mallory, 1973b).

A similar strategy that incorporates a dual format, but for proceduralized information, is one in which major divisions of the information provide "what-to-do" information and subordinate divisions provide "how-to-do-it" information. Figure 11 is an example of this approach in which "what-to-do" are the numbered steps. As users do the tasks over and over, that is, becomes more experienced, they can use the numbered steps as a checklist to remind them what must be done to complete the task.

Such design strategies that provide dual formats are necessary because many users, over time, begin to resent the step-by-step approach every time the task is performed. If instructions can only be used one way, the users, after a time, may stop using the JPA because they feel they do not need that much detail every time. Thus a dual format provides the user with an opportunity to discard the fully detailed or directive JPA crutch. The user can now move on to a situation in which memory and deductive reasoning can be used along with the JPA to complete the tasks. This type of approach appears to provide users with some type of intrinsic reward; that is, they are dependent on themselves for filling in the gaps.

Another design strategy technique that makes JPAs more acceptable to the users is enrichment. Enrichment is information added to a JPA that is relevant to the task but is not related to the task sequence. For example, enrichment information can provide insights to the user by providing purpose statements, that is, explaining why certain task steps need to be performed in a specified way. Enrichment can also be used to add to the user's knowledge, reinforce training previously received, and answer naturally occurring user questions that may arise during task performance. Thus enrichment should increase the user's job satisfaction and further the user's acceptance of the JPA. Figure 12 is an example of a JPA with enrichment information. The enrichment is boxed to set it off from the rest of the task steps.

RESEARCH ON JOB PERFORMANCE AIDS

Although it is difficult to determine when the term *job performance aid* came into existence, the concept came into prominence in the 1950s. During this time period, behavioral researchers at the Air Force Personnel and Training Research Center in Colorado realized that (1) many of the technical jobs in the military were procedural and (2) the approach to the development of technical manuals was inadequate (Folley, 1972).

Technical manuals were written from an equipment perspective with emphasis placed on the physical and functional descriptions of the system. It was during training that instructors demonstrated the procedures necessary to operate and maintain the system. Thus, the newly trained technicians had to remember all the

(a)

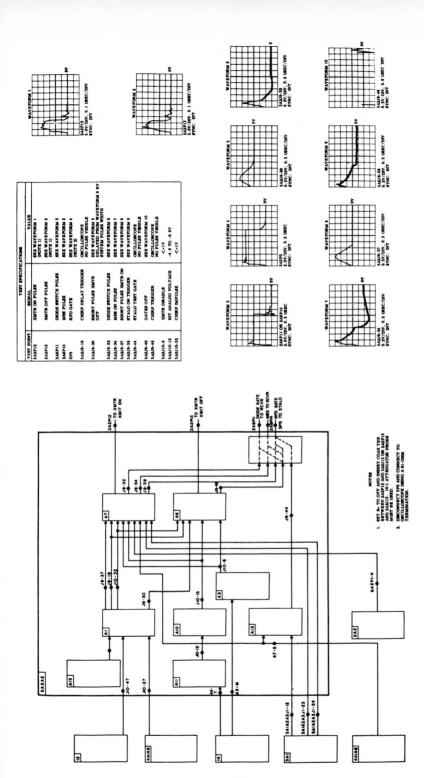

(b)

Fig. 10. An example of a hybrid JPA: (a) directive portion, (b) deductive portion (Products produced under contract to the U.S. Navy Personnel Research and Development Center, EPICS Project Development Office, Code 52E, San Diego, CA 92152).

233

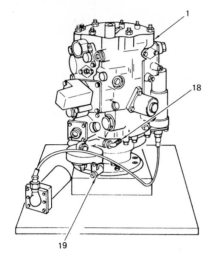

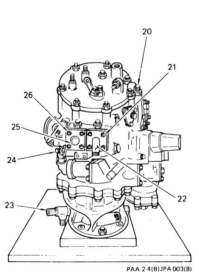

PAA 2-4(B)JPA 003(8)

NOTE

Fuel control pointer (12) must be at 0° to remove bolt (9).

26. **Remove coordinator (8) from fuel control (1):**

a. Remove bolts (9 and 15) and rod (11).

b. Remove bolts (6 and 7) and rod (5).

c. Remove bolt (17).

d. Remove lever (16).

e. Remove three nuts (10) and washers.

f. Remove coordinator (8) from fuel control (1).

NOTE

Tag all parts removed for identification, location, and orientation, as applicable.

27. **Remove fittings from fuel control (1):**

a. Remove elbows (18 and 19).

b. Remove reducer (20).

c. Remove four bolts (21) and inlet adapter (22).

d. Remove four bolts (26) and bypass adapter (25).

e. Remove tee (23).

f. Remove check valve (24).

g. Discard packings.

END OF REMOVAL TASK

Fig. 11.   Dual approach format used to present procedural information (Naval Air Systems Command, 1982).

procedural information they were given during training because the technical manual contained none. Any procedures that were omitted during training had to be learned on the job through experience.

It was Miller (1956) who emphasized an analysis of the job in order to develop complete and concise job instructions that are compatible with the characteristics of the user population. For example, if a given task required the use of a

PROCEDURES

NOTE

On dual system installation, do steps 1 through 3 on both Radar Set Consoles (RSC).

If GENERAL CONTROLS-OFF indicator at RSC is lit, go to step 4.

1. At RSC, depress CONTROL-FIRING CONSOLE/LOCAL pushbutton indicator; verify LOCAL portion of indicator is lit.

2. Depress GENERAL CONTROLS-STANDBY pushbutton indicator; verify STANDBY indicator lights green.

3. Depress GENERAL CONTROLS-OFF pushbutton indicator; verify OFF indicator is lit.

4. At Firing Officer Console (FOC), depress SYSTEM ON/OFF pushbutton indicator; verify OFF portion of indicator is lit.

5. Set all on-board circuit breakers supplying ship's power to FOC to OFF; attach safety tags.

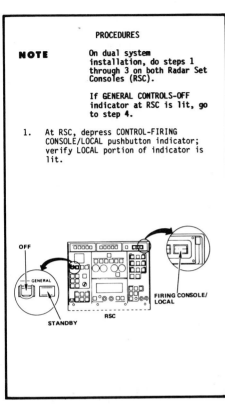

The purpose of the elevation torque receiver marked scale indicator 19A5B1 is to display the launcher elevation position.

For the schematic indicator of 19A5B1, refer to OP 4005, Vol. 2, Part 6, Figure 5-266.

The purpose of the train torque receiver marked scale indicator 19A5B2 is to display the launcher train position in relative coordinates (0 degrees represents ship's head).

For a schematic representation of 19A5B2, refer to OP 4005, Vol. 2, Part 6, Figure 5-265.

Fig. 12.   An example of a JPA with enrichment information. (Products produced under contract to the U.S. Navy Personnel Research and Development Center, EPICS Project Development Office, Code 52E, San Diego, CA 92152).

particular tool and it could not be determined that all expected users would know how to use that tool, then the step-by-step task procedure would have to be expanded to include the additional descriptive steps and illustrations on how to use the tool. Newman (1957) suggested that (1) the specific behavioral processes required by any given task had to be identified and (2) criteria had to be established to evaluate whether or not the identified behaviors had been performed. From these early efforts (see also, Berkshire, 1954; Chalupsky and Kopf, 1967; Folley, 1961) a theoretical basis for a JPA technology was formed in which to evaluate the following hypotheses:

1. Use of JPAs will reduce training because less time would have to be spent teaching procedures.
2. JPAs will improve performance by providing individuals with a complete and accurate description of all the actions that are required for a particular task.

3. Use of the simplified format for performing technical work will be accepted by maintenance technicians.

Review of a key study to support each of these hypotheses is provided.

REDUCTION IN TRAINING

Elliott and Joyce (1971) compared training time and performance (time and errors) of two groups of individuals, one of which was provided with a JPA. One group consisted of 40 Air Force electronic technicians who had training and an average of 7 years experience in the maintenance of electronic equipment. The other group consisted of 20 high school students with no prior training or experience in electronics.

The experimental comparison consisted of 13 problems. For each problem the individual had to find a fault in a piece of electronic equipment. The Air Force technicians were given 7 hours of training with the equipment using the technical manual that contained information on the equipment used for the test. The format of the manual was similar to ones they normally used on the job. The high school students were given 12 hours of training in the use of hand tools and test equipment, and in the use of the JPAs that would guide the individual's performance during each problem.

The high school students were given only one opportunity to solve each problem. It was assumed that, because of the proceduralization of the JPA, additional attempts would only be a repeat of the same sequence of actions from the beginning. The Air Force technicians, on the other hand, were given as many opportunities as necessary within a 90-minute time limit. Performance measures were (1) time to isolate and repair the fault and (2) failure to identify the fault.

All individuals completed the 13 problems. With the JPA, the high school students took significantly less time to find the fault. The Air Force technicians, using the technical manual instead of the JPA, repaired the fault in less time and made fewer errors. The important point, however, is that the high school students could use the JPA to solve problems with no training or experience. When compared to the Air Force technicians who were trained in electronics and had an average of 7 years experience, it is apparent that training time can be reduced if JPAs are used to guide performance on the job. (See Shriver, 1960; Rigney, Fromer, Langston, & Adams, 1965; Gebhard, 1970; and Theisen, Elliott, & Fishburne, 1978, for additional studies in which JPAs were shown to reduce training time.)

IMPROVEMENT IN PERFORMANCE

Perhaps the most comprehensive study of JPA effectiveness was the U.S. Air Force's project PIMO—Presention of Information for Maintenance and Operation (Goff, Schlesinger, & Parlog, 1969; Grieme, Cleveland, & Chubb, 1969;

Inaba & Begley, 1969; Serendipity, 1969; Siciliani, 1969; Straly, 1969; Straly & Dibelka, 1969; Wilmot, Chubb, & Tabachnick, 1969). In this study, performance time and errors of 18 unqualified technicians using JPAs were compared to 18 qualified technicians using JPAs. The unqualified technicians were individuals who had not been trained to maintain, or had experience on, the equipment used in the study (a multiengine jet aircraft). The qualified technicians were individuals who had been trained and had approximately 2 years experience on the job. In addition to the test group comparison, the experienced group was compared to a control group of 18 technicians with approximately 2 years of experience who did not use the JPAs, but rather, relied on their training, experience, and conventional technical manual (a manual that contained convoluted narrative descriptions of how to remove, install, and adjust equipment).

The JPAs that were developed were complete, detailed procedures for each type of removal, installation, and adjustment task used in the study. The JPA employed a fixed format with a limited number of steps per page. The concept was presented in pocket-size book form with illustrations and text on facing pages (Figure 13).

Data was collected over a 4-month period. Using a counterbalanced experimental design, individuals were assigned actual maintenance tasks when these tasks were required. Time to complete the task and number of errors were recorded by trained observers. Control data were also collected.

In comparing the two JPA groups, it was found that neither group had any errors, and the unqualified group took only 33% longer time to complete the maintenance tasks. When comparing the qualified JPA group to the control group, it was found that the control group took 18% less time to complete the assigned tasks. There was also evidence that the time difference tended to decrease as use of the JPAs increased. When errors are considered, the JPA group performed better, that is, with JPAs there were no errors. General maintenance practice, on the other hand, always had some proportion of error.

Thus, taken as whole, the PIMO study indicates that JPAs can be used to improve maintenance performance. By allowing inexperienced technicians to use JPAs to perform procedural maintenance tasks, more experienced technicians will be available to perform the more complex fault-isolation tasks. In addition, using JPAs instead of relying on training and experience alone, reduces the number of errors. (See Post & Brooks, 1970; Potter & Thomas, 1976; Rogers & Thorne, 1965; and Shriver, Fink, & Trexler, 1964, for additional studies in which JPAs were shown to improve maintenance performance.)

ACCEPTANCE

In 1972 the Air Force decided to replace conventional technical manuals for the C-141 aircraft with JPAs. In an effort to evaluate the acceptance of JPAs over time, Johnson, Thomas, and Martin (1977) collected questionnaire data from

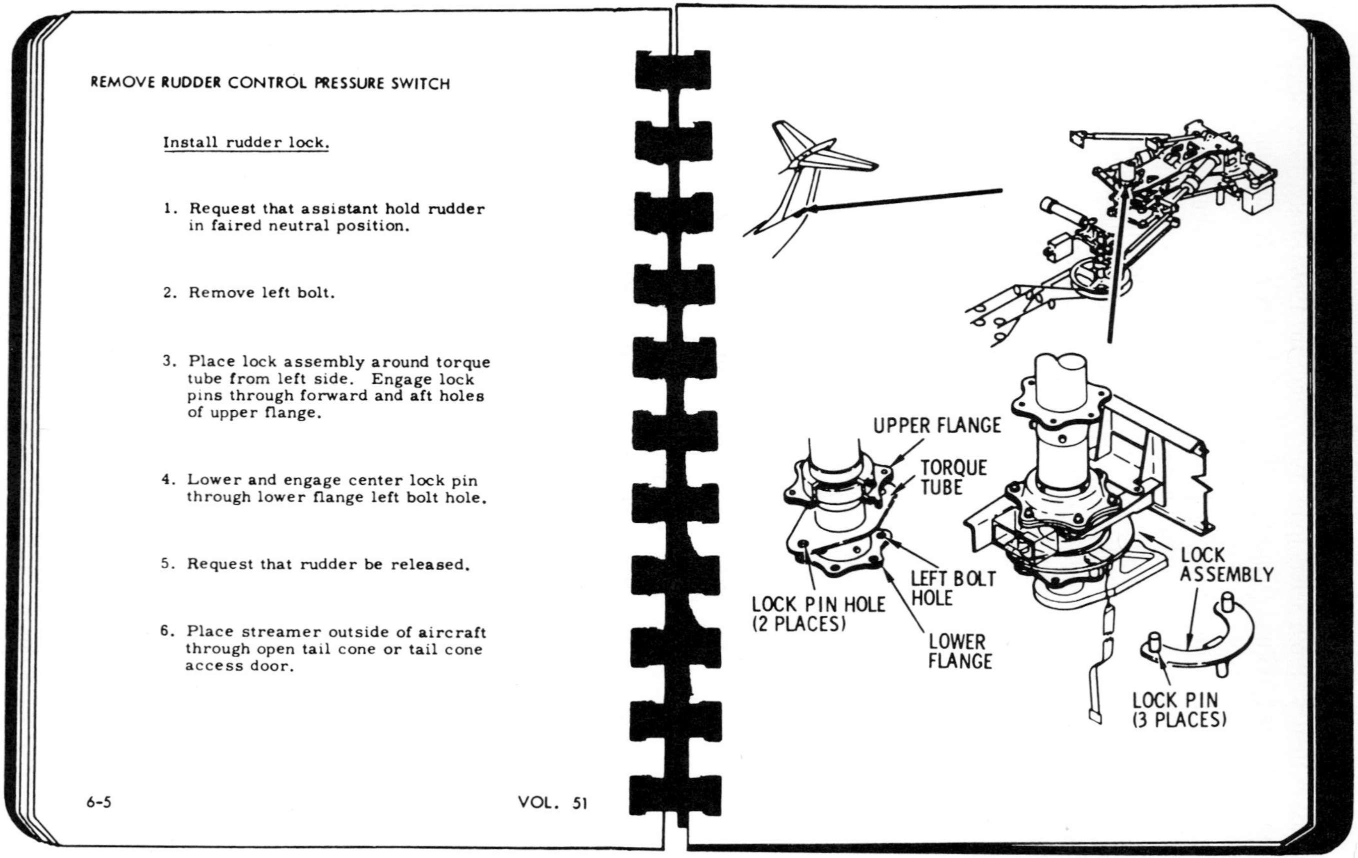

LOCK ASSEMBLY

LOCK PIN (3 PLACES)

UPPER FLANGE

TORQUE TUBE

LEFT BOLT HOLE

LOWER FLANGE

LOCK PIN HOLE (2 PLACES)

REMOVE RUDDER CONTROL PRESSURE SWITCH

Install rudder lock.

1. Request that assistant hold rudder in faired neutral position.

2. Remove left bolt.

3. Place lock assembly around torque tube from left side. Engage lock pins through forward and aft holes of upper flange.

4. Lower and engage center lock pin through lower flange left bolt hole.

5. Request that rudder be released.

6. Place streamer outside of aircraft through open tail cone or tail cone access door.

Fig. 13.   An example of a PIMO format JPA (Serendipity, 1969).

314 technicians. Information was gathered in three phases, the third phase of which was administered 6–8 months after implementation.

All the technicians had been trained in specific maintenance areas that were required to maintain the various equipment in the C-141. Technicians ranged in experience from 2 to 11 years. The skills of the technician ranged from apprentice to master. The questionnaire had 36 multiple-choice questions and was designed to measure attitudes and opinions relative to the acceptance and usability of JPAs.

Results show that 78.7% of all technicians liked the JPAs better than the technical manuals that the JPAs replaced. When given a choice of types of technical data to use on the job, 53.5% chose JPAs; only 20.1% chose the conventional technical manual. There were 69.4% who stated that the JPAs were better sources of information than the conventional technical manual.

When queried about the types of jobs for which JPAs would be useful, 58% preferred JPAs for nonroutine jobs, but only 36.9% preferred JPAs for routine jobs. The most negative responses to JPA acceptance centered around the idea of being required to use JPAs for every job. A total of 50.4% stated they would be somewhat irritated (37.3%) or irritated (13.1%) if they were required to use JPAs for every maintenance task. But, when asked to pick the one factor in six alternatives that would most improve maintenance operations, JPA was picked as the second most frequent alternative (21.7%); more qualified personnel was first (28.0%). Among the other alternatives better training was picked 8.6% of the time and better conventional technical manuals, 9.6%. Thus, even with a slightly negative resistance to use JPAs all the time, overall, the JPAs were well accepted.

SUMMARY AND CONCLUSIONS

To be successful, JPA design strategies have to be centered about the user and the user's acceptance of the JPA because a well-designed JPA is useless if the audience does not want to use it. Therefore, the level required for the anticipated user is a prime concern. Too much detail and users feel they are being seen as less intelligent than they are. Too little detail leaves the user with the responsibility of understanding the intent of the JPA steps. The user may then misinterpret the intended meaning and perform the task incorrectly. Thus the development process should incorporate the user into the JPA design strategy by soliciting user comments and reviews during the JPA development process.

Technical content is also very important. If the user discovers or perceives that information contained in a JPA is wrong, he or she will not use it. Technical content has to be validated. The user must

1. understand why a particular JPA is useful

2. accept the validity of the data source to generate the JPA and

3. understand the logic used to produce the JPA

Some JPAs require training or an explanation before they can be used. This training or explanation has to be considered as part of the JPA design strategy and integrated accordingly.

It is relatively easy to write how JPA designers and developers must focus on the user when one is cognizant of the issues and know where and how trade-offs have to be made. On the other hand, it is quite different trying to put information into a specification that someone who is totally ignorant of JPA technology has to use to procure JPAs. It is unrealistic to expect that individuals without any experience in JPA development will be able to make intelligent decisions about level of detail, enrichment, and so forth. The problem is the same for the individuals who have to comply with the specification when they do not understand that the intent of the specification, satisfying the needs of the user, is more important than rigid compliance.

Unfortunately, the problem is a real one and one that happens too often. If customers are buying JPAs, they have to know and understand exactly what they want. Specifications may seem to fill this requirement, but close examination reveals that there are always areas left for interpretation. As a JPA developer, the specification becomes a convenient metric to determine that all requirements of the contract are satisfied. From a realistic standpoint, it is very hard for customers to purchase something when they can not describe it but ''know it when they see it.'' The solution, of course, is constant interaction between customer and developer until both understand what the customer wants. If only one of them understands the objective, an effective JPA is hard to achieve.

In a recent effort, the customer had to constantly review the JPA development process for all the JPAs that were being developed under that particular contract. If the contractor was left on his own, the level of detail would have varied from one JPA to another. On the positive side, the constant interaction allowed for early identification of problems that were quickly resolved.

A more common occurrence, however, is the failure of the customer to fully understand the intent of a JPA specification. The customer has to be able to intelligently monitor a JPA development. Otherwise the customer will have no alternative but use the specification as written—a rigid set of rules. Such an occurrence, however, usually results in a JPA product that appears to satisfy every requirement of the specification, but is either unusable or unacceptable to the user. The focus on the user's requirements will be lost.

Although the situationally specific JPA (e.g., bicycle assembly, garbage disposal installation) may always be paper, the systems application of JPA technology will eventually use electronic presentation devices. Concern with user acceptance will then be even more important. The system developed to present electronic JPAs will have to be user defined. In a user-defined system, a primary component of the design strategy will be data retrieval, that is, how the users access and interact with the JPA information. In a user-defined system the user defines the format of the JPA information. As the differences within a given audience increases, the need for flexibility also increases, that is, inexperienced users should be able to get the information they need in a format that is meaningful to them, whereas the format for the same information would be very different for experienced users.

The design and development of a user-defined system that is sensitive to the interactiveness parameters of the range of users will require consideration of the advances in artificial intelligence. For an electronic user-defined system, an artificial intelligence environment may be the most logical way to represent an information domain and the most efficient way to represent user interactions with that information domain. User interactions have to reflect that information the user audience possesses and how that information is stored, accessed, applied, and acquired.

REFERENCES

Asimov, I. (1969). *Nightfall and other stories.* Garden City, New York: Doubleday.

Berkshire, J. R. (1954, June). *Field evaluation of a troubleshooting aid* (AFPTRC-TR-54-24). Lackland Air Force Base, TX: Air Force Personnel and Training Research Center (AD 537 25).

Chalupsky, A. B., & Kopf, T. J. (1967, May). *Job performance aids and their impact on manpower utilization* (WDL-TR 3276). Palto Alto, CA: Philco-Ford Corporation, Western Development Laboratory (PB 175 608).

Elliott, T. K., & Joyce, R. P. (1971). An experimental evaluation of a method for simplifying electronic maintenance. *Human Factors, 13,* 217–227.

Folley, J. D., Jr. (1961, October). *Research problems in the design of performance aids* (ASD-TR-61-548). Wright-Patterson Air Force Base, OH: Aeronautical Systems Division (AD 270 866).

Folley, J. D., Jr. (1972). *Transforming JPA results into an operational technology.* Paper presented at the American Psychological Association Convention, Washington, DC.

Gebhard, R. M. (1970). *Development of a training program and job aids for maintenance of electronic communication equipment* (HumRRO-TR-70-19). Alexandria, VA: George Washington University (AD 718 025).

Goff, J., Schlesinger, R., & Parlog, J. (1969, May). *Project PIMO final report. Vol. II. PIMO Test summary* (SAMSO TR 69-155(II)). Chatsworth, CA: Serendipity (AD 852 102).

Grieme, R., Cleveland, D., & Chubb, G. P. (1969, May). *Project PIMO final report. Vol. IV. PIMO technical data format specifications* (SAMSO TR 69-155(IV)). Chatsworth, CA: Serendipity (AD 852 104).

Inaba, K., & Begley, R. (1969). *Project PIMO final report. Vol. III, PIMO operational system analysis* (SAMSO TR 69-155(III)). Chatsworth, CA: Serendipity. (AD852 103).

Johnson, R. C., Thomas, D. L., & Martin, D. J. (1977, June). *User acceptance and usability of the C-144 job guide technical order system* (AFHRL-TR-77-31). Wright-Patterson Air Force Base, OH: Air Force Human Resources Laboratory.

Joyce, R. P., Chenzoff, A. P., Mulligan, J. R., & Mallory, W. J. (1973a, December). *Fully proceduralized job performance aids. Vol. I. Draft specification for organizational and intermediate maintenance* (AFHRL-TR-73-43(I)). Wright-Patterson Air Force Base, OH: Air Force Human Resources Laboratory (AD 775–702).

Joyce, R. P., Chenzoff, A. P., Mulligan, J. R., & Mallory, W. J. (1973b, December). *Fully proceduralized job performance aids. Vol. II. Handbook for JPA developers* (AFHRL-TR-73-43(II)). Wright-Patterson Air Force Base, OH: Air Force Human Resources Laboratory (AD 755–705).

McCormick, E. J., & Sanders, M. (1982). *Human factors in engineering and design* (5th ed). New York: McGraw-Hill.

Marcel, T., & Barnard, P. (1979). Paragraphs of pictographs: The use of non-verbal instructions for equipment. In P. A. Kolers, M. E. Wrolstad, & H. Bouma (Eds), *Processing of visible language* (Vol. 1, pp. 501–518). New York: Plenum.

Meister, D., & Rabideau, G. F. (1965). *Human factors evaluation in system development.* New York: Wiley.

Miller, R. B. (1956, May). *A suggested guide to the preparation of handbooks and job instructions* (ML-TM-56-15). Lowry AFB, CO: Air Force Personnel and Training Research Center.

Naval Air Systems Command. (1982). *P-3 Maintenance instructions* (NAVAIR 01-75PAA-2-4) (Change 5). Washington, DC: Naval Air Systems Command.

Naval Sea Systems Command. (July 15, 1976). *Guided missile fire control system MK91 MODS 0/1* (NAVSEA OP 4005) (3 vols.) Washington, DC: Naval Sea Systems Command.

Newman, S. E. (1957, December). *On identifying effective handbook techniques* (ML-TM-57-26). Lowry Air Force Base, CO: Maintenance Laboratory, Air Force Personnel and Training Research Center.

Post, T. J., & Brooks, F. A. Jr. (1970, December). *Advanced manpower concepts for sea-based aviation systems.* Arlington, VA: Serendipity.

Post, T. J., & Price, H. E. (1972, May). *Development of innovative job aid concepts: Volume I— Description of contents.* Falls Church, VA: BioTechnology (AD 751-044).

Post, T. J., & Price, H. E. (1973, April). *Development of optimum performance aids for troubleshooting* (Final Report). Falls Church, VA: BioTechnology.

Potter, N. R., & Thomas, D. L. (1976, September). *Evaluation of three types of technical data for troubleshooting: Results and project summary* (AFHRL-TR-76-74(I)). Wright-Patterson Air Force Base, OH: Air Force Human Resources Laboratory.

Rigney, J. W., Fromer, R., Langston, E. T., & Adams, H. C. (1965, September). *Evaluation of an experimental fault location device: II Fault location and isolation by experienced electronics technicians* (Tech. Rep. 44). Los Angeles, CA: Department of Psychology, Electronics Personnel Research Group, University of Southern California.

Rogers, J. P., & Thorne, H. W. (1965, March). *The development and evaluation of an improved electronics troubleshooting manual* (Tech. Rep. 65–1). Arlington, VA: George Washington University (AD 614 606).

Serendipity. (1969, May). *Project PIMO final report. Vol. I. Summary* (SAMSO TR-69-155(I)). Chatsworth, CA: Serendipity (AD 852–101).

Shriver, E. L. (1960, June). *Determining training requirements for electronic system maintenance: Development and test of a new method of skill and knowledge analysis.* Alexandria, VA: George Washington University (PB 149 202).

Shriver, E. L. (1975, June). *Fully proceduralized job performance aids: Guidance for performing behavioral analyses of tasks* (AFHRL-TR-75-38). Wright-Patterson Air Force Base, OH: Air Force Human Resources Laboratory.

Shriver, E. L., Fink, C. C., & Trexler, R. C. (1964, May). *Forecast systems analysis and training methods for electronics maintenance training* (Res. Rep. 13). Alexandria, VA: Human Resources Research Office, George Washington University (AD 441 248).

Siciliani, F. (1969, May). *Project PIMO final report. Vol. VIII. PIMO basic technical data storage system* (SAMSO TR-69-155(VIII)). Chatsworth, CA: Serendipity (AD 852–108).

Straly, W. H. *Project PIMO final report. Vol. V. PIMO troubleshooting aid specifications* (SAMSO TR-69-155(V)). Chatsworth, CA: Serendipity (AD 852–105).

Straly, W. H., & Dibelka, G. A. (1969). *Project PIMO final report. Vol. VII. PIMO troubleshooting aid preparations guidelines* (SAMSO TR-69-155(VII)). Chatsworth, CA: Serendipity (AD 852–107).

Swaney, J. H., Janik, C. J., Bond, S. J., & Hayes, J. R. (1981, June). *Editing for comprehension: Improving the process through reading protocols* (Tech. Rep. No. 14). Pittsburg, PA: Carnegie-Mellon University.

Theisen, C. J., Elliott, T. K., & Fishburne, R. P. (1978, December). *Application and evaluation of fully proceduralized job performance aids and task oriented training technologies* (NADC-78286–60). Warminster, PA: Naval Air Development Center.

Wilmot, H. L., Chubb, G. P., & Tabachnick, B. J. (1969, May). *Project PIMO final report. Vol. VI. PIMO technical data preparation guidelines* (SAMSO TR-69-155(VI)). Chatsworth, CA: Serendipity (AD 852–106).

CHAPTER 11

Using Pictorial Language:
A Discussion of the Dimensions
of the Problem

MICHAEL TWYMAN

INTRODUCTION

Of the 14 chapters that appear in this volume, this is the only one to be concerned primarily with pictures. Indeed, the title of this book, *Designing Usable Texts,* would seem to exclude pictures from its terms of reference because all the meanings of the word *text* in the *Oxford English Dictionary* have to do with words (e.g., "the wording of anything written or printed"). The comparative neglect of pictorial language here, and in other general works on graphic communication too, is not easy to explain. But it leads me to suggest how pictorial language may be considered in relation to other branches of language before going on to consider the use of pictures themselves.

Because people from different disciplines view language differently, it may be of value at the outset to look at pictures in relation to some very simple overall models of language. Seen from the point of view of the linguistic scientist, language divides into two major areas: spoken and written. Seen from the point of view of the typographer and graphic designer, the primary breakdown of language tends to be between verbal and pictorial language. These two approaches (Figure 1), which may be more implicit than explicit, appear to be incompatible and certainly lead to difficulties when it comes to studying issues of common concern. Indeed, most linguistic scientists would not accept the use of the word *language* in relation to pictures and therefore consider the term *verbal language* to be a tautology. Such people might like to substitute the word *communication* for *language* in many places in this chapter.

The two major areas of language accommodated by the linguistic model (spo-

Copyright © 1985 by Academic Press, Inc.
ISBN 0-12-223260-7

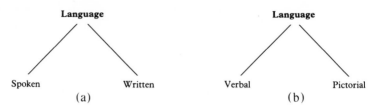

Fig. 1.   The different approaches to language of (a) linguistic scientists and (b) graphic designers.

ken and written) have a common mode (words) but involve different channels (aural and visual). The two major areas of language implicit in the way typographers and graphic designers work have a common channel (visual) but involve different modes (verbal and pictorial). It will be seen that the traditional linguistic model does not accommodate pictures. This is because spoken language—which has no pictorial mode—has been the dominant interest of linguistic scientists for most of this century.

Because linguistic scientists, typographers, graphic designers, and others share an interest in language, it would make sense if a model could be devised that accommodated both words and pictures and at the same time did not conflict with the needs of any of these groups of people. The model presented in Figure 2 is an attempt to satisfy these requirements.

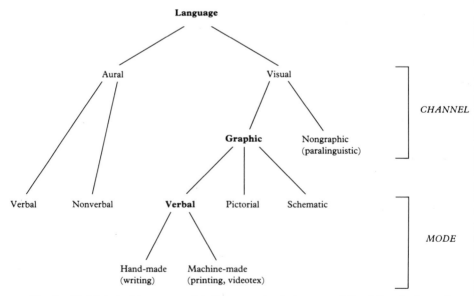

Fig. 2.   Model devised to accommodate the approaches to language of linguistic scientists and graphic designers.

In this model the primary distinction is made through the channel of communication (a model that makes the primary distinction in terms of mode has been rejected as being less appropriate). The channels relate to communication received through the ears (aural) and through the eyes (visual). This approach is not entirely watertight because, for example, some visual images might be experienced through tactile sensations, as when a blind person is allowed to feel a piece of sculpture or a child traces the shapes of raised lettering on a street nameplate. Nevertheless, the aural–visual distinction caters for most normal situations in communication. The visual line in the model has been subdivided into graphic and nongraphic. Graphic language includes the making of marks by hand or machine. Other areas of visual language, such as gesture and facial expression, which are called paralinguistic features by linguistic scientists, are categorized here as nongraphic. Graphic language can be subdivided into three categories: verbal, pictorial, and schematic (Twyman, 1979). The first two of these categories need no further explanation beyond stating that verbal includes the use of numerals and other conventional characters. The third category, schematic, includes all purposeful graphic marks that are not words, numbers, or pictures. In practice, of course, the categories are often combined and have fuzzy boundaries. For the purpose of this all-embracing model, aural language can simply be divided into verbal and nonverbal. It is for the linguistic scientist to state what the nonverbal features of aural language are, but they clearly exist in babies and are rarely absent from adult language, except at its most formal level. Further distinctions can be made at the lowest level of the tree in terms of whether the utterances of language (whether aural or visual) are hand-made or machine-made. For the sake of simplicity, this distinction is made in the model only on the graphic–verbal line, but it can be applied to the pictorial and schematic lines too.

It is hoped that this model may be helpful in providing common points of reference for those approaching from different directions what I am calling language. It does at least have the value of keeping those aspects of language that relate to channel of communication separate from those concerned with mode. At the same time, it highlights the isolation of those concerned with studying different aspects of language. Linguistic scientists have tended to concentrate on the study of aural language, though traditionally they have accepted the importance of paralinguistic features in communication, which function through the visual channel. Epigraphers and palaeographers study hand-made verbal graphic language, whereas the practitioners of machine-made verbal graphic language include printers, typographers, typists, and computer scientists. Pictorial language, which is the concern of this chapter, has been studied by people from quite different disciplines, and particularly by art historians, psychologists, illustrators, graphic designers, and those concerned with child development.

The model presented in Figure 2 also shows the relationship between various kinds of verbal language on the graphic line of the tree. Unfortunately we have no word in English that covers both hand-made and machine-made verbal language (which might loosely be called writing and printing). In this chapter—as elsewhere—I have used the somewhat clumsy term *verbal graphic language* to cover both categories. The derivation of this term can be traced in the model by following its line of descent backwards from *verbal* through *graphic* to *language*.

Because most of those concerned with pictorial language have not been interested in relating it to other aspects of communication, it is not at all easy to place in the overall context of effective communication. The approach I have adopted here is that of the generalist who has worked in a number of areas of picture-making but is more actively involved in writing and in the study and design of verbal graphic language. I have no special desire to promote the cause of pictorial language, though experience in many contexts (particularly in the field of higher education) leads me to appreciate that concentration on such a subject can easily be construed as a threat to the authority of the verbal mode.

The main aim of this chapter is to draw attention to the diversity and complexity of pictorial language and to see it in the context of real communication problems. This is an ambitious and perhaps foolhardy exercise, which may explain why few others have attempted it. One successful attempt has been made recently by Goldsmith (1980, 1984), though her approach—based on Charles Morris's theory of signs—is very different in its scope from the one described here. In this chapter, I merely hope to show that verbal graphic language, which has been more fully studied by those concerned with effective communication than pictorial language, is straightforward by comparison. I can do no more than highlight a few of the dimensions of the problems associated with the use of pictorial language in the hope that some of them will be explored more fully by other people.

Pictorial language has already been discussed briefly in relation to aural and visual language, and it has been suggested that it forms part of the visual branch called graphic. In any situation where graphic language is used, other factors, most of them nongraphic, have also to be taken into account. It may be helpful, therefore, to consider briefly what they are. It is suggested that all graphic language should be considered within an operational framework that identifies the following variable factors:

   a. **Purpose**   whether, for example, to impart information or to persuade
   b. **Information content**   the essence of the information or other message to be conveyed
   c. **Configuration**   the different ways of organizing the graphic elements of language spatially
   d. **Mode**   whether verbal, pictorial, schematic, or a mixture of two or more of them
   e. **Means of production**   from hand-produced to computer-controlled

   f. **Resources**   in terms of available skills, facilities, funds, and time

   g. **Users**   taking into account such factors as age, abilities, training, interests, and previous experience

   h. **Circumstances of use**   whether, for example, the user is working in a well-appointed library or under stressful circumstances in a moving vehicle.

These eight variables need to be considered whenever graphic language is used. In the case of pictorial language the mode (d) has been predetermined, though whether to introduce words along with the picture(s) may not have been decided. Some of these eight variables are referred to again when they appear to have particular relevance to the issues under consideration, but all appear to have some bearing on each of the dimensions of the problem of using pictorial language discussed in this chapter.

For the sake of convenience I have isolated a number of aspects of pictorial language and dealt with them separately, though I accept that many of them interact strongly with one another, just as they do with the aforementioned variables. No graphic model—certainly not one I am capable of devising—would adequately reflect the intricate pattern of interrelationships I should like to be able to present in this chapter. Those aspects of pictorial language I have chosen to discuss are listed under separate headings for the sake of convenience, with the most obvious relationships with one another and with the eight variables noted in passing in each case.

WHAT IS A PICTURE?

I am using the word *picture* to mean some hand-made or machine-made image that relates, however distantly, to the appearance or structure of real or imagined things. This is somewhat different from dictionary definitions of the word *picture,* which are not very helpful in the context of this chapter. Other graphic images that are not letters, numerals, or conventional characters I have called schematic images (Twyman, 1979). Many diagrams fall clearly into the schematic mode of graphic language and are not discussed here. It has been argued (Richards, 1984) that it is not the schematic nature of a graphic display that should lead us to call it a diagram, but its concern with spatial relationships. I have a good deal of sympathy for this view. But in any case it is not always easy to determine whether something is a picture or a schematic image. It does not depend on the image alone, but may relate to the user and the particular circumstances of use. The sound spectrogram shown in Figure 3 was presented as a slide to a group of students. One of these students, who was sitting at the side of the room and had a sharply foreshortened view of the slide, remarked that he saw the image as a view of a petrochemical works. If he did so, and I have no reason to doubt that he did, then that image was for him a picture, at least for a time. But

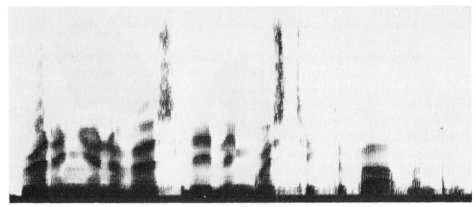

Fig. 3.   A sound spectrogram, interpreted by one viewer as a petrochemical works.

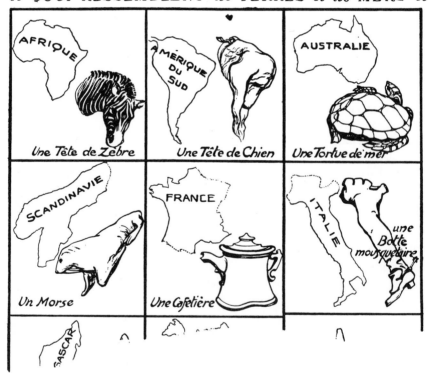

Fig. 4.   Part of a page from a French children's book in which pictures serve as an aid to remembering schematic maps. From H. S. Brès, *Mon premier tour du monde* (Paris: Hachette, nd).

a few minutes later, after I had explained what a sound spectrogram was and after the unromantic truth had been revealed to him, it ceased to be a view of a petrochemical works and had become something else. It had ceased therefore to be a picture and had become a schematic image. Such a phenomenon, which is by no means unusual, hardly needs explanation in a book of this kind, but it serves to highlight the danger of making absolute distinctions between pictorial and schematic images. As Figure 4 shows, practical advantages may stem from the possibility of seeing pictures in schematic images.

Sometimes, however, the distinction between pictures and schematic images does not depend on ambiguities of visual stimuli. The familiar no-entry symbol of a red circle with a white bar across it would, I suppose, be seen by most people in Western Europe as an ideographic symbol (a kind of schematic image). Yet the idea of the white bar stems from the use of a physical barrier that prevents access. For those who know the derivation of the symbol, it is possible that it would be seen as a pictograph (a formalized picture). A similar issue is revealed in Figure 5, which relates to the spacing systems used in printing. The marks shown in this example could be said either to represent metal spacing units or to

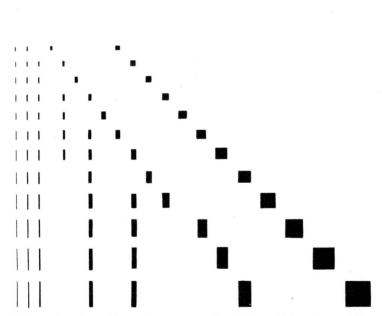

Spaces (Didot)

Fig. 5.   Illustration of one of the spacing systems used in printing, which can be seen either as a set of pictures or as a set of schematic images according to the attitude of the viewer. From A. Froshaug, *Typographic Norms* (Birmingham: The Kynoch Press, 1964).

stand for mathematical notions of space—or both. If they are seen as the former, I would argue that they are pictures of things; if the latter, they denote abstract ideas and are therefore schematic images. Such issues are largely metaphysical and have little relevance to the practical issues that are central to this publication, though it should be stressed that they relate especially to purpose (a), users (g), and circumstances of use (h).

WHAT ARE PICTURES FOR?

This question need not detain us long, but it is the kind of question we ought to try to answer, if only because we tend to avoid doing so. Most obviously many pictures, as in early herbals and recent illustrated encyclopedias, attempt to describe things. Related to the issue of description is that of location, and some pictures have as a prime requirement that they should show relationships of things spatially. Good examples of this are provided by pictorial maps and certain kinds of newspaper illustrations (such as Figure 6). For many people, as the saying goes, "Every picture tells a story." Though this is not strictly true, Western art was preoccupied with storytelling until the nineteenth century. And because children in the Western world are brought up on books that tell stories partially or wholly by means of pictures, this aspect of picture-making is deeply embedded in our culture. In recent years, newspapers and magazines have come to recognize that some kinds of stories can be told better through pictures than through words (Evans, 1978), and this is often because description and spatial relationships play a large part in storytelling (Figure 7). Some pictures are

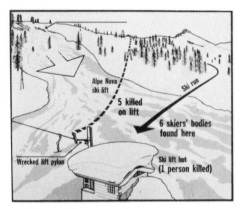

Fig. 6.   Newspaper illustration of an avalanche disaster, illustrating spatial relationships. From H. Evans, *Pictures on a Page* (London: Heinemann, 1978). (Reprinted by permission of William Heinemann Limited)

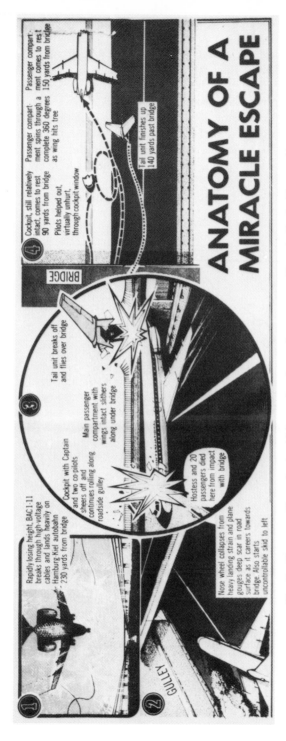

Fig. 7. Newspaper illustration in which narrative plays an important part. From the *Sunday Times* archives.

designed to persuade or exhort: the woodblock print from a fifteenth-century book shown in Figure 8 is an exhortation to the faithful that they should prepare themselves to die gracefully, whereas the Boots advertisement (Figure 9) is more concerned with persuading people to prepare themselves for graceful living.

Other pictures have instruction or the provision of information as their prime objective, and this is the area of picture-making that is most conducive to scientific evaluation. Such pictures may describe a simple operation (Figure 10), designate a service (as in public information symbols), or involve the making of visual comparisons (Figure 11).

In concentrating on the communication of specific information, we must not

Fig. 8.   Page from the fifteenth-century block book, *Ars moriendi*.

Fig. 9.   Double-page cosmetics advertisement for Boots. From *Woman's Own*, 1980.

forget that many pictures were made, and continue to be made, primarily to give pleasure to the spectator or to provide an outlet for an artist's personal expression. Provided it does not conflict with other objectives, there is no reason why the giving of pleasure should not be considered an acceptable ingredient of effective communication. Humor in pictures is a particular kind of device for giving pleasure. It may take the form of visual wit, as in Lear's "Manypeeplia

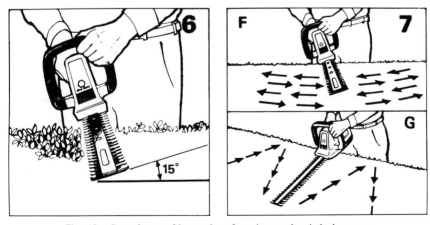

Fig. 10.   Part of a set of instructions for using an electric hedgecutter.

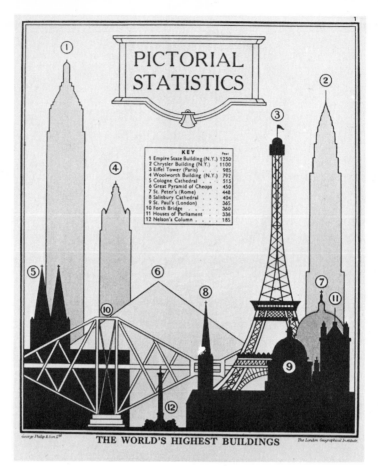

Fig. 11. Picture showing the relative heights of the world's highest buildings in 1934. From *Philips' Universal Atlas* (London, 1934).

Upsidownia'' (Figure 12), or it may take on the deeper significance of social and political satire.

A form of picture that is different in kind from all those discussed so far is the drawing that uses pictorial language as a means of problem solving. Edward de Bono's work in the field (De Bono, 1972) has drawn attention to the value of pictorial language for solving various kinds of problems. Leonardo and Paxton are good examples of men with fertile minds who have used drawing for this purpose: Joseph Paxton's first doodles for the Great Exhibition building, made on a sheet of blotting paper at a Midland Railway Committee meeting in 1850, is shown in Figure 13.

Most of the roles for pictorial language discussed here play some part in effective communication, and they overlap considerably. In a given situation we need to establish what the priorities should be. It would clearly be inappropriate for personal expression or the desire to amuse to come before descriptive or instructive aspects of aircraft safety notices, or for the first exploratory drawings for a new car to be used as a guide to the customer in a maintenance manual. But it would be perfectly reasonable to suppose that persuasion plays a part in the production of pictures for a foreign-language teaching kit. In any real situation it is of the utmost importance to establish priorities in relation to the aforementioned roles, though it is by no means clear how this should be done.

The question, What are pictures for? has a bearing on most of the variable factors already listed, but in practice most consideration tends to be given to its relationship to information content (b), means of production (e), resources (f), and users (g).

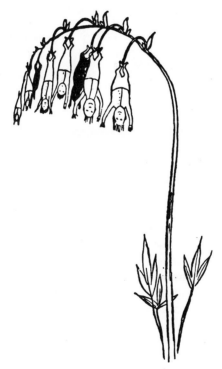

Fig. 12. Edward Lear, ''Manypeeplia Upsidownia,'' from his *Nonsense Songs, Stories, Botany and Alphabets* (London, 1871).

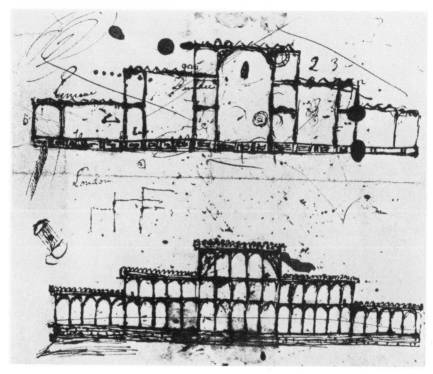

Fig. 13.   Joseph Paxton's first rough drawings for the Great Exhibition building, made on a sheet of blotting paper at a meeting of the Midland Railway Committee in 1850 (Victoria & Albert Museum, London).

DESCRIPTION AND NARRATION

Two of the roles played by pictorial language that were touched on in the previous section, description and narration, are discussed further here because of their centrality when considering effective communication. All narrative pictures must be descriptive to the extent that they allow us to identify the elements of a story; but it does not follow that all descriptive pictures need be narrative. Often, of course, narrative pictures are not interpreted in the ways that were intended because viewers fail to pick up the necessary clues to the story. This is true, for instance, of many works of art when the iconography is not properly understood because it belongs to a different period in time or a different cultural tradition.

The group of pictures of birds shown in Figure 14 is purely descriptive and has no narrative function, though the particular choice of birds suggests to us that some kind of classification has determined what is represented. The botanical illustration (Figure 15) reveals a different level of description in terms of density of information, but is almost identical in kind to the illustration of birds. It can be argued, however, that there is just a hint of narration in the separation of the fruit and seeds from the plants.

The soccer images (Figure 16) are narrative pictures with minimal description. The components that tell the story are depicted in just enough detail to let us know how to interpret them. The goalposts can be recognized as such by those who know about soccer, though there are no nets or supports; the players can be distinguished in terms of the teams they play for, even though no individuals can

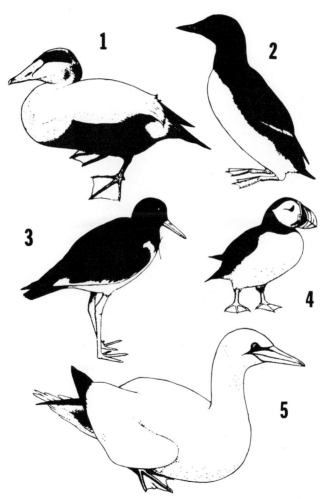

Fig. 14.   Descriptive illustration, without any narrative features, of a set of water birds.

be identified. Nevertheless, the stories can be read by those who share the same sets of experiences. Most comic strips, which are generally held to be a low-level form of picture-making, are much more complex than these in their descriptive features. The story told in the example shown in Figure 17 would mean nothing

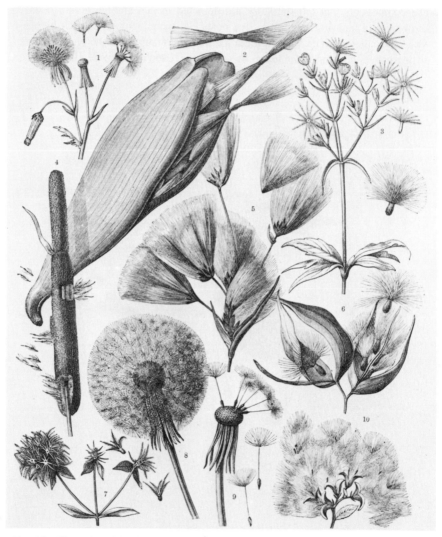

Fig. 15.   Illustration of the dispersion of fruits and seeds by the wind, which is primarily descriptive but has some narrative elements. From Anton Kerner von Marilaun, *The Natural History of Plants* (London, 1894–95).

WHAT HAPPENED LAST WEDNESDAY
The full-back, usually McNab, made ground, hadn't the skill to take on the opposing back, and simply lobbed a high ball into the goalmouth

THE IDEAL SITUATION
The winger beats his full-back on the outside, carries on to the goal-line, and cuts the ball back into the goalmouth

Fig. 16.   Illustrations of moves in soccer, both actual and imagined, which are primarily narrative but necessarily have descriptive features. From the *Sunday Times* archives.

if the figures were not differentiated from one another and if each looked the same in every scene.

In practical situations, questions relating to description and narration are closely associated with the purpose of a picture or set of pictures (a) and with the information that needs to be conveyed (b), though they relate to many of the other variable factors as well.

Fig. 17.   Part of a comic-strip story in which descriptive features are essential to the narrative. From *Buster*, 19 May 1984.

GENERALITY VERSUS PARTICULARITY

Questions of generality and particularity relate to the descriptive dimension of pictorial language discussed in the preceding section; they are concerned with how general or particular pictorial language should be when it is concerned with description.

One of the principal characteristics of pictorial language is that it does not lend itself readily to the making of general statements, and this underlines one of the essential differences between pictorial and verbal language. The word *clock* (or *Clock* and *CLOCK* for that matter) covers all kinds of time pieces, whether digital or analog, French rococo, or institutional electric; but as soon as we try to represent a clock pictorially we cannot avoid being specific in at least some respects. It would, for instance, be extremely difficult to represent through pictures the idea of clocks in general without committing oneself to either an analog or digital approach. More particularly, as soon as we show numerals on a clock face, we have to make a choice between arabic and roman numbers.

Similarly, there are problems in making a pictorial representation of a person (as distinct from a man or woman). It is difficult enough to make a picture of generic man without giving any indication of age, period, color, or of whether he is athletic or sedentary. All pictures of men say things over and above the general idea conveyed by the word *man*. Symbol designers have long been aware of this problem, and few if any "man" symbols have improved on the pictograph (Figure 18) devised by Otto Neurath and Gerd Arntz in the 1930s (Neurath, 1936).

man

group

Fig. 18.   The "man" symbol, together with its plural form, devised by Otto Neurath and Gerd Arntz in the 1930s for what later became known as Isotype (International System of Typographic Picture Education).

Symbol designers are aware also that pictures can change their meaning relatively quickly. Though it is true that words change their meanings (as, for instance, the change from wireless to radio and gramophone to record player), objects that may need to be depicted often change their appearance much more quickly. A telephone of the 1920s is as much a telephone as one designed in the 1980s, though the one looks very different from the other. A symbol depicting a telephone of the 1920s might therefore be read as an "old-fashioned telephone" rather than simply as "telephone." Common things also take different forms in various parts of the world. It is for such reasons that the recommendations of the International Organization for Standardization (1980) for public information symbols take the form of verbal referents to objects rather than to precise visual forms.

The examples mentioned thus far raise the question of generality versus particularity in extreme forms, but the problem has existed less obviously for centuries in the field of natural history illustration. The early herbalists had to decide whether to depict a perfect specimen to illustrate the general characteristics of a

Fig. 19.   Woodcut of cuckoo-pint from Fuchs, *De historia stirpium* (Basel, 1542), which tends toward the representation of the perfect specimen.

Fig. 20.   Woodcut of pasque-flower from Bunfels, *Herbarum vivae eicones* (Strasbourg, 1530), which tends toward the representation of a specific plant with its incidental imperfections.

plant, or to be faithful to the particularities of the actual plant being studied, even though this might involve depicting incidental imperfections. Fuchs is said to have adopted the former practice (Figure 19) and Brunfels the latter (Figure 20) (Blunt, 1950).

Though pictorial language may have difficulties in coming to terms with general concepts, its suitability for representing particularities gives it distinct advantages over verbal language in some situations. For example, how does one describe new things for which there may be no words, and precise shapes or dispositions of things?

Because the question of generality versus particularity belongs to the descriptive dimension of pictorial language, it relates most obviously to the same variables referred to in the section on description and narration: purpose (a) and information content (b).

OBSERVATION-BASED AND CONCEPT-BASED IMAGES

Pictures can be records of visual sensations of observed things, or they can be so carefully constructed as to look as though they have been seen. I am calling the first category of pictures "observation-based" and the second "concept-based." The distinction is by no means a clear-cut one, and the two extremes represent poles of what should be seen as a continuum. These approaches relate in some respects to the idea of "painterly" and "linear" styles developed by the German art historian Wölfflin (1932). Though they have most relevance in connection with the study of art history, they have some bearing on everyday problems of communication.

Observation-based images are particularly liable to what might be called "error" because perception is never a passive activity. What we see is modified by what we know of what we see. Traditionally, therefore, when artists have represented mountains and hills, they have made them far higher than they would have appeared if recorded by a camera. It has been shown that when Cézanne painted Mont St. Victoire he made the mountain higher and the countryside in front of it less foreshortened than images of the same scene captured by the camera (Rewald, 1950). And in a series of experiments Thouless demonstrated that all people, even trained artists, tended to assess the ellipse of a circular card placed on a table as much deeper (more like a circle) than it would have been if the laws of perspective had been applied (Thouless, 1931, 1932). This phenomenon was called by Thouless "phenomenal regression to the real object."

For similar reasons, it can be observed that most children and people inexperienced in drawing make the top halves of heads smaller and place the eyes higher than they normally appear (Edwards, 1979). The supposed reason for this is that the part of a head one responds to in everyday affairs is from the eyes downward, whereas the forehead and cranium are usually neglected because they are more passive. Again, perception is modified by knowledge.

The Thouless experiments and observation of children's drawings of heads help to explain why artists have used devices like perspective and geometric schemata to stop them from going too far "wrong" in their representation of the world. The development of the rules of perspective in Florence in the first quarter of the fifteenth century signaled a new approach to representing the world. By means of such rules images could be constructed in an artificially created space that looked so convincing that they appeared to be a record of things seen though they were often only distantly based on observation. And artists like Uccello made carefully measured drawings of three-dimensional objects which could occupy the space created with the help of the rules of perspective (Figure 21). It may be worth noting that similar approaches are being adopted in computer graphics with what are called wire frame drawings.

Other kinds of drawing props have also been used. The medieval architect Villard de Honnecourt used simple geometric schemata to help him draw such things as figures and animals, and from the Renaissance onward it became commonplace for drawing books to show ways of dividing up the head on a quasi-geometric basis. Such devices were used to stop people from going too far wrong in their drawing, and Gombrich has shown that even artists as committed to observation as Leonardo and Rembrandt could not entirely escape their influence (Gombrich, 1960). The page from a nineteenth-century drawing book (Figure 22) shows the traditional manner of building up an image on the basis of schemata. Such an approach is very different from that of artists who are concerned with making an accurate record of observed things. The bottles in the detail of a painting by Manet (Figure 23) must surely have been painted from observation; they exist only by virtue of their relationship to things around them, while the constructed objects in the Harding drawing book exist independently of their surroundings.

In practice, observation-based and concept-based approaches to picture-making tend to modify one another. Whereas many observation-based pictures reveal traces of the constructs of concept-based approaches, concept-based images must be given some of the trappings of observed effects, otherwise they would not look like the things they represent (Figure 24).

As far as effective communication goes, I suspect that the concept-based approach is generally the more useful of the two; the observation-based approach merely passes on the ambiguities of the real world to the viewer of the picture, as in Impressionist painting. One reason why photography (which must be seen as a special category of observation-based picture-making) is not the answer to all communication problems is that it fails to clarify visual ambiguities. Much will

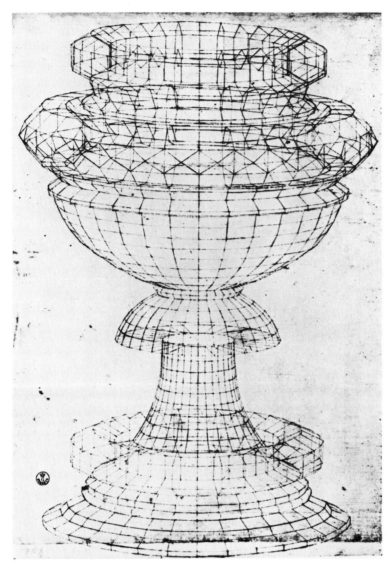

Fig. 21. Paolo Uccello, perspective study of a chalice (Gabinetto Disegni e Stampe degli Uffizi, Florence).

of course depend on the purpose (a) and the information content (b) of the picture; and when communication calls for the understanding of visual effects (such as texture, light, and atmosphere) observation-based approaches, which would include photography, are the only ones likely to be really useful.

Pl. 14

Fig. 1

Fig. 24.   A constructed image that has been given the trappings of observed effects. From D. Beasley, *Design Illustration* (London: Heinemann, 1981). (Reprinted by permission of Heinemann Educational Books).

SYNOPTIC IMAGES AND IMAGES COMPOSED OF DISCRETE ELEMENTS

By a synoptic image I mean a single unified representation of part of the world or of an imagined world. The Degas picture of race horses (Figure 25), though it may have been constructed from separate elements that never existed together, has been organized in such a way as to suggest a slice of the world. It can be compared with the composite set of photographs taken by Eadweard Muybridge in the course of his experiments in recording the movements of horses (Figure 26). The Degas is a synoptic picture, the Muybridge a composite picture consisting of nine discrete elements.

Images composed of discrete elements can be organized in many ways, some of which will be referred to in the next section. This type of image often places considerable demands on the user because it can involve the interpretation of

---

Fig. 22.   Illustration from a nineteenth-century drawing book showing the traditional manner of building up an image on the basis of schemata. From J. D. Harding, *Lessons on Art* (London: 7th. ed. c.1860).

Fig. 23.   Painting based on observation of things seen. Detail from Manet's "Le bar aux Folies-Bergère," 1881 (The Courtauld Institute Galleries, London).

Fig. 25.   Edgar Degas, ''Jockeys in the Rain,'' circa 1881 (Glasgow Art Gallery & Museum, The Burrell Collection). A synoptic image that can be compared with Figure 26.

different styles and conventions of representation, may have different scales, and may not even have clearly defined sequences for ''reading.'' All these points are illustrated in the picture of the Apollo 14 moon landing (Figure 27) and in a more extreme form in the double-page spread from the *TV Times* (Figure 28) in which the insets call for changing viewpoints or relationships between the viewer and the things depicted.

Other images consisting of discrete elements are organized more consistently and conform to conventional patterns of reading verbal language in the Western world (left to right, and top to bottom). Some approaches to the depiction of discrete elements have a long pedigree, most obviously in the field of architectural and engineering drawing in which plans, as well as front and side elevations, are conventionally shown. Such conventions of drawing are sometimes adopted for other kinds of work, as in the early nineteenth-century print about slavery (Figure 29), which shows a plan and elevations of a slave ship together with a synoptic image of the capturing of slaves.

There is good reason to believe that images composed of discrete elements are likely to be more effective than synoptic images under some circumstances.

Fig. 26. Eadweard Muybridge, "The Trot," from his *Animals in Motion* (3rd impression, London, 1907). A set of discrete images that can be compared with Figure 25.

After all, a synoptic image cannot reveal those parts of the world it depicts that have to be seen from other viewpoints. When making a choice within this dimension of pictorial language, much will clearly depend on purpose (a), information content (b), users (g), and circumstances of use (h). There may also be considerable practical difficulties in the production of images composed of discrete elements because it is not as easy as it may seem to describe step by step even a simple operation like making a cup of tea. Such an exercise, which may well require as many as 50 discrete images, is analogous to computer programming and points to the value of using picture language as an exercise in clear thinking (Neurath, 1936).

CONFIGURATION

Some of the ways in which discrete pictorial elements are organized relate to the configurations of verbal graphic language. Such configurations have been described in the context of a schema which attempts to provide a means of thinking

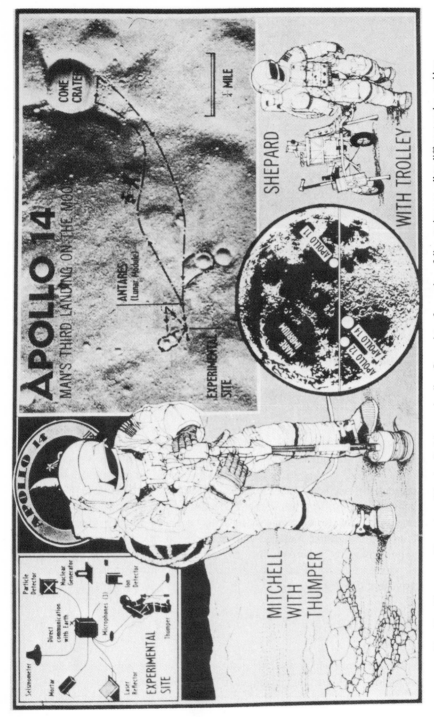

Fig. 27. Newspaper illustration of the Apollo 14 moon landing. It consists of a number of discrete images, all to different scales, and has no clear sequence of reading. From the *Sunday Times* archives.

Fig. 28. Double-page spread from the *TV Times*, October, 1980, showing an even more complex use of discrete images than Figure 27.

Fig. 29.   Early nineteenth-century etching relating to slavery. It combines a synoptic image of the capturing of slaves with discrete images (two elevations and a plan) of conditions on a slave ship.

about graphic language as a whole (Twyman, 1979). Configurations of graphic language range from pure linearity at one end of the scale to extreme nonlinearity at the other. In the middle of the scale are some configurations with long pedigrees that the verbal mode of graphic language shares with the pictorial. Comic strips, for example, are organized in much the same way as text presented in the ''linear interrupted'' configuration (Figure 30); that is, breaks are made at

Fig. 30.   Discrete pictorial images organized in the ''linear interrupted'' configuration. From *Buster*, 19 May 1984.

Fig. 31. Discrete pictorial images organized as a list.

the end of lines without much regard to their relationship to information units. On occasion, pictures composed of discrete elements are also organized as lists (Figure 31), as branching structures (Figure 32), and in matrix form (Figure 33). Because these configurations are common in verbal graphic language, it may well be that they have special relevance when words need to be combined with pictures.

In general, however, pictorial language is not as rule-bound as verbal graphic language. Though the maker of a picture may have clear intentions in terms of how a picture should be interpreted, many pictures, whether synoptic or composed of discrete elements, are nonlinear and leave options wide open in terms of user strategies. Synoptic pictures, and many others composed of discrete elements (such as Figures 27 and 28), fall into something of a rag-bag category described as ''non-linear directed viewing'' (Twyman, 1979). When words are combined with pictures, as, for instance, when keys are included, it is quite possible that they will exert a strong influence on the way a picture is ''read.''

A decision has to be made with regard to configuration whenever we use graphic language, though often the decision is almost preempted by precedent. Choice of configuration should relate to all the variable factors discussed at the

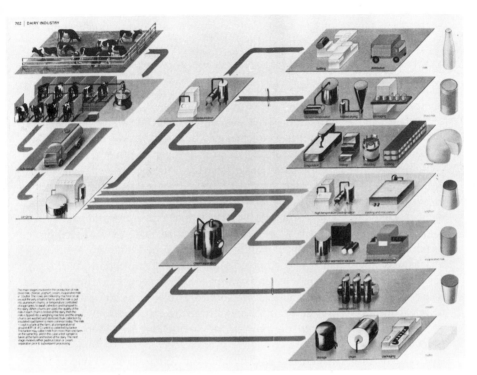

Fig. 32.   Discrete pictorial images showing the structure of the dairy industry, organized in a branching configuration. From *How It Works* (London: Marshall Cavendish, 1974–5).

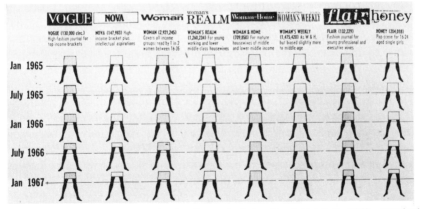

Fig. 33.   Discrete pictorial images showing changes in the lengths of skirts in the 1960s, organized in a matrix configuration. From the *Sunday Times* archives.

beginning of this chapter, but especially to purpose (a), information content (b), resources (f), and circumstances of use (h).

CONVENTIONS OF DRAWING

Because pictures, at least as defined in this chapter, are concerned with the appearance or structure of things or imagined things, the conventions of representational drawing deserve consideration as a separate issue. The potential conflict between different conventions of drawing is nicely resolved—and hence acknowledged—in the copper-engraved plate (Figure 34) from Perrault's *Mémoires pour servir à l'histoire naturelle des animaux* (1576). Each plate from this publication includes a representation of an animal in its natural habitat in a form that would be described here as a synoptic and more or less naturalistic picture. Above each representation of the animal is a set of discrete, formalized images of some of its organs and other parts. The two conventions of drawing have as a common feature a sheet of paper, which is depicted in the synoptic image as a real (though somewhat extraordinary) object; at the same time, it serves as the carrier for the set of discrete, formalized images.

Numerous approaches to the problem of representing the structure or appearance of things have been developed over the centuries, and some of these have become firmly established as conventions in certain fields. Many of them are illustrated in specialist handbooks on illustration (André, 1874; Beasley, 1981; Clutterbuck, 1966; Gill, 1973; Ridgway, 1938). Some of these conventions are very old, such as the foldaway or roll-back convention seen in the woodcut from Berengario da Carpi's treatise of 1521 (Figure 35). This is not the place to review the many conventions of drawings, but examples are given of the following: cutaway (Figure 36), ghosted (Figure 37), and exploded (Figure 38). Some drawing conventions, such as those used in building and engineering, have been developed for specific purposes; they must be considered as having the status of sublanguages, the precise rules of which are often understood only by specialists (British Standards Institution, 1969, 1972). For example, the planometric worm's-eye-view of the Palazzo Farnese in Rome (Figure 39) may well present difficulties of interpretation for some readers of this chapter.

There are occasions when the "grammar" of a drawing needs to be understood in very precise terms before it can be "read" accurately. In the accompanying sketch of the frame of a tent (Figure 40), the user needs to be able to tell at a glance whether the drawing is isometric or in perspective before knowing where to place three long poles and three short poles in the roof structure. If it is an isometric drawing, the three long poles should go at the front; if it is a perspective drawing, they probably go at the back. Only close inspection of the drawing or experience of erecting the tent will establish what one needs to know

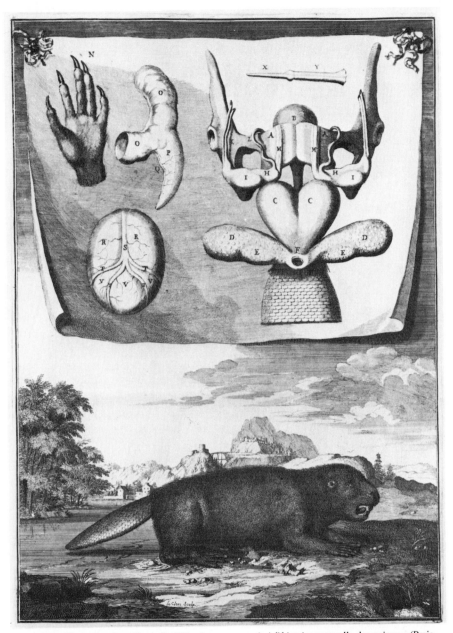

Fig. 34. Illustration from Perrault, *Mémoires pour servir à l'histoire naturelle des animaux* (Paris, 1576), in which the differences between two conventions of drawing are resolved by the inclusion of a sheet of paper that is common to both of them.

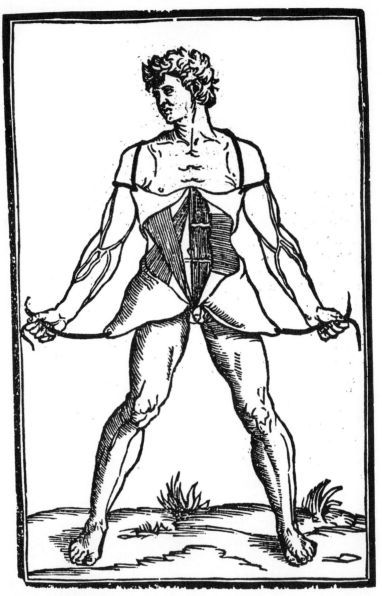

Fig. 35.   An early example of the use of a specialized convention of drawing. From Berengario da Capri, *Commentaria super anatomia Mundini* (Bologna, 1521).

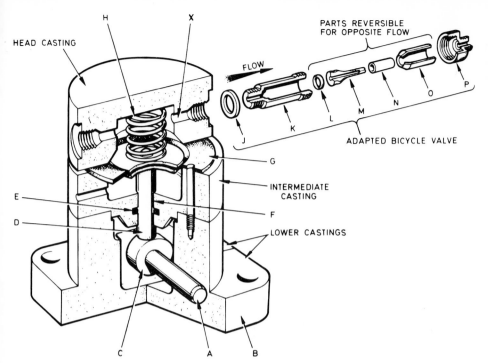

Fig. 36. Cutaway drawing (with exploding parts). (West Glamorgan Institute of Higher Education).

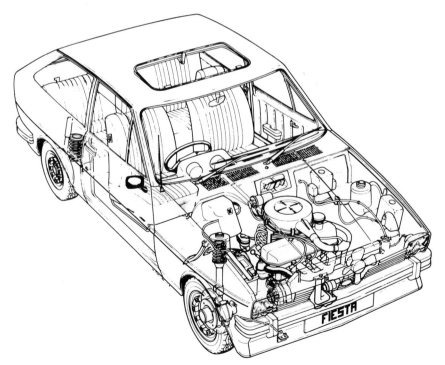

Fig. 37. Ghosted drawing.(West Glamorgan Institute of Higher Education).

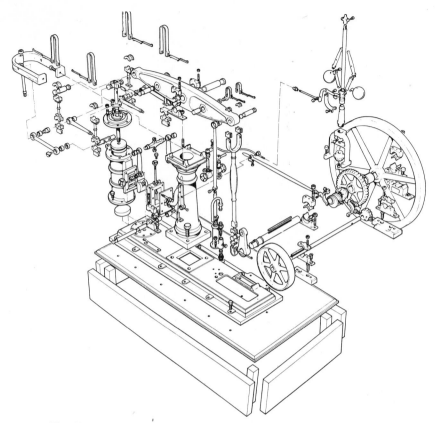

Fig. 38.   Exploded drawing.(West Glamorgan Institute of Higher Education).

at the outset—that the long poles go at the back. This example illustrates the importance of considering conventions of drawing in the context of purpose (a), content (b), users (g), and circumstances of use (h). Other factors, such as resources (f), would normally need to be taken into account because some conventions of drawing make heavy demands in terms of human skills and time.

STYLE

By style I mean those ingredients or qualities that make it possible to distinguish one person's or one group of people's treatment of a subject from that of others. In pictorial language the dimension of style applies to all means of production, including photography. It may take the form of a propensity for such

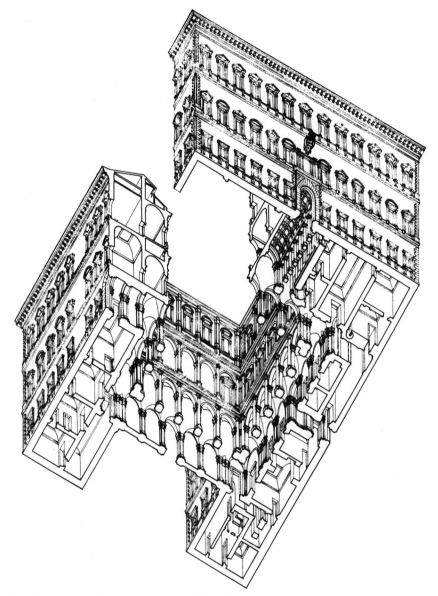

Fig. 39.   Planometric worm's-eye-view of the Palazzo Farnese in Rome. From P. Portoghesi, *Rome of the Renaissance* (London: Phaidon Press, 1972).

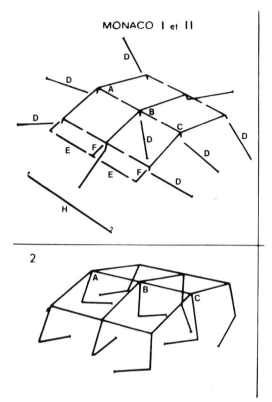

Fig. 40.   Part of a set of instructions for the erection of a tent. The user has to decide whether the drawing is isometric or in perspective before knowing which tent poles go where.

features as horizontals and verticals, particular spatial relationships, and strong contrasts of tone; or it may reside in what might be called the graphology of the image. This dimension of pictorial language is probably the most elusive of all and is not easy to describe in words. But whatever it is that makes the Beardsley illustration (Figure 41) different in style from the Van Gogh drawing (Figure 42), or the two heads (Figure 43 and 44) different from one another, is clearly of importance.

A very helpful approach to describing such differences has been provided by Ashwin (1979). He identifies seven ingredients of style (consistency, gamut, framing, placement, proxemic, kinetic, and naturalism) and argues that stylistic characteristics of an image can be determined by the presence and relative degree of these seven ingredients. Ashwin's approach was developed as a means of coming to terms with contemporary illustration, and his examples are all of the synoptic kind. No doubt this approach could be adapted and extended to embrace other kinds of pictorial language but, as it stands, it does not accommodate sets of discrete images or some specialized conventions of drawing.

The inescapable presence of stylistic characteristics ensures that pictorial language cannot be neutral, and decisions have to be made on matters of style whether consciously or otherwise. A sensible choice in relation to this dimension of pictorial language requires consideration of all the factors that affect graphic communication, though it would seem that the most crucial of these factors is information content (b).

Fig. 41.   Aubrey Beardsley, invitation card for the opening of a ladies' golf club, 1894.

Fig. 42.   Van Gogh, ''Mlle Gachet Playing the Piano,'' 1890.

Fig. 43.   A. M. Cassandre, poster for Grand Sport caps.

VERISIMILITUDE

This dimension of pictorial language relates to Ashwin's naturalism. I have chosen to give it some emphasis here because it has provided such a challenge to artists in the Western world, at least on and off, for 2000 years. But what is it? Is it achievable? And what is its value in relation to effective communication? Such issues are too large to begin to consider properly here, though a few points can be made in passing.

Important though the goal of verisimilitude may have been in the context of Western art, it may be much more questionable in relation to effective communication. This is because it leaves out the element of selection, which seems to be essential when messages have to be conveyed purposefully through pictures. Even among its staunchest supporters, therefore, verisimilitude has to give way to other goals from time to time.

True verisimilitude when representing isolated things would involve same-

Fig. 44.   W. G. Easton, scraper-board drawing.

scale images, or at the very least representing them the size they are seen—
which means that pictures of elephants and fleas might present more of a problem than pictures of mice. In practice, things are rarely represented the size we
see them; but because pictures often assume a single viewing point, they look
convincing enough for us to get over the barrier of scale. The principal characteristics of verisimilitude in Western picture-making appear to be the achievement of an illusion of depth and solidity; the rendering of color, tone, texture,
and effects of light; and, when necessary, good resolution of detail. But who is to
say whether the Egyptian picture (Figure 45) of a girl painting her lips with the
mirror she holds in her hand shown full-face to the viewer, is less satisfactory in
terms of effective communication than the Pompeian wall painting (Figure 46)
with its tabletop foreshortened to such a degree as to belie Thouless's findings
(Thouless, 1931, 1932)?

The ideal of verisimilitude in ancient times is illustrated by the anecdote,

Fig. 45. Egyptian drawing of the Twentieth Dynasty depicting a woman painting her lips with the mirror she holds in her hand shown full-face to the viewer (Museo Egizio, Turin).

Fig. 46. Pompeian wall painting of the first century A.D. with a table in the foreground with its circular top shown convincingly as an ellipse (Museo Nazionale, Naples).

Fig. 47. Hand-produced artwork by Ian Cole for an advertisement for Cadbury's chocolate biscuits, rendered to look as much like real biscuits as possible.

related by Pliny, that the Greek artist Zeuxis painted grapes in such a life-like way that birds used to fly down to peck at them; but the real roots of verisimilitude in painting were put down in Renaissance Italy with the discovery of the laws of perspective and the growth of a scientific attitude to the representation of nature. Since then all sorts of artists have teased us, from commercial artists working in advertising (Figure 47) to major painters such as Magritte (Figure 48). In the particular Magritte picture shown here the artist delights in his ability to match nature, albeit painted nature, by painting a canvas on an easel in front of the view that would have existed had the canvas not been there.

Fig. 48.   Magritte, "La condition humaine," 1933 (Private collection). A painting that teases us by depicting a canvas on an easel in front of the view that would have existed had the canvas not been there.

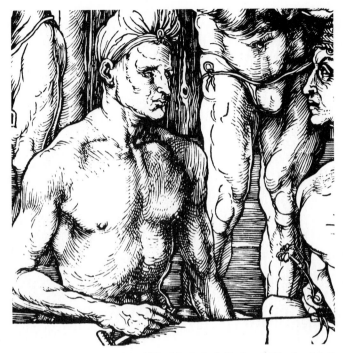

Fig. 49.   Detail from Dürer's woodcut "The Men's Bath," circa 1496, showing the syntax of marks he developed for representing form, tone, and texture by means of swelling and tapering lines, sometimes cross-hatched.

Today, because verisimilitude has been mastered in painting, and photography is available to all, the real problem often arises when we want to transmit images through printing. In the late fifteenth century, Dürer (Figure 49) developed a syntax of making marks in woodcuts that represented form, tone, and texture by means of swelling and tapering lines that could cross one another (Ivins, 1953; Panofsky, 1943); and by the seventeenth century incredible illusions of three-dimensionality were being achieved in copper engraving (Figure 50). Such skills were frequently put to scientific use, as in the illustration from Cowper's *The Anatomy of Humane Bodies* (1698), in which verisimilitude is heightened by the inclusion of a fly on the drapery (Figure 51).

Having looked at such examples it is hard to accept that printing still imposes limitations on verisimilitude. But an example from a low-cost horticultural research publication (Figure 52) shows that it does. The published caption to the two pictures suggested that we should be able to detect differences in the lettuce seedlings arising from the use of different light sources in their cultivation; but what comes over to my horticulturally untutored eyes stems primarily from the

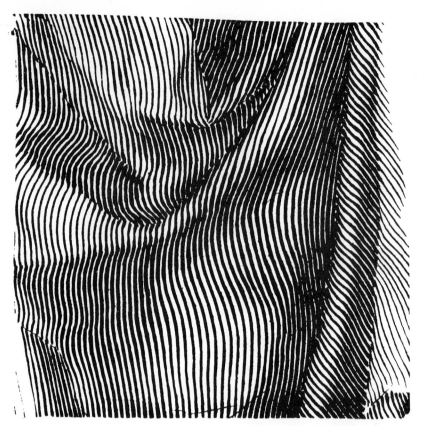

Fig. 50.   Detail of an eighteenth-century copper-engraving by Claude Mellan after Poussin showing an effective illusion of three-dimensionality by means of swelling and tapering lines.

differences in the photography of the two samples. In another low-cost publication of a similar kind I happen to know that no expense was spared on one occasion in order to produce an illustration in full color that showed the subtle differences between two similar kinds of apples. Only color reproduction could have revealed such differences. The argument of this paragraph—that printing still imposes limitations on verisimilitude—is underlined by the fact that I am unable to include a color illustration to make this point visually because of the cost of color printing in short-run publishing.

Verisimilitude relates particularly to such variable factors as purpose (a), information content (b), means of production (e), and resources (f), and also to the question of transmission and repeatability to be discussed later in this chapter.

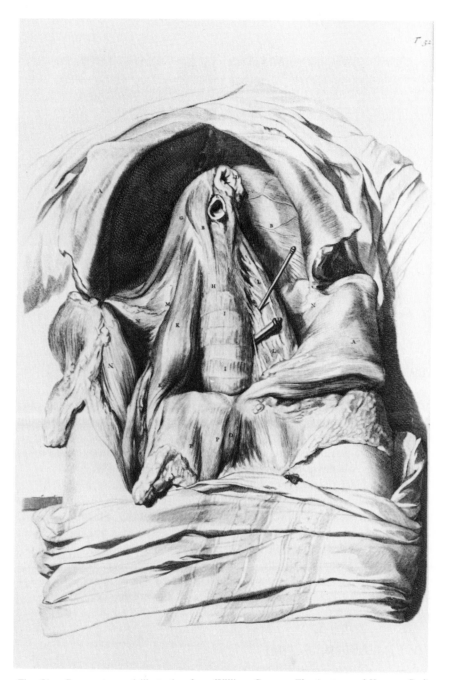

Fig. 51. Copper-engraved illustration from William Cowper, *The Anatomy of Humane Bodies* (London, 1698), in which verisimilitude is heightened by the inclusion of a fly on the drapery.

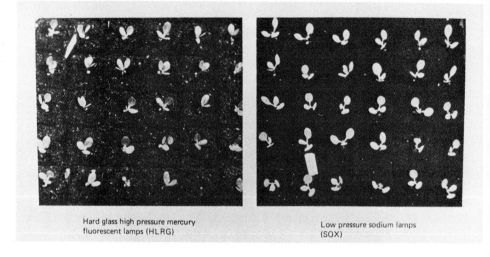

Hard glass high pressure mercury
fluorescent lamps (HLRG)

Low pressure sodium lamps
(SOX)

Fig. 52. Page from a low-cost horticultural report that aims to show through a comparison of photographs the difference between lettuce seedlings grown under different light sources.

BERTIN'S GRAPHIC VARIABLES

The French cartographer Bertin (1967) has defined a number of graphic variables that have a bearing on pictorial language. He presents his variables—again the magical number seven—in graphic form (Figure 53). These variables of shape, scale, value [that is, tonal value], texture, color, orientation, and location must all apply whenever graphic forms of communication are used.

There is a clear overlap here with Ashwin's breakdown of style (1979), but Bertin's graphic variables have a wider application than Ashwin's because they can be related to virtually every kind of graphic language, whether pictorial, schematic, or verbal. They have a particular relevance when considering content (b) and means of production (e), but must have some bearing on all other factors that need to be taken into account when using graphic language. Bertin provides us with a useful checklist of graphic variables, and his approach has the value of completeness, but I am not sure whether it takes us very far along the road to understanding pictorial language.

THE DIMENSION OF TIME

To Bertin's variables we must add the dimension of time, both in the sense of sequences of discrete images, as in a slide presentation or a succession of pages

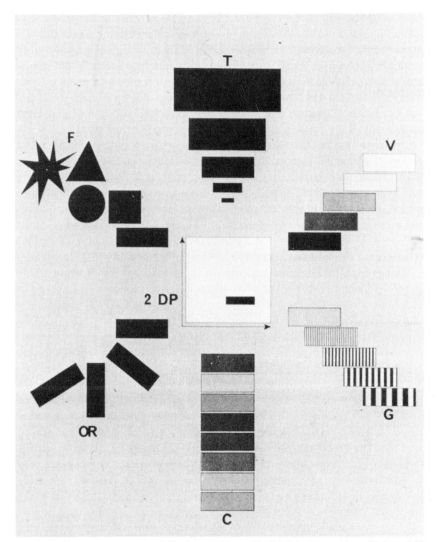

Fig. 53. The graphic variables defined by Bertin in his *Sémiologie graphique* (Paris and The Hague: Mouton and Gauthiers-Villars, 1967). The variables are coded for the French language. Reading from the northwest position they are: shape, scale, value, texture, color, and orientation, with location in the center.

of a book, and in the sense of what appear to be continuously moving images, as in film and television. Besides straightforward recordings of happenings in the real world, moving images can, of course, be animations of drawings or generated by means of computers.

It is well known that the development of means of making and transmitting pictorial images along the dimension of time has opened up whole new realms of understanding. Specialized techniques, such as time-lapse photography and the freezing of frames for analysis, have been particularly valuable in this respect because they combine the advantages offered by still and moving images. It may be worth remarking that there is no real equivalent to moving pictures in the field of verbal graphic language; for although words can be made to move, this does not normally affect the message they carry in any significant way.

In practice, the choice as to whether to use moving or still images relates mainly to information content (b), means of production (e), and circumstances of use (h). Were it not for the expense of making moving pictures and the resources needed for showing them, they might well be the answer to many communication problems. However, in a British television series on newspapers Evans (1981) demonstrated convincingly from the field of war reporting a point made earlier by Hopkinson (1970, p. 20) that a good still photograph can have much more impact on our memory than a passage of film. Along with evidence from everyday experience, this suggests that purpose (a) should play an important part in determining whether still or moving images should be used.

REPEATABILITY AND TRANSMISSION

It was argued by Ivins (1953) that it was not so much the development of picture-making itself that was important for the growth of science as the development of means of making exactly repeatable pictorial statements. He pointed out that it was no accident that the two branches of science that flourished in ancient Greece, astronomy and geometry, had appropriate visual images in repeatable form: the clear Mediterranean skies were available for all to see and the images of geometry could be defined by precise verbal statements. Words mean much the same however they are presented, and when errors of transcription occur they can often be identified by context, but the message of a picture can be distorted in such a way that the distortion may not even be noticed.

The message of a picture can be distorted through errors of interpretation by its maker or through technical degradation in production or transmission. In the presentation of the paper from which this contribution arose, I showed a sequence of slides of details from reproductions of the Bayeux Tapestry from 1824 to 1973 in order to make this point. In general, as would be expected, information content increased and became more accurate the later the date of the reproduction, and there can be no doubt that the extent of the variation in image content and treatment must have led to different interpretations of the things depicted. Every printed half-tone involves some degradation, and the amount of the degradation depends largely on the choice of half-tone screen, the kind of

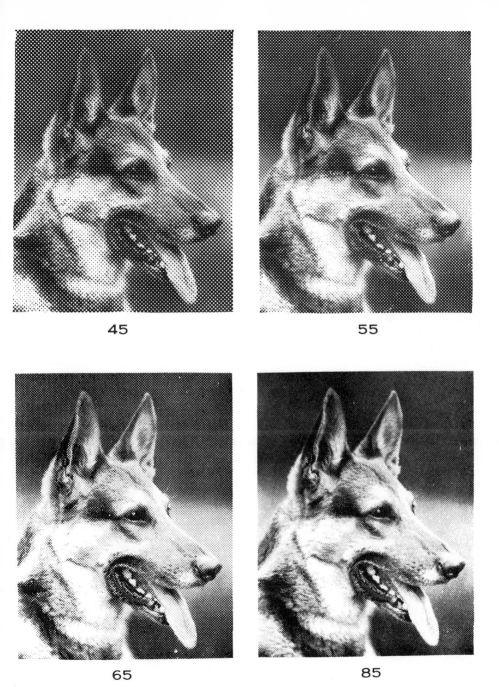

Fig. 54.   Half-tone screens originally printed at 45, 55, 65, and 85 dots to the inch. Though in general terms the information carried by these photographs may not vary much with the coarseness of the screen, it may well do so if we have to count the dog's teeth or describe their shape.

paper on which the printing is done, and the skill of the printer. Figure 54 shows how the coarseness of the half-tone screen can affect the information carried by a picture. We may think that the information carried by each of these examples is the same until we are asked to count the number of the dog's teeth that are visible, or describe their shape. The screens traditionally used in newspaper production are very coarse compared with those used in general printing and inevitably lead to loss of information. Can we really see ''The full glory of the Victorian arched roof at Kings Cross Station'' (Figure 55), or are we merely responding to the verbal message of the caption that accompanied it?

The question of technical degradation arises also in relation to electronic means of transmission. In such cases it may be even more crucial than in printing because it is possible to have local variations in transmission that affect information content. And if, after 500 years, printing still has difficulties reproducing color images accurately, it might be unwise to pin too much faith on the ability of the newer technologies to meet all our demands in terms of faithful and reliable transmission of information.

BRIGHT OUTLOOK : The full glory of the Victorian arched roof at Kings Cross station, London, is revealed again after being cleaned as part of British Rail's new environmental policies

Fig. 55. View of Kings Cross station, published in the *Guardian* newspaper. The caption of the original reads, ''The full glory of the Victorian arched roof at Kings Cross station, London, is revealed again after being cleaned as part of British Rail's new environmental policies.''

Fig. 56. "Derwentwater, Looking Towards Borrowdale," 1826, by an anonymous artist working in the idiom of English lithography of the period. From E. H. Gombrich, *Art and Illusion* (London: Phaidon Press, 1960).

Issues touching on repeatability and transmission seem to be of special importance in relation to purpose (a), information content (b), and means of production (e).

CROSS-CULTURAL PROBLEMS

Because it is often held that pictorial language differs from verbal language by being universally effective, it may be necessary to remind ourselves that there are strong cultural differences in picture-making. The two pictures shown here were reproduced by Gombrich (1960) to illustrate this point. The view of Derwentwater (Figure 56) produced by an anonymous lithographer in 1826, is very much in the idiom of English topographical lithography of the period. It shows an interest in detail and effects of light and in the soft edges of vegetation. It is certainly very different from Chiang Yee's treatment of the same subject (Figure 57), with its emphasis on broad distribution of shapes and well-defined edges. As Gombrich has shown, each artist emphasized—or perhaps could only accommo-

Fig. 57. "Cows in Derwentwater," 1936, by Chiang Yee, drawn in a very different idiom from the lithograph reproduced in Figure 56. From E. H. Gombrich, *Art and Illusion* (London: Phaidon Press, 1960).

date—those aspects of the subject that fitted into his schema for representing things.

If there are recognizable cultural differences in picture-making, it is reasonable to assume that similar differences exist in the interpretation of pictures. Some research into the reaction of non-Westerners to Western conventions of picture-making seems to support this view. It was claimed by Hudson (1960), for instance, that perspective cues, such as changes in scale and the converging lines of a road (Figure 58), were not picked up by many of his subjects from "subcultural groups" in southern Africa. Consequently it was the proximity of things on the picture plane that determined how they interpreted the picture.

Though it may be right to question some early stories from far-off lands, which claimed that people unfamiliar with Western conventions of picture-making looked at photographs upside down, it hardly needs research to establish that cultural influences play a part in the interpretation of pictures of all kinds. Every day we are bombarded with evidence to the effect that people read into pictures—as indeed they read into words—things that relate to their own experience. And if things do not relate to a viewer's experience there can be problems too. This was brought home to me many years ago at an extramural class when I showed a slide of a painting of the Deposition of Christ (I forget now whose painting it was). I had assumed that everyone understood the essence of the subject depicted until an Indian in the audience asked me what the three tiny sets of sticks on the hill in the background were. Though they were very small, he was well aware that they must have been important for the reading of the picture; and he was quite right to ask the question. This experience made me realize how much we miss or fail to understand properly when looking at pictures from cultures other than our own. If cultures are different, then picture conventions are also likely to be different; and if picture conventions are different, then so too will be the ways in which people interpret them.

Cross-cultural problems clearly have most bearing on the user variable (g), though they should be taken into account when considering other factors, including information content (b) and configuration (c).

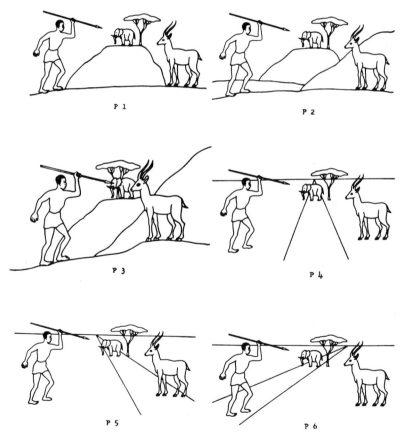

Fig. 58.   Illustrations used by Hudson to test the extent to which his subjects from "subcultural groups" in southern Africa responded to perspective cues.

LEARNING TO MAKE AND "READ" PICTURES

There is ample evidence to suggest that mark-making and, following on from this, picture-making, are natural activities for young human beings (Arnheim, 1956; Kellogg, 1959, 1969; Lowenfeld & Brittain, 1975). The central thesis of Gombrich's seminal book *Art and Illusion* (1960), that making comes before matching, is certainly borne out by observation of some children. The drawing shown in Figure 59 was done by a child at the age of 27 months and was his first purposeful drawing. What prompted the mark-making I do not know, but when he was asked the somewhat stupid and stereotyped adult question, "What is it?" he replied, after some hesitation, that it was a hedgehog. It does not look much like a hedgehog to me, and I have no doubt that it was not a hedgehog, nor indeed anything, until its maker was asked to identify it. But thereafter it was a hedgehog. Within a few months the same child had developed a method for drawing cars based on a simple schema not very different from the "hedgehog." These cars came in all shapes and sizes and in great profusion around the age of 3 years (Figure 60). At this stage drawing was for him, as it is for many children, a natural language. This was demonstrated most delightfully on one occasion when the same child was asked to say a few words on the telephone to a relative. The family had just bought its first car and he was very excited about it. The relative

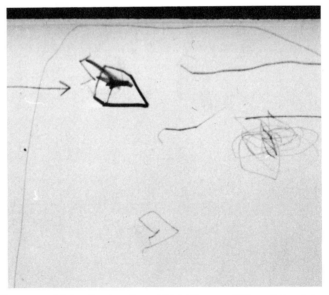

Fig. 59.   First purposeful drawing done by a child (at the age of 27 months) and described after questioning as a hedgehog.

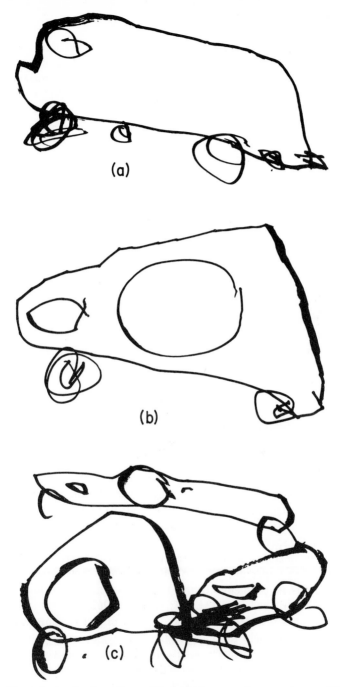

Fig. 60. Three of many drawings of cars, all based on the same schema, made around the age of 3 years by the child who made the drawing reproduced in Figure 59.

must have asked him what it looked like because he was heard to say the child's equivalent of "hold on a moment" and then add, "I'll draw it for you." Can there be better evidence of the use of drawing as a natural language?

It hardly needs stating that children's pictures are usually different from those of adults, but it is not often realized that some of the ways children represent things have a bearing on effective communication. The drawing of a room with furniture in it (Figure 61) shows the objects as they relate to the child's experience of them, and they are placed around the edge of the paper as they were placed in the room, with their most characteristic view presented to the observer. Such a drawing reflects total experience of the room rather than a simple visual experience and is similar in kind to many medieval views of cities and present-day tourist maps. How is it that we manage to stifle such approaches to drawing, which can be so effective in terms of transfer of information, as children grow up?

It seems important to distinguish between the ability to make pictures and to understand them. Most people in adult life continue to be able to interpret and comprehend many kinds of pictures, but our concentration on other things in education has led to the making of pictures being neglected. In general, adults only originate pictures (apart, that is, from photographs) when they work in specialist capacities as, for example, architects, geographers, botanists, and engineers. Consequently, as far as origination goes, pictorial language has been broken down into specialist sublanguages, the conventions of which have been found appropriate for particular purposes.

To counteract the neglect of graphic skills and the mental apparatus associated with them, a campaign was launched in Britain some years ago by two geographers (Balchin & Coleman, 1965). They coined the term *graphicacy* for the facility that they saw providing, along with numeracy and literacy, an essential underpinning of education. After some initial success, the campaign lost impetus; it made no real impact on the British educational world and has done little to change attitudes. Unfortunately, therefore, we have to accept that pictorial language is by no means a natural language for adults insofar as origination goes, except in certain specialist areas.

Although the teaching of picture-making is neglected, presumably because it is not held to be important, we also tend to assume that learning to interpret pictures presents no problems. In this respect it seems to me that Hochberg's well-known experiments (Hochberg & Brooks, 1962) can be misinterpreted. These experiments revealed that a child deprived of pictorial images for 2 years from birth was still able to label pictures of things correctly. However, the 'reading' of pictures is a much more complex business than correct labeling. Learning to understand the different configurations, conventions, and styles of pictorial language is surely something that has to be considered seriously from an educational standpoint if we are to treat pictures as serious carriers of informa-

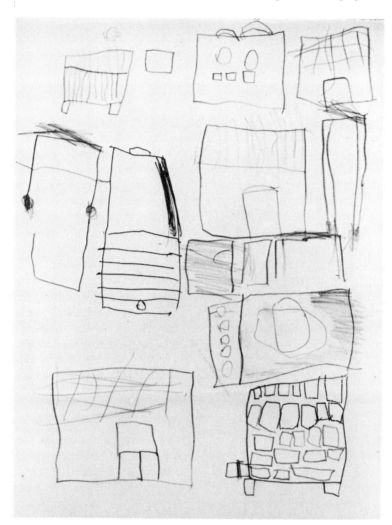

Fig. 61.   A child's drawing of a room with furniture positioned on the paper more or less as it was in the room, but with the most characteristic view of each item presented to the viewer.

tion. Learning to "read" pictures means learning not just one "grammar" but a whole set of grammars for different kinds of pictorial language.

The question of education in relation to pictorial language is central to all the communication variables listed at the beginning of this chapter, though some relate more to the origination of pictures than to their use. The problem is a circular one. Picture-makers will not attach importance to pictorial language as a carrier of information until it is treated as such by users (g); but users are not likely to respond to it in this way until they can learn to trust pictures in terms of information content (b).

FEEDBACK AND EVALUATION

Graphic language, whether written or pictorial, differs from most spoken language in that it has no direct way of providing feedback for its producer. The "extended conversations" found on some internal memoranda and in graffiti provide the nearest approaches to feedback in pre-electronic graphic language I can think of. The pictorial branch of graphic language presents a specially difficult problem in this respect because it has no real "language of dialogue." And because no ways of talking to one another through pictures have been developed, feedback from pictorial language usually comes—if it comes at all— in the form of verbal queries or modifications. The drawn instructions of an artist to his wood-engraver in Figure 62 underline the rarity of feedback through drawing. The development of computer-controlled interactive systems may change all this, but at present pictorial language suffers doubly in terms of feedback. It suffers because it is graphic, and it suffers because it is pictorial.

All this means that we usually have less chance of finding out whether we have made ourselves understood when using pictorial language than we do when using verbal language, particularly spoken language. We must therefore turn to controlled experimentation for help in finding out what works and does not work. As we have already seen, there are so many graphic variables in pictorial language—quite apart from all the variables that are common to all communication—that it is difficult to know on what basis to make decisions.

Action research, which deals with specific issues in relation to particular situations and learning objectives, of the kind that led Fuglesang to use photographs with painted out backgrounds in Botswana (Figure 63), clearly has considerable value (Fuglesang, 1973). Action research does not aim to come up with findings from which one can generalize, but even longer-term research into pictorial language has found it difficult to tease out issues of general significance over and above those that relate to perception generally. Such comments are not intended as criticism of the wide range of research work undertaken in the field (Goldsmith, 1984, Kennedy, 1974) but as an acknowledgement of the extreme difficulty of the problem. At present it has to be admitted that research has precious little to offer the picture-maker in practical situations. Conversely, it is only fair to say that many practitioners do not even recognize that users can have problems in understanding their work.

When evaluating the effectiveness of pictorial language, we need to consider such variables as the purpose of the communication (a), the information content (b), the users (g), and circumstances of use (h); we might also need to consider

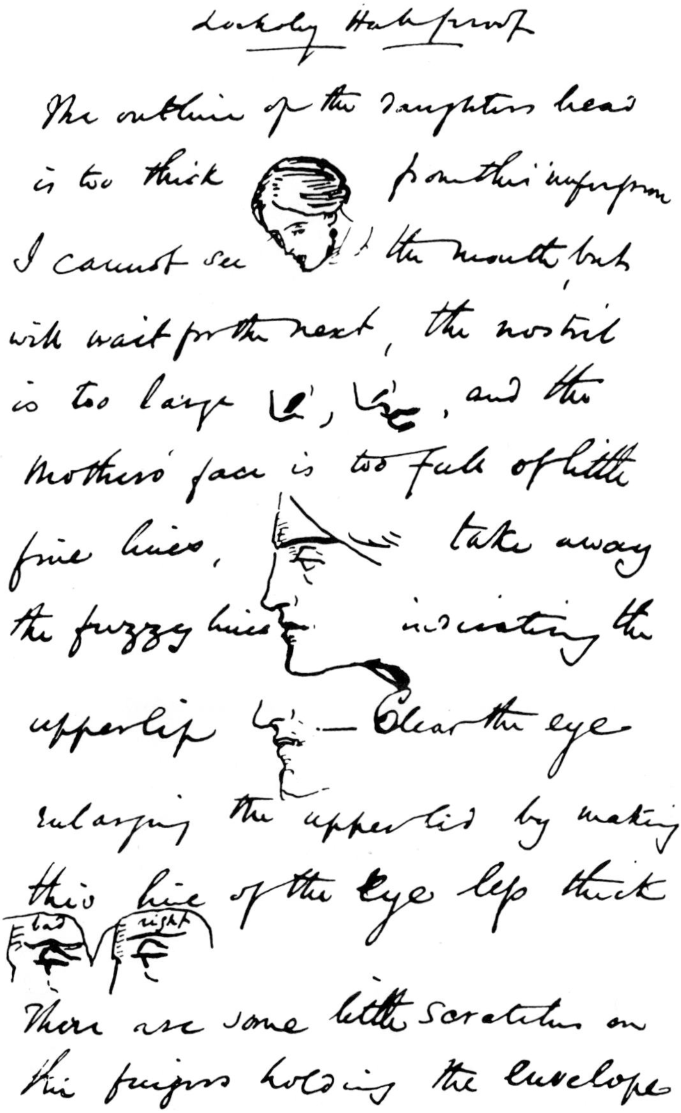

Fig. 62. Part of one of a number of letters from the artist Millais to his wood-engraver in which he provides feedback through drawings. From G. and E. Dalziel, *The Brothers Dalziel* (London: Methuen, 1901).

Fig. 63.   One of a series of posters designed by A. Fuglesang for the Health Education Unit in Botswana. On the basis of action research, Fuglesang decided to use photographs with painted out backgrounds.

its configuration (c) and the effect of the means of production (e). We should also question whether the pictorial mode (d) is the right one to use.

CREDIBILITY OF PICTURES

Pictures have had a rather bad track record in terms of reliability and accuracy and, along with the difficulty of getting effective feedback and the neglect of pictorial education, this has affected their credibility as information carriers. The Nuremberg Chronicle of 1493 is well known for having used the same wood-blocks over and over again for views of different towns (Figure 64). Sometimes illustrators get things wrong because of difficult circumstances, as in the picture of Nelson's funeral car which appeared in *The Times* in 1806 (Figure 65). Last-minute changes in the arrangement of the funeral pall affected its appearance, but the wood-engraving of it had already been made and the editor could only apologize rather lamely in the caption that there was no time to make any alterations. Instances from the field of illustrated journalism in which pictures were inadvertently or deliberately altered are numerous and must have played a part in undermining the credibility of pictures (Evans, 1981; Twyman, 1970).

But we have to ask whether the track record of pictures is really any worse than that of text, or merely more noticeable. In some cases it can even be argued that illustrations were more accurate than the text they were illustrating. In Vesalius's famous treatise *De humani corporis fabrica* of 1543, the text is said to follow Galen's orthodox and often erroneous views almost to the letter, whereas the pictures, which were drawn by an artist who must have made careful observations of the human body, were often very accurate (Ivins, 1952).

Despite this case, and many others in which pictures come out well as reliable carriers of information, pictorial language has had to work against a background of suspicion, particularly from those working in the humanities. Doubtless this has something to do with the respect, amounting almost to reverence, accorded to classical texts since the Renaissance. Edward Gibbon, for example, was quite prepared to take on trust evidence from ancient written sources when writing his *History of the Decline and Fall of the Roman Empire,* but when referring to a pictorial source of information in connection with the exotic animals slain by the Emperor Commodus, he revealed his suspicion of pictures by noting that these

Fig. 64.   Identical illustrations used to represent both Damascus and Mantua in the *Nuremberg Chronicle* (Nuremberg, 1493).

Fig. 65.   Wood-engraving of Nelson's funeral car printed in *The Times*, 10 January 1806. In the caption, the editor apologized for the fact that neither the coronet nor the pall appeared on the coffin during the funeral procession and that there was no time to change the wood-engraving.

Fig. 66.   A verbal translation of a picture. Illustration published in the *Observer* on 4 February 1979 from a photograph submitted by a reader, James Trimmer.

animals had been seen "only as representations of art, or perhaps of fancy" (Gibbon, 1776–1788). Gibbon may well have been right to be suspicious of the pictures of exotic animals he had seen, but his doubts, which are deep-rooted in Western culture, help to account for the way advertisers and others use pictures to deceive us. There have been cases recently where the overt message of an advertisement presented primarily in pictures says one thing while the truthful statement is made discreetly in words, thereby, it seems, covering the advertiser legally. Is it any wonder therefore that the credibility of pictorial language is called into question and that absurdities of the kind shown in Figure 66 occur?

The issue of the credibility of pictures must have a bearing on the choice of mode (d) and this in turn will be influenced by the purpose of the communication (a), the attitudes of users (g), and the circumstances of use (h).

REFERENCES

André, G. G. (1874). *The draughtsman's handbook of plan and map drawing, including instructions for the preparation of engineering, architectural, and mechanical drawings* London: Spon.

Arnheim, R. (1956). *Art and visual perception*. London: Faber & Faber.

Ashwin, C. (1979). The ingredients of style in contemporary illustration: A case study. *Information Design Journal, 1*(1), 51–67.

Balchin, W. G. V. (1972). Graphicacy. *Geography, 57*, 185–195.

Balchin, W. G. V., & Coleman, A. M. (1965). Graphicacy should be the fourth ace in the pack. *Times Educational Supplement*, 5 November.

Beasley, D. (1981). *Design illustration*. London: Heinemann.

Bertin, J. (1967). *Sémiologie graphique*. Paris and The Hague: Mouton and Gauthiers-Villars.

Blunt, W. (1950). *The art of botanical illustration*. London: Collins.

British Standards Institution. (1969). *Building drawing practice, BS 1192.*

British Standards Institution. (1972). *Engineering drawing practice, BS 308.*

Clutterbuck, C. K. (1966). *3-D scale drawing*. London: English Universities Press.

De Bono, E. (1972). *Children solve problems*. Harmondsworth: Allen Lane/Penguin Books.

Edwards, B. (1979). *Drawing on the right side of the brain*. Los Angeles: Tarcher.

Evans, H. (1978). *Pictures on a page: Photojournalism, graphics, and picture editing*. London: Heinemann.

Evans, H. (1981). Evans on newspapers. BBC television series.

Fuglesang, A. (1973). *Applied communication in developing countries*. Uppsala: Dag Hammarskjöld Foundation.

Gibbon, E. (1776–1788). *The history of the decline and fall of the Roman Empire* (first ed., 6 Vols). London.

Gill, R. W. (1973). *Rendering with pen and ink*. London: Thames & Hudson.

Goldsmith, E. (1980). Comprehensibility of illustrations—an analytical model. *Information Design Journal, 1*(3), 204–213.

Goldsmith, E. (1984). *Research into illustration: An approach and a review*. Cambridge: University Press.

Gombrich, E. H. (1960). *Art and illusion*. London: Phaidon Press.

Hochberg, J. E., & Brooks, V. (1962). Pictorial recognition as an unlearned ability: A study of a child's performance. *American Journal of Psychology, 75*, 624–628.

Hopkinson, T. (Ed.) (1970). *Picture Post 1938–50*. Harmondsworth: Penguin.

Hudson, W. (1960). Pictorial depth perception in sub-cultural groups in Africa. *Journal of Social Psychology, 52,* 183–208.

International Organization for Standardization. (1980). *Public information symbols,* ISO 7001.

Ivins, W. M. (1952). What about the "Fabrica" of Vesalius? In S. W. Lambert, W. Wiegand, & W. M. Ivins, (Eds.), *Three Vesalian essays*. New York: Macmillan.

Ivins, W. M. (1953). *Prints and visual communication*. London: Routledge and Kegan Paul.

Kellogg, R. (1959). *What children scribble and why*. Palo Alto.

Kellogg, R. (1969). *Analyzing children's art*. Palo Alto.

Kennedy, J. M. (1974). *A psychology of picture perception*. San Francisco and London: Jossey-Bass.

Lowenfeld, V., & Brittain, W. L. (1975). *Creative and mental growth,* 6th ed. New York: Macmillan.

Neurath, O. (1936). *International picture language* (Psyche Miniatures, General Series, 83). London: Kegan, Paul, Trench, Trubner.

Panofsky, E. (1943). *Albrecht Dürer,* 2 vols. Princeton: Princeton University Press.

Potter, T. C. (1983). The structural features of pictorial experience. Unpublished doctoral thesis, Brighton Polytechnic.

Rewald, J. (1950). *The ordeal of Paul Cézanne*. London: Phoenix House.

Richards, C. J. (1984). Diagrammatics: An investigation aimed at providing a theoretical framework for studying diagrams, Unpublished doctoral thesis, London, Royal College of Art.

Ridgway, J. L. (1938). *Scientific illustration*. Stanford: Stanford University Press.

Thouless, H. (1931). Phenomenal regression to the real object. *British Journal of Psychology, 21,* 339–359; *22,* 1–30.

Thouless, H. (1932). Individual differences in phenomenal regression. *British Journal of Psychology, 22,* 216–241.

Twyman, M. L. (1982). The graphic presentation of language, *Information Design Journal 3*(1), 2–22.

Twyman, M. (1970). *Printing 1770–1970*. London: Eyre & Spottiswoode.

Twyman, M. (1979). A schema for the study of graphic language. In P. A. Kolers, M. E. Wrolstad, and H. Bouma (Eds.), *Processing of visible language* (Vol. 1, pp. 117–150). New York and London: Plenum.

Wölfflin, H. (1932). *Principles of art history*. London: Bell. (first German, edition, 1915).

PART IV

Identifying Information Requirements

CHAPTER 12

Understanding Readers and Their Uses of Texts

T. STICHT

The whole duty of a writer is to please and satisfy himself, and the true writer always plays to an audience of one. . . . If one is to write, one must believe in the truth and worth of the scrawl, in the ability of the reader to receive and decode the message.

Strunk and White, *The Elements of Style*

INTRODUCTION

These quotes from the classic volume on writing by Strunk and White (1959) remind us that reading plays a dual role in the making of a text. On the one hand, texts are designed, written, and produced by people who, in the very course of their work, read what they produce and evaluate their work by their own standards as "an audience of one." On the other hand, texts are usually produced to be read by someone other than the producer. In this case, The producer designs and develops text on the basis of his or her understanding of the readers for whom the document is being prepared, including an understanding of the readers' abilities "to receive and decode the message."

From the perspective of Strunk and White, it is clear that the design of a text may suffer if the producer is faulty as "an audience of one" or if the producer holds incorrect beliefs about the abilities of prospective readers "to receive and decode the message." Unfortunately, as I illustrate later on, there are often situations in which both conditions apply.

PLAN FOR THIS CHAPTER

In this chapter I discuss certain problems that text producers face when they serve as readers of their own materials in order to judge the adequacy of their

DESIGNING USABLE TEXTS

texts for other readers. In this discussion, I focus on text producers who are developing materials for youth and adults in high schools or technical schools, and for workers in a variety of jobs. Thus, my focus is on the producer of youth and adult functional as contrasted with recreational texts. Also, I use the term *text* or *document* interchangeably to include narrative prose texts as well as documents such as forms, charts, tables, and so forth. If the distinction between prose and other materials is needed, I make it.

The first problem that I discuss concerns the text producer's understanding of the differences between the types of tasks readers perform in schools and those they perform on the job. The point is made that failure to properly understand these differences has, at times, resulted in a failure of the text producer as "an audience of one" capable of judging the appropriateness of his or her product to the needs of the prospective users of the document. In this discussion I review research aimed at understanding readers' uses of texts in schools and on the job.

The second problem concerns the text producer's understanding of the ability of the reader "to receive and decode the message." Here the major focus will be on the information and techniques, such as readability formulas, that the text producer may draw upon to try to judge the reader's ability to read and understand the text. Limitations to the use of readability formulas due to special aptitudes of readers and the conditions and manner of text use on the job are noted. (See also Chapter 6 by Duffy in the present volume for a discussion of the problems with readability formulas.)

THE TEXT PRODUCER AS "AN AUDIENCE OF ONE"

The ability of a text producer to read and evaluate her or his own material and to judge its appropriateness for users will be conditioned by the understanding that the producer has of the types of tasks that readers will perform with the document. For a great many people who are asked to produce texts in their work, their major experiences with functional literacy (i.e., reading for applied, in contrast to recreational, purposes) are obtained first in their elementary and secondary schooling and only later in their experiences in the world of work. For people new to the working world, or who have been in the work force for some time but have never been required to produce a major work of technical writing, such as a new procedures manual, we can expect that their general ability as "an audience of one" will largely reflect their past schooling experiences. As the following research indicates, schooling experiences may produce an inappropriate knowledge background for people who are later called upon to produce functional documents for work.

PRIMARY READING TASKS
IN THE SCHOOL-TO-WORK TRANSITION

The U.S.Navy sponsored research in which Sticht,Fox,Hauke,and Welty-Zapf (1977) identified reading tasks performed by students in Navy technical training schools, by their instructors, and by job incumbents in 10 job fields. Subsequently, Mikulecky (1981) applied the approach of Sticht *et al.* to the study of reading tasks performed by high school students, technical school students, and job incumbents in civilian settings.

The research by Sticht *et al.* (1977) and Mikulecky (1981) was based on an analysis of written language that indicated that it differs from spoken language in three major features: Written language is more or less permanent, it can be arrayed in visual space, and it utilizes properties of light, that is, brightness contrast and color. These features make possible the use of written materials in two broad, primary classes of reading tasks. In the first class of tasks, the features of permanence and spatiality are drawn upon to permit the written language to serve as an external "memory" that can be consulted by the user to acquire information needed to do some task at hand. Once located and applied, the information can be forgotten. Because the information is stored in the book, it does not have to be "stored in the head"; it can simply be looked up if needed again. This type of reading task, in which information is looked up, used, and may then be forgotten I call a *reading-to-do* reading task.

The second general class of reading tasks identified by Sticht *et al.* (1977) is actually a subset of the set of reading-to-do tasks and is called a *reading-to-learn* task. In a reading-to-learn task, the features of permanence and spatiality are drawn upon in various study strategies, such as previewing and reviewing (based on permanence) and outlining and underlining (based on the use of visual space and contrast), to permit the reader to extract and retain information in one or another representation "in the head" so that it may be drawn upon at a later time.

In the research of Sticht *et al.* (1977) and Mikulecky (1981), interviewers obtained information on the frequency with which high school students, technical school students (civilian and military), technical school instructors (military), and job incumbents (civilian and military) performed reading-to-do and reading-to-learn tasks. As indicated in Figure 1 there is a complete reversal in the frequency with which these two classes of tasks are performed in the transition from the traditional academically oriented high school, through technical schools that prepare one for particular jobs, and into the world of work. In the high school, 66% of reading tasks were reading-to-learn tasks, whereas only 15% were reading-to-do tasks. At the work site, on the other hand, civilian job incumbents in professional, clerical, and blue-collar jobs reported 78% reading-to-do tasks and 15% reading-to-learn tasks. Altogether, the civilian and military

318   T. Sticht

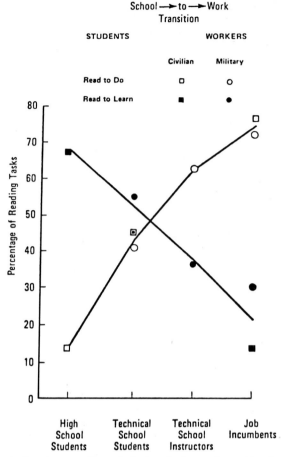

Fig. 1.   Changes in the primary reading tasks in the school-to-work transition for read-to-do tasks for civilians and the military and for read-to-learn tasks for civilians and military.

data are quite consistent and mutually confirmatory in indicating that the school-to-work transition reverses the primary uses of literacy skills.

In addition to the differences in primary reading tasks for school and work, Mikulecky (1981) also reported finding large differences in the types of written materials used in school and at work. In the case of the high school students, 95% of the materials they reported using were textbooks. Job incumbents, on the other hand, rarely used textbooks, and instead they reported a wide variety of materials such as manuals, flyers, labels, forms, and even computer screens, which they consulted in the course of performing job tasks.

The Textbook Reader as Job Materials Writer

If one's primary exposure to functional reading prior to joining the work force is textbook reading to satisfy school learning requirements, there is reason to suspect that when called upon to produce job materials, the school-reader-turned-job-writer may lack the appropriate experience to serve as "an audience of one" for judging the suitability of job texts for job performers.

This situation was, in fact, found by Kern and Sticht (1974) in a study in which they conducted interviews with close to 100 writers of Army training and job performance literature to find out who the writers were, what their qualifications for producing materials were, how they work, and what kind of guidance they thought might be helpful to them in producing better materials.

For the most part, it was found that Army writers were usually college graduates with no formal training in technical writing but were considered subject matter experts in the assigned writing area. Also, because all of our interviews were with writers in Army school settings, in keeping with our focus on Army training literature, it was found that most writers were (or had been) instructors in the subject matter area.

Generally it was found that the Army writers received writing assignments as an extra duty at the direction of the school management. Such recommendations resulted from the periodic review that each school conducted of the field manuals, technical manuals, and so forth, for which the school was responsible. If there was the need for a revision or a new manual, the school management would assign a person to write the material, frequently with only a directive to write a manual on a certain subject.

Given this general guidance, the writers tended to view their jobs as that of assembling, organizing, and recording what was known about the topic they were assigned to write about. They generally assumed that if a manual contained a reasonably complete exposition of the topic, it could serve as a general text or reference source and could be used by anyone for any purpose, whether initial learning (reading-to-learn); looking up previously learned information; or consulting for directing the training, learning, and job performance of others (reading-to-do).

By taking this topic-oriented approach to writing, then, these Army, college-educated writers tended to bring the orientations and formats of the textbooks they had had extensive experience with to the preparation of materials for Army students whose primary tasks were to learn to perform specific job tasks. Further, once this practice was established, this topic-oriented, textbook type material tended to be perpetuated by the writer's primary method of document design, which consisted simply of producing a new manual that looked like one of the old ones.

The topic-oriented, textbook-type approach to writing that the Army personnel took reflected itself in the types of guidance that the writers said they might find helpful, though most of them said that they did not use writer's guides of any type. Of 12 types of information the writers thought might be helpful, 8 were concerned with activities involved in researching a topic and writing about it (how to conduct a literature search, how to identify reference sources for literature review, how to develop outlines, etc.), 2 were concerned with how to determine and write a given reading level, 1 was concerned with how to obtain copyright release, and 1 factor concerned the need for guidance in determining user, purpose, and scope of materials.

Interviews with *users* of Army training literature in the study discussed in the preceding (Showell & Brennan, 1974) again revealed the inappropriateness of the Army writer's "textbook schema" for judging audience needs. Both supervisors at work and students in training programs reported excessive generality of information as being a problem. This caused reader problems on two counts: (1) They were required to make their own interpretations of requirements or other information and (2) there was the possibility that their interpretations were different from the actual requirements intended by the writer of the document.

Other major problems cited by the users were that publications were not giving sufficient emphasis to job relevance and job performance. In this regard, when asked for recommendations for new Army publications, the most frequent type of new publication requested was one oriented around job duties, in effect, a how-to-do-it handbook instead of an textbook on everything you always wanted to know about the topic.

In this Army research, then, the Army officer or noncommissioned officer assigned a writing task failed as "an audience of one" with respect to content (too much irrelevant, general information; not job-oriented enough); purpose (multipurpose text for learning, reference, and procedural directions in contrast to limited-purpose, job-performance orientation); and audience (everyone of the rank of private through general in a military unit in contrast to the job learner–performer). The workers-turned-writers had only vague, amorphous images and understandings of the production task because they were informed by nothing but their own apperception of text, developed primarily in school settings prior to entering the world of work. This, at times, resulted in concerns about (1) the reading levels of potential users, (2) techniques for measuring the grade level of difficulty of materials, and (3) writing for a particular grade level. Writers were concerned about readability levels even as they contemplated multipurpose, general, topic-oriented texts for use by privates to generals. Such reading material would surely call for skills in locating, extracting, and integrating information. Thus no matter what the reading level of the words and sentences, many users would either not use the manuals or find their use difficult.

TEXTBOOK PRODUCTION AND THE VIOLATION OF AUDIENCE

Perhaps the naive writer's willingness to place so much of the information-processing burden on the reader is also a product of her or his experiences with textbooks and schooling in secondary and postsecondary education. In research on textbooks and student's use of textbooks in a community college, I found what appears to be a major conflict between textbook producers and their concepts of learning in their student audience (Sticht, in press). The concept seems to be held that, in order to best promote learning, information should be presented in a logical, meaningful sequence, with later learning building on earlier learning. The conflict was found in the study of textbook prefaces, which, although stating that the organization and sequencing of the textbook followed a logical development, also stated that the chapters could be taught in any order the teacher desired.

Another indication of the conflict between textbook authors, teachers, and their theories of learning was revealed by the presence of statements regarding the use of extensive cross-references to help integrate learning across loosely interrelated or chapters that could stand alone. Thus, although textbook authors and teachers believe that materials should be sequenced in such a manner as to promote learning, they are willing to shift the burden of this sequencing and integration to the learner, aided by such tools of design as cross-references, end-of-chapter questions that require cross-chapter reading for finding answers, and additional workbooks that students can use to improve learning. This shift in the responsibility for sequence and organization from the text producer to the text user occurs, I suspect, because of the need to market the textbook to a wide range of professors who have their own ideas about what is important and what is not in a given discipline. To accommodate the widest range of teachers, then, the textbook producers develop stand-alone chapters that permit the teacher to intrude her or his own proclivities for content and order into the teaching process.

There may be two significant outcomes of the attempt by producers to accommodate the teacher at the expense of the students. First, student learning is made more difficult. Integrated bodies of knowledge are not likely to be sought by either teachers or students, and learning may become a fragmented enterprise characterized by cramming to pass multiple-choice or other objective tests that call for the recall of isolated bits of information from one or more chapters covered between tests. This belief was reinforced in conversations with the students who participated in the community college study of textbooks. These students reported that they had very little past experience with integrating learning across textbook chapters at any level of their previous schooling. They did not use cross-references, nor did they understand well the use of any analysis—

synthesis tools such as matrices, tree structures, flowcharts, or, for some, outlining for organizing information across chapters. For the most part these students had simply read assigned chapters and taken an objective test that covered the assigned material.

The second major outcome of producing texts that appeal to teachers is a type of implicit learning about how textbooks are designed and used. This type of implicit learning may have affected the approaches to materials production by the aforementioned Army writers. If people are constantly exposed to topic-oriented, multiuser texts in school, it is not too surprising to find these same people produce similar texts at work. Unfortunately their experiences in school will most likely fail to prepare them to serve as "an audience of one" for preparing texts for workers.

UNDERSTANDING THE ABILITY OF THE READER TO "RECEIVE AND DECODE THE MESSAGE"

One of the contributing factors to the interest in the improved design of documents in the last decade has been the mounting evidence that, for many citizens in Western industrialized societies, there is reason to question their ability "to receive and decode the message" as expressed by Strunk and White (1959, p. 70). In Great Britain, for instance, the British Association of Settlements (1974) formulated a national "right to read" policy on the basis of an analysis of newspapers, medicine bottle labels, recipes on food packets, government documents, and assorted other "functional literacy" materials. Based on applications of the FORCAST readability formula (Sticht, 1975) to these materials, and on comparisons of the reading skill levels of adults in England and Wales to the readability levels of the materials, the British Association of Settlements concluded that 6% of the adult population in those countries were not able "to receive and decode the message" in the materials.

In the preceding research on Army writers, the concern that the writers expressed for guidance on how to determine and write to specified reading levels was stimulated in large part by additional research that indicated that, in certain Army jobs, the reading difficulty level of the materials exceeded the readers' measured reading skills by anywhere from one and one-half to three grade levels on the average; and in many cases the difficulty level of materials exceeded the reading levels of lower-aptitude personnel by some three to five grade levels (Sticht, 1975, p. 112). The extent to which problems of readability of materials and reading levels of personnel are of concern to the U.S. armed services is indicated by the fact that in 1975 and again in 1978 representatives from the Air Force, Army, and Navy gathered in national conferences to discuss problems of literacy and readability of materials in the military services (Curran, 1980; Sticht & Welty- Zapf, 1976).

Concerns about the level of difficulty of materials in training programs and on the job and in other functional life contexts has led to several strategies for better matching materials to readers. In one approach the reading skills of people are assessed and the data used to either screen them out of positions in which they might be expected to have difficulty coping with the materials, or to assign them to positions (training programs and jobs) in which their reading skills match the readability of the materials they are expected to use (this I call the selection-and-assignment strategy). In a second approach, an attempt is made to cope with the lower reading skills of people by redesigning the materials to reduce the reading difficulty of the materials (the document design strategy). In the third approach that I consider, the attempt is made to to, in a manner of speaking, "redesign" the person to make him or her a better, more functional reader (the literacy training strategy).

Notice that in each of these three strategies two assessments are made: The person's reading skills are assessed and the reading difficulty of the materials is assessed. Each strategy then aims at making a match between the two assessments. Now, in order to accomplish this feat, it is necessary that the two assessments be founded on a common metric. For this purpose, the various readability formulas are used to state the difficulty of materials in units of reading grade levels (RGLs) (Harrison, 1980). To assess people's reading skills, standardized tests that give a RGL are typically administered, even to assess the skills of adults who have been out of school for some time (Sticht, 1982a, pp. 46–48).

Problems with the use of readability formulas as measures of the reading difficulty of materials have been documented by Kern (1980). His focus is upon the imprecision of the RGL estimates of the formulas. In the present case, I discuss problems that can arise in attempting to match people to materials on the basis of the assessment of general RGL of ability. The problem that I discuss concerns the concept of general literacy and its measurement by standardized tests. The point that I make is that beliefs about people's ability "to receive and decode messages" based on measures of general literacy may be inaccurate and particularly discriminatory against lower-ability readers who may have special interests and competence in one or more limited domains of literacy. I discuss this general problem within the contexts of the three strategies for matching readers to materials summarized in the preceding: selection and assignment, document design, and literacy training.

SELECTION AND ASSIGNMENT TO MATCH READERS TO MATERIALS

Quite clearly, the producer of texts who is faced with the task of attempting to rewrite materials to lower levels of difficulty would have his or her job greatly simplified if poorer readers were simply screened out of the training program, job, or other situation for which the materials are being produced. And, in fact, such screening is used in certain organizations, such as colleges and the military, to prevent less apt readers from entering into the organization.

There is evidence, however, from research in the military to suggest that measures of general literacy may be too exclusive when applied to lower-ability readers who have special aptitudes for various job fields (Sticht, 1975, pp. 39–49). In this research, special job-reading task tests (JRTTs) were constructed from materials used in Army jobs for automotive repairmen and supply clerks. These JRTTs included tests on the use of indexes, following procedural directions, looking for and extracting information from job manuals, and filling out forms. The JRTTs were administered to three groups of personnel: one group consisted of men new to the Army who had not yet received assignments to jobs and who represented the total range of abilities and aptitudes in the recruit population; a second group consisted of men who had been selected for a particular job field based on their special aptitude test scores, such as aptitude for mechanical or clerical career fields; the third group of men tested on the JRTTs had been both selected for aptitude in a given job and had completed 8 weeks of job training to develop job knowledge and skills particularly relevant to the JRTTs.

Each of the three groups of Army personnel was also administered a standardized test of general reading ability. This made it possible to determine how men who performed at different reading levels on the general reading test performed on the JRTT if they (1) had no special aptitude for the job represented on the JRTT (the general recruit sample), (2) had special aptitude for the job, or (3) had both special aptitude and training in the job to which the JRTT was appropriate.

The results for the testing using the JRTT for supply clerks are presented in Figure 2. Similar findings were found for the automotive repairmen's JRTT. The data of Figure 2 show that, across the range of general reading abilities given on the abscissa, men selected for special clerical aptitude performed better on the JRTT than did the general recruit population. Further, this difference was more pronounced for the least able general readers. In the case of Figure 2, the group with special clerical aptitude who read at a general level of grade 5.0 actually performed on the supply clerk's JRTT like a person in the general recruit sample who read at a 6.5 RGL. Thus possession of special aptitude for the job had the effect of adding 1.5 years of reading ability when assessed by JRTTs.

The effect of training on the job is also shown in Figure 2. For the supply clerk's JRTT, selection for special aptitude plus completion of the supply clerk's training program made it possible for personnel reading at a general level of grade 5.0 to perform on the JRTT like people with a general level of grade 7.5— a $2\frac{1}{2}$-year increment in "apparent" reading ability for the job.

These data, and similar data for the automotive repairmen's JRTT, suggest

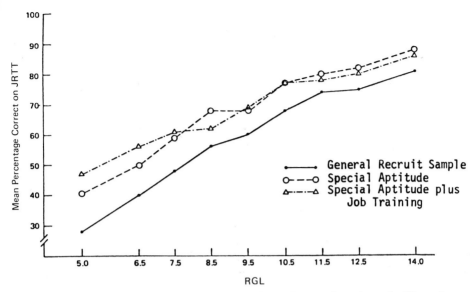

Fig. 2.   Performance on JRTT as a function of RGL for (1) the general recruit sample, (2) recruits selected for special aptitude, and (3) recruits with special aptitude plus job training.

that if general measures of literacy are used to match personnel and text, then significant numbers of personnel might be screened out on the basis of their reading score even though they might be able to adequately use the job materials due to their interests and knowledge of the field. If they are screened out of the career field based on their general literacy scores, there is a useless waste of human resources. Perhaps the extent of this waste could be reduced if JRTTs were used to assess people's ability to use materials in their areas of special aptitude, and if readability formulas were developed for special aptitude groups using job relevant materials. Using computers, such specialized assessments are increasingly feasible.

TEXT USE ON THE JOB

Typically, readability formulas and tests of general literacy are composed of relatively brief paragraphs followed by questions about the passage. The reader encounters new materials and interprets them alone, with no help from others. Based on such procedures, the readability formulas may be used to establish reading levels required for entry into a given job field, and the reading test will be used to determine if applicant's reading skills match the readability levels of the job (e.g., Mockovak, 1974).

Apart from the difficulties for this approach to matching people to jobs due to the effects of special aptitude discussed in the preceding, this use of readability formulas and tests of reading fails to consider the effects of the conditions of text use on the job in contrast to the conditions of text use in the development of the readability formulas and reading tests. An increasing body of research indicates that, on the job, personnel are likely to read materials repeatedly, (2) use materials of a familiar nature, (3) use materials composed of a variety of texts (prose and nonprose graphs, tables, schematics, etc.), and (4) utilize information sources in addition to the printed documents to comprehend and perform job tasks (Kirsch & Guthrie, 1982; Sticht, 1982b; Diehl & Mikulecky, 1980).

It seems likely that the differences in the conditions of use of materials in the readability and reading skill assessments and on the job may account, at least in part, for the fact that, contrary to predictions based on these assessments, many low-literacy skill personnel do, in fact, perform quite satisfactorily on the job (Sticht, 1975, 1982a). It may also be that, because the conditions of readability and reading ability assessment are similar to the conditions of text use in training programs, in which there is an abundance of new information to be comprehended and learned, there is a higher relationship between literacy skills and satisfactory performance (Sticht, 1982, pp. 13–20).

In summary, the use of selection and assignment strategies for matching reading skills to readability requirements of training programs and jobs should be tempered by the role of special aptitudes for career fields and by the conditions of use of texts in work settings. Reading ability measures and readability formulas that are developed taking aptitudes and conditions of use into consideration may permit a more accurate matching of people and materials (see also Duffy, Chapter 6 in the present volume).

DOCUMENT DESIGN TO MATCH READERS TO MATERIALS

The second strategy for matching people to materials mentioned in the preceding is to redesign the materials. Ordinarily, because of the interest in accommodating less literate readers, the approach to the redesign of materials has consisted of attempts to reduce the reading difficulty level of materials. In one such approach, research has aimed at doing away altogether with the requirement for reading and to substitute audio or audiovisual materials for the printed page (Sticht, 1975, pp. 96–104). In a second approach the attempt has been made to rewrite materials to increase their readability (i.e., lower their reading difficulty). Because this latter approach has been reviewed by Kern (1980), I focus the present discussion on the approach to overcome literacy limitations by the substitution of audio or audiovisual materials.

For the message designer who is faced with preparing training or reference materials for marginally literate youth and adults, one of the first factors to be considered is the choice of media to convey the message. Typically the reasoning may proceed as follows: Because the target audience lacks the ability "to receive and decode the message" in the written medium, let us present the message in the spoken medium, *which the audience can receive and decode.* The latter is the usually implicit assumption that the message designer makes in deciding to substitute listening for reading requirements for illiterate or marginally literate audiences.

Although there is much information about the reading skills of adults, little information exists about the listening skills of adults. Thus it is difficult for designers to determine if audio rather than printed materials should be produced for marginally literate adults. If designers elect to produce audio materials, research gives little guidance as to the grade level for which they should produce material. However, limited research suggests that adults who read, on the average, at around the fifth-grade level are likely to listen at the fifth- to sixth-grade level (Sticht, 1982c). This finding of near parallelism of listening and reading skills in adults of marginal literacy was confirmed for the full range of young adult readers spanning RGLs from the second through the eleventh-grade level (Sticht, Hooke, & Caylor, 1982). These data, based on over 2000 applicants for military service in 1978, are summarized in Figure 3.

As indicated in Figure 3 it is only at the very lowest level of reading that listening exceeded reading performance in the paragraphs test. Above the second-grade reading level, these young adults consistently scored higher by reading than by listening, though only slightly. For the vocabulary data, however, the results are different, reflecting, for this study, differences in the vocabulary and paragraph tests. In the latter, examinees were tested for paragraph listening comprehension by having the paragraphs read aloud to them. In the vocabulary test, however, items in the listening–reading test were read aloud while the examinees also read the item silently. Because the listening–reading vocabulary test was force-paced by means of an audiotape that performed the reading-aloud component of the test, examinees were more likely to try all items than when they read the reading vocabulary test silently to themselves. Apparently, the forced pacing resulted in higher scores in the combined listening–reading vocabulary test than in the reading-only vocabulary test across the full range of reading ability scores. In and of itself, this is an interesting result because it suggests that such a combined listening–reading procedure provides an overall better evaluation of peoples' vocabulary knowledge than the reading-only condition, and further suggests that such combined listening–reading presentations might result in better learning from textual materials than reading alone, especially with poorer readers.

In general, the research studies summarized in the preceding suggest that simply substituting the spoken for the written language as a means of redesigning materials to accommodate less literate users is not likely to be very productive. In the present-day United States, youth and adults who have poor reading vocabu-

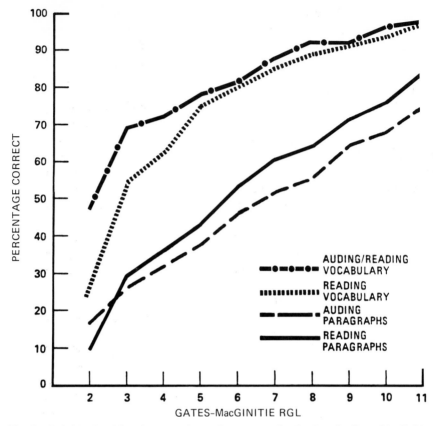

Fig. 3. Relationship of listening to reading performance reading level on the Gates–MacGinitie reading test.

laries and abilities to comprehend materials of paragraph length are also likely to have poor oral language comprehension skills.

Although the foregoing is a valid conclusion from the available research, (see Sticht, 1972, for additional reviews of relevant studies), it should be noted that these studies have all been conducted using academic testing materials and conditions in which a premium has been placed on efficient listening or reading and immediate recall of information. Just how marginally literate adults would compare on their performance of more ecologically representative reading and listening tasks is not known by me. There are, however, studies of media use (Sticht, 1974) that suggest that the information media used by the marginally literate adults tend toward the more transient, electronic media rather than the more permanent, print media. These studies also suggest that people who use print media are more likely to have *access* to extended, systematic knowledge (in contrast to bits of information typical of audio-media), and they are more likely to *possess* knowledge about science, health, and similar topics (i.e., they are better able to answer questions about information presented in various printed sources) than are the users of the electronic media, and particularly the less-educated users of such media.

Although the media studies are important in suggesting differences in the ecology of use of listening and reading among youth and adults of various education and literacy levels, they do not provide information about

1. The development of vocabulary and oral comprehension skills by the less literate in listening to electronic broadcast or audio playback media.
2. The ability of the less literate to efficiently extract, store in memory, and recall information obtained from various electronic media,
3. Comparative studies of information processing from printed sources in the environment by the marginally literate.

Such studies are needed to permit message (and media) designers to establish more accurate beliefs about the ability of the marginally literate "to receive and decode the message" in both spoken and printed form.

LITERACY TRAINING TO MATCH READERS TO MATERIALS

Earlier, in my discussion of the selection and assignment strategy for matching readers to materials, I noted how special aptitudes and training could produce specialized literacy skills that might go undetected by tests of general literacy. Then, in my discussion of the strategy of document redesign for matching readers' skills to the medium of the message, I pointed out that beliefs about the oral language skills of less literate adults may be incorrect and that this could lead to unwise decisions regarding the removal of literacy demands of tasks by substituting listening for reading.

Now, in this section, these two lines of thought come together in a discussion of problems involved in teaching reading in adult literacy programs. The focus of of the discussion is on adults whose literacy skills, in today's high-technology, information-oriented world, are so poorly developed as to render them of only marginal utility, in an economic sense. When the economy is robust, the marginally literate may be hired into jobs that require only a modicum of literacy. When the economy weakens, however, the marginally literate, though the last to be hired, are frequently the first to be fired.

Today the plight of marginally literate adults appears to be deepening. With the development of computer capabilities, many blue-collar jobs that require only low levels of literacy are being automatized. Industrial robots are increasingly displacing blue-collar workers from factory jobs (Gunn, 1982). Additionally, the development of computerized aids for designing and preparing documents, such as programs that correct spelling, perform certain technical editing functions, and even assist in authoring documents threaten the jobs of many white-collar workers whose literacy skills are average or above average in the adult population (Guiliano, 1982).

Given the foregoing state of affairs, we face the possibility that the range of literacy skills included in the margin of utility will increase faster than we can alleviate the problems of the least literate today. There is, therefore, a sense of urgency in our need to understand the marginally literates' ability "to receive and decode the message" and how best to go about improving that ability.

The present discussion centers around the beliefs about the marginally literates' oral language skills and the nature of general literacy that are widely held among the adult education profession, text and curriculum developers, and the public in general. These beliefs have lead, so I argue, to the frequent use of brief, remedial programs of adult literacy training that attempt to overcome long-term literacy problems with short-term, intense, concentrated programs of instruction. For instance, in a review of adult literacy programs in industry, the armed forces, and penal institutions, commissioned by the National Academy of Education, Ryan and Furlong (1975) note that the programs they reviewed "have been of short duration—from 16 to 20 weeks—and the average progress has been only 1.5 to 2 grade levels" (p. 187). They go on to state that for these programs to have practical effects upon employability or other uses of reading "it is obvious that the programs must be extended in length and that the trainees must be motivated to continue" (p. 185).

The demand for brief programs of basic skills development arises, at least in part, from a point of view recognized by Ryan and Furlong (1975). They note that, if people reach adulthood without developing what are though to be requisite literacy skills, then there is reluctance on the part of employers, in industry or government, to provide extensive literacy education because "that is the school's job." Managers in these organizations "point out that their institutions are not rightfully burdened with the failures of public education" (p. 185).

Because the improvement of adult literacy skills requires an investment in human resources development beyond the K–12 school years and curriculum, programs of adult literacy development are eschewed, and, when implemented, they are considered as remediation rather than continuing development; they are expected to be of limited duration, fast-acting, far-reaching, and to bring about improvement not only in basic literacy skills, but in job performance, parenting, community participation, and so forth.

CONCEPTS OF ADULT MARGINAL LITERATES AS LEARNERS

The demand for brevity in adult basic skills programs is reinforced by the willingness of many adult educators to offer such programs on the strength of beliefs that adults can and will learn at much faster rates than children in the school system. This belief is frequently supported by statistics that show that adult literacy students in a particular program make 1, 2, or even more years of gain in reading in as few as 14, 50, or 100 or so hours of instruction (Sticht, 1982a). Thus, what the *typical* child in the public school system requires up to 2 years to learn, the adult illiterate is said to learn in just a few hours. How can this be so?

Rather than suspecting the psychometric tests and, procedures by means of which improvement in reading is assessed in adult basic skills programs (in which in most cases a year or two of "learning" can be achieved simply by answering three to five items correctly), Many adult educators seem to assume that if adult literacy students score at a given grade level on a basic skills test, then the adult student is probably just as proficient, or more so, in that skill, as the student in the grade school who scores the same as the adult. If an adult literacy student scores on a reading test at the fifth-grade level, the assumption may be made that the adult can now perform fifth-grade literacy tasks as effectively and efficiently as can a typical fifth-grade child.

The "Reading Potential" Concept

The belief that adult marginal literates can make rapid increases in literacy is frequently expressed in textbooks for adult literacy teachers. For instance, in their textbook entitled *Teaching Reading in Adult Basic Education,* Bowren and Zintz (1977) state

> Since his experiences are much broader, the adult nonreader generally has more words in his oral vocabulary that can be converted to the reading vocabulary than does the child nonreader. This is one of the reasons that the reading skills may be taught more quickly to adults than to children. (p. 61)

The presumed higher capability in oral language of marginally literate adults as compared to grade school children is said to provide the adult with a higher "reading potential." Therefore, it is argued, it is possible for adult marginal literates to make more rapid increases in learning to read as they close the gap between what they can already comprehend in oral language and what they can comprehend in the written language.

In effect, then, the reading potential argument for brief literacy programs rests upon the same beliefs about the oral language skills of the marginally literate adults as were discussed in the section on document design and the substitution of listening for reading. And, as discussed there and illustrated in Figure 3, this belief appears to be incorrect. For the most part, the adult marginally literate does not appear to have much reading potential, defined as having listening skills much higher than reading skills.

To further evaluate the reading potential concept for adult literacy training, research was conducted to determine (1) the reading potential of a sample of adult literacy students and (2) the relationship between reading potential and achievement in an adult literacy program (Sticht, 1982c). Of particular interest in the second objective was the hypothesis from the reading potential concept that students with greater potential should make the greatest gains in a brief literacy program.

The research was conducted using students in an adult literacy program conducted by the U.S. Army. As determined by the U.S. Armed Forces Institute (USAFI) Intermediate Achievement Test administered upon entry into the literacy program, the average RGL of the students was 5.3. For this research, in addition to the USAFI test, which provided a measure of general literacy, a specially constructed JRTT was administered at the end of the program to measure gain in job-related reading skills. The latter was of special interest because the literacy program was a job-oriented program in which Army students received training in performing the kinds of reading tasks they would encounter in their jobs following graduation from the literacy program.

The Durrell Listening–Reading Series (DLRS), Intermediate Level, Form DE (Durrell and Brassard, 1970) was used to assess differences between listening and reading skills of students upon entry into the program. From this difference score, a ''reading potential'' score was derived, which indicates how well the person would be reading if his or her reading score was as high as his or her listening score.

Figure 4 presents the reading and reading potential scores obtained with the DLRS for students at different entering levels of reading as indexed by the USAFI test of general reading. These data indicate that students who entered the literacy program reading at the fourth-grade level or below showed the greatest amount of reading potential (about 1.5 grade levels), and that reading and reading potential curves tend to converge at the higher USAFI reading levels. Thus these data are consistent with those of Figure 3 in demonstrating a close fit of listening to reading scores. Although there is *some* degree of reading potential at the very lowest levels of reading, there is not enough to warrant expectations for extensive, rapid increases in reading skills in brief programs of literacy.

The latter interpretation was corroborated by the study of the relationships between amount of reading potential and improvement made in the 6-week, 180-hour program. Figure 5 shows the amount of gain made on the USAFI test of general literacy and the JRTT test of job-related literacy as a function of the amount of entering reading potential. (The ''negative potential'' [<0.0] category resulted from subtracting normative RGL scores from reading potential scores that were less than the normative reading scores.) As Figure 5 indicates, there is no systematic increase in gain scores on the USAFI or JRTT as the amount of reading potential increases from negative to 3 years or more of potential for reading.

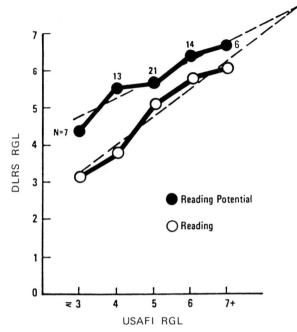

Fig. 4.   Reading score and reading potential score for adult remedial literacy students at different levels of reading skill as measured by the USAFI reading test.

Additional correlational analyses indicated that there was no systematic gain in general or job-related reading as a function of reading potential for the data as a whole, or for students scoring at the third to fourth grades, the fifth grade, or the sixth to seventh grades on entry into the program, indicating a lack of relationship between reading potential and gain in the literacy program regardless of the students' entering RGLs.

The foregoing research suggests that the beliefs held by many text and education program producers regarding the marginally literates' abilities "to receive and decode messages" presented in spoken or written forms may be erroneous. Brief programs of adult literacy training may not be as effective as is commonly thought due to the fact, at least in part, that the marginally literates' oral language skills may be about as low as their written language skills. Furthermore, additional research (Sticht, 1982c) indicates that the reading tests used to measure progress in literacy training programs for adults may provide an inaccurate indication of the adult's actual range of skills in processing print. In that research it was found that adults in a remedial literacy program who scored at the fifth-grade level on a commercially available, nationally normed (normative scores were determined) test based on the elementary and secondary school system,

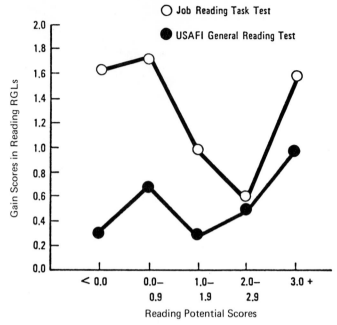

Fig. 5.   Gain in JRTT and USAFI General Reading Test as a function of reading potential scores.

actually performed more poorly than typical fifth-grade students on a set of literacy tasks. Thus, for instance when it is reported that students in an adult literacy program entered the program reading at the fifth-grade level and left the program reading at the 6.5 RGL, it is not certain just exactly what that implies relative to the school system in which the reading tests are normed.

This problem is compounded by the fact that literacy programs use a variety of reading tests to evaluate gains in literacy, and the various tests do not generally provide the same estimates of reading skills. Table 1 presents comparative data for three tests widely used to assess adult literacy skills: the Gates–MacGinitie, Adult Basic Learning Examination (ABLE), and the Tests of Adult Basic Education (TABE). As the table indicates, a person scoring at the Grade 6.0 level in reading on the Gates–MacGinitie would have a score of Grade 6.9 on the ABLE and 8.1 on the TABE—a 2.2-year spread in the estimate of the person's reading skills. A question of concern for text producers is raised by these data; to what level should materials be designed for this person or the class of persons whose skills are assessed by these three tests? For literacy program operators, the question arises as to just where, in a structured, grade-oriented literacy program, the person should be assigned.

SPECIFIC LITERACIES VERSUS GENERAL LITERACY

In addition to the difficulties in understanding adult reading skills posed by the differences in the available standardized tests, the data of Figure 5 raise, again, the problem posed earlier with regard to the role of special aptitudes and training in reading assessment. Figure 5 shows that, in the job-oriented literacy program for adults in the Army, improvements in the job-related reading tasks assessed by the JRTTs far exceeded the gains in general literacy indicated by the USAFI test. In other words, the students made the greatest gains in the domain in which they were given direct instruction and, although there was some impact of the job-related reading training on general literacy, the growth in the latter was much less than in the former.

In additional research on job-related literacy training, Sticht (1975, p. 136) reported data comparing performance on JRTT for students who had attended general literacy programs in the Army and in the Air Force to students who had attended the Army job-oriented reading program. The results showed that the

Table 1

Comparative Data for the Gates–MacGinitie, ABLE, and TABE[a]

Gates–MacGinitie	ABLE	TABE	Gates–MacGinitie	ABLE	TABE
4.0	5.5		7.4	7.9	9.1
4.1	5.6		7.5	8.0	9.2
4.5	5.7		7.7	8.1	9.4
4.6	5.8		8.1	8.2	9.5
4.8	6.0		8.4	8.3	9.6
5.1	6.2		8.7	8.5	9.7
5.3	6.3		8.9	8.6	9.8
5.4	6.5		8.9	8.6	9.8
5.6	6.6		9.0	8.7	9.8
5.7	6.7		9.3	8.8	9.9
5.8	6.8	8.0	9.5	8.9	9.9
6.0	6.9	8.1	9.7	9.0	10.0
6.1	7.0	8.1	10.0	9.2	10.1
6.2	7.2	8.1	10.4	9.4	10.2
6.3	7.3	8.2	10.6	9.5	10.3
6.4	7.4	8.3	10.8	9.6	10.4
6.6	7.5	8.4	11.0	9.8	10.5
6.7	7.6	8.5	11.3	10.1	10.8
7.0	7.7	8.9	11.5	10.3	11.2
7.2	7.8	9.0	11.7	10.4	11.3
			11.8+	10.5+	11.4+

[a]From Sticht, Hooke, & Caylor (1981).

students who received job-oriented literacy training did as well on general literacy tests as did the students who had received the general literacy training. Additionally, however, the students who received job-oriented training in reading made over three times the gain in job-related reading as did the general literacy students. Thus there appears to be an asymmetry in the consequences of specific versus general literacy training such that the transfer from specific literacy training to general literacy ability is greater than the transfer from general literacy training to specific literacy skills.

The differences in transfer from specific and general literacy *programs* to specific or general literacy *tasks* is understandable when it is recognized that specific literacy training is concerned with reading speed; problem solving using various formats (indexes, tables of contents, tables, figures, forms, narrative prose descriptions and directions, lists); special vocabulary and concepts; *and* such generally applicable knowledges and skills as are involved in the use of function words (a, and, the, etc.); syntactical constraints (verb–object agreement, number); and the use of "world knowledge" to understand and comprehend special bodies of information. In the case of job-oriented literacy training, all of these activities are understandable by the student within a high-order schema (Rumelhart, 1980) called the job. Thus the activities, words, exercises, formats, and materials form a more or less coherent frame of reference for learning that is motivated by an understandable, and generally desirable, goal— to learn a job.

In contrast to specific literacy training, which ordinarily will take place within some more or less well-constrained body of knowledge, general literacy training has as its goal the improvement of the student's ability to perform reading tasks in an unspecified set of domains. Thus, rather than teaching job-related reading, or parenting-related reading, the general literacy program teaches reading-related reading: reading to recognize words known in the spoken language, to get faster at reading, to understand sequence, to get literal meaning, to grasp the main idea, to follow directions, to make inferences, to reason critically, to increase vocabulary, and to use figures, tables, and graphs, and so forth.

In the general literacy program the *content* of the reading materials and exercises is not important, though the readability level of the materials (the average sentence length, number of one syllable words per 150-word passage etc.) is. Finally, unless the goal of the program is aimed at obtaining an academic credential, such as the high school equivalency certificate, there is likely to be only a vaguely understood reason or set of reasons for participating in the training, such to improve oneself, to prepare for a better job, to read to children at home, and so forth.

A consequence of the wide variation in the contents of the general literacy program is that the assessment tests are not likely to be sensitive to the specifics of the program instruction. For instance, the reading tests may test for vocabulary knowledge that was not taught in the program—even though reading to increase vocabulary was taught. The problem with the latter as a content-free skill is that it actually involves the learning of some quite specific knowledge—specifically, the meanings and uses of particular words. Furthermore, because general reading tests are used to sort out high- and low-ability readers at a given grade level in the K–12 school system, they will include some vocabulary words and paragraphs that are very unlikely to be known by students at the particular grade used to norm the test. Thus, a 5th-grade student who reads at an 8th-grade level will know words and comprehend paragraphs that are unknown to most 5th-graders in the norming group. Because these words and concepts are not taught to 5th-graders on the average, how can an adult literacy teacher know what to teach to a group of 5th-grade reading adults to move them to the 7th- to 8th-grade level as assessed by the standardized test? It would seem that only extensive, wide-ranging reading would increase the likelihood that the adult literacy student would encounter the rarer words and ideas used to distinguish high-ability 5th-grade students from the lower-ability or average students of the same grade.

For the same reason, it is unlikely that a general literacy program will teach a person the special vocabulary, concepts, formats, and so forth, involved in reading in a job-oriented or other specialty domain of reading. At the very least, we can expect that, in order for a general literacy program to develop the levels of skills and knowledges needed to read and perform literacy tasks in a wide variety of domains, as the data of Figure 2 suggests is possible for persons reading at the higher grade levels, a great deal more time will have to be devoted to such programs than is the usual case today. Additionally, students will have to devote considerable time outside of classes reading materials of ever-increasing complexity and abstraction. Only through such extensive and wide-ranging reading can we expect the student to develop the vocabulary, semantic networks, and format knowledge that can be drawn upon to perform reading tasks in a wide range of specialty domains. (See Chall's 1983, discussion of reading stages for a further explanation of the difficulty of achieving high levels of literacy in brief programs.)

Given the finding that literacy training aimed at improving job-oriented or other specialty domain reading may also improve general literacy, research is needed to determine the effects on general literacy of training in a number of specialty domains. Is it possible that, by offering adults literacy training in a variety of specialty domains, they will, over timed develop much higher levels of general literacy? What might be the effects on general literacy of developing very high levels of skill within a given specialty domain rather than a set of such domains? There is some research to suggest that although extensive practice in reading within a speciality domain can lead to high levels of skill in performing reading tasks within that domain, there is likely to be little transfer to other domains (Kirsch & Guthrie, 1982). However, the latter findings were not based on training studies but rather on studies of frequency of and time spent in the performance of tasks of job incumbents. The job-oriented training research suggests that some transfer from the specific domain of job-reading task performance to general literacy may occur. But additional research is needed to more fully understand the nature and limits of transfer among reading domains resulting from literacy training.

Although research on general and specific literacies is very sparse, there is sufficient evidence to suggest that text producers or program developers who believe that the abilities of adult literacy students to receive and decode written language messages can be rapidly developed through brief programs using general literacy materials are wrong on several accounts.

1. The listening skills of adult literacy students are not much higher than their reading skills, and hence they do not show high degrees of reading potential for making large increments in reading in brief amounts of time.
2. General literacy tests that index adult reading skills in terms of the grade scale used to assess children's skills are not accurate indicators of the adult's reading skills. They mistakenly imply that an adult who reads at a given grade level on such tests can read as well as the children upon whom the tests were normed.
3. The tests do not provide the same estimates of reading skills when applied to the same samples making it impossible to accurately know the reading levels of persons in the sample.
4. Relatively large increments in specific domains of literacy can be made in brief literacy programs while only slight increments in general literacy are achieved.

SUMMARY

In this chapter I have approached the understanding of readers and their uses of texts from the writer's or, more broadly construed, the text or program producer's perspective. I have explored aspects of the writer's understandings of readers and their uses of texts in school and work settings, and in so doing I questioned the relevance of the writer's experiences with textbooks in school for preparing her or him to serve as "an audience of one," as suggested by Strunk and White (1959), for judging the suitability of functional materials for practical, performance-oriented purposes. In this discussion I focused on the school-to-work transition and the reversal of the primary reading tasks from that of reading-to-learn in high school, to reading-to-do a job task in the world of work. Research was reviewed to suggest that student's experiences with textbooks and learning in school may lead to the development of school-like, topic-oriented manuals when, in fact, workers want job-related, performance-oriented guidance. Perhaps high school and college students would be better prepared to serve as ''an audience of one'' for producing functional materials if composition and other English courses were to introduce students to the functional uses of texts beyond the literature and textbooks that make up the bulk of school life experiences with texts.

In a second line of thought, I questioned the accuracy of text and program producers' beliefs about the abilities of adult marginal literates ''to receive and decode messages'' presented in spoken or written forms. Strategies for matching readers to materials were discussed, including strategies of selection and assignment, redesign of materials, and literacy training to raise reader's skills to the levels demanded by the materials they are expected to use. Problems in implementing these strategies due to faulty beliefs about readability formulas, reading tests, and concepts of marginally literate adults' listening and reading skills were noted, and several directions for research to better understand readers and their uses of texts were suggested.

REFERENCES

British Association of Settlements. (1974). *A right to read: Action for a literate Britain*. London.

Bowren, F., & Zintz, M. (1977). *Teaching reading in adult basic education*. Dubuque, IO: Brown.

Chall, J. (1983). *Stages of reading development*. New York: McGraw-Hill.

Curran, T. (Ed.) (1980, March). *Tri-service literacy and readability: Workshop proceedings* (NPRDC SR 80-12). San Diego, CA: Navy personnel Research and Development Center.

Diehl, W., & Mikulecky, L. (1980). The nature of reading at work. *Journal of Reading, 24,* 221–227.

Durrell, D., & Brassard, M. (1970). *Durrell listening-reading series: Intermediate level*. New York: Harcourt.

Guiliano, V. (1982). The mechanization of office work. *Scientific American. 247,* 124–134.

Gunn, T. (1982). The mechanization of design and manufacturing. *Scientific American, 247,* 86–108.

Harrison, C. (1980). *Readability in the classroom*. London: Cambridge University Press.

Kern, R. (1980, January). *Usefulness of readability formulas for achieving Army readability objectives* (Tech. Rep. 437). Alexandria, VA: U.S. Army Research Institute for the Behavioral and Social Sciences.

Kern, R., & Sticht, T. (1974, March). *Guidebook for the development of Army training literature: Rationale and policy implications from interviews with Army writers*. (Interim Rep.). Alexandria, VA: Human Resources Research Organization.

Kirsch, I., & Guthrie, J. (1982, August). *Prose comprehension and text search as a function of reading volume* (Tech. Rep. No. 3). Newark, DE: International Reading Association.

Mikulecky, L. (1981). *Job literacy: The relationship between school preparation and workplace actuality*. Final Report, Indiana University.

Mockovak, W. (1974, December). *Literacy skills and requirements in Air Force career ladders. AFHRL-TR-74-90*. Lowry, AFB: CO: Air Force Human Resources Laboratory.

Ryan, T., & Furlong, W. (1975). Literacy programs in industry, the armed forces, and penal institutions. *In* J. Carroll & J. Chall (Eds.), *Toward a literate society*. New York: McGraw-Hill.

Rumelhart, D. (1980). Schemata: The building blocks of cognition. *In* R. Spiro, B. Bruce, & W. Brewer (Eds.), *Theoretical issues in reading comprehension.* Hillsdale, NJ: Erlbaum.

Showel, M., & Brennan, M. (1974). *A survey of user attitudes towards Army training literature.* Alexandria, VA: Human Resources Research Organization, Final Report.

Sticht, T. (in press). The learning process and the text in use. *In* T. Sticht, J. Cole, & R. Selden (Eds.), *The textbook in American education.* New York: Academic Press.

Sticht, T. (1982a, March). *Basic skills in defense.* Washington, DC: Office of the Assistant Secretary of Defense (Manpower, Reserve Affairs, and Logistics).

Sticht, T. (1982b). Literacy at work. *In* B. Hutson (Ed.), *Advances in reading language research* (Vol. I). Greenwich, CT: JAI Press.

Sticht, T. (1982c). *Evaluation of the reading potential of marginally literate adults* (Tech. Memorandum 82-5). Washington, DC: Office of the Secretary of Defense, Directorate for Accession Policy.

Sticht, T. (Ed.) (1975). *Reading for working.* Alexandria, VA: Human Resources Research Organizations.

Sticht, T. (1974, April). *Mentally marginal men (MMM): Information processing skills of the last hired and first fired.* Paper presented at the Annual Meeting of the Adult Education Research Conference, Chicago.

Sticht, T. (1972). Learning by listening. *In* R. Freedle & J. Carroll (Eds.), *Language comprehension and the acquisition of knowledge.* New York: Wiley.

Sticht, T., Fox, L., Hauke, R., & Welty- Zapf, D. (1977, September). *The role of reading in the Navy* (NPRDC TR 77-40). San Diego, CA: Navy Personnel Research and Development Center.

Sticht, T., Hooke, L., & Caylor, J. (1981, May). *Manual for the administration and interpretation of the literacy assessment battery (LAB)* (FR-ETSD-81-10). Alexandria, VA: Human Resources Research Organization.

Sticht, T., Hooke, L., & Caylor, J. (1982, March). *Literacy, oracy, and vocational aptitude as predictors of attrition and promotion in the Armed Services* (Professional Paper 2-82). Alexandria, VA: Human Resources Research Organization.

Sticht, T., & Welty- Zapf, D. (Eds.) (1976, September). *Reading and readability research in the Armed Services* (HumRRO FR-WD-CA-76-4). Alexandria, VA: Human Resources Research Organization.

Strunk, Jr., W., & White, E. (1959). *The elements of style.* New York: Macmillan.

CHAPTER 13

Modeling Users and Their Use of Technical Manuals*

RICHARD P. KERN

INTRODUCTION

Content and design of a job manual can be viewed as reflecting the developer's predictions of the information, the organization and format, and the method of packaging that users are most likely to find comprehensible and usable in the job setting. This idealized perspective assumes that developers base their predictions on a model of the users, the job activities they perform, and the way they are most likely to use information in the job setting. Within this framework of ideal conditions, "goodness" of the manual is directly related to "goodness" of the developer's model of the users and their information needs in the job setting.

Ideal conditions, of course, are not reality. Currently, development of a model of users and their information needs is an intuitive process, and very little of the model is articulated and available for examination. To complicate the art of modeling the user, writers frequently have no direct contact with the users, the job, or the job setting. The writer's assignment may not specifically identify the user and the purpose or function the manual is intended to serve (Kern & Sticht, 1980; Kern, Sticht, Welty, & Hauke, 1977). The intended user may turn out to be several different groups of users performing different types of job activities and sharing only a general type of relationship to the same piece of equipment or content area. In addition, the manual is frequently required to serve the multiple functions of a general reference text, a training text, and a procedural guide for performance of specific tasks. Finally, as Orna (Chapter 2 in the present volume)

---

*Views and conclusions contained in this chapter are those of the author and should not be interpreted as representing official policies or position, either expressed or implied, of the U.S. Department of Defense.

DESIGNING USABLE TEXTS

and Duffy (1981, 1985) have indicated, usability and comprehensibility of completed manuals suffer from the competitive claims of developers' organizational practices and business goals regardless of the goodness of their model of the user. Although these complications are easy to deplore, they can be expected to persist as long as we are unable to articulate the knowledge of how to model users and their use of information for different purposes.

A major thesis of this chapter is that a good model of the user is a necessary, if not sufficient, condition for producing a good manual. Lacking a good model, design and cost trade-off decisions made during manual production are likely to be based primarily on administrative and short-term considerations. Under these conditions, content and design features important in enabling the users to efficiently and effectively use the manual get lost in the shuffle. And finally, in the absence of an explicit model of the users, criteria are lacking for evaluating how well manuals are achieving their objectives. Without this type of feedback, we lack a basis for developing the knowledge needed to advance the uncertain art of modeling the user into a more certain methodology.

A major question, as yet unanswered, is, What should be modeled to produce a good model of the user? In the sections that follow I first summarize and critique techniques currently considered useful in assisting developers in producing more usable manuals. I then describe how vehicle mechanics interacted with manuals and other job information sources during routine performance of maintenance assignments. These findings were obtained as part of a broader research project undertaken to develop a methodology for evaluating usability and effectiveness of job information sources under normal work-site conditions. Research conducted using this methodology served two objectives:

1. to develop baseline data for use in evaluating future manuals, or other sources of job information, introduced to replace existing maintenance manuals and
2. to extend our knowledge of when and how technicians use job information sources, factors that affect this use, and the relationship between use of job information sources and quality of performance

I then summarize what I see as the implications of the previous and recent research for developing better technology for designing technical manuals.

RESEARCH ON COMPREHENSIBILITY AND USABILITY OF MILITARY MANUALS

Questionnaire and interview surveys on use of technical manuals in the work setting have consistently concluded that people on the job seldom consult their manuals (Johnson, Thomas, & Martin, 1977; Losee, Allen, Stroud, & Ver Hulst, 1962; Showel & Brennan, 1978; Sticht, Caylor, Kern, & Fox, 1972;

Thomas, Johnson, & Dalezman, 1978). Reasons commonly cited include complaints such as content is not accurate, content is not current, there are gaps in content, it takes too long to find desired information, the manual is too cumbersome to use while performing the task, and the manual is not available. Research to address the problems of how to design more usable manuals has generally reflected one or the other of two perspectives. For ease of discussion I have labeled one a content perspective and the other a readability perspective. These two perspectives reflect differences in the definition of the basic problem to be dealt with in improving manuals. Although they are not mutually incompatible, researchers' adherence to one or the other perspective has led to different research approaches involving different user characteristics and different criteria of comprehensibility and usability.

THE CONTENT PERSPECTIVE: MODELING USERS' TASK PERFORMANCE

Research on military manuals, conducted since the early 1950s, has focused on the areas of troubleshooting and maintenance of equipment. Objectives of this research have progressively narrowed over the years to focus on development and evaluation of prescriptive-style manuals called job performance aids or guides. Research in this area has been reviewed extensively by Booher (1978), Foley and Camm (1972), Folley and Munger (1961), and Rowan (1973). (See also Smillie, Chapter 10 in the present volume.)

Since the beginning of this work in the 1950s, researchers in this area have considered difficulty of text, as reflected by readability formulas, to be primarily a side-effect of a more basic problem. The basic problem from this perspective was that the content and organization focused on engineers' design of equipment as opposed to focusing on how to identify faults and repair equipment (Folley & Munger, 1961; Hoehn & Lumsdaine, 1958; Johnson et al., 1977). Thus, whether or not the text was comprehensible, the information was not usable for performance of technicians' tasks.

Consistent with the identification of this problem, the approach under the content perspective has been to develop and use task analytic procedures to identify the specific behaviors required of technicians in performing each equipment maintenance task. An overview of these procedures, as presented by Shriver (1977), is given in Table 1. Contents of the new manuals are dictated by the behavioral acts identified during the task and behavioral analyses of each specific maintenance activity. Thus the major thrust of this approach is to model the job activities the user is expected to perform and use this model as the basis for predicting users' information needs and the way this content should be organized.

In addition to modeling task performance, this approach has taken users'

Table 1

Analytic Techniques for Developing Task-Oriented Content[a]

Technique	Description
Equipment analysis	Identification of all parts of an equipment system (e.g., a vehicle) to show those parts that each different type of technician will work on in performing maintenance
Functional analysis	Conducted for troubleshooting maintenance requirements; an analysis to accomplish a logical relationship of part failures to indications of failure and a guide for user maintenance actions on the basis of indications
Task analysis	Develops a detailed step-by-step description of the procedures required to perform each maintenance task, condition under which each task is performed, and identification of the tools to be used.
Behavioral task analysis	A refinement of task analysis to identify specific cues (equipment detail) technicians will need to identify in performing detailed actions embedded in the grosser task analysis; these cues are identified for presentation in a graphic display
Intelligibility standards	Specifications for making the graphic and written instructions intelligible to personnel with grade school reading ability; requires verbs used to describe actions be restricted to those on a list of single-syllable verbs; specifies how graphic cues take the place of nouns and how words relate to pictures; restricts sentence length.

[a]From Shriver (1977).

cognitive skills into consideration by generating specific rules for formatting text and illustrations. The specific formatting rules were based on state-of-the-art judgments and on generalizations drawn from research literature on short-term memory (Joyce, Chenzoff, Mulligan, & Mallory, 1973a, 1973b; Serendipity, Inc., 1969). These rules include standard verb lists for use in expressing procedural steps: rules for formatting procedural steps in a list fashion; and rules placing stringent limits on number of words, sentences, and steps per page to facilitate scanning and chunking of information. These rules also require the pairing of each page of procedural steps with a facing page containing an outline drawing that shows location of parts and focus of action for each step. In short, the objective of producing more usable manuals has been pursued by focusing on a method for providing detailed, prescriptive directions. These directions are formatted and expressed in ways believed to facilitate technicians' ability to rapidly retrieve information from a page and to retain this information in short-term memory while carrying out the performance. Aside from improving clarity of job instructions, this approach is perceived as a way of reducing the need for developing technicians' job knowledge through initial or entry-job training.

Evaluation of the new instructions has usually been conducted by placing the technician in some type of controlled performance test setting. The major hypothesis tested has been that technicians, given the new instructions, will perform maintenance tasks in less time and with fewer errors than technicians not using the new instructions. Thus success of the new instructions has been judged against criteria linked only indirectly to the printed page. Observations on how technicians used or did not use the printed instructions (new or old) during the process of performing the task are not reported in this literature. Conclusions generally reported have been that inexperienced technicians, given the new proceduralized instructions, perform as well, or with fewer errors, than experienced technicians performing as they normally perform, with or without using the traditional (engineer-oriented) manual. In addition, it has been concluded that experienced technicians also made fewer errors when using the new instructions under performance test conditions (Foley, 1973).

The focus on the development and evaluation of improved content has been at the expense of testing assumptions regarding conditions that affect when and how technicians use manuals in their normal job settings. These untested assumptions complicate the problem of generalizing from present evaluation results to the design of new manuals for use at the job site.

A network of implicit and explicit assumptions have been made that represents a model of the user and how this user interacts with manuals and equipment during task performance. A basic assumption of this model is that, given good manuals, technicians will make full use of them (Collins, 1977). It is also assumed that the function of the manual is to direct and control the technicians' performance in a way that requires the technician to be dependent on the text for directions during performance of each step in a maintenance task (Eames & Starr, 1965). Consistent with these two assumptions, it has been assumed that there is a direct causal link between quality of the manual and quality of the technicians' performance. Thus the basic evaluation methodology has been to contrast performance test scores of technicians using the new instruction with the scores of technicians provided with the old instruction and/or free to pursue their normal practices. Conclusions supporting this approach for evaluating design of more usable job-site manuals are dependent on their model of how technicians should be required to use manuals and the performance test conditions of their evaluation methodology.

Time and cost considerations during the developmental research have precluded testing the usability of an entire new manual. Typically, evaluation has been restricted to use of new task instructions that represent only a small segment of a complete manual. It is only recently that research has been conducted to explore usability of the new job guide manuals under operational as opposed to experimental conditions.

Johnson, Thomas, and Martin (1977) interviewed and observed technicians in their work setting 7 months after new manuals, designed using guidelines developed under the aforementioned approach, were introduced into unit work sites.

Their observations illustrate the importance of modeling users and their use of manuals in relation to work-site conditions and organizational factors that determine how tasks are performed in the work setting. Johnson *et al.* found that many technicians were not using the new manuals. They attributed this lack of use to lack of training in how to use these manuals. However, use of these improved manuals may not increase even if technicians are given training on how to use them. The technicians' apparent ability to perform tasks without using the new manuals suggests, as it did with the old manuals, that technicians are not typically dependent on manuals for instructions during performance of many types of maintenance tasks. If the technicians' attention is not "manual-centered" during task performance, this suggests that other sources and types of information used by technicians during task performance need to be considered in determining the purpose and the design of more usable manuals. Step-by-step procedural instructions may not provide the kind of information assistance the technician needs while interacting with the equipment.

The sheer volume of pages required to satisfy the requirements for the detailed, step-by-step instructions and the associated formatting rules also detract from usability. In the job setting observed by Johnson *et al.* (1977), 63 volumes of job manuals were required to present the tasks one type of technician was expected to perform in maintaining one type of equipment on one large airplane. Technicians using the manuals reported having difficulty in locating the information they were seeking and, in many cases, complained of having to use too many different volumes to accomplish a single work assignment.

The task analytic techniques developed under the content perspective provide important tools for use in developing job manuals. However, it is important to emphasize that these techniques enable manual developers to model the task activities the user is expected to perform, not the users' knowledge base or expected information needs. Research from the content perspective has not been designed to identify user, task, and job-site variables that affect technicians' use of manuals in the job setting. As a result, this research has not provided criteria for identifying and discriminating among levels of importance or need for various kinds of information. Research is needed to develop better ways of assessing the relevant knowledges and skills the technicians bring to the task and the kinds of inferences they are capable of making in using manuals to identify and solve problems arising during task performance.

THE READABILITY PERSPECTIVE: MODELING USERS' READING COMPREHENSION SKILLS

Research from the readability perspective has focused on the reading achievement level of personnel in relation to the difficulty level of printed materials and measures of job proficiency. Growth of research from this perspective has been primarily due to the military services' concern over effectively utilizing personnel entering the services with poor to marginal reading skills. Contrasted with the content perspective, the readability perspective focuses on how to cope with reading skill requirements of manuals.

Application of readability formulas to military job and training literature from the 1950s through the 1970s consistently revealed that these materials were written at levels of difficulty considerably above the general reading achievement level of the average military user (Burkett, 1976; Curran, 1976; Duffy, 1976; Kern, 1976). This disparity has been viewed as an important factor in the failure of workers to use their manuals and in the difficulty they have comprehending the content when the manuals are used. Data consistent with this conclusion are reported by Sticht *et al.* (1972). They found that the lower-skilled readers assigned to jobs requiring difficult manuals were less likely to use these manuals than were the more highly skilled readers. In contrast, there was no relationship between reading skill and reported use of printed materials for cooks, whose job instructions (recipe cards) were written at difficulty levels nearly equal to the average reading grade level of the personnel. In response to evidence of this type, the military services undertook additional research to develop training to improve the job-related reading skills of their marginally skilled readers and to develop approaches and techniques for improving the comprehensibility of their printed materials.

Major reviews of the research undertaken to identify and address reading skill and readability problems in the military services are presented by Sticht and Welty-Zapf (1976), Curran (1977, 1980) and Duffy (Chapter 6 of the present volume). Research most directly related to the problem of modeling the user has addressed a broad range of applied objectives. This research has included development of readability formulas based on military personnel and manuals (Caylor, Sticht, Fox, & Ford, 1973; Kincaid, Fishburne, Rogers, & Chissom, 1975), development of special military writers' guides (Kern *et al.*, 1977; Miller, 1974; Post & Price, 1974; Siegel, Lambert, & Burkett, 1974), and development of computerized authoring and text editing aids (Braby & Kincaid, 1981–1982). In addition, research has been conducted to assess the relationship of reading skill to job performance, to develop methods for identifying reading requirements of jobs (Burkett & Hooke, 1980; Caylor *et al.*, 1973; Duffy & Nugent, 1980; Sticht *et al.*, 1972; Sticht, Fox, Hauke, & Welty-Zapf, 1977a, 1977b), and to identify readability standards for job manuals (Mockovak, 1974). Finally, research has addressed the effectiveness of readability formulas and standards in improving comprehensibility of text (Duffy & Kabance, 1982; Hooke, DeLeo, & Slaughter, 1979; Kern, 1980; Kniffin, Stevenson, Klare, Entin, Slaughter, & Hooke, 1980). The contributions this body of research has made to the problem of modeling comprehension skills of the user are examined in the remainder of this section.

MODELING THE ORGANIZATION'S MODEL OF THE USER

Style manuals and writers' guides are developed for the use of editors and writers in preparing documents to meet specific standards adopted by their organizations (Walter, 1971). The major function of style manuals and writers' guides is to standardize virtually every aspect of the printed displays produced for an organization's manuals. These guides give models of text that company employees or customers are expected to find usable and comprehensible. Thus the writer's task is writing to conform to the model contained in the guide rather than attempting to directly model users. If the manuscript meets the guidance standards, it is assumed that employees or customers will find the resulting materials comprehensible and usable.

Although style manuals and writers' guides share the same objective of standardizing materials, these two types of guides address different domains of manual development and differ greatly in influencing writers' performance and the organization's acceptance of their product. Style manuals establish rules and developmental procedures that must be observed in producing an acceptable manual. Developers of military manuals are required by contract to conform to style manual guidance contained in a particular set of military specifications. In addition to the usual types of rules found in style manuals, the task analytic techniques advanced under the content perspective and the use of readability formulas advanced under the readability perspective have been incorporated into military specifications. Duffy (1985) cites these new military specifications as representing the "penultimate" of guidelines based on research technology. However, he finds the usability of manuals produced on the basis of these or similar specifications disappointing. He concludes that "rules alone—even when they are 'good' rules and are contractually required—will not yield usable text." Duffy's observations and conclusions perhaps illustrate the dilemma an organization encounters when it contracts writers to write to the model of the user defined by detailed specifications. The core problem identified since at least the early 1950s appears to be unchanged.

Writers' guides, in contrast to style manuals, provide general writing guidance rather than specifications. Perhaps, as a consequence, they have exerted little apparent influence on comprehensibility of military manuals. Kern and Sticht (1980) found that Army writers did not consult writers' guidebooks. Instead they used other manuals as a model and revised or developed the new manual to look like the other manuals that had met the Army's style manual criteria. The guidebook for Army writers developed by Kern *et al.* (1977) was designed to capitalize on writers' practice of intuitively modeling other manuals by providing a large number of "before" and "after" pages from a wide range of Army manuals. The development of computerized authoring and editing programs (Braby & Kincaid, 1981–1982; Macdonald, Frase, Gingrich, & Keenan, 1982) offers an approach that organizations may use to place greater emphasis upon meeting criteria set for syntax and even specific writing styles for specific types of documents. However, as discussed later, these criteria do not address the need for ways to identify or, in effect, predict when content will effectively meet users' information needs.

MODELING USERS' READING ACHIEVEMENT LEVELS

Assessments of the reading difficulty level of manuals obtained through the use of readability formulas have challenged the effectiveness of writers in modeling the reading comprehension skills of military personnel. These manuals were generally written at an advanced college level of difficulty. This level of difficulty remained uniformly high regardless of the educational level of the intended users. To address this problem, writers needed some way of improving their ability to produce material appropriate to the reading comprehension skills of the users, and literature managers needed some method for ensuring that materials were written at an appropriate level.

Readability formulas were developed to relate reading difficulty level of military text to reading achievement levels of military personnel (Caylor *et al.*, 1973; Kincaid *et al.*, 1975). This was accomplished by selecting passages from military manuals to represent a wide range of levels of difficulty. These passages were then converted to cloze test formats. Those cloze tests and a standardized reading test yielding reading grade level (RGL) scores were administered to samples of military recruits. Through regression analysis, formulas based on syllable counts and/or sentence length were developed to predict the lowest standardized reading test scores (RGL) at which 50% of the personnel had achieved a passage cloze score at or above the 35% criterion level.

The RGL scores obtained from standardized reading achievement tests have been traditionally viewed as reflecting an ordering or ranking of developmental levels of reading comprehension skills. Thus the readability formulas developed for use in the military appeared to provide a way of appropriately placing printed materials along this same developmental scale. Mockovak (1974) cited the arithmetic discrepancy between RGL test scores of personnel and the higher RGL readability scores for their job materials as evidence of a "literacy gap." As a result, he developed an approach for identifying RGL standards for writers to use in preparing materials. In developing this approach, he compared the distribution of RGL readability scores (formula scores) for printed job materials with the distribution of RGL achievement scores for personnel in each of a large number of Air Force jobs. As a result of these comparisons he recommended a decision rule and provided data tables for identifying the RGL readability score writers should use as a standard in preparing materials for each of the different jobs. The rule he used states that the average RGL readability score for material prepared for a specific job must be equal to or less than the RGL achievement scores of 85% of the people in the job.

Managers of military literature have welcomed approaches such as the one developed by Mockovak as providing a valuable tool that will enable them to improve the comprehensibility of their manuals and other literature. However, in practice, approaches of this type have led to a misinterpretation of both RGL test scores and the meaning of a literacy gap.

The most serious misinterpretation of the RGL concept occurs as a result of the wide acceptance and use of the literacy gap notion as a basis for establishing readability standards for printed materials. The RGL scores have been obtained from standardized reading tests, developed and normed (normative values were determined) on grade placement of students in the public schools. These RGL scores have been misinterpreted to represent a single, continuous dimension of skill development. Comparisons of these reading test scores with RGL scores from the readability formulas have led literature managers to set readability standards based on the mistaken assumption that the users' reading achievement level is important only in relation to the readability level of the material. Thus it is frequently assumed that, if material is rewritten to lower its RGL readability score to the level of the user's RGL test score, lower-skilled readers will be able to achieve the same type and criterion level of comprehension achieved by higher-skilled readers. Research on rewriting materials to match the lower reading-test scores of users has failed to support this hypothesis (Duffy & Kabance, 1982; Kniffin *et al.*, 1980). In addition, numerous reviews, only a few of which are cited here, conclude that readability formulas are not useful for matching difficulty level of materials to the reading comprehension skills of users (Bruce, Rubin, & Starr, 1981; Kern, 1980; Plung, 1981; Redish, 1981; Duffy, chapter 6 of the present volume).

SUMMARY CRITIQUE:
CONTENT AND READABILITY PERSPECTIVES

The task analytic techniques advanced under the content perspective and the use of readability formulas advanced under the readability perspective have both been incorporated into military manual specifications. These specifications are contractural requirements manual developers must satisfy. Research leading to this present state-of-the-art of manual design and development has focused on the manual as the only source of job information. In addition, it has not dealt directly with variables affecting use of manuals in the job setting. The content perspective has been based on an evaluation methodology that tests users' performance on job sample tests when the user is restricted to the manual and instructed to use it. This methodology can not shed light on factors affecting the use and effectiveness of manuals in the normal work setting. The readability perspective has focused on difficulty indexes yielded by readability formulas and on reading achievement level of personnel. In doing so, this research has generally not considered type of content, the job-related purpose the content is expected to serve, and users' prior knowledge of the content area.

RESEARCH ON USE OF INFORMATION SOURCES AT THE JOB SITE

TESTS TO MODEL JOB READING TASKS

Standardized reading tests developed in the public school setting are not designed to provide writers with information on the level of proficiency adults can be expected to demonstrate in performing the various types of reading tasks encountered on the job. Sticht *et al.* (1972) and Caylor *et al.* (1973) developed Job Reading Task Tests (JRTT) to better assess reading skill requirements of jobs. The JRTTs are based on the concept of a job reading task (Kern, 1970), that is, a task in which personnel on the job use printed materials to obtain information to support performance of their work activities. This concept of a job reading task requires that a test item reflect both a question that occurs among personnel on the job and the specific material used in attempting to answer the question.

Sticht *et al.* identified specific job reading tasks through semistructured interviews conducted with individuals at their job sites. Interviewees were asked to describe up to five specific instances in which they had used printed materials to assist them in performing their work. After citing each incident, the worker was asked to describe the task or activity that had been performed and the information that had been sought from the printed material. In addition, the worker was asked to obtained the printed material, usually a manual, and show the interviewer the portions of the material used in obtaining the information. Thus the nature of the information the worker had sought and the specific material used in obtaining this information identified a job reading task.

The JRTTs were constructed to simulate reading tasks identified from the interview protocols. In constructing these tests, materials used on the job were classified into four format–content types: indexes, tables, textual discourse, and procedural directions (Sticht, 1975). Items were selected to represent commonly occurring reading tasks in each of the four categories. Each item consisted of an exact copy of the printed materials used in performing a reading task on the job; the facing page contained questions based on the types of information commonly sought from the respective materials. Thus JRTTs provide a method for assessing how well personnel can use different types of printed displays encountered on the job to obtain the type of information normally sought on the job. Subsequently, a machine-scorable form of these JRTTs was developed for use by the Army (Claudy & Caylor, 1982).

The JRTTs developed by Sticht *et al.* (1972) were specifically designed for use with personnel at time of entry into the service. For this reason, questions were based on types of information sought that required only identification and retrieval of factual data. In other words, these questions did not require job-specific knowledge. Questions were purposely designed this way; this restriction does not reflect a limitation intrinsic to this approach.

The research conducted by Sticht *et al.* (1972) shifted the focus of the readability research discussed in the preceding to use of information sources at the job site. This research highlighted the importance of supervisors and co-workers as important sources of job information that frequently compete with use of the manual as the source. Information sought from other people on the job is important to take into consideration in attempting to model or predict technicians' information needs. However, the recall methodology of the interview necessarily places severe restrictions on the kinds of information that can be obtained to identify when and how workers use information sources during the process of performing a task. Presumably there are characteristics of work activities in addition to characteristics of the worker that are more or less likely to cause the worker to seek information sources. The JRTT has proved to be a useful approach for identifying the level of proficiency a worker must have to enable them to use the printed job materials as needed to accomplish their work. However, when a job reading task is converted to a test item, the test, unlike the job, does not require the worker to recognize the need for information, generate the question needed to obtain the information, and identify the source to consult.

MODELING INFORMATION-SEEKING BEHAVIORS

In developing the concept of a job reading task a distinction was made between two general types of job activities based on the function print serves in accomplishing a task (Caylor *et al.*, 1973). This distinction contrasted job activities in which use of print is physically intrinsic to performance of the work activity with those in which performance of the work activity can be performed independently of print. For example, use of print is physically intrinsic to the task of researching court decisions in preparing a legal brief. In contrast, use of print is physically extrinsic or only supportive to the performance of many tasks dealing with the operation and maintenance of equipment. The majority of the work activities cited by cooks, vehicle mechanics, and supply clerks interviewed by Sticht *et al.* (1972) were of the type in which print was physically extrinsic. As a result, the model of a job reading task developed during this earlier research focused on the type of reading tasks that occur when print is extrinsic to performance of the work activities. When performing this type of work activity, a reading task occurs only as a result of workers recognizing the need for supportive information and identifying print as the source they want to use to obtain the information.

Thus job reading tasks are embedded in a process model of information-seeking behaviors presented in Figure 1.

The model presented in Figure 1 implies that use of a manual during performance in the job setting is dependent on a far broader range of factors than have been considered in research conducted under the content and readability perspectives described earlier. Those perspectives have focused on the use of print under directed reading assignment and test-taking conditions. In contrast, the model in

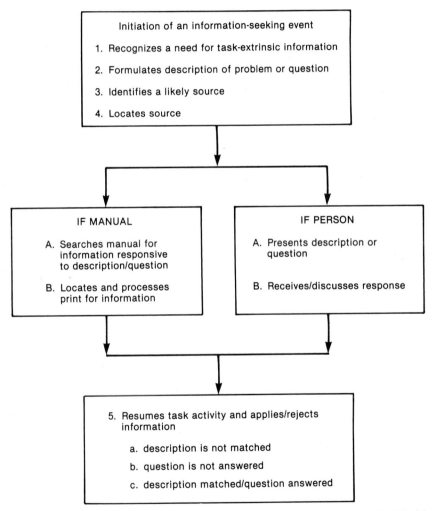

Fig. 1.   Modeling use of a manual or person as an information source during performance at the job site.

Figure 1 asserts that, for information-seeking behaviors to occur, the worker must first, at some level of awareness, recognize the need for information. Recognition of the need for information does not necessarily result in a well-formulated question. Articulation of this need can range from a vague description of what was observed at one extreme, to identification of the crux of the problem and a well-formulated question at the other extreme. In addition to the extent of the technician's success in formulating the question, the identity of other factors that influence choice and effective use of an information source has received very little attention. This model of information-seeking behaviors in the work setting raises questions that are important to the issue of how to design more usable manuals. For example, are there characteristics of the materials or equipment the person works on that are consistently linked with information seeking from manuals or people? Can we predict the occurrence of this information seeking and the type of information sought? What factors influence the choice of an information source? Is use of this information associated with a higher quality of task performance?

MODELING PERFORMANCE AT THE WORK SITE

THE OBSERVATIONAL METHODOLOGY

Research conducted for the U.S. Army Research Institute by Schurman, Porsche, and Joyce (1980) had the objectives of (1) developing a method for evaluating use and effectiveness of information sources in the natural job setting and (2) testing hypotheses for predicting occurrence of information-seeking behaviors. The observational methodology developed is described by Schurman, Porsche, Garbin, and Joyce (1982). This methodology involved three phases: preobservation analyses of task activities likely to be observed; observation of performance in the work sites, and postobservation interview with each technician.

This methodology was developed to focus on the observation of information-seeking behaviors in relation to the specific task activities being performed. In order to understand and interpret the information-seeking behaviors in an unobtrusive manner, the observers must fully understand the activities required to accomplish the tasks observed. Thus the task analysis was a critical first step in applying this methodology. This analysis was performed by maintenance experts on a large pool of tasks likely to be observed at the work site. The analysis of a task describes each step; how it is performed; and, as appropriate, special tools, tolerances or other specifications, and serviceability judgments identified with the step. In addition, these analysts applied a rating procedure (information-demand rating or IDR) to certain physical characteristics of the equipment worked on in performing each task. The purpose of these ratings was to test hypotheses predicting the extent to which specific task activities required by characteristics of equipment design are more or less likely to cause mechanics to seek information. The ratings were based on visual and manual accessibility of the specific parts or components of the vehicle requiring maintenance and on the degree to which the physical relations among parts or components clearly identified steps to be performed.

The methodology used during the observational phase provided a detailed description of the performance of maintenance tasks by mechanics under their normal work assignment and performance conditions. Thus this method represents a restricted or focused application of the ethnographic approach. The observer did not intervene during the performance of the work assignment. In contrast to the performance test methodology characteristic of earlier research, no special arrangements were made to ensure that the proper tools, manuals, or other resources were readily available to the mechanic while performing the assigned work. In other words, with the exception of the presence of the observer, conditions were just as they would have been if the observer had not been present. During the mechanic's performance the observer recorded in step-by-step fashion:

1. activity being performed and how it was performed
2. when information was sought in the context of the ongoing activity
3. source and identify of information sought and obtained and
4. errors made (corrected, uncorrected, and omissions)

Following the observation, information was obtained to provide indexes of the mechanical knowledge of each mechanic. These indexes included number of times the mechanic had previously performed the task observed, length of time as an Army mechanic, and prior civilian experience and training in vehicle maintenance. In addition, estimates of the individual's reading proficiency in comprehending language of technical maintenance manuals were obtained by administering passages selected from a basic mechanics' training manual that were made into cloze tests. Finally, any questions the observer might have regarding the mechanic's performance were resolved during this interview.

Reliability and Replicability of Observational Data

Schurman et al. (1980) initially collected observations on 149 Army mechanics. This initial collection was replicated 1 year later on a similarly selected sample of 97 mechanics. In using this methodology they demonstrated interobserver agreement ranging from 92 to 97% on recording and coding of steps when two observers independently observed the same mechanic's performance. Consistency of data obtained across the initial and replication year was tested based on a technique for comparing the full correlational matrices obtained for each year. A *t* test for correlated data produced by this technique was not statistically significant (5% level). This finding supports the conclusion that the data obtained in the second sampling represent a simple random replication of the first collection. Because no systematic changes in job-site information sources or shop procedures had occurred during this period, it was important to demonstrate that data obtained from this methodology produced a stable source of baseline data. As a result, this research provides a methodology and baseline data for use in evaluating effectiveness of new manuals, other new information sources, or training and management techniques in achieving desired changes in mechanics' use of information sources and quality of their performance.

THE WORK-SITE CONTEXT

Actual work-site contexts are remarkably different from the usual performance test setting. For example, in the usual performance test setting the mechanic is isolated from others and placed in a fully equipped test station. The following birds-eye view of the mechanics' work-site context illustrates the importance of considering these contexts in any effort to improve the art of modeling users of job manuals.

The Army mechanics observed by Schurman *et al.* (1980) were assigned to tank and mechanized infantry company maintenance shops. The mechanics in each shop are responsible for maintaining from 20 to 30 motor vehicles. These vehicles are tanks, armored personnel carriers, and trucks ranging from jeeps to large 10-ton wreckers. The mechanics work in a relatively informal, small-group setting. There may be approximately 12 people staffing a company-level maintenance shop. Of these 12, anywhere from 3 to 6 will be vehicle mechanics. The separate shop area occupied by each armor or infantry company's maintenance personnel contains office space for the motor sergeant and parts clerk, a parts room, a toolroom, and two to three bays or areas for working on vehicles. Each bay is only large enough to accommodate two vehicles at a time. As a result, a lot of the work is done outside the building on a large hardtop area where the vehicles are parked. This means a lot of work is done while being exposed to some very messy weather conditions.

Many of the maintenance tasks require an assistant who can supply additional muscle power or observe and report the effects the mechanic's activities are having on parts of the vehicle that the mechanic cannot observe while performing the task. Sometimes this assistant is another mechanic but frequently is a vehicle driver. The mechanic does not have a fixed work station as one often sees in a large civilian garage. Each mechanic has his or her own toolbox containing hand tools most frequently used. However, if the mechanic needs a larger, heavy-duty tool or a special tool such as a torque wrench, it is necessary to go to the toolroom and sign out the tool. Technical manuals are usually kept in the office, and frequently there is only one copy of each. Thus the mechanic must travel back and forth through the maintenance work areas to obtain parts, tools, and information as the need arises. During these travels the mechanic may stop and provide muscle assistance or offer suggestions to resolve problems another mechanic appears to be experiencing. There is a lot of talking back and forth among co-workers, even when they are not sharing a task assignment. This, then, is a birds-eye view of the work-site context in which Schurman et al. (1980) conducted their observations.

ANALYSES OF OBSERVATIONAL DATA

Analyses performed by Schurman et al. (1980) revealed that many of the personnel characteristics that have yielded important relationships with performance in restricted research settings were simply not related to performance in the actual work setting. Length of time on the job, civilian experience as a mechanic, and military aptitude scores were not related to either the use of task-extrinsic information sources or the quality of task performance. In addition, no relationship was found between reading proficiency in comprehending technical manuals and either use of manuals or quality of task performance. This latter finding may be contrasted to the positive effects obtained by Sticht et al. (1972) in a controlled setting.

Findings reported in this chapter are based on an independent analysis (Kern & Hayes, 1983) of data collected by Schurman et al. (1980). To conduct this analysis the database was restructured to focus on three specific types of maintenance activities (remove, install, and adjust activities) and to ensure that the same mechanic was represented in only one activity type and only once within that type. Tests of statistical significance reported here are based on chi-square adjusted for Yates correction as appropriate. When aggregated, this database provides results consistent with those reported by Schurman et al. for all observations aggregated over all types of maintenance tasks.

MODELING FACTORS AFFECTING
PERFORMANCE AT THE WORK SITE

Previous research (Johnson et al., 1977) and observations conducted at job sites in this research clearly indicate that use of job manuals is dependent on factors other than quality of the manual. If one predicts that provision of the good manual will, by itself, effect improved quality of performance at the work site, one neglects the full range of work-site factors usually considered to affect job proficiency. A model of the major factors and how they interrelate to affect performance at the work site is presented in Figure 2. This model was developed as a result of the work-site observations and has served to organize the analyses and interpretation of results that are presented in the remainder of this chapter.

Major factors affecting mechanics' performance of maintenance tasks are designated by the solid lines in Figure 2. Work-site policies and resources are linked to the other factors with a solid line bearing only one arrowhead. This signifies (from the worker's perspective) a directive rather than an interactive relationship. Work-site policies include such things as general work-site rules and the manner in which work scheduling and assignment is accomplished. These policies serve to regulate quality of the mechanic's performance through various direct and indirect ways of establishing and supporting maintenance standards. Work-site resources serve to restrict or enhance the mechanic's ability

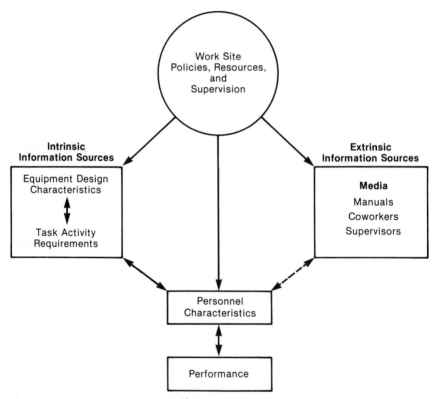

Fig. 2.   Factors affecting performance at the work site.

to perform to technical manual standards through availability of tools, parts, manuals, and knowledgeable personnel who can check and correct mechanics' performance. Work-site policies and resources were treated as a constant rather than as a variable in the research reported here. These maintenance shops were sampled from a larger population of such shops, all established and operated by the Army on the basis of a common core of regulations governing policies and resources. Variations observed from shop to shop appeared to represent a random type of fluctuations from a common core of policies and resources.

The interactive nature of the relationship between the mechanic ("personnel characteristics" in Figure 2) and equipment, media, and performance is shown by the lines with arrowheads at each end. The mechanic's interaction with task-extrinsic information sources is represented in Figure 2 by a dotted line to denote the possible, but not essential, nature of this relationship. That is, maintenance tasks can be performed without using people or manuals as sources of information, and, thus, these sources are physically extrinsic to the actual performance of these activities.

The solid line in Figure 2 linking the mechanic to equipment characteristics and performance signify that the mechanic is engaged in continuous information processing involving interpretation of the stimulus properties of the equipment and the monitoring of feedback obtained as actions are performed based on these interpretations. These linkages represent the mechanic's task-intrinsic information processing. Difficulty experienced in processing task-intrinsic information should trigger recognition of the need for task-extrinsic information and result in the occurrence of the type of information-seeking behaviors modeled in Figure 1. That is, task-intrinsic information processing is interrupted when the mechanic cannot interpret stimulus properties to identify actions to be performed or when the action performed does not produce the expected effect.

The information-demand rating (IDR) developed for this research represents an attempt to identify equipment design characteristics that affect the relative difficulty of accomplishing tasks based on task-intrinsic information processing. It was assumed that this type of equipment design characteristic makes task-intrinsic information processing either more or less difficult by regulating the amount and kind of task-specific knowledge a mechanic must possess to accomplish the task based only on task-intrinsic information sources. If successful, this approach can provide manual developers with a technique for designing manuals to more directly satisfy mechanics' task-extrinsic information needs.

PREDICTING TASK-EXTRINSIC INFORMATION SEEKING

The IDR developed for this research (Schurman et al., 1982) simply assumed that the probability of extrinsic information seeking would increase as equipment design made it more difficult to visually and manually access components and trace their physical interrelationships. These ratings were made for each of a large number of maintenance tasks analyzed as part of the task analysis performed before initiating job-site observations. Ratings were based on visual inspection of the vehicles in the intact state before any disassembly was performed that might be required. The distribution of the ratings for the tasks actually observed was separated at the median into high and low IDR scores.

Analyses reveal that more mechanics used extrinsic information sources when performing tasks that received high, as opposed to low, IDR scores ($p < .01$). Thus 48% of the mechanics performing tasks rated at the higher information-demand level sought task-extrinsic information as opposed to 28% of those performing tasks rated at the lower level. This greater number of mechanics seeking extrinsic information is statistically significant for both use of another person as an information source ($p < .01$) and use of a manual ($p < .05$).

Major Conditions Affecting Use of Task-Extrinsic Sources

Although the IDR predicts tasks either more or less likely to trigger extrinsic information seeking, two other major conditions strongly influence the probability that mechanics will use extrinsic information sources. These two conditions are prior task-specific experience and working with or without assistants during performance of the task. Mechanics were classified into three levels of prior task experience based on the number of times they reported having previously performed the same task. These three levels were (1) task not previously performed (none), (2) performed one to six times (few times), and (3) performed seven or more times (many times). Working with one or two assistants is a condition frequently encountered in the natural job setting. For this analysis, mechanics were classified as either working alone or working with assistants.

The effects of these two conditions on extrinsic information seeking when performing high and low IDR tasks are shown in Figure 3a for mechanics working alone and in Figure 3b for mechanics working with assistants. As stated earlier, mechanics in general were more likely to see extrinsic information when performing tasks rated high as opposed to low on the IDR. However, comparison of the two sets of bar graphs in Figure 3 reveal the interactive effects of task experience and assistant conditions on IDR predictions. When mechanics were working alone (Figure 3a) the high versus low IDR clearly separates the tasks that were either more or less likely to trigger use of extrinsic information sources ($p < .01$). In contrast, when working with an assistant (Figure 3b), more mechanics, especially the task-experienced ones, used extrinsic information sources whether tasks were those rated high or low on the IDR.

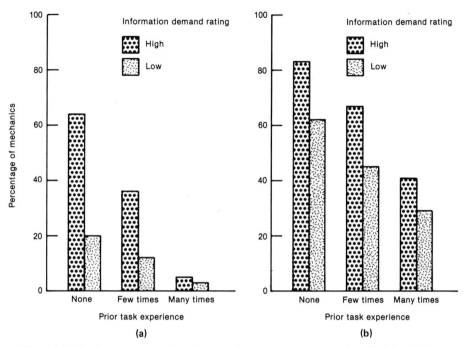

Fig. 3. Mechanics' use of task-extrinsic information sources one or more times for (a) mechanics working alone and (b) mechanics working with assistants.

USE OF MANUALS AND PEOPLE AS INFORMATION SOURCES

Figure 4 shows the number of mechanics who used people and manuals as extrinsic information sources. Those choosing people as the source account for the larger number of mechanics who sought extrinsic information when working with assistants. The number of mechanics who used manuals as a source remained essentially the same whether mechanics worked alone or with assistants. Thus the questions, comments, or perhaps just the presence of assistants tended to trigger the mechanics recognition of the need for information but biased choice in favor of people as sources. However, under both working conditions, consulting a manual was usually in addition to consulting a person source. Considering only the mechanics who used manuals, 69% also sought information from other personnel. This percentage remained the same regardless of whether mechanics worked with assistants or worked alone. Thus a manual was considered more as a secondary rather than as a primary source of information.

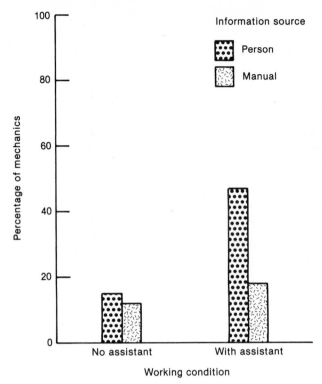

Fig. 4.   Mechanics' use of task-extrinsic sources one or more times.

TYPES OF TASK-EXTRINSIC SEEKING BEHAVIORS

The 86 mechanics who sought extrinsic information did so on an average of three times during performance of their task. These information-seeking behaviors were classified into the four types of information shown in Table 2. This table shows the relative frequency by which each type of information was obtained from person and manual sources. The types of information sought and the relative frequency with which each type was sought were essentially the same whether working alone or with assistants. The difference between these two conditions was simply the source of information used. Mechanics working alone tended to obtain identification–location and procedural information primarily from manuals, whereas those working with assistants obtained these two types of information primarily from person sources. However, both groups used primarily person sources for technique and standards–specification types of information.

RECOGNIZED AND UNRECOGNIZED NEEDS
FOR INFORMATION

Note in Figure 3 that the mechanics who were most likely to seek extrinsic information were those who had never performed the task before. The number who sought task-extrinsic information then rapidly declined with increased task experience. Based on this decline it is tempting to conclude that with repeated performances mechanics quickly learn how to perform a task and hence no longer need task-extrinsic information aids. However, there are three types of evidence that suggest this conclusion would not be correct. One type of evidence is provided by comparing the number of mechanics who sought extrinsic information in Figure 3a with those in 3b. Mechanics working with an assistant were more likely to seek task-extrinsic information than were mechanics working alone ($p < .001$). Most importantly, this effect was strongest among mechanics who had prior task experience (few times, $p < .01$; many times, $p < .001$).

Table 2

Distribution of Extrinsic Information-Seeking Behaviors
by Type of Information and Source

Type of information	Source used		% of total behaviors
	Person (%)	Manual (%)	
Condition: mechanics working with assistants			
Identification–location of component (What and/or where is it?)	70	30	13
Procedural directions (What do I do?)	65	35	18
Technique (How do I do it?)	79	21	47
Standards–specifications (What are they?)	71	29	22
Condition: mechanics working alone			
Identification–location (What and/or where is it?)	33	67	9
Procedural directions (What do I do?)	20	80	28
Technique (How do I do it?)	65	35	43
Standards–specifications (What are they?)	60	40	20

Thus presence of assistant appears to have triggered experienced mechanics' recognition of the need for information but, when task-experienced mechanics were working alone, this need was not recognized.

A second type of evidence illustrating the continued need for information in spite of having performed the task many times is presented in Figure 5. This figure presents the percentage of mechanics at each experience level who made one or more errors during the task process (process errors) and who, after completion of the task, left one or more errors uncorrected. As this figure illustrates, experienced mechanics were just as likely to make errors as were mechanics who had never performed the task before. This is consistent with earlier findings based on administration of maintenance performance tests (Smith, 1964; Post & Brooks, 1970). Thus performance of a task many times tended to extinguish mechanics' use of manuals or people as information sources, but it did not eliminate their need for information that would enable them to perform tasks to maintenance standards.

The third type of evidence illustrating that the need for information does not decline with increased task experience is presented in Figure 6. Mechanics'

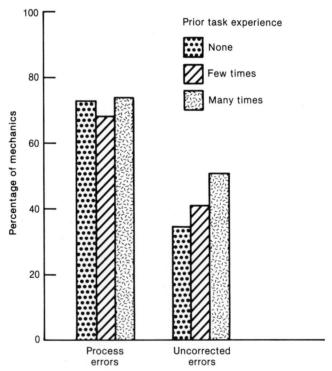

Fig. 5.   Occurrence of one or more errors by mechanics at different task experience levels.

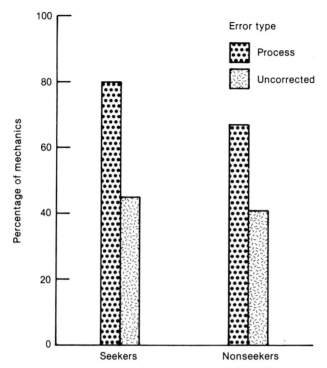

Fig. 6. Occurrence of one or more errors for mechanics who did and did not seek task-extrinsic information.

performance in using or not using task-extrinsic information sources was not related to their performance in making or not making errors. This finding suggests that use of extrinsic information sources and occurrence of errors provide two independent definitions of mechanics' information needs. Use of extrinsic information sources represents mechanics' recognized need for information. Occurrence of errors represents unrecognized need for information.

MODELING INFORMATION PROCESSING DURING TASK PERFORMANCE

Mechanics' reliance on task-intrinsic information sources is evidenced by 63% of the 234 mechanics who never used people or manuals to obtain information. A large amount of information exchange occurs by virtue of the mechanics' continuous examination or, by analogy, "reading" of the components on which the work is being performed. To some extent this reading process can be inferred from the detailed recording Schurman *et al.* (1982) made of the mechanics' overt behaviors. When the mechanic's performance is proceeding smoothly and he or she is not seeking extrinsic information, it is difficult to detect how he or she is processing task-intrinsic information. However, use of task-intrinsic information is clearly revealed when a mechanic's action proved unsuccessful and the work flow was physically blocked. Such blocking of the work flow does not necessarily reflect performance errors. For example, if a part that a mechanic was attempting to install would not slip into place, the mechanic would then examine the mechanism with which the part was expected to mate, examine the part itself, try different ways of aligning the part with the mechanism, and, perhaps, locate another vehicle and examine how the part was installed on it.

Mechanics who had performed the task many times were less likely to experience blocking of the work flow than were mechanics who had little or no prior task-specific experience ($p < .01$). The highly task-experienced mechanics resolved these problems by relying exclusively on the type of task-intrinsic information processing described in the example given in the preceding paragraph. Thus, with increased task-specific experience, mechanics appear to gain a type of task-specific knowledge that enables them to obtain all of the information they recognize the need for (right or wrong) by "reading" and, if necessary, "rereading" the equipment.

Task-intrinsic information sources did not satisfy the information needs of mechanics who had little or no task-specific experience. This is suggested by the greater incidence of work flow problems among these mechanics and their use of extrinsic information sources in attempting to resolve these problems. Thus these mechanics had not yet learned a way of performing the task (right or wrong) by "reading" the equipment.

Performance of mechanics who have little or no task-specific experience appears to reflect their general recognition of the need for information from people or manuals that will aid the mechanic in "decoding" the equipment. The need for procedural information (What do I do?) was recognized and sought from manuals and people in an anticipatory fashion (Table 3). By anticipatory I mean the information was sought before the action was initiated. When the work flow of task-inexperienced mechanics was physically blocked (as exemplified in the preceding) recognition of the need for extrinsic information occurred as reactive seeking. Technique (How do I do it?) information was the type of information most frequently sought and was predominantly sought in this reactive fashion and from person sources.

As suggested earlier, errors, particularly uncorrected errors, reflect unrecognized information needs. A considerably larger number of mechanics at all levels of task-specific experience made uncorrected errors when performing the type of tasks that, to be performed to maintenance standards, require use of special tools and specific tolerance specifications ($p < .001$). These are errors that do not physically block the performance process. As a result, errors of this type were

Table 3

Distribution of Extrinsic Information-Seeking Behaviors
by Style and Type of Information Sought

Type of information	Behavioral style		% of total behaviors
	Anticipatory (%)	Reactive (%)	
Condition: mechanics working with assistants			
Identification–location of component (What and/or where is it?)	17	83	13
Procedural directions (What do I do?)	59	41	18
Technique (How do I do it?)	28	72	47
Standards–specifications (What are they?)	39	61	22
Condition: mechanics working alone			
Identification–location (What and/or where is it?)	50	50	9
Procedural directions (What do I do?)	75	25	28
Technique (How do I do it?)	29	71	43
Standards–specifications (What are they?)	60	40	20

frequently not recognized as such, and the mechanic considered the task successfully completed. This type of errors was associated with equipment that is not physically designed to identify certain types of activities as ones required for proficient performance. For example, requirement for torquing a given nut to certain specifications can not be "read" from the equipment. The mechanic can tighten the nut with a common wrench and, to all appearances, has successfully completed the task. Given these conditions, as mechanics repeatedly perform the same task, they develop confidence in their ability to read the equipment while remaining unaware of the need for this type of task-extrinsic information.

SUMMARY: MODELING PERFORMANCE AT THE WORK SITE

Research conducted by Schurman *et al.* (1980) represents a systematic effort to develop a methodology for obtaining baseline data on mechanics' use of information sources and quality of performance under natural work-site conditions. Manuals available in the work sites during this research were traditional maintenance manuals that were scheduled to be replaced by newly designed job guide manuals. Thus the baseline data were intended to provide a standard for evaluating use and effectiveness of new manuals or other media. The contribution this methodology can make to the establishment of a technology for improving manuals by modeling users will be discussed in the final section of this chapter.

Results from this research emphasize the continuous interaction between the mechanic and the equipment. Increased task-specific experience, as opposed to time on the job, is the most potent factor affecting the probability that mechanics will consult a manual or person for information during task performance. The mechanic learns a way (right or wrong) of performing these tasks by "reading" the equipment. With repeated performance of the same task the probability of mechanics seeking information from manuals or people rapidly decreases. In other words, with increased task experience, information seeking shifts from task-extrinsic sources (manuals and people) to task-instrinsic sources (the equipment).

As indicated in the preceding, information seeking at these job sites is largely problem solving initiated when the mechanic can not "read" the equipment or an activity did not produce the effect the mechanic expected. Reading-to-do as opposed to reading-to-learn is frequently interpreted as simply requiring the worker to transfer information in the manual to their short-term or working memory. This interpretation may apply to other jobs but does not describe the majority of the information-seeking behaviors observed by Schurman *et al.* (1980). The major share of the information-seeking behaviors of these mechanics represented an effort to resolve the discrepancy between their expectations and the observed effect of their action. For example, mechanics described the effect, however well or poorly articulated, to another person and these two proceeded to interactively interrogate each other to identify the problem and a solution.

Manuals are seldom designed to "interrogate" users to help them identify the problem and the solution. Observation of mechanics' performance suggested that manuals were not found useful when the mechanic appeared to have only a vague conception of the problem encountered before consulting the manual. Possibly the closest a manual can come to simulating an interactive exchange with the mechanic and an expert is through use of tables presenting symptoms, their probable causes, and remedial actions to be taken in each case. The apparent need for information sources that can satisfy this function points to the need for research in the applied setting that carefully examines the role of prior knowledge in the ability to effectively use job information sources. As underscored by theoretical research reported by Miyake and Norman (1979); Hayes-Roth and Walker (1979); Chiesi, Spilich, and Voss (1979); and Spilich, Vesonder, Chiesi, and Voss (1979), effectiveness of a technical manual is probably more dependent upon mechanics' prior knowledge than "goodness" of its design.

IMPLICATIONS OF RESEARCH FOR AN IMPROVED TECHNOLOGY

My perception of the current technology for designing technical manuals is presented in Figure 7. The functional, task, and behavioral analytic techniques discussed under the content perspective have been incorporated in at least some, if not all, of the contract specifications for development of military manuals. Readability formulas discussed under the readability perspective have also been incorporated into these contract specifications.

The current methodology for evaluating manuals is restricted to the types of methods appropriate for developers' use during the developmental process. Hence in Figure 7, I have labeled these "process evaluation methods. " These

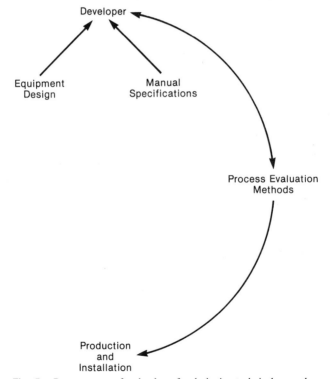

Fig. 7.   Present status of technology for designing technical manuals.

methods include a line-by-line review by subject matter experts to ensure correctness of data and procedures. Subsequently, a verification procedure is performed. This consists of selecting individuals from the user population, providing them with the new materials and the equipment, and checking on their ability to use the new instructions to perform a few selected tasks. Obviously, it is impractical to test the ability of mechanics to use all parts of a manual or set of manuals to perform all of the tasks assigned to their job position. Duffy (1985) discusses the problems with these current methods of validation and verification in detail. Note, as depicted in Figure 7, these process evaluation methods represent the final step in current application of technology for designing manuals. As a result, feedback regarding usability of the manuals at the job site depends solely on comments volunteered by users in the field. Thus the current technology is based primarily on experts ability to predict what users will need and how it should be designed to meet their needs. This technology does not provide the type of feedback needed to enable ''design experts'' to become ''user design experts.''

Improving the technology of modeling users to produce usable and effective manuals (or other media) requires a fully developed methodological base. As shown in Figure 8, the observational method developed by Schurman et al. (1982) represents an important contribution to establishing this type of methodological base. Once in place, the technology for developing manuals (or other media) gains feedback from users' performance at the work site and also gains a memory (the database) for improving the technology.

The types of feedback from the job site that can be obtained via the observational methodology will provide a basis for improving current process evaluation methods for verification of users' ability to use the manual. Because not all parts of a draft manual can be subjected to process evaluation, baseline data provided by this methodology furnishes a basis for strategies in sampling tasks and materials for process evaluation. These data identify the types of task performance during which mechanics are most likely to need information aids, the types of information most frequently sought, and the types of errors most frequently made. Usefulness of the manual during performance tests does not mean it will be used on the job. However, using these criteria, the content selected for testing can represent task instructions that, if used, have the most potential for improving performance at the job site.

As shown earlier in Figure 2, there are a large number of factors that affect use and usability of manuals in the natural work setting. Thus the baseline data shown in Figure 8 must be structured to provide feedback to equipment designers, trainers, and job-site management as well as to manual developers. Actions taken in any one of these four areas can make manuals more or less usable and technicians more or less likely to make errors. Little is known about the interactive effects and practical trade-offs among these four areas. Working with the

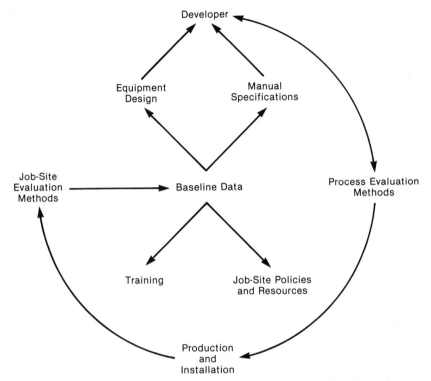

Fig. 8.   Requirements for an improved technology for designing technical manuals.

methodological base shown in Figure 8 will increase our knowledge of these interactions and how effectiveness of manuals and other media can be improved.

The major objective of the approach proposed here is to establish a base for developing a technology of manual (or other media) design. The goal in producing a usable manual is to produce one that meets the users' needs in the work-site context. A technology that develops manuals and other media in isolation from the users' performance at the work site can not achieve this goal.

REFERENCES

Booher, H. R. (1978, July). *Job performance aids: Research and technology state-of-the-art* (NPRDC TR 78-26). San Diego, CA: Navy Personnel Research and Development Center. (NTIS No. AD A057562)

Braby, R., & Kincaid, J. P. (1981–1982). Computer aided authoring and editing. *Journal Educational Technology Systems, 10*(2), 109–124.

Bruce, B., Rubin, A., & Starr, K. (1981, March). Why readability formulas fail. *IEEE Transactions on Professional Communication, PC-24*(1), 50–52.

Burkett, J. R. (1976, September). A review of research and development on literacy and technical writing in the Air Force. In T. G. Sticht & D. W. Zapf (Eds.), *Reading and readability research in the armed services* (HumRRO Final Rep. FR-WD-CA-76-4). Alexandria, VA: Human Resources Research Organization. (NTIS No. AD A034 730)

Burkett, J. R., & Hooke, L. R. (1980). *Analysis of the functional literacy requirements of Air Force job*. Paper presented at the meeting of the American Psychological Association.

Caylor, J. S., Sticht, T. G., Fox, L. C., & Ford, J. P. (1973, March). *Methodologies for determining reading requirements of military occupational specialties* (HumRRO TR 73-5). Alexandria, VA: Human Resources Research Organization. (NTIS No. AD 758 872 ERIC No. ED 074 343)

Chiesi, H. L., Spilich, G. J., & Voss, J. F. (1979). Acquisition of domain-related information in relation to high and low domain knowledge. *Journal of Verbal Learning and Verbal Behavior, 18,* 257–273.

Claudy, J. G., & Caylor, J. S. (1982, November). *Development of job-based reading tests* (TR 479). Alexandria, VA: U.S. Army Research Institute for the Behavioral and Social Sciences. (NTIS No. AD A123 324)

Collins, J. J. (1977, May). Some perspectives on the job performance aids technology base. In H. R. Booher (Ed.), *Symposium proceedings: Invitational conference on status of job performance aids technology* (NPRDC TR 77-33). San Diego, CA: Navy Personnel Research and Development Center. (NTIS No. AD A040 540)

Curran, T. E. (September, 1976). Readability research in the Navy. In T. G. Sticht & D. W. Zapf (Eds.), *Reading and readability research in the armed services* (HumRRO Final Rep. FR-WD-CA-76-4). Alexandria, VA: Human Resources Research Organization. (NTIS No. AD A034 730)

Curran, T. E. (1977, June). *Survey of technical manual readability and comprehensibility* (NPRDC-TR-77-37). San Diego, CA: Navy Personnel Research and Development Center. (NTIS No. AD A042 335)

Curran, T. E. (Ed.) (1980, March). *Tri-service literacy and readability: workshop proceedings* (NPRDC Special Rep. 80-12). San Diego, CA: Navy Personnel Research and Development Center. (NTIS No. AD A083 04310)

Duffy, T. M. (1976, September). Literacy research in the Navy. In T. G. Sticht & D. W. Zapf (Eds.), *Reading and readability research in the armed services* (HumRRO Final Rep. FR-WD-CA-76-4). Alexandria, VA: Human Resources Research Organization. (NTIS No. AD 034 730)

Duffy, T. M. (1981). Organising and utilizing document design options. *Information design journal, 2*(3, 4), 256–266.

Duffy, T. M. (1985). Preparing technical manuals: Specifications and guidelines. In D. Jonassen (Ed.), *The technology of text* (Vol. 2). Englewood Cliffs, NJ: Educational Technology Publications.

Duffy, T. M., & Kabance, P. (1982). Testing a readable writing approach to text revision. *Journal of Educational Psychology, 74*(5), 733–748.

Duffy, T. M., & Nugent, W. (1978, April). *Reading skill levels in the Navy* (NPRDC SR 78-19). San Diego, CA: Navy Personnel Research and Development Center. (NTIS No. AD-A054859)

Eames, R. D., & Starr, J. (1965, August). Technical publications and the user. *Human Factors, 7,* 363–369.

Foley, J. P., Jr. (1973, November). *Description and results of the Air Force research and development program for the improvement of maintenance efficiency* (AFHRL-TR-72-72). Brooks Air Force Base, TX: Air Force Human Resources Laboratory. (NTIS No. AD 771 000)

Foley, J. P., Jr., & Camm, W. B. (1972, August). *Job performance aids research summary*. Wright-Patterson Air Force Base, OH: Air Force Human Resources Laboratory. (NTIS No. AD 697 034)

Folley, J. D., Jr., & Munger, S. J. (1961, October). *A review of the literature on design of informational job performance aids* (ASD TR 61-549). Wright-Patterson Air Force Base, OH: Behavioral Sciences Laboratory, Aeronautical Systems Division, U.S. Air Force. (NTIS No. AD 270 867)

Hayes-Roth, B., & Walker, C. (1979). Configural effects in human memory: the superiority of memory over external information sources as a basis for inference verification. *Cognitive Science, 3,* 119–140.

Hoehn, A. J., & Lumsdaine, A. A. (1958, January). *Design and use of job aids for communicating technical information* (AFPTRC-TR-58-7). Lowry Air Force Base, CO: Air Force Personnel and Training Research Center. (NTIS No. AD 152 109)

Hooke, L. R., DeLeo, P. J., & Slaughter, S. L. (1979, September). *Readability of Air Force publications: a criterion referenced evaluation* (AFHRL-TR-79-21). Brooks Air Force Base, TX: Air Force Human Resources Laboratory. (NTIS No. AD A075 237)

Johnson, R. C., Thomas, D. L., & Martin, D. J. (1977, June). *User acceptance and usability of the C-141 job guide technical order system* (AFHRL-TR-77-31). Wright-Patterson Air Force Base, OH: Advanced Systems Division, Air Force Human Resources Laboratory. (NTIS No. AD A044 001)

Joyce, R. P., Chenzoff, A. P., Mulligan, J. F., & Mallory, W. J. (1973a, December). *Fully proceduralized job performance aids. Draft military specification for organizational and intermediate maintenance* (AFHRL-TR-73-43-I). Brooks Air Force Base, TX: Air Force Systems Command. (NTIS No. AD 775 702)

Joyce, R. P., Chenzoff, A. P., Mulligan, J. F., & Mallory, W. J. (1973b, December). *Fully proceduralized job performance aids. Handbook for JPA developers* (AFHRL-TR-73-43-II). Brooks Air Force Base, TX: Air Force Systems Command. (NTIS No. AD 775 705)

Kern, R. P. (1976, September). U.S. Army research and development on readability and useability of printed materials. In T. G. Sticht & D. W. Zapf (Eds.), *Reading and readability research in the armed services* (HumRRO Final Rep. FR-WD-CA-76-4). Alexandria, VA: Human Resources Research Organization. (NTIS No. AD A034 730)

Kern, R. P. (1980, January). *Usefulness of readability formulas for achieving Army readability objectives: research and state-of-the-art applied to the Army's problem* (TR 437). Alexandria, VA: U.S. Army Research Institute for the Behavioral and Social Sciences. (NTIS No. AD A086 408/2)

Kern, R. P., & Hayes, J. F. (1983, November). *Research findings to aid supervisors and trainers in improving maintenance performance* (RP83-14). Alexandria, VA: U.S. Army Research Institute for the Behavioral and Social Sciences. (NTIS No. AD A144 655)

Kern, R. P., & Sticht, T. G. (1980, January). The study of writing in functional contexts: The Army writer and the design of a guidebook for developing Army training literature (HumRRO Special Rep.). In R. P. Kern (Ed.), *Usefulness of readability formulas for achieving Army readability objectives: research and state-of-the-art applied to the Army's problem* (TR 437). Alexandria, VA: U.S. Army Research Institute for the Behavioral and Social Sciences. (NTIS No. AD A086 408/2)

Kern, R. P., Sticht, T. G., & Fox, L. C. (1970, June). *Readability, reading ability, and readership* (HumRRO PP 17-70). Alexandria, VA: Human Resources Research Organization. (NTIS No. AD 709 629 ERIC No. ED 043 834)

Kern, R. P., Sticht, T. G., Welty, D., & Hauke, R. N. (1977, November). *Guidebook for the development of Army training literature* (P-75-3). Alexandria, VA: U.S. Army Research Institute for the Behavioral and Social Sciences. (NTIS No. AD A033 935)

Kincaid, J. P., Fishburne, R. P., Jr., Rogers, R. L., & Chissom, B. S. (1975, February). *Derivation of new readability formulas (automated readability index, FOG count and Flesch reading ease formula) for Navy enlisted personnel* (Research BR 8-75). Naval Air Station Memphis, Millington, TN: Chief of Naval Technical Training. (NTIS No. AD A006 655)

Kniffin, J. D., Stevenson, C. R., Klare, G. R., Entin, E. B., Slaughter, S. L., & Hooke, L. (1980, May). *Operational consequences of literacy gap* (AFHRL-TR-79-22). Brooks Air Force Base, TX: Air Force Human Resources Laboratory. (NTIS No. AD A084 782/2)

Losee, J. E., Allen, R. H., Stroud, J. W., & Ver Hulst, J. (1962, August). *A study of the Air Force maintenance technical data system* (AMRL-TDR-52-85). Wright-Patterson Air Force Base, OH: 6570th Aerospace Medical Research Laboratories. (NTIS No. AD 288 636)

Macdonald, N. H., Frase, L. T., Gingrich, P. S., & Keenan, S. A. (1982). The writer's workbench: computer aids for text analysis. *Educational Psychologist, 17*(3), 172–179.

Miller, E. E. (1974, December). *Designing printed instructional materials: content and format* (HumRRO RP-WD-TX-75-4). Alexandria, VA: Human Resources Research Organization. (NTIS No. AD A052 761)

Miyake, N., & Norman, D. (1979). To ask a question, one must know enough to know what is not known. *Journal of Verbal Learning and Verbal Behavior, 18*, 357–364.

Mockovak, W. P. (1974, December). *Literacy skills and requirements in Air Force career ladders* (AFHRL-TR-74-90). Brooks Air Force Base, TX: Air Force Human Resources Laboratory. (NTIS No. AD A008 770)

Post, T. J., & Brooks, F. A., Jr. (1970, December). *Advanced manpower concepts for sea-based aviation systems* (AMSAS). Washington, DC: Advanced Systems Concepts Division, Research and Technology Group, Naval Air Systems Command. (NTIS No. AD 880 542)

Post, F. J., & Price, H. E. (1974, November). *Requirements and criteria for improving reading comprehension of technical manuals*. Falls Church, VA: Biotechnology Inc. for Naval Sea Systems Command. (NTIS No. AD A070 369)

Plung, D. L. (1981, March). Readability formulas and technical communication. *IEEE Transactions on Professional Communication, PC-24*(1), 52–54.

Redish, J. C. (1981, March). Understanding the limitations of readability formulas. *IEEE Transactions on Professional Communication, PC-24*(1), 46–48.

Rowan, T. C. (1973, March). *Improving DOD maintenance through better performance aids*. Arlington, VA: Information Concepts Inc. for Advanced Research Projects Agency, Department of Defense. (NTIS No. AD 758 713)

Schurman, D. L., Porsche, A. J., Garbin, C. P., & Joyce, R. P. (1982). *Guidelines: assessing use of information sources and quality of performance at the work site* (Res. Note 82–7). Alexandria, VA: U.S. Army Research Institute for the Behavioral and Social Sciences. (NTIS No. AD A125 366)

Schurman, D. L., Porsche, A. J., & Joyce, R. P. (1980). *Assessing use of information sources and quality of performance at the work site*. Valencia, PA: Applied Science Associates, Inc.

Serendipity Inc. (1969, May). *PIMO final report: Volume 1*. Norton Air Force Base, CA: Space and Missle Systems Organization, Air Force Systems Command. (NTIS No. AD 852 101)

Showel, M., & Brennan, M. F. (1978, October). *A survey of user attitudes towards Army training literature* (Research Memorandum 78–14). Alexandria, VA: U.S. Army Research Institute for the Behavioral and Social Sciences. (NTIS No. AD A075 432)

Shriver, E. L. (1977, May). New directions for information transfer research in maintenance jobs. In H. R. Booher (Ed.), *Symposium proceedings: Invitational conference on status of job performance aids technology* (NPRDC-TR-77-33). San Diego, CA: Navy Personnel Research and Development Center. (NTIS No. AD A040 540)

Siegel, A. I., Lambert, J. V., & Burkett, J. R. (1974, August). *Techniques for making written material more readable/comprehensible* (AFHRL-TR-74-47). Lowry Air Force Base, CO: Air Force Human Resources Laboratory, Technical Training Division. (NTIS No. AD 786 849)

Smith, J. P. (1964, March). *The performance of organizational maintenance by track vehicle mechanics and maintenance sergeants* (HumRRO TR-87). Alexandria, VA: Human Resources Research Organization. (NTIS No. AD 478 720)

Spilich, R. J., Vesonder, G. T., Chiesi, H. L., & Voss, J. F. (1979). Text processing of domain related information for individuals with high and low domain knowledge. *Journal of Verbal Learning and Verbal Behavior, 18,* 275–290.

Sticht, T. G. (1975, June). *A program of Army functional job reading training: development, implementation, and delivery systems* (HumRRO FR-WD-CA-75-7). Alexandria, VA: Prepared by Human Resources Research Organization for the U.S. Army Research Institute for the Behavioral and Social Sciences. (NTIS No. AD A012 272)

Sticht, T. G., Caylor, J. S., Kern, R. P., & Fox, L. C. (1972). Project REALISTIC: Determination of adult functional literacy skill levels. *Reading Research Quarterly, 7,* 424–465.

Sticht, T. G., Fox, L. C., Hauke, R. N., & D. Welty- Zapf (1977a, September). *The role of reading in the Navy* (NPRDC-TR-77-40). San Diego, CA: Navy Personnel Research and Development Center. (NTIS No. AD A044 228)

Sticht, T. G., Fox, L. C., Hauke, R. N., & D. Welty- Zapf (1977b, September). *Integrated job skills and reading skills training system* (NPRDC-TR-77-41). San Diego, CA: Navy Personnel Research and Development Center. (NTIS No. AD A044 227)

Sticht, T. G., & Zapf, D. W. (Eds.) (1976, September). *Reading and readability research in the armed services* (HumRRO Final Rep. FR-WD-CA-76-4). Alexandria, VA: Human Resources Research Organization. (NTIS No. AD A034 730)

Thomas, D. L., Johnson, R. C., & Dalezman, J. J. (1978, July) *Opinions of Air Force maintenance personnel about conventional technical orders* (AFHRL-TR-78-32). Wright-Patterson Air Force Base, OH: Advance Systems Division, Air Force Human Resources Laboratory. (NTIS No. AD A058 340)

Walter, J. A. (1971). Style manuals. In S. Jordan (Ed.) *Handbook of technical writing practices* (Vol. 2). New York: Wiley (Interscience).

CHAPTER 14

Testing Design Alternatives: A Comparison of Procedures

GARY M. SCHUMACHER
ROBERT WALLER

INTRODUCTION

Writers, editors, and designers possess an enormous amount of knowledge and skill, often tacit and unarticulated. Because they are essentially separated from their audience (unlike those who communicate face to face, such as teachers), they are only able to benefit from feedback about the effectiveness of their decisions by making a conscious effort to do so—and a considerable investment in time and money. This chapter reviews a range of techniques that can be used by such people to find out how their products affect readers, to pretest new products, or to compare alternative designs.

THE IMPACT OF RESEARCH
ON DOCUMENT DESIGN

There exists already a large literature on text-related issues. It is notoriously hard, however, for professional producers of texts (who we refer to here as document designers to cover the range of job descriptions in use in different contexts) to access and interpret it. It is scattered among a wide range of disciplines and is not easy to find without the aid of proper research library facilities—and when research material is located successfully it rarely seems applicable to the problem in hand.

A major problem is that research on texts is undertaken for a variety of reasons other than to provide guidelines to practitioners. Indeed, many studies are not primarily investigations of "texts" in the everyday sense of the word, but simply use them as a way of looking at some other point of interest—cognitive processes, for instance. To the scientist, the text medium may simply be a convenient way of controlling the presentation of a stimulus so that all subjects receive the same treatment. Although a better theoretical understanding of memory or cognition may eventually help us write better textbooks, the writer's problem is not the immediate concern of the researcher—in spite of the gestures toward the practical that can be found in the conclusion sections of many theoretical papers. Not only may the results of such studies be inapplicable by document designers, but the methods used may also be inappropriate in the practical context; the degree of control properly required by cognitive researchers may be unacceptably restrictive to those whose purpose is to test prototype textbooks or to compare graphic formats.

Because of this difference in purpose, then, care must be taken that the methods used to evaluate real texts are appropriate to the immediate needs of the document designer. For example, learning (insofar as that is measured by tests of recall) is not the only goal of textbook readers, and it is certainly not the main goal of readers of technical manuals, timetables, or catalogs. Even when learning is a goal, the use of a text may just be one component in a wider range of activities. The concept of a text as a tool that is used within a framework of individual purposes and task environments is central to the criterion of usability (discussed further by the editors in the preface to the present volume). To accept it is to accept that an essential characteristic of the text medium (and the source of its power) is that the users are in control of the time, pace, and pattern of interaction. Because of this we put considerable emphasis in our review on evaluation procedures that monitor the pattern of this interaction (process measures) in addition to those that measure static factors (outcome measures).

EVALUATION AS RESEARCH

The aim of all research is the production of knowledge—a concept that is by no means straightforward to define. Words like *expertise, science, theory, rules, guidelines,* or a *craft* all refer to knowledge systems, but the precise distinctions are elusive. It is much easier to distinguish between the different outcomes or embodiments of "public" knowledge (knowledge that is generally available such as diagrams, tables of data, laws, methods, etc.) than between styles or types of personal knowledge (knowledge that has been internalized, learned, or otherwise developed by an expert). The knowledge systems used (or at least claimed) by scientists and designers have traditionally been polarized—the goal of the former is the discovery of general principles underlying the natural world; the latter seeks to bring problem-solving ability, expertise, experience, and a skill in making connections to bear on specific problems, with no pretense to generality.

To a large degree the distinction is confirmed by the difficulties faced by those who have attempted to cross the boundary. The relationship between pure and applied research has always been a problem for the social sciences (in the context of text research, Wright, 1978, discussed approaches to their integration), and efforts to create a "science of design" as envisaged by Simon (1969) have met with difficulty and disillusionment (reviewed by Cross, 1980).

However, as Polanyi (1958) has demonstrated, even the traditional hard sciences involve a considerable degree of unarticulated personal knowledge and take place in a social context (Ravetz, 1971). This element of personal skill is especially significant in the case of research on document design as a linking factor between the researcher and the practitioner. In an ideal world the objective data provided by research activity would inform and enhance the designer's expertise; in turn, this expertise would be articulated to provide pertinent hypotheses, to generate suitable and relevant test materials, and to make sensible interpretations and generalizations from the data.

It could be further argued that the normal distinction between research and evaluation does not apply in the case of research on document design. The complex interaction of variables and the context dependency of text comprehension mean that even the most controlled laboratory study is in essence an evaluation of a particular set of materials in a particular context. Of course, the degree of control exercised in that context may be such that generalizations may be more reliably drawn from the resulting data than from, say, the outcome of a market research exercise for a particular textbook. However, in practice this has often been questionable. Although researchers are expected to apply rigorous standards of statistical analysis to their data (and publicly demonstrate this analysis in their reports), their stimulus materials are rarely subjected to the same scrutiny. A research hypothesis is thus confirmed or denied in a strictly limited context— limited to the combination of those variables that the researcher has happened to notice and control. In practice, lack of insight and expertise in the domain of application can lead to naive or misleading conclusions and recommendations.

Evaluation exercises, on the other hand, rarely address theoretical hypotheses but are undertaken by or for designers who, it is to be hoped, possess a proper awareness of the interaction of variables such as the content of the document, the conditions of use, and the goals of the users. Thus the resulting data are less reliable for theoretical purposes but should be highly valid in the immediate context.

Although in a strict technical sense the validity of evaluation data is restricted to its immediate context, in practice designers cannot help but generalize from it. They make connections through insight rather than formally stated models of how variables interact, but the reliability of this insight is enhanced by an accumulation of such design and evaluation experience. If adequately expressed and synthesized, insight acquired in this way can provide as fruitful a source of generalizable guidelines as properly controlled research. The validity of guidelines, whatever their source, must always be determined by their users, who are the only ones with full knowledge of the circumstances of application.

The use of evaluations as sources of generalizable guidelines (or indeed, of research data) is an essential argument for an additional reason. Publishing is not a leisurely operation, and the addition of an extra cycle of testing and rewriting (for there is little point in testing unless you are prepared for quite considerable rewriting) needs strong arguments to succeed. There is no doubt that evaluation is costly and disruptive, and, even when there is a strong commitment to it, only a selection of documents will receive the full treatment. Those documents that are selected for testing will be of two kinds: particularly important ones for which there are substantial safety or financial implications (e.g., government forms on which expensive administrative procedures and legal processes are based) and documents that are seen as typical of their kind and likely to yield information of general applicability.

Comparing Evaluation Procedures: Desirable Characteristics

In order to compare various procedures for testing the design of documents, it would be preferable to compare each procedure against an ideal assessment procedure. But because of the broadness of the criteria we group together under the concept of usability, such an ideal is not particularly easy to define.

In assessing the impact of text design we can consider expert opinions, outcome measures of text (e.g., readability or structural analyses), or processing measures (e.g., eye movements or verbal protocols). In addition, sometimes we are interested in ongoing feedback in the midst of document preparation, whereas at other times we are concerned with developing a general understanding of the important characteristics of good document design. These varying approaches and concerns make it impossible to describe any ideal measurement procedure; document design evaluation is as heavily context dependent as document use.

Although it may not be possible to describe an ideal procedure, it is possible to describe some general characteristics of all evaluation procedures. By keeping these characteristics in mind as various document design procedures are considered, it is possible to compare and contrast the procedures on these characteristics and hence see the strengths and weaknesses of the procedures. Six such general characteristics are described in the following paragraphs.

Time

For the document designer the amount of time it takes to receive useful information is a key variable in evaluating various measurement procedures. Although timely information is important in any evaluation process, it is crucial if the evaluation is providing ongoing feedback during document preparation. Delays in the publishing industry can be extremely expensive; this probably explains why publishers make little use of ongoing evaluation.

Because of the importance of ongoing feedback, some institutions build in time in their text design process for obtaining such feedback. For example, the Open University in Britian, which produces all its own instructional materials for a large number of correspondence students, uses pretesting with typical students. Obtaining this information at the right time is a continually difficult problem, and only a proportion of students can receive the full treatment.

It is apparent that procedures that fail to provide information quickly are of little use in document preparation. Time is, then, a key variable on which evaluation procedures must be judged.

Usable Form

Many evaluation procedures can produce large amounts of data that need to be heavily processed (analyzed, summarized, and correlated) before any useful message becomes clear. For example, structural analyses may provide detailed descriptions of the hierarchical layering in a text; eye-moving procedures may supply reams of information regarding micro-eye-movements. It is crucial that these data can be summarized and described in a form that is useful to the individual developing the document. Time constraints and a potential lack of knowledge about or sophistication in the use of certain kinds of data may make those data useless or misleading.

Goodness-of-Fit

There are different levels of concern in document design. At one level, for example, an author might be concerned about the structuring of ideas or whether he or she should use inserted study aids. At another level a text editor may be concerned about whether to use boldface type for key terms. At still another level a graphic designer may be concerned about the layout of a specific page or where to place certain figures or photographs to achieve maximum effect. Each of these individuals may be able to make use of evaulation procedures, but they need a certain kind of data. It is important therefore that the appropriate type of pro-cedure be used that provides the right level of information.

Reliability

Test construction specialists expend substantial effort in determining whether their tests are reliable, that is, whether the test is producing consistent results. This issue is also important in considering different kinds of document design evaluations. If a performance assessment is repeated, will it provide comparable answers at each assessment? Do eye-movement measures reliably show where the individual is looking? Without such consistency the measures are of no use in improving the design of documents.

Validity

Perhaps the single most important issue in evaluation is validity—whether the measurement procedure is accurately reflecting the underlying phenomenon. Validity is frequently glossed over with a cursory comment or simply not considered, but some major concerns arise here. A few questions serve to show the importance of the issue. Do eye fixations accurately reflect what is being processed at the time of the fixation? Are individuals sufficiently aware of their own processing activities to accurately describe how they use a text either in written questionnaires or in spoken protocols? Are the measurements obtained on individuals in laboratory situations reflective of how they will perform in a natural setting?

Ease of Use and Cost

In many situations the individuals involved in making text design decisions do not have access to or skill in the use of expensive equipment or elaborate statistical and measurement procedures. So an important characteristic of a good text design evaluation procedure is the ease with which the procedure can be used, the types of skills required to use the procedures, and the cost of setting up and carrying out the evaluation. An elaborate eye-movement camera may provide a reliable and valid measure of how text design changes influence reading, but the cost of such a system is often prohibitive.

These six characteristics are not exhaustive but do provide a set of issues to consider as we take up each of several text design evaluation procedures that are available.

PROCEDURES FOR EVALUATING DOCUMENT DESIGN

The evaluation procedures we review here may be loosely divided into two categories: outcome measures and process measures. Outcome measures are those in which a completed document (or part of a document) is tested. These frequently involve ratings or user tests. Process measures, on the other hand, are those in which the emphasis is on how the reader interacts with the document during usage. This may involve recording eye-movement patterns or text-accessing patterns.

These two major categories are not cleanly separable, but they do allow us to see the particular emphasis of a technique. The purpose of this section is to describe several examples of each of these types of procedures. We evaluate these against the six characteristics already described and indicate the benefits and drawbacks of the procedures and their potential uses. In the case of two process measures, we provide data comparing these methods and discuss the implications of the findings for the use of these two systems.

Outcome Measures

We review four major types of outcome measures that have been used in evaluating document characteristics. These are readability formulas, performance tests based on document use, structural analyses, and ratings or questionnaires based on usage trials.

Readability

Of all evaluation procedures of document design, readability formulas have probably had the widest use. Generally these procedures provide a numerical estimate of the level of reading skill a person needs to understand a particular document. Because there is extensive discussion of the issues involved in the use of such devices in Chapter 6 by Duffy in the present volume, we limit our comments.

Most of the myriad of readability formulas measure two aspects of a completed document: word characteristics such as length or familiarity and sentence length. Because it is now generally accepted that many variables beyond these two factors contribute to the success of a given document (e.g., goal of the reader, textual cohesion, typography), these measures have come under considerable attack.

Relevant to our list of six characteristics, the following summary may be made. Because of the simplicity involved in most readability formulas, they are relatively easy to use, they are typically low in cost, they are quite reliable (because they usually involve counts of syllables and words), and they can be obtained in very timely fashion. The very simplicity that leads to positive remarks in these categories, however, makes such formulas vulnerable in the other areas. Because the formulas rely on a few simple properties of the completed text, they do not provide a valid index of the many factors of document design that have impact on a document's usefulness. Similarly the simplicity means the goodness-of-fit is very restricted because many issues that authors, editors, and typographers are concerned with are not treated. Finally, the form in which information about the document is conveyed (typically reading grade levels) is too general to provide those interested in document design with much help.

Generally readability formulas are too global a level of information; they provide little help in determining either how to produce a well-designed document or how to improve the design of an already existing document. One way to decide whether they are likely to be useful is through a set of questions to be asked before applying them. Klare (1981) describes one such set of questions.

In summary, readability formulas appear useful only in giving a global assessment of documents for general audience use and perhaps in aiding the making of some administrative decisions, although some researchers contend that even this latter point is not the case (Bruce, Rubin, & Starr, 1981).

Performance Tests

There is a large collection of research literature, particularly in the fields of psychology and education, that has investigated the impact of various text features on the ability of readers to remember, understand, and use text. This work has generally looked at a particular type of design feature such as the use of inserted questions (reviewed by Rickards & Denner, 1978), advance organizers (reviewed by Barnes & Clawson, 1975), headings (Hartley & Trueman, 1982), or passage organization (Schumacher, Liebert, & Fass, 1975). The procedure (or set of procedures covered by the term *performance tests*) is more suited to experiments on these kinds of discrete devices with identifiable borders than multivariate aspects of textual argument, typography, or the use of pictures and figures.

The typical approach in using this procedure has been to present to a set of subjects in a laboratory setting passages of material manipulated on some particular text feature and then to assess the impact of this feature on a memory or comprehension test. These tests may take many forms but have frequently included multiple-choice or short-answer questions (most basic textbooks on educational research or experimental design give more detailed guidance about these procedures). On the basis of subject performance, conclusions are reached as to the efficacy of some particular text design feature.

Evaluations based on performance tests can usually be accomplished quite quickly, easily, and inexpensively. The data obtained are generally some score on a test, so although the procedure can provide information on a number of different design features, it can only indicate whether the features enhance the subjects' ability to recall the text. It provides little guidance to the author or designer of a document as to how the particular feature was used by the subjects and so provides only limited specific guidance as to how to modify the text to improve it.

It is possible that design features may modify any number of other variables such as reading time, interest, or even willingness to complete the study of a document. This raises a validity issue because the response measures may be too narrow to capture the richness of complex interactions of design features. There are also validity issues that deal with whether the specific questions used even tap memory or comprehension of the particular document, and whether the laboratory conditions under which most of the investigations are carried out so restrict the generalizability of the findings as to make them of little practical use. Reliability issues must also be considered. Are the tests reliably constructed so that they would show a similar pattern of results on a retest, or does the test show an adequate level of internal consistency?

In summary, performance tests have an important, but limited, role in document design. They are generally most useful in establishing general principles of design but can also aid in designing a specific document. They can help designers see the final impact of a particular design feature on one particular measure, but they are of limited use in specifying exactly how to redesign a document to make it more effective.

Structural Analyses

During the early 1970s there was considerable interest in developing procedures for analyzing the structure of written documents (e.g., De Beaugrande, 1981; Frederiksen, 1977; Kintsch, 1977; Meyer, 1977), and they took several different forms. The structural analysis procedures were generally aimed at specifying the nature and relationship of the various ideas presented in a text. The emphasis therefore was on text content rather than on presentation.

Because these analyses are typically quite detailed, they can require considerable expertise and time to execute and result in very elaborate "maps" of the text. The outcome of the application of these procedures may be overwhelming to a person unfamiliar with them and consequently of limited use without the help of individuals sophisticated in the procedures. The reliability with which structural analyses can be accomplished is frequently not addressed in these models, leaving this issue in the air. Some sticky validity issues arise because the same text can be analyzed with different systems resulting in different outcomes; there is no reliable rule to decide which system is the most useful or defensible. In addition, the recent work suggesting the importance of what the reader brings to the reading situation and its impact on comprehension indicates that text structural analyses need to be interpreted cautiously.

In summary, structural analyses appear to be of limited usefulness in document design evaluations. They can provide a formal way to look at the argument the author is presenting, but they provide too little direct guidance as to how the various structural properties influence comprehension and usability to be of major value in the design of a particular document. They may eventually provide useful information regarding general characteristics of effective documents.

User Ratings

Some institutions and groups make use of a less formal outcome measure that we refer to as user ratings. Text book publishers frequently make use of several different forms of this type of measure. They may, for example, ask teachers or professors to respond to a questionnaire regarding a certain text or even to write a formal review at various stages in the development of a text. Similarly, they may request observations from faculty and students who have used a text to aid in the design of a new edition of the text or to determine particular features of text design that have proved effective or ineffective.

Little formal research has been conducted on the role of such user ratings in the document design process. This procedure suffers from several problems. Specifically, these user ratings typically take a substantial amount of time to obtain and are less reliable than readability formulas. The lack of reliability is chiefly due to the more open-ended character of such ratings and the small and potentially biased sample of raters that may be used. Because user ratings may be obtained on levels of document content, style, or even text layout, they may have a reasonable goodness-of-fit. However, the observations made are often at a general level and thus fail to provide specific information by which the document designer can improve the document. Because it is often not possible to verify what aspects of document design are being considered in such ratings, it is not possible to consider issues of validity systematically. However, such ratings are relatively easy to obtain and (in small numbers) relatively inexpensive.

In summary, user ratings provide a means of obtaining global impressions about a particular document. These are helpful in making certain macrolevel decisions regarding content coverage and organization. They are at too large a level and too time-delayed in many cases to be of use in most ongoing design decisions.

PROCESS MEASURES

Until recently these outcome measures were the principal procedures by which document designers could obtain empirical information about their documents. It is not surprising that designers relied upon their own intuition obtained over years of experience in making design decisions. What information these techniques could produce was typically of a very general level and hence failed to provide specific help to solve a design problem. On other occasions the information was so delayed that it could have little impact on ongoing decisions.

Since the mid-1970s, more process-oriented measures of text design and use have become popular. Researchers have shown considerable ingenuity in devising ways of tapping information on how individuals process and use various documents. Although some of the procedures necessitate special types of equipment, others can be carried out with a minimum of equipment. We begin by considering some procedures that necessitate little equipment.

User Edits

One of the simplest and easiest ways to assess how an individual is using a document and to determine potential design problems is the user edit. In this procedure, inexperienced individuals are given a document, such as a technical manual for a machine, and are asked to work with the machine with the manual as their only aid. Careful observations of pauses and errors can provide insight into document design problems or weaknesses in specific documents (Atlas, 1981). User edits are similar to laboratory evaluations originally used in developing programmed instructional materials.

The British Open University pretesting procedure uses a type of user edit (Henderson & Nathenson, 1977), which has become known as "developmental testing." Questionnaires are inserted at frequent intervals in the draft text. This is given to a number of students who study as for a normal course (they are tested and awarded credits in the normal way); their opinion of particular sections or diagrams is thus canvassed while it is still fresh in their minds.

The user edit procedure is usually carried out with relatively small numbers of individuals and is more oriented toward a feedback or troubleshooting approach to a single document than a scientific procedure for determining general principles of document design. The procedure is most effective for "action" documents where one can quickly see where comprehension is failing.

Most user edits have the individual work through the document page by page. This allows for content information to be checked, such as missing, misleading, or poorly designed instructions. Atlas (1981) notes that the procedure can also help identify stylistic problems although it probably will not capture all such difficulties. Because a page-by-page use of a document may fail to determine if material is accessible when needed, Atlas recommends formal testing procedures to determine if directory, index, and cross-referencing procedures are adequate.

Generally it would seem that user edits can be carried out in a timely fashion so as to be useful in troubleshooting a particular document. The procedure should generate information that is linked to specific design problems and provide information relevant to content and some stylistic questions. It probably is not optimal for picking up information relevant to typographical or text layout problems: first, it is rarely possible to use a professionally printed document at this preproduction draft stage; second, students are not always sensitive to typographical problems, and may attribute difficulties to some other cause. There should be reasonable reliability to the approach, although individuals with different levels of background knowledge may generate substantially different feedback about the text. Finally, the procedure is quite easy to use and is inexpensive; it should provide reasonably valid information on "action" documents.

In summary, a user edit is an inexpensive and easy-to-use procedure for the evaluation of specific documents, but because the procedure is quite time-consuming with each subject and the data are difficult to summarize, it is probably not an optimal procedure for deriving general principles of document design.

Protocol Analyses

In 1972 Newell and Simon introduced a technique for investigating human problem-solving activities—protocol analyses. This procedure has become a prime tool for investigating writing processes (Flower & Hayes, 1980, 1981) and has also been used for studying how individuals read and comprehend governmental regulations and forms (Flower, Hayes, & Swarts, 1980; Holland & Redish, 1981).

Using the protocol analysis procedure in evaluating document design involves asking individuals to "think aloud" as they attempt to understand a document or complete a form. The request to think aloud typically involves a request to say everything they are thinking about, writing, or reading as they are carrying out a task. This procedure produces a massive amount of information from each subject. The experimenter then takes this information and attempts to analyze the comments in order to determine what difficulties or problems are being generated for the reader or what general processes readers employ in trying to generate meaning from the text.

Holland and Redish (1981), for example, used protocol analyses to study how individuals completed the federal government's job application form. They found that three levels of strategies were used by subjects in successfully filling out the form. These included decoding strategies that involved efforts to understand lexical and syntactic aspects of the form, form-using strategies that involved attempts to relate items across the form, and global strategies that involved attempting to predict how answers will be interpreted or looking for the intention of a particular question. It is argued that information of this type can reveal general principles that individuals use in comprehending documents.

Protocol analyses can also be used in a feedback-oriented procedure to help in the design of a particular document. In this case, individuals would be asked to think aloud as they worked on a version of a document. The comments generated could then be used by the authors to produce a revised version of the document that would be subjected to a second protocol analysis. In this manner the procedure is similar to a user edit, except in the latter case the emphasis is more on performance activities of the readers rather than on their comments.

Depending on how protocol analyses are done, they can vary widely in the time needed to carry them out. If, for example, protocols are obtained from several subjects on lengthy documents, compiling and analyzing the protocols can be very time-consuming. In addition, because subjects are usually told to comment on whatever they are thinking about, there can be considerable variability in what is noted from subjects—one may get a wide variety of information from a protocol but not necessarily in particular areas in which an author or designer is interested. The goodness-of-fit of the technique as a design tool is therefore questionable.

One particular reliability issue relates to the scoring of protocols. This process typically involves little structure so it is possible that different individuals scoring the protocols will pay attention to different things. It is usually necessary, therefore, to have more than one judge and to provide the judges with considerable training. Several validity issues arise with protocol analyses also. Because individuals generating the protocol must expend some cognitive effort in producing the protocol, it is possible that their actual processing of the document is modified. That is, because readers are limited in the amount of activity they can carry out at any one time, asking them to do an additional activity (in this case talking about their reading) may alter the actual reading process. It is also possible that being asked to externalize their thoughts about their processing of the document may lead individuals to make the process sound more regular, or suppress what they feel to be poor habits or techniques. Finally, it is unclear how consciously aware we are of many aspects of text processing. Many key aspects of our processing may be missed if attention is paid only to those aspects that come into conscious attention.

In summary, protocol analysis is a relatively easy and inexpensive process by which to collect data relevant to the design of a document and how that document is processed. However, there can be several problems in analyzing the data collected. There are potential scoring problems and possibly biases in the reporting of data by the subjects. Nevertheless, protocol analyses, if used cautiously and carefully, can be a major source of ideas both for the refinement of a particular document and the development of general principles regarding the importance of certain design features on the usability of documents.

Micro-Eye-Movement Procedures

There has been extensive interest in the last couple of decades in developing techniques for measuring the cognitive activities that individuals carry out while doing various types of mental tasks. Such techniques can provide windows on the processing needed to carry out these tasks. A technique that has been increasingly used in text-processing work is to monitor the eye-movement patterns of individuals as they read. The large majority of these studies have focused on what might best be called micro-eye-movements. In these studies the interest has been on eye fixations, regressions, and movements that focus on individual letters, words, and occasionally sentences. There has been, however, a small amount of work that has focused on macrolevel eye movements across paragraphs and pages of text. The focus of this work has frequently been on studying processes and macroreading strategies and how these are influenced by variables such as text design or subject variables. Because these two traditions represent quite different types of work, we treat them in separate sections. In the remainder of this section we deal with micro-eye-movements; in the next section we consider the macrolevel work.

The process measures of document design that we have considered in the preceding have relied on either rather large action sequences (e.g., operational mistakes in doing a user edit) or comments from the reader about what he or she is thinking or doing at a given point in a document. There are, however, cognitive processes occurring on many levels while a document is being read and used. For example, letters and words are being recognized; inferences are being drawn; comparisons are being made; and words, sentences, and larger text blocks are being integrated. Because speech and reading comprehension occur at rates well above 100 words a minute, these numerous processes must be carried out quickly and automatically, often making them unavailable for conscious inspection (Carpenter & Just, 1977). As a consequence, methods that rely on large-scale behaviors or subject comments are unable to tap many of these processes. In order to get at this very detailed level of processing, techniques that monitor the numerous processes involved in reading, comprehending, and integrating words and sentences need to be employed. Perhaps the major technique used for this fine level of analysis is micro-eye-movements.

There are numerous ways of recording eye movements. Many of the procedures make use of the corneal reflection process, which determines where the eye is looking by reflecting a small light off the cornea of the eye. The systems vary widely in cost and in availability. Some demand that the reader be very constrained in his or her movements and make use of bite bars, chin rests, or head restraints to achieve immobility. Some need the text to be displayed a single line at a time, perhaps on a computer terminal display. These characteristics severely limit the generalizability of the information generated to the design of real documents.

In addition, some important issues had to be settled before these systems could be used to investigate language processing and document design. McConkie *et al.* (1979) considered a number of these issues in detail. We mention only two here. The first concerns the lag between the time information is visually fixated and the time when it is used in reading. If there is considerable delay between these two points, the use of eye movements in the investigation of document design would be extremely difficult. Although McConkie *et al.* argued that this question could not be definitely answered, these researchers did review evidence suggesting that manipulations such as changing the content of a line during a fixation did inflate the duration of that fixation. The second issue concerns whether information from the same region of a document is being seen in more than one eye fixation. If a region is being seen in more than one fixation, it would be difficult to judge which fixation is critical for that region. Generally the research seems to indicate that a single region is fixated only once unless there is a regression back at a later time (McConkie *et al.*, 1979).

Micro-eye-movement procedures have been used to generate theoretical models of the reading process (e.g., Just & Carpenter, 1980). They are just beginning to be used to help understand how some basic features of texts such as linguistic cues in paragraphs influence the understanding of pronoun reference and the effect on reading performance of the need to make direct or indirect inferences in documents.

Micro-eye-movement procedures can be quite time-consuming to carry out because they frequently involve individual data collection and substantial data processing and equipment set-up time. They involve the use of sophisticated and costly equipment and necessitate extensive data summarization to collapse the data into usable form. The better systems appear able to generate reliable data on eye movements and fixations, but there is some question about the validity of the data generated because of the constraints necessitated for use of the equipment (e.g., head restraints, reading from video screens).

In summary, it appears that micro-eye-movement procedures are useful in helping to determine theoretical principles of document design that influence reading behavior. But the large cost factor and the specialized skills needed to use the equipment indicate that these procedures will have little use in the forseeable future in ongoing evaluation of particular documents. Because most micro-eye-movement techniques necessitate the use of small segments of text that must be read under unusual contexts, there is serious question about the generalizability of the results to more natural materials and contexts.

Macro-Eye-Movement Procedures

The difficulty of using micro-eye-movement techniques for practical document development has led to interest in developing procedures for recording macrolevel reading behavior in more natural settings. These procedures have usually allowed the use of regularly presented documents, hence allowing for a greater diversity of textual materials, and usually involve less costly equipment. We describe three different examples of such procedures here. In a later section we present briefly the results of a methodological study of two of the procedures.

The first procedure, using a light-pen recorder, involves a small light source attached to a joystick suspended from above; the joystick is then linked to a microcomputer (see Figure 1). The prototype light-pen recorder was developed by Peter Whalley (Whalley & Fleming, 1975) who used it to evaluate the placement of diagrams. Individuals read in a semidarkened room (i.e., there is just a small lamp several feet away from the reader) and move the light source over the material to be read. The microcomputer records the coordinates of the joystick location over the text. The light beam can be adjusted for both width and height allowing for a variable-sized lighted rectangle on the text, while the room is kept light enough for individuals to overview the page structure but not to read in detail except with the light pen. The insertion of page-grid definitions into the computer makes it possible to record the time on each subblock of a page and to print graphic plots of the accessing pattern subjects use in reading each text page. The printouts can also be scored for lookbacks (looking at a prior page) and lookforwards (looking at a subsequent page).

The procedure has been used to test principles of document design by Whalley and Fleming (1975) and Schumacher and Waller (1983). Because it involves no

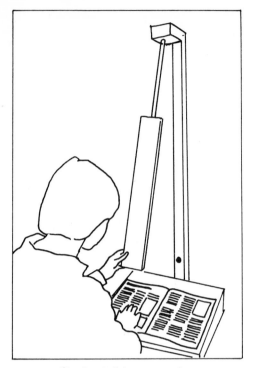

Fig. 1.   A light-pen recorder.

special document preparations, it can be done in a sufficiently short period of time to be effective in ongoing development of a particular document. The output from the computer program allows for direct observation of the reading pattern a subject is using in reading a document, and the time that is being spent in each text block. The procedure can provide useful data for several design features such as text layout and some typographical characteristics. The output is not sufficiently precise, however, to allow for processing issues related to letter-, word-, or even phrase-level processing. Because all data recording is done by the computer, reliability appears to be quite good. There are some validity issues that the system raises. Specifically, the necessity of individuals reading in a semi-darkened room may influence reading strategies and hence may lead to different conclusions regarding design characteristics. Some aspects of this problem are discussed in a later section describing the results of the methodological study. The cost of the system is moderate; the actual light device can be produced very inexpensively whereas any basic microcomputer should be able to handle the data recording and analyzing necessitated. (Directions for construction and programs for an Apple microcomputer are available from Robert Waller.)

In summary, the procedure provides a reasonably inexpensive method for obtaining information about either general design principles or specific characteristics of documents under development. It is restricted to testing certain macrofeatures of text design.

The second macro-eye-movement procedure involves the use of a specially constructed reading stand and a videotape system. The reading stand consists of a platform on which the reading materials can be placed. About 6 inches above this platform a semisilvered piece of glass is mounted (see Figure 2). The glass is positioned so that the readers view the material through the glass but can have their hands beneath the glass to turn pages, underline, or write. With appropriate lighting the glass appears transparent to the reader. A videotape camera placed above the individual's shoulder records both the material that is being read and the face and eye movements of the reader. A number of different measures can be scored directly from the videotapes. These include lookbacks, lookforwards, note taking, hesitations at text locations, and reading pattern. The general system

Fig. 2. A specially constructed reading platform with a semisilvered piece of glass mounted over it. A videotape camera is placed above the reader and records both material being read and eye movements.

was originally used by Pugh (1979) to investigate reading patterns and provide students in a study skills course with feedback about their reading styles. Pugh adapted it from a related system developed by Karslake (1940) to investigate the way individuals looked at advertisements in magazines.

The procedure can be used both in investigations of general principles of reading and studying activities and document design (Pugh, 1979; Schumacher, Moses, & Young, 1983; Schumacher & Waller, 1983) or in an ongoing fashion to improve the design of a particular document. In the former situation the use of at least two judges to score the various measures is recommended. Generally the level of reliability has been found to vary from a high of about .95 for lookbacks and lookforwards to .75 for scoring reading pattern. These measures are obviously markedly influenced by the degree of refinement that is desired.

In using the system to aid in the design of a particular document, the procedure works much as an user edit. It has the advantage of not interrupting the individual as he or she is using the document. Such interruptions may significantly influence how the document is used. Nor does it require an experimenter to be present while the document is being used. The presence of the experimenter can also alter the way a reader uses a document by making the user self-conscious. The videotape showing the document and the eye movements serves as an excellent prompt for readers to recall what they were doing at a particular location in their reading. This procedure also has the advantage of allowing more normal lighting and reading conditions than does the light-pen recorder. It is, however, substantially less reliable than the light-pen recorder in determining reading pattern.

When being used for feedback in designing a document, the procedure can be accomplished in a timely fashion. However, when it is used for a scientific investigation, the scoring process can become laborious and time-consuming. Information from the system can be put into a usable form to aid document design relatively easily, although the system is not optimal for providing detailed information on aspects of design such as typography. Its main use would appear to be for larger design issues such as the use of various study aids (e.g., inserted questions). Because the system can use regular documents in a relatively normal setting, it would appear to be a generally valid usage test of a document. There is some concern about reliability, particularly if one is attempting to determine fine details of text usage. The cost of the system is moderate—particularly if a video system is already available—and it requires little special training in its use.

In summary, this system could have some use both in the design of a particular document and in establishing general principles of design. Its strengths are in its creation of a relatively normal reading situation that involves no interruption of the reading process. Its weaknesses are in the laborious scoring and potentially low reliability for assessing the impact of detailed aspects of document design.

The third macro-eye-movement process in this review has been developed by Bernadette van Hout Wolters of Katholeke University in Nijmegen, The Netherlands (Hout Wolters, 1982). It involves a combination of measures recorded while a document is being read. It makes use of an *X*- and *Y*-coordinate grid on which the document to be read is placed. The reader moves a special pen down the text locating it on the text line that is being read. The coordinates of the pen are recorded by a computer. By recording the line coordinates of the document in the computer, it is possible to determine the line being read at any point in time. The system is set to record time on each line and the pattern of line access. Two videotape cameras record the reading platform and subjects' head and facial movements.

In addition to the macro-eye-movement information, the system also records the galvanic skin response (GSR) continually throughout a reading session and latency to respond to an oral sound presented at various spots in the text. This latter measure allows for a measure of the depth of processing the reader is engaged in at various locations in the text. This allows for a determination of the impact of various document design properties on processing level. Currently that type of information is not available from other measurement procedures. Information from all measures is coordinated by the computer and is digitally displayed on the videotape of the subject.

Because this procedure involves some rather complex and costly equipment and may involve considerable set-up and scoring time, it is most useful in investigations of general principles of reading and studying than for practical document development. It is best used for investigating larger design issues and content characteristics of text because, like the other macrolevel systems, it does not have sufficient refinement to address very detailed design issues. Because all data recording is automated, reliability should not generally be an issue, but a serious validity issue may arise from the need for readers to move the pen to indicate where they are reading. It is possible in highly involved portions of text that the reader may fail to move the pen promptly leading to errors on time on line and location. In addition, when all data recording systems are being used (GSR, pen movement, delayed response time), individuals may become overloaded, resulting in changes of normal reading pattern. The necessity of moving the pen to lines being read may be sufficiently unusual to lead to strategy changes also. This question, though, remains an open one until data are available from the use of the system.

In summary, this system holds promise for investigating some general design issues that have not been addressed by other process measures. Specifically, the ability to investigate processing load issues simultaneously with eye movements may allow the tapping of some content and structural issues of documents that other systems cannot. It remains to be seen how generalizable information obtained from this procedure is to real-world settings.

Macroprocessing Procedures

In the section on macro-eye-movement procedures we noted that there were many aspects of text processing beyond the word and sentence level that play important roles in text comprehension and use. The procedures we described to get at these processes typically dealt with passages several paragraphs to several pages in length. The argument has been made that even these measures fail to tap the types of complex text processing that individuals are frequently asked to do. Specifically, in coming to understand some new topic area, we may read several chapters or books of information and integrate this information to obtain new skills and understandings. This type of reading is extremely difficult to access in laboratory settings because it is so time-consuming and subject to individual motivational levels. Therefore, procedures that allow us to tap the processes involved at this level would be of critical importance to understanding not only the reading process but how to design large-scale documents (chapters and books) to lead to effective comprehension and use.

Although the macro-eye-movement processes we described could be used to analyze this type of reading, they would have a couple of major drawbacks. First, the equipment involved would usually require readers to come into some central facility. This could result in significant changes in the reading process and raise serious validity questions. Second, the systems could produce such voluminous amounts of data that it would be very difficult to summarize the information effectively. It seems inefficient, at best, to collect microlevel data and then collapse these data by averaging to look for macrostrategies.

To overcome these problems, Whalley (1982) designed a Study Protocol Recorder, which can be sent home with students. The text material that the students are reading (potentially book-length) is placed on the recorder, which is an adapted ring binder of the sort typically used by students to store notes. A special page sensor device on the recorder "reads" a binary pattern of marks placed on each page of the document that indicates to which page the document is opened. As the reader turns the pages to read, the recorder keeps track of the page sequences. The recorder also has an internal clock to record the date and time of each page turn, obviating the need to store continuous data in real time; it can thus store several weeks worth of data on a single microcassette, which can be sent to the experimenter at periodic intervals. One version of the recorder has been made into a convenient folding arrangement so that texts that are not being used may be set aside or shelved. This version thus makes it possible to investigate the simultaneous use of several interrelated texts (Whalley, 1982). One evaluation study using the Study-Protocol Recorder investigated the use of flowcharts in a microprocessor engineering course (Whalley, 1981).

Because this system is primarily for investigating the use of large blocks of text over considerable periods of time, its main usefulness should be in deriving general design principles integrating large text segments. Because data collection and analysis will take place over sizable blocks of time, the process will probably be of little use for the design of a specific document, although an important exception to this is in producing a revised version of a book. Some effective means of data categorization will be needed to ensure that the information gained from the procedure is useful for design considerations. Because the system provides information in page-sized blocks, it will not be of use in very detailed analyses, but it should provide efficient information about the pattern of text usage. Because data collection is highly automated, reliability should not be a problem with one major exception. Some procedure needs to be developed to ensure that individuals do not get up, leave the room but keep the recorder on; this could show a long reading time on a page when, in fact, the text was not being read. Because the device can be used in the home to record normal reading activity, it should provide a valid index of whole text use. The basic recording unit is relatively inexpensive and demands no special skills to use.

In summary, the Study-Protocol Recorder is the first system to allow systematic measurement of long-term reading behavior on large text segments. The resulting data can aid in large-scale design decisions and provide previously unobtainable information about study habits.

OUTCOME OR PROCESS MEASURES

Because the final test of a document is whether it communicates effectively with the reader, some may claim that outcome measures are sufficient. Process measures, it is claimed, are superfluous because there may be many processing routes to the same outcome. We think, however, that process measures are an important, but under-used measure. Outcome measures frequently indicate that a particular document fails to accomplish its goal but provide little specific information as to why or where the document fails. Process measures are frequently able to pinpoint specific trouble-spots and make remedies more apparent. Also, of course, it is possible for a document to succeed but at a considerable cost to the reader. This situation may result in a person being reluctant to use similar documents in the future. Process measures may result in documents that are equally effective but more efficient.

Many of the process measures described here have been developed or have become popular since the mid-1970s. It will be important in the next few years to determine if these procedures provide us with effective information to aid design. Two types of information will be useful in making this determination. One will be systematic use of the systems to investigate various aspects of reading and the design process. If the systems are providing good data, there should be convergence in the reported results. The second type of information should come from systematic methodological comparisons of those procedures that appear to be tapping information about similar levels of reading. Although these types of studies are not often done, they can provide valuable information. In the next section we report the results of one such investigation comparing two of the macro-eye-movement procedures.

A METHODOLOGICAL COMPARISON OF TWO MACRO-EYE-MOVEMENT PROCEDURES

The light-pen recorder and video recorder eye-movement procedures are both designed to tap macro-level reading strategies. In using these procedures to investigate reading processes and text design, it is important to know whether they produce similar outcomes of the reading process. It is possible that one or the other (or both) of the systems lead readers to adopt unusual reading practices. If this were the case, the usefulness of the information gained from the systems regarding reading procedures and text design would be called into question. It would obviously be best, then, if we could compare each of the systems against normal reading practices. But how do we know these practices? To study them we must measure them, and measuring them will potentially change them. Although it is not possible to unequivocally solve this dilemma, we can obtain some useful information by using the two systems on identical materials under the same reading conditions and determine if comparable results are obtained. This would provide us with hard data about at least the equivalency of the two systems. This is one important step. Judgments by the experimenter and subjects about the normalcy of the reading would provide some basis to determine if the monitoring procedures were influencing the reading process. The purpose of the study reported in the following is to accomplish this immediate comparison.

Thirty-two adult subjects from a semirural area of England were obtained by advertisement in a local paper. These individuals ranged in age from 20 to over 70 in a ratio of one-third men to two-thirds women. They came from a variety of occupations and had a diverse background of educational training.

The stimulus materials were two sections from a British Open University health education text. They were selected as representative of the sort of complex typographic pages that, it was hypothesized, might cause problems of reading sequence and about which little data have been gathered previously. The material is written and designed in a journalistic style; blocks of text, pictures, activities (short quizzes, mainly), and activity discussions are set out in a three-column layout. Figure 3 shows one of the double-page spreads tested.

An analysis of the content suggested that a particular reading sequence was intended by the author but that several potential problems might arise from the typographic design of the spread. A full account of the critique and resulting evaluation cannot be given here, but, as an example, the following points were raised about the pages shown in Figure 3. First, readers were expected to inspect the three cartoons and return to the first column of the left-hand page; would they distinguish between the second and third ones properly (they appear to be visually merged) and remember to return? Would they look at each cartoon and its discussion in turn or all three cartoons and then all three discussions? Second, an activity is spread over two pages but does not cohere as a visual unit (it starts at

Asserting yourself

Relationships are a matter of give and take. You tell people what you want. You try to understand what they want.

How can you do it without falling into the traps we talk about in the earlier topics? Look at the cartoons on these two pages and decide which is most typical of you when you try to stick up for yourself.

Passive, hostile or assertive?

The first cartoon shows a passive exchange. Mabel approaches Bill timidly. She is apologetic. She is vague about what she wants. Bill hardly bothers to listen. He doesn't even register that there is a problem.

The second cartoon shows a hostile exchange. Mabel is really steamed up. She attacks Bill but she doesn't really say what she wants him to do. The conversation escalates. They exchange insults. Bill slams out of the house.

In the third cartoon strip, Mabel gets what she wants. Bill agrees to talk about the problem. Why? What has happened that is different? Mabel has asserted herself. She has worked out beforehand what she wants to say. She is concrete about exactly what she wants Bill to do.

Asserting yourself, or asserting your rights is part of good, clear communication. People sometimes think that being assertive means being pushy, selfish or manipulative. It doesn't.

You are more likely to be manipulative if you adopt a passive role. This Mabel in the first cartoon. This Mabel will probably get back at Bill by sulking, crying or secret acts of revenge. She might forget to wash his socks.

You are more likely to be selfish and pushy if you adopt the hostile approach. The hostile approach assumes that no compromise is possible. The only gains will be those won by force. Blaming, anger and making others feel guilty are the weapons in both cases.

What do you do?

Most people have times when they find it difficult to assert themselves. Someone puts you down. Someone takes advantage of you. You get bad service in a shop. You can't stand up to someone in authority. You feel timid, anxious or shy. You find a good reason for not making a fuss. And you don't get what you want.

Think of some occasions where this sort of thing has happened to you recently. Write them down, on a separate piece of paper, like the example from Mabel below. For each one make sure you write down what happened, who you were with, where you were, when it happened, how often this has happened before.

Think of at least four events of your own to write down.

What happened?	Who with?	Where?	When?	How often has this happened before?
When I made a comment about politics to Jane, Bill and Bob said and 'Oh you don't know what you're talking about'	Bill	At a party	Last week	Every time we meet, his friends

For the four events you have written down, tick any of the following feelings you experienced at the same time:

	1	2	3	4
sad				
hostile				
bewildered				
frightened				
shy				
resigned				
inadequate				
self-conscious				
stupid				
inferior				

Tick any of the following bodily reactions you felt:

	1	2	3	4
butterflies in the stomach				
blushing				
going weak at the knees				
dry mouth				
increased pulse				
heart thumping				
shallow breathing				
hot flushes				
sweating				

And any of the following rationalisations you made to yourself!

	1	2	3	4
it's not worth making a fuss about				
perhaps I'm being selfish				
it's only once				
no-one else is complaining				
it won't make any difference				
I don't want to make a scene				

You now have the information you need to start changing your behaviour to become more assertive. Look through your list of situations. Decide which was the most threatening to you. Decide which was the least threatening to you. And which came in between. The more ticks you made on the three checklists above the more threatening or upsetting the situation probably was. Use this as a rough guide to help you judge.

Now pick one of your medium-threat situations. This is the situation you are going to work on for the rest of this topic. If you choose a very threatening situation to work on it is likely to be too upsetting for you to do too much about at first. If you pick one with very little threat it will be such a pushover that you won't learn anything.

Fig. 3. Example of materials used to test two macro-eye-movement procedures.

"What do you do?" and ends after the tables near the bottom of the right-hand page). Third, the second half of the activity section (the three columns of tabular matter) appears visually merged with three columns of text just below it. Is the thin horizontal rule adequate to prevent readers from following straight down each column in turn instead of studying the two three-column blocks separately in turn?

On the basis of this critique, the materials were redesigned. The redesigned materials keep the same textual and illustrative content (with some minor exceptions) but differ typographically on too many variables to be directly comparable in the traditional way—the exercise is, rather, a holistic comparison of alternatives in the sense suggested by Macdonald-Ross and Waller (1975) aimed at enhancing sensitivity to design issues in a general sense rather than providing detailed general guidelines.

The subjects were randomly assigned to one of the two reading procedures (already described) and received one version of each of the text sections (seven pages in all). They were allowed to read at their own pace and to take notes or write in their booklets if they desired. They were told that they would have to answer some questions about the material. Upon completion of their reading, subjects were given a brief retention test and were asked a set of questions about the materials and the apparatus.

For scoring purposes the seven pages of text were divided into a set of subblocks based on section headings, pictures, and other text design features. These page-grid definitions were inserted into the microcomputer of the light-pen recorder, and the time on each subblock and the accessing pattern of the blocks were determined. The participants' protocols were then scored for lookbacks, lookforwards, and page turns. The videotapes from the video recorder system were scored by a judge for the same variables. In order to assess scoring reliability from the videotapes, a second judge scored half of the tapes. The reliabiity for scoring the accessing order was .75. Reliability for lookbacks and lookforwards was not determined because a prior study using this procedure reported reliabilities above .95 (Schumacher, Moses, & Young, 1983).

Data from the retention test, questionnaire, and reading records of the two methodologies were compared using parametric and nonparametric procedures. One-way analyses of variance showed the following results:

1. There were no differences between subjects using the light-pen recorder and video recorder in reading time on the passages, on the number of lookbacks, or in recall.
2. Subjects reading wih the video recorder made more page turns compared to those on the light-pen recorder and made more lookforwards.
3. Subjects reading with the light-pen recorder spent more time on pictures and cartoons than subjects did on the video recorder.

Chi-square analyses were conducted on several variables. These showed the following results:

1. Subjects using the video recorder indicated that they carried out activities recommended in the articles more frequently than those on the light-pen recorder.

2. There were no differences in the proportion of subjects who took notes on the passages or who indicated that they studied as they normally did.

From the point of view of comparing the two designs, visual inspection of the reading records showed that certain of the layouts generated consistent strategies, while others produced a variety that defies analysis. Most, but not all, of the redesigned features appeared to work better than the original versions, and the exercise was felt to be useful in providing the designer with objective feedback; a detailed discussion is outside the scope of this report, which is presented here only for the purpose of comparing methodologies.

This study provides one of the first systematic comparisons of methodologies aimed at allowing researchers to tap issues related to text design and studying strategies. The results of this study indicate that the two methodologies investigated here do lead to different performance on some measures. Subjects studying with the video recorder seem more likely to read and reread text segments beyond the two-page spread in front of them. In addition, they appear more likely to carry out activities suggested in the text. However, data from this system are more difficult and time-consuming to score, particularly if one is scoring for specific reading patterns. This indicates that the video recording system may be more appropriate than the light-pen recorder for investigating issues such as macrostudying strategies across large numbers of pages. Because the light-pen recorder and video recorder systems lead to similar studying times and text interaction patterns within a two-page spread, and because the light-pen recorder can be easily set up to test various design hypotheses, this system seems better that the video recorder system for testing more detailed design questions such as page layout and the usefulness of certain access structures. These conclusions are restricted to the particular systems tested here; modifications to the light-pen recorder are under way as a result of this study to facilitate note-taking and page-turning activities.

In summary, both systems appear to allow for accurate tapping of relatively normal studying activity on normal texts. Generally, the systems produce comparable data; specific characteristics of the present systems for recording and scoring data suggest somewhat different uses.

SUMMARY

It is apparent that those individuals faced with developing useful documents now have an array of procedures to aid in this complex process. A wide range of outcome procedures are available to determine the impact of design characteristics on the comprehension and use of documents.

However, since the mid-1970s, there has been remarkable growth in developing new process measures to aid document design. These process measures provide those interested in text design with the means to conduct direct assessments of the processes subjects use as they attempt to handle the documents with which they are faced. Such direct tests are not aimed at replacing decisions made on the basis of tacit knowledge gained by those who design documents. Rather, these procedures can come to play a useful role in providing evidence on difficult aspects of a particular text design, in helping to externalize the knowledge that good designers of text have gained, and to derive general principles of document design. If they can accomplish these ends, they will become an important cog in the wheel of designing usable text.

REFERENCES

Atlas, M. A. (1981). The user edit: Making manuals easier to read. *IEEE Transactions on Professional Communication, PC-24*, 28–29.

Barnes, B. R., & Clawson, E. U. (1975). Do advance organizers facilitate learning? *Review of Educational Research, 45*, 637–660.

Bruce, B., Rubin, A., & Starr, K. (1981). Why readability formulas fail. *IEEE Transactions on Professional Communication, PC-24*, 50–52.

Carpenter, P. A., & Just, M. A. (1977). Reading comprehension as eyes see it. In M. A. Just & P. A. Carpenter (Eds.), *Cognitive processes in comprehension*. Hillsdale, NJ: Erlbaum.

Cross, N. (1980). An introduction to design methods. *Information Design Journal, 1*, 242–253.

De Beaugrande, R. (1981). Design criteria for process models of reading. *Reading Research Quarterly, 16*, 261–315.

Flower, L., & Hayes, J. (1980). The dynamics of composing: Making plans and juggling constraints. In L. W. Gregg & E. R. Steinberg (Eds.), *Cognitive processes in writing*. Hillsdale, NJ: Erlbaum.

Flower, L. & Hayes, J. (1981). The pregnant pause: An inquiry into the nature of planning. *Research in the Teaching of English, 15*, 229–243.

Flower, L., Hayes, J., & Swarts, H. (1980, March). Revising functional documents: The scenario principle (Document Design Project Tech. Rep. No. 10). Pittsburgh, PA: Carnegie-Mellon University.

Frederiksen, C. (1977). Semantic processing units in understanding text. In R. Freedle (Ed.), *Discourse production and comprehension*. Norwood, NJ: Ablex.

Hartley, J., & Trueman, M. (1982, March). *Headings in text: Issues and data*. Paper presented at the Annual Meeting of the American Educational Research Association, New York.

Henderson, E. S., & Nathenson, M. B. (1977). Developmental testing: Collecting feedback and transforming it into revisions. *Journal of the National Society for Performance and Instruction, 16*, 3.

Holland, V. M., & Redish, J. C. (1981). Strategies for understanding forms and other public documents (Document Design Project Tech. Rep. No. 13). Washington, DC: The American Institutes for Research.

Hout Wolters, B. van (1982). Methoden voor procesqericht onderzoek tijdens het bestuderen van studieteksten In M. van de Kamp & L. van de Kamp (Eds.), *Methodologie van de onderwijsresearch*. Lisse, The Netherlands: Swets en Zeitlinger.

Just, M. A., & Carpenter, P. A. (1980). A theory of reading: From eye-fixations to comprehension. *Psychological Review, 87,* 329–354.

Karslake, J. (1940). The Purdue Eye-Camera: A practical apparatus for studying the attention value of advertisements. *Journal of Applied Psychology, 24,* 417–440.

Kintsch, W. (1977). On comprehending stories. In M. A. Just & P. A. Carpenter (Eds.), *Cognitive processes in comprehension.* Hillsdale, NJ: Erlbaum.

Klare, G. R. (1981). Readability indices: Do they inform or misinform? *Information Design Journal, 2,* 251–255.

McConkie, G. W., Hogaboam, T. W., Wolverton, G. S., Zola, D., & Lucas, P. A. (1979). Toward the use of eye movements in the study of language processing (Center for the Study of Reading Tech. Rep. No. 134). Champaign, IL: University of Illinois.

Macdonald-Ross, M., & Waller, R. H. W. (1975). Criticisms, alternatives and texts: A framework for improving typography. *Programmed Learning and Educational Technology, 12,* 75–83.

Meyer, B. F. (1977). What is remembered from prose: A function of passage structure. In R. Freedle (Ed.), *Discourse production and comprehension.* Norwood, NJ: Ablex.

Newell, A., & Simon, H. (1972). *Human problem solving.* Englewood Cliffs, NJ: Prentice-Hall.

Polanyi, M. (1958). *Personal knowledge.* London: Routledge & Kegan Paul.

Pugh, A. K. (1979). Styles and strategies in silent reading. In P. Kolers, M. Wrolstad, & H. Bouma (Eds.), *Processing of visible language* (Vol 1). New York: Plenum.

Ravetz, J. R. (1971). *Scientific knowledge and its social problems.* London: Oxford University Press.

Rickards, J. P., & Denner, P. R. (1978). Inserted questions as aids to reading test. *Instructional Science, 7,* 313–346.

Schumacher, G. M., Liebert, D., & Fass, W. (1975). Textual organization, advance organizers and the retention of prose material. *Journal of Reading Behavior, 7,* 173–180.

Schumacher, G. M., Moses, J. D., & Young, D. (1983). Students studying processes on course related texts: The impact of inserted questions. *Journal of Reading Behavior, 15,* 19–36.

Schumacher, G. M., & Waller, R. H. W. (1983, April). *Recording study behavior on normal text: A methodological comparison.* Paper presented at the Annual Meeting of the American Educational Research Association, Montreal.

Simon, H. (1969). *The sciences of the artificial.* Cambridge, MA: MIT Press.

Whalley, P. C. (1981). *Macro level recording of reading behavior.* Paper presented at the Conference of the European Group for Eye Movement Research, Bern.

Whalley, P. C. (1982). *Argument in text and the reading process.* Unpublished paper. Institute of Educational Technology, Open University, Milton Keynes, England.

Whalley, P. C., & Fleming, R. W. (1975). An experiment with a simple recorder of reading behavior. *Programmed Learning and Educational Technology, 12,* 120–123.

Wright, P. (1978). Feeding the information eaters: Suggestions for integrating pure and applied research on language comprehension. *Instructional Science, 7,* 249–312.

Author Index

Numbers in *italics* show the pages on which complete references are cited.

A

Aagard, J. A., 114, 125, *142*
Adams, H. C., 236, *242*
Aldrich, P., 44, *59*
Allen, R. H., 342, *374*
Amiran, M., 134, *140*
Anderson, M. C., 168, *176*
Anderson, R. C., 168, 173, *176*
Anderson, T. H., 160, 161, 162, 168, *176*
André, G. G., 278, 302, *311*
Armbruster, B. B., 160, 161, 162, 165, 168, *176*
Arnheim, R., 278, 302, *311*
Ashwin, C., 284, 294, *311*
Asimov, I., 213, *241*
Atlas, M., 46, *59,* 387, 402, *402*
Ausubel, D. P., 151, *156,* 186, *211*

B

Bailey, V., 55, *60*
Baker, C., 34, *40*
Baker, L., 161, *176*
Balchin, W. G. V., 304, *311*
Barba, M., 45, *61*
Barnard, P., 67, 71, *94, 96,* 222, *242*
Barnes, B. R., 151, *156,* 384, *402*
Bartlett, E. J., 66, *94*
Barton, W. A., 161, *176*
Basescu, B., 181, *211*
Battison, R., 97, *111*
Beasley, D., 278, *311*
Begley, R., 236, *241*
Bell, M., 134, *142*

Bentley, T. J., 34, *40*
Berkenkotter, C., 48, *59*
Berkshire, J. R., 235, *241*
Berlyne, D., 151, *156*
Berry, P. C., 182, *211*
Bertin, J., 294, *311*
Bever, T., 54, *60*
Bever, T. G., 100, *111*
Biersner, R. J., 117, 125, *140*
Bishop, R. L., 106, *111*
Bloom, B. S., 181, *211*
Blunden, B., 65, *94*
Blunt, W., 265, *311*
Bobrow, R., 51, *59*
Bolin, S., 45, *61*
Bond, S., 47, *59,* 222, *243*
Booher, H. R., *371*
Bormuth, J. R., 123, 134, *140*
Boutwell, R. C., 151, *156*
Bowren, F., 331, *339*
Braby, R., 347, 348, *371*
Brady, M. E., 129, *143*
Bransford, J. D., 7, *15,* 51, *60,* 87, *94,* 168, *176*
Brassard, M., 332, *339*
Brennan, M. P., 320, *340,* 342, *374*
Brent, S., 168, *177*
Briem, J., 86, *94*
Briggs, L. J., 133, *140*
Brittain, W. L., 302, *312*
Brookes, B. C., 21, *40*
Brooks, Jr., F. A., 237, *242* 364, *374*
Brooks, L. W., 168, *176*
Brooks, V., 304, *311*

Subject Index

effect on comprehension, 173
readability guidelines, 128–129
technical terms, 174

W

Word processing
  as support for editorial work, 64
WRITER'S WORKBENCH, 107, 111
  writer–user relationship, 3–11, 20–21, 27–
    29, 148, 315–340, 341
Writers, 19–41
  awareness of audience, 45–46
  composing styles, 48
  as content experts, 153–154
  editing skills, 46–48
  educational background, 44
  evaluation of text, 48
  as evaluators of own text, 316–322
  experienced–novice comparison, 46–47
  failures in structuring knowledge, 21–23
  as illustrators, 93
  influence of organisational standards, 48–
    50, 126
  job background, 44, 48–49
  lack of knowledge of production process,
    22–23

as own editors, 32–33, 65–66, 93–94
relationship with designers, 23–25
relationship with editors, 23–25, 67
rhetorical knowledge, 45–46
role in design of instructional text, 153–154
of textbooks, 321–322
training, 36–40, 43–61, 139, 207–210, 319
training background for technical writing,
  319–320
writing skills, 44–48
views of style, 90–92
Writing
  by committees, 49
  definition of purposes, 26
  effectiveness of texts on writing, 33–36
  organization of ideas, 25–33
  organizational standards, 49–50
  structured writing, 179–212
  topic-oriented approach, 319
Writing guidelines, *see* Guidelines
Writing instruction, 106, 127–133
  computer applications, 106–111, 139
Writing manuals, 33–36
Writing scenarios, 53–55
Writing Service Standards, 179–212
Writing skills, 22, 32, 44–48, 106
Written language
  difference from spoken, 317